RECENT
AMERICA

Arthur S. Link
Princeton University
GENERAL EDITOR FOR HISTORY

Recent America

America

THE UNITED STATES SINCE 1945

DEWEY W. GRANTHAM

VANDERBILT UNIVERSITY

Harlan Davidson, Inc.
Arlington Heights, Illinois 60004

Library of Congress
Cataloging-in-Publication Data

Grantham, Dewey W.
Recent America

Bibliography: p.
Includes index.
1. United States—History—1945-   .
2. United States—Foreign relations—1945-   .
I. Title.
E741.G73   1987   973.92   86-6321
ISBN 0-88295-841-0

91 90 89 88 87   1 2 3 4 5 6 7

For Scott and Lesley

Contents

Contents

Preface

FROM THE VANTAGE POINT of the 1980s, the years since 1945 constitute a new and in many respects revolutionary period in American history. "The gulf separating 1965 from 1943," the cultural anthropologist Margaret Mead wrote in the mid-sixties, "is as deep as the gulf that separated the men who became builders of cities from Stone Age men." The break may not have been as sharp as Mead thought, but it is clear that the Second World War ushered in a new era in the nation's history. The war acted as a catalyst for social change and dramatized the apocalyptic nature of modern society. The most compelling of all the contrasts with former times was the bomb. The explosion of the first atomic bomb in July 1945, in a remote New Mexico desert, cast its shadow over the entire postwar period.

The years that followed transformed the United States in many ways. This transformation was manifested in the centralization of power in the federal government, in the nation's sustained prosperity, in perplexing problems such as the "crisis of the cities," in the success of the black struggle for equality, in the new role of women in American society, in the pervasive impact of the consumer culture, and in much else. Among the multiple revolutions in American life since the end of World War II, none was more portentous than the involvement of the United States with the rest of the world. Americans soon discovered that in the cold war it was virtually impossible to discuss domestic questions without referring to foreign affairs; almost every political issue was affected with a global interest. Geographically, the nation's diplomatic and security concerns became far broader than ever before, and many new agencies and instruments were soon involved in the conduct of foreign relations.

Change was not always the dominant force in the new era, and a common commitment to shared values persisted. Americans themselves were ambivalent about change, and it was ironic that the United States, itself the product of a revolution, should have come, in a new age of national revolutions, to be viewed by many people in other countries as a conservative society, dedicated to the maintenance of the status quo. But the rate of change in the United States, as elsewhere, accelerated after the war, whether one welcomed it or not. One result was that, despite certain uniformities, the postwar period was essentially an era of disruption and discontinuity. The striking alterations associated with World War II, the increase in the velocity of history, and the transformation of many features of American life gave a distinctive cast to the postwar period.

Historians, increasingly drawn to the study of the recent past, have contributed to the recognition of the years after 1945 as a distinctive era. An impressive amount of scholarly research and writing, as well as many useful popular histories, has been devoted to the United States since 1945, especially to such developments as the cold war, the civil rights movement, the Vietnam War, and presidential leadership and administrations. The growing acceptance of contemporary history as a legitimate field of scholarly specialization has encouraged this historiographical concentration on the very recent period.

This book is based on my earlier work, *The United States Since 1945: The Ordeal of Power*, published in 1976. It draws on the extensive historical writing about postwar America and on the work of social scientists, journalists, and other analysts especially concerned with the contemporary scene. *Recent America* seeks to provide a relatively brief but comprehensive survey of the American experience since 1945. The emphasis is on national politics and national affairs, including international issues and diplomacy, but some attention is given to economic, social, and cultural trends. I hope that the volume will serve as a useful introduction to a fascinating historical epoch and that it will interest students and general readers alike. In organizing and interpreting the events of this tumultuous period, I have tried to bring new perspectives to bear on our recent history and to engage in the process the historian Felix Gilbert describes as "reconstructing a historical consciousness that integrates the present with the past."

I am grateful to the late Harlan Davidson for his interest in this project, and I wish that he had lived to see it published. I am indebted to Arthur S. Link for reading the manuscript and offering a number of helpful suggestions; to Maureen Gilgore Hewitt for her efficient supervision of the bookmaking process; to Brad Barrett for his help in the treatment of popular music; and to Henry M. Mc-Kiven, Jr., for his valuable research assistance. I want to thank Kiddy Moore, Julia Buzzell, and Pamela Allen for their good cheer and efficiency in typing several drafts of the manuscript. I am also happy to acknowledge the support of my colleagues in the department of history at Vanderbilt University. It gives me special pleasure to dedicate this book to my two favorite young Americans, my grandchildren, Scott and Lesley Grantham, who started their personal odysseys at about the time their country entered the third century of its political independence.

Dewey W. Grantham

CHAPTER ONE

The Transition from War to Peace

WHEN THE JAPANESE formally surrendered to the Allies on September 2, 1945, the United States was vastly different from the nation that had been propelled into war by the surprise attack on Pearl Harbor on December 7, 1941. To most Americans in the late summer of 1945, the war seemed very old, its beginnings already shrouded in the mists of the retreating past. Part of this feeling was no doubt an illusion produced by the sacrifices and weariness of wartime, abetted by the tumultuous events of a global conflict. But the impression was also based on the reality of alterations that had taken place in the United States during the past four years. The war led to the creation of a mighty military force, brought about a great mobilization of industry and other resources, banished unemployment and freed the economy from the grip of the depression, helped redefine the role of government, invoked new international policies, and changed the nation's social structure. It also precipitated new social tensions and problems.

WORLD WAR II: CATALYST FOR CHANGE

The first part of the war was a grim and sobering experience for Americans, and in those dark days it sometimes seemed that it would be impossible for the Allies to stem the powerful tide of the Axis onslaught. Yet the people and their leaders set about the forbidding task in a spirit of remarkable unity. Pearl Harbor ended the great debate on foreign policy and united Americans in a common purpose. While the extravagant idealism that attended the nation's involvement in World War I was noticeably absent from that in the Second World War, most people would have agreed with Vice President Henry A. Wallace's characterization of the conflict as "a fight between a slave world and a free world." Divisions and disagreements in the United States continued to be evident, as might be expected, but there was little intolerance or hysteria compared with 1917–18, and except for the treatment of Japanese-Americans on the West Coast, violations of civil liberties were relatively few.

The war resuscitated the U.S. economy and brought a new era of prosperity in place of the devastating depression of the previous decade. In spite of serious flaws in its mobilization schemes, the United States became, in the phrase of the day, an "arsenal of democracy." So great was its increase in plant capacity that production almost doubled between 1939 and 1945. By late 1943 an incredible flow of tanks, airplanes, ships, and guns was pouring out of American factories, and the national output was more than twice that of the combined Axis powers. The economy was transformed in many ways: in the modernization and consolidation of industry, the growing industrialization of the South and the western regions, the expansion of organized labor, the massive internal movement of workers, and the increase in agricultural productivity despite a substantial decline in farm population during the war. "At the end of the war," Richard Polenberg observes, "the United States was a more urban, technological and industrial society than when it had entered."

Governmental intervention during World War I and the period of the New Deal appeared limited when compared with the mobilization of manpower, industry, finance, and technology during the early 1940s. Though the American home front was not subjected to the thoroughgoing controls imposed by most of the major belligerent powers, the extent of the federal government's involvement in the economy was unparalleled in U.S. history. The war enhanced the power of the president and the federal bureaucracy, thereby accustoming people to Washington's expanded role. This development was associated with a revolutionary change in the national government's fiscal policy; wartime expenditures were so enormous that they amounted to twice as much as *all* federal appropriations before 1941! The heightened influence of the national government centered on Franklin D. Roosevelt, in whose deft hands the responsibility for coordinating mobilization and production rested. Roosevelt's leadership symbolized the nation at war, and his influence and personality were indelibly stamped on the great transformation of American life during those hectic years.

Although the Roosevelt administration continued to win the support of a majority of the voters, the war weakened the influence of liberals and intensified the strength of conservatives. The New Deal

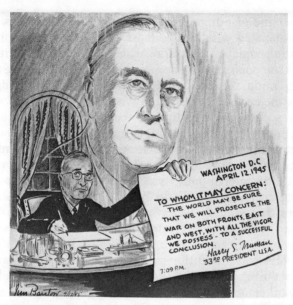

Truman carries on for Roosevelt (*Jim Barstow in the General Electric News, courtesy Harry S. Truman Library*)

seemed to be waning. Power in the Democratic party shifted in the direction of more moderate and conservative elements, and in Congress a bipartisan coalition of conservatives strongly resisted further domestic reform. "The new shape of American politics," Alonzo L. Hamby has written, "included a reform-oriented presidential Democratic party able to control presidential nominations and a moderate-to-conservative congressional Democratic party."

No feature of the war years contrasted more sharply with the situation in the 1930s than the abandonment of isolationism in the United States. The Japanese attack on Pearl Harbor destroyed the old myth of American impregnability, and during the war the United States became the organizer and leader of the Grand Alliance in destroying the Axis powers and establishing an international organization for peace. A war-born American empire had taken shape by 1945, and at the end of the war U.S. influence had become dominant in Western Europe, Japan, Latin America, and throughout the Pacific. Most Americans seemed to think that it was both possible and desirable for the United States to use its immense power to help reshape the world along the lines of its own democratic capitalism.

The transformation of U.S. foreign policy was directly related, of course, to certain changes in the rest of the world. One such change was the decline of Europe's preeminence in world affairs, a development associated with the collapse of Western imperialism, the revolt of the peoples of Asia and Africa, the rise of Eastern nationalism, and the polarization of power between the United States and the Soviet Union. A second impetus to America's changing foreign policy was the end of what C. Vann Woodward has described as "the era of free security"—the physical security from attack and invasion the country had enjoyed through most of its history. The end of this era came so suddenly that Americans could hardly bring themselves to face its practical implications. A third factor in altering the nation's foreign policy was the revolution in weapons technology that began during World War II. Historic changes in weapons, tactics, and strategy were insignificant when contrasted with the distance separating the preatomic and the nuclear ages.

Wartime prosperity and economic mobility had begun to reshape the fabric of social institutions. A vast redistribution of population took place during the early 1940s, with millions of soldiers and civilian workers moving around the country, large numbers of southern blacks migrating to the North and West, and many rural inhabitants going to cities and towns. Women assumed a much more important place in the industrial labor force. Although American society in 1945 was still divided along class, ethnic, and racial lines, the war years blurred many of the traditional distinctions among Americans. Full employment and favorable governmental policies resulted in a more equitable distribution of national income, while the war experience softened ethnic distinctiveness. The war also brought employment opportunities and economic advances to American blacks, without, however, noticeably reducing the level of racial intolerance and proscription. Yet the war heightened the expectations and dissatisfaction of Negroes in the United States. By linking racial discrimination at home with fascism abroad, black leaders formulated the rationale for a "Double V" campaign—a demand for victory at home as well as abroad.

Americans in 1945 seemed to be better prepared for the postwar period than they had been in the autumn of 1918. As Franklin Roosevelt remarked at a press conference in May 1944, "Today, we are a little older; we have gone through some pretty rough times together. And perhaps we are not saying that we can devise a method of ending all wars for all times." After the signing of the formal surrender documents on September 2, 1945, on the deck of the battleship *Missouri* in Tokyo Bay, General Douglas MacArthur spoke by radio to the American people, warning them of the "utter destructiveness" of war in the new atomic age and urging the need to devise "some greater and more equitable system." The general noted that "a new era is upon us." How the United States would adjust to the new era only the future would tell.

DEMOBILIZATION AND RECONVERSION

Although the anticipated blessings of peacetime did not come easily or quickly, many of the mistakes of the heedless demobilization process in 1918 and 1919 were avoided in the aftermath of the Second World War. For one thing, the War Production Board and other agencies began to plan for reconversion as early as 1943, and before the end of the war, the president and Congress had approved an essential blueprint to guide the economy in the transition from wartime to peacetime. The widespread fears of a major postwar recession proved to be unfounded, and despite momentary uncertainty the nation experienced continuing and expanding prosperity. Industry adjusted quickly to civilian production, and by the end of 1945 its reconversion had largely been completed. Unemployment did not become a severe problem, and by August 1946 the number of men and women at work in the United States had reached 60 million! Corporate profits were high, personal income went up, and farmers prospered in the aftermath of the war.

Even so, the strains of resuming normal peacetime arrangements were very great. The first order of business, dictated by an irresistible demand, was the demobilization of the armed forces. The process went forward so rapidly that some military and civilian leaders became alarmed at the prospect of a complete disbandment of the mighty force created to fight Germany and Japan. President Harry S Truman and the military representatives urged the maintenance of substantial forces, but there was little support for such a policy in the early postwar period. The pressure to "bring the boys back home" was inexorable, and by April 1946 almost 7 million men had been released from the armed forces. Congress reluctantly agreed to continue Selective Service but refused to adopt the administration's plan for universal military training.

In one respect, at least, the government had given thought to the future needs of those who had served in the armed forces. The Servicemen's Readjustment Act—soon dubbed the G.I. Bill of Rights—had been enacted in June 1944. It provided support for education and training, unemployment benefits, veterans' hospitals, and loans for homes, farms, and businesses. By 1947 more than 4 million young men and women were receiving benefits from this legislation, and by 1950 the annual expenditures of the Veterans Administration had reached a peak of over $9 billion. Of all the reconversion plans, none received more popular approval or proved more beneficial in human and social terms.

Governmental planning in many other respects worked out less well. The structure of the mobilization machinery was rapidly dismantled after the war. Billions of dollars worth of war contracts were canceled immediately, many wartime agencies were soon abolished, and numerous controls were removed early in the postwar period. In October 1945 the War Production Board was replaced by the Civilian Production Administration. In January of the next year the War Assets Administration was established, and it proceeded to dispose of hundreds of government-owned war plants, often at bargain prices to corporations that had operated them during the war. The government also showed its concern for business in other ways; in November 1945, for example, Congress reduced taxes by almost $6 billion, thereby providing a further boost to the peacetime economic lift-off.

President Roosevelt's annual message to Congress in 1944 had included an "Economic Bill of Rights," in which Roosevelt looked ahead to the establishment in postwar America of "a new basis of security and prosperity." During the campaign of 1944 the Democrats had talked about full employment in peacetime as well as in war, and early in the Truman administration Congress began to consider a so-called maximum employment bill. The Employment Act was passed in 1946 and became a landmark in recent U.S. history. It provided for a three-member Council of Economic Advisers to study economic trends and to recommend to the president policies to alleviate downturns in the business cycle. It required the chief executive to make an annual report on the economy, and it created a congressional joint committee on the economic report to recommend stabilization steps. While the act did not guarantee government action against recessions, Section 2 declared it to be "the continuing policy and responsibility of the Federal Government to use all practicable means . . . to promote maximum employment, production, and purchasing power."

THE STRUGGLE OVER ECONOMIC CONTROLS, 1945–46

Following V-J Day most Americans wanted a quick return to "normal" conditions, but they disagreed over what constituted normality and over the best means of bringing it about. The strong pressures for higher prices and increased wages, coupled with continuing shortages of many critical products, presaged a serious inflation unless effective governmental controls could be maintained during the reconversion period. The Truman administration hoped to provide such controls. But the task was fraught with complexities and difficulties. Organized interest groups were determined to throw off governmental restraints. Businessmen and farmers were eagerly buying new equipment and machinery. Consumers, with billions of dollars in wartime savings and plenty of credit, were in no mood to delay the purchase of long-sought durable goods. The Office of Price Administration (OPA), the heart of the postwar stabilization program, was widely disliked. According to the journalist Cabell Phillips, "it inspired a devious, illicit sort of gamesmanship not unlike that of the prohibition era, with black marketers taking the place of the bootleggers." Meanwhile, the administration's honeymoon period had ended; the president was now expected both to remove wartime controls and to prevent inflation.

Industrialists, businessmen, and farm representatives pressed Congress to abolish all controls. Such action, they contended, would enable the "natural forces of the marketplace" to bring abundance and low prices within a few months. Business representatives argued that controls were delaying full production, encouraging the black market, and preventing producers from getting their rightful profits. Many trade association executives denounced the OPA as a "socialistic" bottleneck that was damaging production, employment, and the heart of the free enterprise system. Business interests mounted a concerted campaign to destroy the agency.

Organized labor tended to favor price controls, but only if it could secure higher wages. Labor had acquired great strength and confidence during the war. But at the same time, its leaders believed that workers had not shared equally with capital in the war prosperity. Concerned about the return to a forty-hour week and the loss of overtime pay after the war and apprehensive of the possibility of massive unemployment or of drastic inflation, they were determined to protect labor's interests in the postwar era.

Labor's restiveness quickly manifested itself. Half a million workers went out on strike within a few weeks of Japan's surrender, and the following autumn and winter witnessed widespread work stoppages when union demands for wage increases and other benefits were not met by management. The loss of man-days reached 23 million in February 1946. A series of strikes in the steel, automobile, meat-packing, and electrical industries threatened to disrupt the entire economy. Although a labor-management conference in late 1945 failed to reach agreement on reconversion wage policies, a recommendation by a presidential fact-finding board eventually provided the basis for the settlement of the great industrial strikes in the winter of 1945–46. In general, labor received a little over two-thirds of what it sought, while management was allowed substantial price increases in return. A new round of labor-management disputes began in the fall of 1946, with an agreement in April of the next year providing for an hourly wage increase of about 15 cents. A third encounter was settled in 1948. In these and subsequent confrontations, management showed a willingness to accede to labor's demands, but with the understanding that the added costs would be passed on to the consumer in the form of higher prices.

The general settlement of 1946 did not end the Truman administration's problems with organized labor. A national emergency was created when John L. Lewis of the United Mine Workers (UMW) led 400,000 miners out of the coal pits on April 1, 1946. The strike continued until the government finally decided to take over the mines. Eventually, a settlement gave the UMW most of what it wanted. Lewis made new demands that October, and when negotiations failed, the labor leader called another strike. In December 1946, Lewis and his union were fined for contempt for disregarding a temporary restraining order. But when the mines were returned to their owners in July 1947, Lewis secured a new contract that provided virtually all he had sought.

In the meantime, the troubled spring of 1946 had confronted the administration with still another labor controversy. When the railroad brotherhoods called a nationwide railroad strike in mid-May, the president seized the railroads under the provisions of the Smith-Connally Act and won a compromise settlement with most of the unions. But two of the brotherhoods—the Locomotive Engineers and the Railroad Trainmen—decided to strike anyway. "If you think I'm going to sit here and let you tie up this whole country," Truman exclaimed to the leaders of the two unions, "you're crazy as hell." When they went ahead with the strike, Truman scheduled an appearance before Congress on May 25 to request authority to prevent the paralysis of transportation and to curb labor disputes in essential industries. The railroad unions gave in just before the chief executive spoke, and the crisis ended.

Many members of Congress applauded President Truman's get-tough policy toward John L. Lewis and the railroad brotherhood leaders. Yet these same legislators were often critical of Truman's economic controls in 1945 and 1946. Senator Edward H. Moore of Oklahoma declared in June 1946, "A controlled economy leads to an authoritarian psychology which results in the oppression and destruction of individual rights and liberties under a gestapo system." Truman sought "continued stabilization of the national economy" through a policy of gradually relaxing the wartime regulation of prices, wages, and commodities in short supply. Most rationing was ended in the early postwar period. Unfortunately, the administration itself was divided over the implementation of its economic controls. Chester Bowles, the head of OPA, wanted to follow a more stringent program of price ceilings than did the more conservative John W. Snyder, the director of the Office of War Mobilization and Reconversion. The president leaned toward Snyder's position and allowed higher prices, a concession he described as a "bulge in the line." Bowles became discouraged and soon resigned. Nevertheless, the administration's anti-inflation record during the first ten months following the war was fairly good; wholesale prices during that period rose only 7 percent.

The brunt of the Truman administration's battle against inflation was carried by the OPA, whose statutory authority would expire on July 1, 1946. The administration urged that the agency be continued for another year, and a congressional struggle ensued during the spring of 1946 over the issue of extension. A price control bill was finally passed on June 27 providing for a one-year extension, but it gave the agency little power and ordered it to decontrol prices "as rapidly as possible." This weakness led the president to veto the measure, which he described as "a sure formula for inflation," and allowed price controls to end on July 1. Prices immediately zoomed, climbing 25 percent in a little over two weeks—an increase almost twice as great as that of the previous three years. Congress then passed a second bill on July 25, almost as weak as the first, authorizing a one-year extension of price and rent controls. The damage had been done by that time, however, and thereafter the administration could do little to halt the inflationary spiral. Soon after the November elections, the president ended all controls over wages and prices except on rents, sugar, and rice.

If the Democrats had won the 1946 congressional elections, President Truman might have continued the fight against inflation. But the Republicans won a sweeping victory in 1946. During the campaign they indicted the administration for inept and discriminatory price control policies, high prices, and continuing shortages. As they put it to the voters, "Had enough? Vote Republican." The Democrats were also vulnerable in other ways. Union labor was disaffected. Truman was unpopular with many members of his own party—with conservatives because of his liberal domestic proposals and his economic policies, and with liberals because of certain of his appointments and his support in some instances of conservatives against liberals within his own administration. The president's popularity with the public was at a low ebb, for he presented a spectacle of executive incompetence. There was a rash of Truman

The fire ball of a nuclear test rises over the Eniwetok Atoll during Operation Sandstone (*National Archives/Imagefinders, Inc.*)

jokes going around, including the quip that "to err is Truman." The Republicans won majorities in both houses of Congress and would control the legislative branch for the first time since 1930.

NATIONAL DEFENSE AND WORLD AFFAIRS

In the new era no feature of national defense could be considered without taking the atomic bomb into account, and the American monopoly of this awesome power made it imperative that policies be adopted for its control at home and abroad. Most political leaders accepted the need for governmental control over the production and use of atomic energy, but there was sharp disagreement over the nature of such regulation when Congress debated the matter in the fall of 1945. Brien McMahon of Connecticut, chairman of a special Senate committee investigating the problem, prepared a bill with the backing of the administration to establish an atomic energy commission with exclusive civilian control. Senator Arthur H. Vandenberg of Michigan, also a member of the special committee, and others insisted that military representatives be given a key role in the work of the commission. While this position won the approval of the special committee, President Truman strongly opposed it, as did much of the public, and the issue was heatedly debated in the spring of 1946. A compromise was finally worked out that resulted in the Atomic Energy Act of 1946. The law created a five-member Atomic Energy Commission, with civilian control but with provision for a military liaison committee to work with the commission. Complete control over fissionable materials was vested in the government, and the act stipulated that the president alone would have responsibility for ordering the use of atomic weapons in warfare.

Meanwhile, the administration was giving thought to the need for international control. Early in 1946 the United Nations General Assembly established the UN Atomic Energy Commission, and soon afterward the so-called Acheson-Lilienthal plan for the international control and inspection of atomic energy was formulated under the aegis of the Truman administration.[1] In mid-June 1946, the U.S. representative to the commission, Bernard M. Baruch, submitted a proposal based on this plan to the UN. American spokesmen hoped that it would win quick approval.

Administration leaders also made progress in solving another problem, the need to reorganize and unify the country's armed forces. The disaster at Pearl Harbor had revealed fundamental defects in military organization, and the war provided much more evidence of duplication, waste, and inefficiency resulting from overlapping and competing services. Many informed people urged the

creation of a common command and a more streamlined organization. But a major reform of this character was not easy to effect; a
bitter controversy swirled around the question for two years following the war's end. Representatives of the Navy were especially re-
calcitrant, since they feared that unification would diminish the
role of seapower and eliminate the Marine Corps. President Truman
actively endeavored to secure a workable arrangement, and the unification legislation was enacted in July 1947. The National Security
Act, as it was called, provided for a secretary of defense with Cabinet rank, under whom were secretaries of Army, Navy, and Air
Force. The Joint Chiefs of Staff, representing the three services,
would assist in coordinating the armed forces and be responsible for
defense plans and strategy. The new legislation placed procurement,
research, and intelligence in the three services under central boards
in an effort to prevent duplication. The act created the Central Intelligence Agency to take charge of intelligence work at the highest
level, and it established the National Security Council and the National Security Resources Board to advise the president and Congress on national security. Secretary of the Navy James V. Forrestal,
who had lent his support to the unification drive, became the first
secretary of defense. Although the National Security Act was a major accomplishment, it did not do away with interservice rivalry and
bickering, as was demonstrated in the long controversy over long-
range bombers versus super aircraft carriers.

Meanwhile, the U.S. posture toward other nations was also revealed in the organization and early operation of the United Nations. The United States was, from the very beginning of its involvement in World War II, the leading advocate of a new world
organization. President Truman was as enthusiastic as his predecessor had been in supporting the creation of the peace organization.
Congress was also strongly in favor of the idea, and the Senate's
ratification of the UN Charter by a vote of 89 to 2 on July 28, 1945,
made the United States the first nation to approve the plan. The
American public welcomed the new organization, whose permanent headquarters were located in New York City.

While the UN was impressive in design, experience soon showed
that it could work only to the extent that its members voluntarily
cooperated. Though empowered to use force against aggressor nations, the organization was unable to force compliance over the opposition of its strongest members. Permanent members of the Security Council had the right to veto all but procedural questions,
and the charter permitted "regional" agreements and agencies. The
United States, despite its ardent efforts to create the new world organization, had insisted on both the veto and the legitimacy of re-

gional defensive associations, and these two features of the UN Charter played an important part in the troubled international history of the postwar era.

During this period, the United States was a generous contributor of international aid. Its financial support was indispensable in launching the United Nations' far-flung activities. American contributions channeled through the UN and other agencies were vitally important in bringing a measure of relief and rehabilitation to millions of starving and homeless people in war-ravaged Europe and Asia. Relief was also afforded in large amounts through the aid of such private groups as the Red Cross. The United States, moreover, made funds available to needy nations through such agencies as the Export-Import Bank, and in 1946 the American government extended Britain a $3.75 billion loan. Meanwhile, the United States worked to ease restrictions on trade, to stabilize foreign currencies, and to stimulate American investments abroad.

As these relief and rehabilitation efforts were being made, the United States was deeply involved in the formulation of peace treaties with the Axis Powers and in their political reconstruction. In the case of Germany, the United States occupied one of the four zones agreed upon by the Allies, proceeded with the task of destroying the German military potential, and joined in the victors' policy of "denazification." The Americans were also instrumental, between November 1945 and October 1946, in the trial at Nuremberg of a group of leading Nazi officials by the International Military Tribunal. Twelve of the Reich leaders were sentenced to death for war crimes and atrocities. The United States alone controlled the occupation and reconstruction of Japan. General MacArthur was appointed supreme commander for the Allied powers, and under his imperious control a thoroughgoing program was carried out to demilitarize Japan, to establish a system of social democracy there, and to reconstruct the country's economy. Twenty-eight top officials of wartime Japan were tried before the International Military Tribunal for the Far East, and seven of these men were executed.

PEACETIME PURSUITS

International problems and matters of statecraft did not much concern the majority of Americans during the immediate postwar months. They were too preoccupied with the exhilaration of homecoming, throwing off wartime restraints, and settling down in peacetime pursuits. As jobs were found for the returning G.I.s and new business ventures were undertaken, the fears of a crippling depression in the reconstruction period soon dissipated, and most people began to achieve an unaccustomed sense of security and to be aware of marvelous possibilities in the future. "Times have changed," one labor representative remarked early in the new era. "People have become accustomed to new conditions, new wage scales, new ways of being treated." In the prosperous transition from war to peace, Americans busied themselves with the myriad plans of an energetic people in a society that still seemed uniquely open and promising.

The prosperity of the war and its aftermath expanded the middle class in the United States and raised the economic and social expectations throughout the population. As the historian Eric F. Goldman wrote a few years later, "The boom rolled out in great fat waves, into every corner of the nation and up and down the social ladder." For a time it seemed that almost all elements of American society could, if they chose, change their status and enjoy a better life than ever before. Although the reality of inequality and discrimination, not to mention inflation, soon revealed the limitations of the postwar boom, economic abundance had never been available to such a large percentage of Americans. Incomes that went up year after year, new leisure time, regular vacations, expensive hobbies, and the spectacular development of tourism in states like Florida and California were available not merely to the privileged few but also to millions of middle-class people who had achieved new levels of well-being. The nation had never experienced such a dynamic consumer culture.

One evidence of postwar America's social buoyancy was the sharp increase in the birthrate. There was a trend toward earlier marriages, and the marriage rate (as well as the divorce rate) rose steeply. The growing number of new households and the large crop of new babies gave a strong impetus to the economy. But they also produced social problems. For example, the veterans' return, the growth of population, and the rapid movement of people to the cities and suburbs contributed to a severe housing shortage, a shortage that was not relieved for several years after 1945. The educational system also faced a major crisis during this period. Wartime neglect, the shift of many teachers from the classroom to better-paying jobs, and the crowded schools resulting from an expanding and migratory population confronted many school districts with an impossible situation. Higher education was also entering a period of remarkable expansion, caused in part by the influx of veterans studying under the G.I. Bill of Rights. The nation's campuses had never witnessed anything like this G.I. invasion, but the veterans generally proved to be serious and hard-working students, who adjusted well to the requirements of academe.

Abundance in postwar America had its limits, of course. The good times did not greatly improve the condition of many disadvantaged Americans. A group of U.S. senators reported in 1944, for instance, that twenty million of their fellow-citizens "dwell constantly in a borderland between subsistence and privation, where even the utmost thrift and caution do not suffice to make ends meet." Even the beneficiaries of the burgeoning economy sometimes expressed doubts. A reporter in St. Louis asked a young mother about her personal expectations. "Oh, things are going along just wonderfully," she exclaimed. "Harry has a grand job, there's the new baby—" But then she paused and asked, "Do you think it's really all going to last?" At a deeper level, affluence was tinged with anxiety, most profoundly by a pervasive awareness of the possibility of nuclear destruction.

The United States, it seemed, had entered a new and radically different stage in its historical evolution. Just how different the new era was became more apparent in 1947, when the cold war became a dominant concern in the nation's policy and consciousness. It is to that extraordinary development that we must now turn.

NOTE

1. Under Secretary of State Dean G. Acheson and David E. Lilienthal, former chairman of the Tennessee Valley Authority, were the plan's principal authors.

SUGGESTIONS FOR FURTHER READING

Richard Polenberg, *War and Society: The United States, 1941–1945* (1972), offers a fresh and balanced analysis of the impact of World War II on American government, politics, economy, and society. The effects of the war are also explored in a thoughtful and illuminating book by John Morton Blum, *V Was for Victory: Politics and American Culture during World War II* (1976). Less scholarly but useful is Geoffrey Perrett, *Days of Sadness, Years of Triumph: The American People, 1939–1945* (1973). James MacGregor Burns, *Roosevelt: The Soldier of Freedom* (1970), while emphasizing foreign policy and military affairs, is valuable for developments on the home front during the war. The war as a catalyst for social change is considered by Frances E. Merrill, *Social Problems on the Home Front: A Study of War-Time Influences* (1948); Richard Polenberg, *One Nation Divisible: Class, Race, and Ethnicity in the United States since 1938* (1980); and William H. Chafe, "The Paradox of Progress: Social Change Since 1930," in James T. Patterson (ed.), *Paths to the Present: Interpretive Essays on American History Since 1930* (1975), pp. 1–55.

The American role in the creation of the United Nations is described by Robert A. Divine in *Second Chance: The Triumph of Internationalism in America during World War II* (1967). The movement to control atomic energy is treated in Richard G. Hewlett and Oscar E. Anderson, *The New World: A History of the United States Atomic Energy Commission* (1962), and Gerard H. Clarfield and William M. Wiecek, *Nuclear America: Military and Civilian Nuclear Power in the United States, 1940–1980* (1984). Stephen E. Ambrose's *Rise to Globalism: American Foreign Policy Since 1938* (4th rev. ed., 1985) contains a critical but balanced account of U.S. foreign policy during the war, as well as a cogent interpretation of the wartime origins of the cold war.

For inflation and economic issues in the postwar years, see Lester V. Chandler, *Inflation in the United States, 1940–1948* (1951). Stephen Kemp Bailey's *Congress Makes a Law: The Story behind the Employment Act of 1946* (1950) is a classic study of the techniques and processes involved in the enactment of Public Law 304. For the G.I. Bill and other veterans' benefits, see Davis R. B. Ross, *Preparing for Ulysses: Politics and Veterans during World War II* (1969).

Eric F. Goldman's *The Crucial Decade—and After: America, 1945–1960* (1960) contains some intriguing glimpses of the domestic scene after 1945. Broad perspectives are provided in John Brooks, *The Great Leap: The Past Twenty-five Years in America* (1966). Two very different but quite useful works on the broad period beginning during the Second World War are William H. Chafe and Harvard Sitkoff (eds.), *A History of Our Time: Readings on Postwar America* (1983), and Alonzo L. Hamby, *Liberalism and Its Challengers: FDR to Reagan* (1985).

CHAPTER TWO

The Cold War: Confrontation and Containment

AFTER THE WAR Americans settled down to enjoy the fruits of the Allied victory, confident that the major threats to international peace and stability had been destroyed. But to their dismay they soon discovered that the United States faced a new time of testing— a far-reaching conflict with the Soviet Union that seemed ready at any moment to precipitate a worldwide holocaust. This "cold war," as it was labeled, polarized many nations of the world into Communist and anti-Communist blocs, produced a generation of recurrent confrontations and crises, and profoundly influenced almost every consideration of foreign policy and national politics on the part of the principal protagonists. Most Americans eventually came to believe that drastic steps must be taken to counter Soviet moves, that vast amounts of aid were required by friendly allies, and that U.S. military power must be available around the globe.

AMERICA FACES RUSSIA

The immediate origins of the momentous struggle that developed between the United States and the USSR lay in the wartime relations between the Russians and the Americans and British, in the way the war changed the earlier balance of power in Europe and Asia, and in the fact that the United States and the Soviet Union had emerged as the two most powerful nations on earth. The two superpowers were soon at loggerheads over treatment of the occupied countries of Eastern Europe, the fate of Germany, the economic reconstruction of Europe, conditions in the eastern Mediterranean, the future of East Asia, and control of atomic energy. In July 1945 at the Potsdam Conference, the last wartime meeting of the Big

Three heads of state, the fundamental differences between the USSR and the Western Allies became clear. Agreements were finally reached on the questions of reparations and the occupation of Germany, and the Russians reluctantly conceded permission for British and American observers to move about freely in occupied countries in Eastern Europe. But these agreements were not self-enforcing, and even at Potsdam they scarcely concealed the deep cleavage that now divided the former allies. At the Potsdam Conference the West accepted Polish occupation of German territory as far as the Oder-Neisse line and approved the Russian annexation of eastern Poland. President Truman and his advisers were unhappy about the Soviet spheres of influence in Eastern Europe, but they had no real alternative in view of the fact that the Red Army already occupied most of these areas. They could only hope that Joseph Stalin would live up to his earlier commitments to permit free elections and minority rights in the East European nations.

At Potsdam a Council of Foreign Ministers was approved to draft definitive peace treaties with Italy and the former Axis satellites. The council held numerous conferences and struggled between September 1945 and the end of 1946 to overcome the chronic disagreements and hostility between East and West. Treaties with Italy, Finland, Hungary, Rumania, and Bulgaria were finally concluded. The Italian settlement was favorable to the Western Allies, but in the other treaties the Western powers acquiesced in Soviet control of Hungary and the Balkans. No agreement could be reached in the case of Austria, part of which was being occupied and exploited by Russia. A Russian regime was also imposed on Albania, Marshall Josip Tito's Communists controlled Yugoslavia, and a Communist movement shared power in Czechoslovakia.

The United States gradually adopted a firmer posture in its dealings with the Soviet Union. In October 1945, President Truman delivered what some officials described as a "getting tough with the Russians" speech. American policy, he declared, was "based firmly on fundamental principles of righteousness and justice." The United States would "refuse to recognize any government imposed on any nation by the force of any foreign power." In early January 1946, an exasperated Truman told Secretary of State James F. Byrnes, "Unless Russia is faced with an iron fist and strong language another war is in the making. Only one language do they understand—'how many divisions have you?' . . . I'm tired of babying the Soviets." In March 1946 Winston Churchill delivered a memorable address at Westminster College in Fulton, Missouri, an appearance Truman helped arrange. The former prime minister warned his audience that an "Iron Curtain" had descended across Europe "from Stettin in the Baltic to Trieste in the Adriatic," and he asserted his conviction that there was nothing for which the Russians had "less respect than for weakness, especially military weakness."

A series of incidents in 1946 heightened the increasing tension between Russia and the West. While doubtless fortuitous in their timing, several of these developments appeared almost as a direct response to Truman's stiffening position and Churchill's Iron Curtain warning. The Russians created a crisis over Iran by refusing to withdraw their troops from that country in accordance with a previous agreement. They made demands on Turkey for naval bases and a "joint defense" of that country. They refused to become a member of the World Bank and the International Monetary Fund, agencies that were largely supported by American economic strength. They launched a new five-year plan and made a significant change in their economic policy toward East Germany. And they timed their evacuation of Manchuria in such a way as to leave valuable matériel to benefit the Chinese Communists in their struggle with Chiang Kai-shek's Nationalist forces. The Soviet reaction to the plan for international control of nuclear energy that the United States presented to the United Nations in June 1946 was incomprehensible to Americans. The Russians refused to accept the provi-

The Big Three at Potsdam (*U.S. Army photograph, courtesy Harry S. Truman Library*)

sions calling for international management and supervision, while vociferously demanding that the United States show its good faith by unilaterally destroying its atomic weapons. Meanwhile, as the world soon learned, the USSR was rapidly completing the development of its own atomic bomb.

The major bone of contention between the Soviet Union and the West, however, was the "German question." The Russians were fearful of a reunited Germany that they could not control; the West was afraid of a Soviet-dominated Germany that would destroy the possibility of a balance of power in postwar Europe. Russia's obstructionist tactics soon produced friction within the four-power Allied Control Council, and with help from France, still uneasy about German power, the Soviet Union blocked all efforts to unite Germany economically and politically. The Russians also stripped the eastern zone of industrial equipment and exploited its economy, while claiming a share of the industrial plant in the other three zones. In May 1946 the Western powers ended German reparations to the Soviet Union, and in the autumn of that year the United States gave up the attempt to secure a united Germany. Within a short time, the USSR and the Western Allies were involved in a propagandist and ideological contest to win the support of the Germans—the dreaded enemy only two years before!

Neither side fully understood the objectives of the other, and neither appreciated the source of the other's suspicions and fears. The overriding significance of the Second World War, for Soviet leaders, was security on their country's borders and control over nearby governments. American leaders were genuinely alarmed by the Soviet Union's expansion into regions of Eastern and Central Europe formerly dominated by Germany. They expected the Russians to live up to the Yalta Conference's "Declaration on Liberated Europe," which affirmed the principles enunciated in the British-American Atlantic Charter of 1941 and pledged its signatories to self-government through free and open elections. Although the United States was motivated by self-interest, including foreign investments and open markets in Europe, its spokesmen were also committed to traditional American values of self-determination, democracy, and humanitarianism. The central problem, Secretary of War Henry L. Stimson declared in July 1945, grew out of "the fundamental differences between a nation of free thought, free speech, [and] free elections . . . with a nation which is not basically free but which is systematically controlled from above by Secret Police and in which free speech is not permitted."

The situation that existed two years after the close of World War II was startlingly new to Americans. As Dean Acheson expressed it in June 1946, "We have got to understand that all our lives the danger, the uncertainty, the need for alertness, for effort, for discipline will be upon us. This is new for us. It will be hard for us." It proved to be a remarkably accurate forecast.

THE ARCHITECTS OF CONTAINMENT

The containment doctrine that President Truman urged Congress to approve in the spring of 1947 was the product of no single leader, group, or party, even though it rightly came to be identified most closely with Truman and his administration. The consensus that quickly formed in support of containment may tempt one to assume that, given the Russian position in postwar Europe, such a policy was inevitable, almost foreordained. The question arises, however, as to whether containment would have become a national policy had Franklin D. Roosevelt lived to serve out his fourth term. It is impossible to know. Perhaps Roosevelt's supreme confidence and great flexibility would have made possible a broad settlement with the masters of the Kremlin. Roosevelt accepted the concept of big-power domination, and he hoped to integrate the USSR into the structure of postwar security. Yet when FDR died, he was moving toward a position of insisting that the Russians honor their agreements. One suspects that the cold war would have come even had Roosevelt lived on in the White House.

Harry Truman continued Roosevelt's policy of cooperation with the wartime allies and his efforts to work out an accommodation with the Soviet Union. He lent wholehearted support to the organization of the United Nations, sent Harry L. Hopkins, Roosevelt's most trusted adviser, on a special mission to talk with Marshal Stalin in May 1945, and helped arrange the conference of the Big Three at Potsdam during the following summer. But he came to the presidency with an abiding distrust of Communist ideology, and when suddenly faced with awesome responsibilities for which he had virtually no preparation, he was naturally less patient, flexible, and confident than his illustrious predecessor. Heeding the advice of W. Averell Harriman and other advocates of greater resistance to the Soviet Union, the new president quickly moved to a showdown with the Russians over the issue of Poland. Although his transition from wary friend to implacable foe of the USSR was gradual, he became increasingly demanding in his relations with Moscow in 1946. In September of that year he dismissed Secretary of Commerce Henry Wallace when Wallace openly criticized the administration's policy toward Russia. Truman was influenced, like many other American leaders, by the assumption that the Soviet Union's great need for economic assistance in the postwar period would make Stalin more amenable to United States demands. His "get-tough" posture was also bolstered by the immeasurable weight of the American monopoly of the atomic bomb in all calculations involving the national interest and perhaps by his frustrating setbacks on domestic issues in 1946 and 1947. Tending to personalize foreign policy and to approach international issues in terms of his own political experience, Truman was determined to avoid the trap of appeasement and to do all he could to prevent the recurrence of another Munich.

The principal spokesman for the Truman administration's foreign policy during the crucial eighteen months between the Potsdam Conference and the end of 1946 was James F. Byrnes, who succeeded Edward R. Stettinius, Jr., as secretary of state in June 1945. The genial, quick-witted, and urbane Byrnes, a South Carolinian, had little experience in foreign affairs. But he hoped to maintain the Grand Alliance and to achieve a stable world order after the war. He assumed that a *quid pro quo* strategy in negotiating with the Soviet Union would make possible a series of acceptable compromises between the two powers. Yet like the president, he gradually adopted a harsher line in dealing with the Russian leaders, a toughness, the historian Richard D. Burns observes, "anchored, not to military and economic strength, but to a moral rhetoric which created the illusion of ultimate success."

Byrnes was succeeded in January 1947 by George C. Marshall, a distinguished military officer who had served as Army chief of staff during the war. While Marshall shared the fundamental assumptions of President Truman and Secretary Byrnes about the nature of the East-West split, he was not one of the major architects of containment. Rather, his role was that of presiding over the process of transforming the doctrine into a national policy. A more important contribution to the formulation of containment was made by Under Secretary of State Dean Acheson. A diplomatic "realist," Acheson did not accept Woodrow Wilson's faith in international organization as an adequate foundation for American foreign policy or the achievement of stability in the world, nor did he agree that the purpose of U.S. policy abroad was "to carry out a 'crusade' or 'mission' to bring about equal justice or to vindicate international law." The great task in the conduct of American foreign policy, he believed, was to apply morality *and* power in handling international relations. As for the Soviet Union, Acheson had long been distrustful of its policies, which he termed "aggressive and expanding."

No member of Congress contributed more to the creation of an American consensus on the doctrine of containment than Senator

Arthur H. Vandenberg of Michigan, chairman of the Senate Foreign Relations Committee in the Eightieth Congress (1947–48). A Republican and a staunch isolationist before Pearl Harbor, Vandenberg experienced a dramatic change of heart during World War II, becoming a strong supporter of a world peace organization and his party's leading advocate of an internationalist foreign policy. Vandenberg more than any other Republican leader prepared the way for the bipartisan foreign policy that flourished during the early years of the Truman administration. The Michigan senator was in complete agreement with the get-tough policy that Truman and Byrnes gradually adopted in dealing with the Russians in 1945 and 1946. And he played a key role in congressional approval of the containment program in 1947. Vandenberg, as well as such internationalist Republicans as Thomas E. Dewey and John Foster Dulles, sometimes differed with Truman over tactics, but he was no less critical of the Soviet Union and no less insistent that American strength be exerted to counter Russian expansionism.

The American who provided the ideological base for the containment doctrine was George F. Kennan, a Foreign Service officer who was serving in Moscow when the war ended. Kennan, who believed in the diplomacy of "reality," had become convinced of the Soviet Union's deep-seated expansionist aims. In a long cable to the State Department in February 1946, the diplomat outlined the strategy that later became official national policy. In explaining Soviet behavior, he expressed the increasingly strong feeling among American leaders that it was futile to seek further agreements with the Russians. Soviet leaders, Kennan warned, had a "neurotic view of world affairs. And they have learned to seek security only in patient but deadly struggle for total destruction of rival power, never in compacts and compromises with it." Yet Soviet power was "neither schematic nor adventuristic," Kennan contended. "It does not take unnecessary risks. For this reason it can easily withdraw—and usually does—when strong resistance is encountered at any point." The main element of any U.S. policy toward the USSR, Kennan later wrote in a famous article published in *Foreign Affairs*, "must be that of a long-term, patient, but firm and vigilant containment of Russian expansive tendencies." This would increase "the strains under which Soviet policy must operate," force the Kremlin to show more "moderation and circumspection," and promote tendencies that "must eventually find their outlet in either the break-up or the gradual mellowing of Soviet power."

Kennan's cogent and eloquent language expressed the views and predispositions that had come to prevail among American leaders by early 1947. The formulation of specific policies to implement the containment doctrine awaited only the formal decision of the Truman administration. And the precipitant of such a decision would almost certainly be another in the recurring crises in East-West relations.

THE TRUMAN DOCTRINE AND THE MARSHALL PLAN

The crisis came in the eastern Mediterranean early in 1947. Russian pressure on Iran continued, despite the withdrawal of Soviet troops from that country in the spring of 1946. Nor had the Russian leaders given up their demands on Turkey for territorial cessions and naval bases in the Bosporus. Although the USSR was not an active force in Greece, the Greek royalist regime was encountering mounting pressure from Communist-dominated rebels in the northern part of the country. In late February 1947, the British quietly informed Washington that they could no longer bear the burden of supporting the Greek government; British troops would soon be withdrawn, thus ending that nation's historic role as a great power in the eastern Mediterranean. Greece and Turkey turned for financial and military assistance to the United States, which was keenly aware of the vital importance of the region in the East-West conflict. "If Greece was lost," Truman later wrote in his *Memoirs*, "Turkey would become an untenable outpost in a sea of Communism. Similarly, if Turkey yielded to Soviet demands, the position of Greece would be extremely endangered."

President Truman and Secretary Marshall were determined to prevent the Russians from taking advantage of the British withdrawal to move into the eastern Mediterranean. After being informed of the British decision to withdraw from Greece, Truman conferred with congressional leaders of both parties, obtaining their backing of his plan of action. Senator Vandenberg was later quoted as saying at that conference, "Mr. President, if that's what you want, there's only one way to get it. That is to make a personal appearance before Congress and scare hell out of the country." Truman took Vandenberg's advice, and in an appearance before a joint session of Congress on March 12, 1947, he requested approval of a $400 million program of military and economic assistance to Greece and Turkey.

The president proclaimed what came to be called the Truman Doctrine. He described in grim words the way in which "totalitarian regimes" were threatening to snuff out freedom in various parts of the world. The United States, Truman declared, must "support free peoples who are resisting attempted subjugation by armed minorities or by outside pressures." If Americans faltered in their leadership, Truman warned, "we may endanger the peace of the world—and we shall surely endanger the welfare of our own nation." Congress approved the administration's request, and the Greek-Turkish Aid bill became a law in May 1947.

It was soon evident that the Truman Doctrine was working. The United States spent over $650 million in aid to Greece and Turkey between 1947 and 1950, and the eastern Mediterranean remained within the Western sphere. Turkey was able to strengthen its economy and modernize its armed forces. The Greek problem was more difficult, but the government there succeeded in reorganizing the army and accelerating its campaign against the Communist insurgents. After Yugoslavia broke with the Soviet Union in 1948, the Greek guerrillas were deprived of a major source of support, and the civil war was finally ended in the fall of 1949.

The Truman Doctrine cleared the way for a gigantic American aid program abroad. The former was essentially a military program, and its application was intended to be specific and limited. But it was a natural first step in the evolution of a much more comprehensive and imaginative enterprise to strengthen European nations against the challenge of Communist domination. This broader and more audacious undertaking emerged not only from the Kremlin's growing recalcitrance, the bitter conflict between the Western Allies and Russia over the future of Germany, and the precedent for bold American action provided by the Truman Doctrine, but also from the terrible internal conditions that existed in the countries of Western Europe in 1946 and 1947. Although the United States had already committed $11 billion in postwar relief, loans, and other kinds of aid to these countries, they were experiencing severe food and fuel shortages. Their leaders were also haunted by the specter of social upheaval. Europe, declared Churchill, had become "a rubble heap, a charnel house, a breeding ground of pestilence and hate."

Soon after Secretary Marshall returned from Moscow, where a Council of Foreign Ministers meeting on Germany ended in failure in late April 1947, the Truman administration began to develop a program to provide further aid to Western Europe and at the same time to resist Russian expansion. Much of the work on this European aid program was done by the Policy Planning Staff in the State Department, a special committee recently created by Marshall and headed by George Kennan. This group worked at a furious pace in May. It recommended that short-term assistance be provided to arrest the deterioration of the European economy and that a long-range program be launched to encourage the economic integration of Western and Central Europe. Kennan and his colleagues had devised a bold plan to contain communism by eradicating the poverty and misery that provided much of its sustenance.

The essentials of what was soon labeled the Marshall Plan were set forth in a commencement address delivered by Marshall at Harvard University on June 5, 1947. The secretary proposed a gigantic reconstruction of the European economy, to be financed largely by the United States but to be worked out as a joint plan between the United States and the European nations. Marshall spoke less in terms of anticommunism than of humanitarianism. But there was no mistaking the diplomatic and ideological objectives of the scheme. "Our policy is directed not against any country or doctrine but against hunger, poverty, desperation and chaos," Marshall asserted. "Its purpose should be the revival of a working economy in the world so as to permit the emergence of political and social conditions in which free institutions can exist."

Western Europe responded immediately. Great Britain and France took the lead in convening a European conference in Paris in July 1947. Since the American plan did not exclude Eastern Europe in this preliminary stage, Soviet leaders hesitated briefly before deciding to boycott the Paris meeting; they were joined in doing so by their satellite nations and by Finland and Czechoslovakia, where Russian influence was great. But the representatives of sixteen nations met in Paris and prepared an elaborate plan for European recovery, estimated to cost $22 billion over a period of four years. In December 1947, President Truman submitted this plan to Congress, with his own recommendation for an appropriation of $17 billion over a four-year period.

The novelty of the request and the enormous amount of money it called for shocked many Americans and provoked sharp criticism in Congress. The strongest congressional opposition came from Senator Robert A. Taft of Ohio and his supporters, whose ranks included some of the nation's traditional isolationists. Men of the Taft persuasion feared that the Marshall Plan would wreck the American economy and lead to a third world war. It was a huge "international WPA," one critic asserted. The support for the proposal was impressively large, however. Liberals of both parties backed it. A powerful array of business, farm, and labor organizations endorsed the plan, recognizing the beneficial effects it would have on the national economy. Vandenberg led the bipartisan supporters of the administration measure, calling it a "calculated risk" to "help stop World War III before it starts." Events in Europe also contributed to congressional approval, particularly the Communist coup in Czechoslovakia, a nation to which Americans had a strong sentimental attachment.

Congress approved the aid program in March, and it was signed by the president on April 3, 1948. Under Vandenberg's leadership the four-year commitment sought by the administration was eliminated and the first installment was reduced somewhat, from $6.8 billion to $5.3 billion. But no one could doubt that the Truman administration had won a great victory and that its foreign policy had been given an overwhelming vote of confidence. The law established a European Recovery Program (ERP) to be carried out by the Economic Cooperation Administration, which in turn was supposed to work with the Committee of European Economic Cooperation.

By the end of 1952 the United States had spent about $13 billion on this program. The results were very encouraging. Industrial production in the Marshall Plan countries had increased by 64 percent within three years. An impetus was given to the economic integration and unification of Western Europe—to such eventual developments as the European Steel and Coal Community and the Common Market. West Europeans had regained their confidence, and the Communist threats in France and Italy had been substantially lessened.

The Truman Doctrine and the Marshall Plan constituted a revolutionary shift in American foreign policy. For the first time in a period of peace, the United States had committed its military and economic strength to the defense of nations outside the Western Hemisphere. The United States had involved itself directly in the internal affairs of countries like Greece, and a host of American experts and advisers were soon swarming over Europe to help implement a vast program of reconstruction. Even more significant, perhaps, was the primary justification for these striking new policies. Their purpose, it was endlessly proclaimed, was to prevent the expansion of the Soviet Union and to halt the spread of international communism.

FORGING NEW COALITIONS

The Marshall Plan exacerbated the differences between the United States and the Soviet Union and, in combination with the worsening controversy over Germany, provoked the Russians into drastic action and created still another crisis in East-West relations. The Kremlin denounced the European Recovery Program as an example of American imperialism and an effort to establish continental bases for aggression against the USSR. The Soviet leaders had not been idle in the face of American and Western European activities in 1946 and 1947. They had set up a new Communist Information

Bureau (Cominform) to ensure unity throughout Eastern Europe. In February 1948 Communist workers in Czechoslovakia had carried out a successful coup and forced that country into the Russian orbit. Nevertheless, the Russians were profoundly disturbed by the Marshall Plan and the unity it inspired in Western Europe. Moscow had also suffered a setback when Yugoslavia, its strongest satellite, refused to follow the Soviet line and succeeded in striking out on an independent course.

Then there was the acute problem of Germany, where the Western powers were moving rapidly to effect an economic and political consolidation of their zones. In June 1948, the three Western Allies announced consolidation. The resulting "Trizonia" comprised a rich industrial area with a population of 50 million people, in contrast to the 17 million residents of the Soviet zone. The consolidated western region was brought into the recovery machinery of the Marshall Plan, and a drastic reform of the West German currency was carried out. The Russians resisted these efforts to unify western Germany, and in the early spring of 1948 they began to obstruct the traffic between the western zones and Berlin, located a hundred miles inside the eastern zone. There were violent scenes in the four-power Control Council for Berlin. When the Western powers extended their currency reform to their sectors of Berlin on June 23, Soviet leaders responded by stopping all surface traffic between the western zones and the capital city. They cited the fact that the Western Allies had never secured a written agreement guaranteeing land access to Berlin. Although the Russians maintained that they were blockading the city because of the new currency reform, it was obvious that they were trying to force the Western powers to abandon their plans for a united West Germany or, failing in that, to bring about their withdrawal from Berlin and thus achieve a great symbolic victory in the cold war.

American leaders refused to give ground. General Lucius D. Clay, deputy military governor of the American zone, wanted to use an armed convoy to break the blockade. "When Berlin falls, western Germany will be next," the general warned. President Truman was equally adamant, declaring, "We [are] going to stay period." But Truman did not resort to the provocative action recommended by General Clay and some other advisers. He imposed a counterblockade against the Russians in Germany and, with the British, supported the non-Communist majorities on the Berlin City Council, forcing the Soviet representatives to set up a separate administration for their sector of the city. But most important of all, he decided to prevent the starvation of West Berliners by using air transport to supply their needs. This continuous airlift, operated by the U.S. Air

Force and the British Royal Air Force, was maintained for 324 days, with 277,264 flights in all and a total cargo of 2.5 million tons of food, coal, and other supplies. The airlift was a spectacular success; it saved West Berlin and lifted the morale of its people. Early in the blockade, the Truman administration did resort to a little saber rattling: the president ordered two groups of B-29 bombers—planes designed to carry atomic bombs—sent to England.

In the end, Western resistance and the success of the airlift caused the Russians to give in. They agreed to lift the blockade if the Western powers would reopen the whole German question and discuss the Austrian peace treaty at a new meeting of the Council of Foreign Ministers. After more than ten months, the blockade was ended on May 12, 1949, on the same day the foreign ministers met in Paris. The Paris conference made no real progress on the German problem, but it provided the Soviet Union with a diplomatic pretext for abandoning the Berlin blockade. In the meantime, the United States and its West European allies were completing the formation of a West German state, the Federal Republic of Germany. The Russians also acted. In October 1949 they created the German Democratic Republic, with its capital in East Berlin. Thus, instead of a single reunited Germany, there were now two German nations.

While these developments were taking place, Western Europe and the United States had formulated and adopted an extensive military alliance that was designed to counter Soviet expansionism. The Truman Doctrine and the Marshall Plan had pointed the way. But the Western European nations had also done their part. France and Belgium had signed a mutual defense agreement in March 1947. Great Britain had indicated a willingness, in January 1948, to join in a Western European union. And in Brussels on March 17, 1948, Britain, France, and the Benelux countries had entered into a fifty-year treaty of economic cooperation and military alliance. Early the following year the Council of Europe was established. The Council, which included the Federal Republic of Germany, had broader representation than the Brussels Pact. These agreements stimulated the interest of American leaders in a still broader military alliance, for despite this evidence of West European unity, they were dubious about the effectiveness of military strength in Western Europe. At the time of the Brussels agreement, there were only about a dozen inadequately equipped and poorly trained divisions in the whole region. A significant indication of American interest and intent came from Washington in June 1948, when Arthur H. Vandenberg introduced a resolution in the Senate to encourage "the progressive development of regional and other collective arrangements" for defense and to promote the "association of the United States" with

North Atlantic Treaty Organization

such organizations. The Senate speedily approved the Vandenberg resolution, by a vote of 64 to 4.

The Truman administration, which was already searching for means to this end, took advantage of the Vandenberg resolution to begin discussions the following month with the Western European powers. A conference of most of the Marshall Plan countries met in Washington early in 1949 and drafted the North Atlantic Treaty. It was formally adopted on April 4, 1949, by the United States, Canada, and ten West European countries. Greece and Turkey joined NATO in 1952, and three years later West Germany became a member. The treaty constituted a twenty-year military pact. Each member pledged itself to lend military support, which was to be jointly organized and supervised by the North Atlantic Council, the secretary-general, and the Military Committee. The members also agreed that

> an armed attack against one or more of them in Europe or North America shall be considered an attack against them all; and consequently they agree that, if such an armed attack occurs, each of them, in exercise of the right of individual or collective self-defense recognized by Article 51 of the Charter of the United Nations, will assist the Party or Parties so attacked by taking . . . such action as it deems necessary, including the use of armed force, to restore and maintain the security of the North Atlantic area.

The U.S. Senate ratified the treaty on July 21, 1949, by an overwhelming majority of 82 to 13. In late September, while Congress was still considering the initial appropriation for NATO, President Truman informed the public that the Soviet Union a few weeks earlier had exploded an atomic device. Within six days Congress voted $1 billion for NATO arms and equipment under the Mutual Defense Assistance Act, with an additional $211 million for Greece and Turkey.

Efforts to construct a formidable military force under the North Atlantic Treaty Organization began in earnest in 1950. Late that year General Dwight D. Eisenhower was appointed supreme commander, and soon afterward the Supreme Headquarters of the Allied Powers in Europe (SHAPE) was established near Paris. The president had also directed that the development of a more powerful nuclear weapon, the hydrogen bomb, be accelerated. American military authorities, acting within the framework of the administration's policy, were determined to build a large conventional European army, an army that would include German military units. The commitment to NATO meant that the United States had abandoned its long tradition of avoiding permanent peacetime alliances. As Secretary Acheson put it, the United States had learned "that the control of Europe by a single aggressive unfriendly power would constitute an intolerable threat to the national security of the United States."

While American leaders concentrated on European reconstruction and the containment of Russian communism on that continent, they also tried to devise policies and machinery in other parts of the world that would strengthen the nation's position in the cold war. The United States was eager to present a united front in the Western Hemisphere toward the Soviet Union and the challenge of international communism. Canada, whose relations with the United States had grown closer during World War II, became an ally in NATO. Latin America was less predictable, although the Good Neighbor Policy of the 1930s had resulted in some relaxation of tension between the United States and the twenty nations to the south, and all of the Latin American countries except Argentina had cooperated to some extent in waging war against the Axis powers.

The United States took the first step in the direction of postwar unity in Latin America by arranging a special conference in Mexico City in February 1945. The result was the Act of Chapultepec, which was eventually signed by all Latin American states; it stipulated that any attack upon one American state would be met by the combined forces of all of them. In June 1947, after the Truman Doctrine had been announced, President Truman indicated that the United States was seeking a mutual defense agreement that would guarantee concerted hemispheric action. In the late summer, delegates from twenty-one American republics met at Rio de Janeiro to consider enforcement machinery for the Act of Chapultepec. On September 2, 1947, they adopted the Inter-American Treaty of Reciprocal Assistance. This agreement established a broad security zone around the North and South American continents, declared that an attack anywhere in this zone would constitute an attack against all American states, and provided for collective self-defense for the Western Hemisphere, as a regional association permitted under Articles 51 and 52 of the United Nations Charter. In the spring of 1948, at the Ninth Inter-American Conference at Bogotá, the charter for the Organization of American States was drafted, giving full constitutional status to the inter-American system. As the historian David Green has written, "All non-American military and political power had been successfully excluded from the hemisphere."

In spite of this evidence of hemispheric unity, Latin America was a caldron of social misery and potential upheaval. Economic colonialism flourished, the gap between rich and poor continued to widen, the army assumed an ever larger role in politics, and few countries were able to maintain political stability for any length of time. Many Latin Americans remained suspicious of the United States, which was clearly giving priority to European recovery over Latin American development. Truman's Point Four program, announced in his inaugural address in January 1949, promised U.S. technical aid "to supply the vitalizing force to stir the peoples of the world into triumphant action, not only against their human oppressors, but also against their ancient enemies—hunger, misery, and despair." This new program to make the benefits of American scientific and industrial progress available for the improvement of underdeveloped areas was aimed primarily at Latin America. But one of its goals was the stimulation of private investment in the region, and ironically, it had the effect of helping to perpetuate the colonial and extractive character of the Latin American economy.

During the early months of 1950, the National Security Council, in response to an order from the president, carried out "an over-all review and re-assessment of American foreign and defense policy." The resulting study—NSC 68—was a comprehensive statement of the nation's defense strategy. After reviewing the various policy alternatives in the cold war, the authors of NSC 68 concluded that the only logical course open to the United States was the development of free-world military capabilities. They advocated an immediate and large-scale buildup in the military and economic strength of the United States and its allies in order to meet "each fresh challenge promptly and unequivocally." Although Truman did not immediately make the document public, its recommendations were to provide a blueprint for the United States in waging the cold war during the next two decades. NSC 68, Stephen E. Ambrose writes, "represented the practical extension of the Truman Doctrine, which had been worldwide in its implications but limited to Europe in its application. The document provided the justification for America's assuming the role of world policeman."

THE COLD WAR CONSENSUS

As the rift between the Western powers and the Soviet Union widened during the first eighteen months after V-J Day, American opinion seemed to be divided into three fairly distinct positions. At one extreme was the view that the breakup of the Grand Alliance and the intransigence of the Russians required the United States and its European allies to resort to balance-of-power politics to protect Western interests. At the other extreme stood those who believed that British and American aggressiveness was provoking Soviet hostility and that the United States had no business interfering with Russian control in Eastern Europe. The U.S. government and the largest part of the public, representing a third position, seemed for a time to waver between the two extremes. Yet by 1947 a large number of Americans, probably a majority of the population, had come to approve a get-tough policy toward the USSR. Many people in the United States viewed the struggle with communism in terms that were reminiscent of the recent war against fascism. This gave currency to the image of "red fascism," the idea that the Soviet Union was a replica of Nazi Germany and that Joseph Stalin was the "Russian Hitler."

Nevertheless, general agreement on the containment of the Soviet Union did not emerge overnight, and several obstacles had to be overcome before such a consensus was created. At the end of the war most Americans were unprepared for the demands of the new international age—for the responsibilities of world leadership, the complexities of European politics, the enormous costs of national defense and foreign aid that containment entailed, the imposition of internal security controls, and the powerful effect that foreign policy came to have on almost every domestic consideration. The idealism associated with the vision of "one world" and the strong faith in the United Nations challenged the assumptions that supported the containment program. There was also some reluctance in the United States to support reactionary governments like that of Greece in the name of democracy and morality.

The most spectacular dissent from the Truman administration's hardening opposition to the Russians was led by Henry A. Wallace, who was dismissed from the Cabinet after calling for a softer line toward the Soviet Union. Wallace and his supporters saw no reason why the wartime collaboration with the Russians could not continue. They discounted the charges of Soviet aggression and contended that the USSR would cooperate with the Western powers if the West recognized the Russian sphere in Eastern Europe and otherwise showed that it had no intention of "encircling" the Soviet Union. Wallace lost much of his support when he attacked the Marshall Plan, and as a Progressive party nominee for president in 1948 he was tellingly assaulted by Democratic spokesmen, including the Americans for Democratic Action, for opposing the containment policies and allegedly making common cause with Communist groups in this country.

Meanwhile, there had also been some conservative opposition to the Truman policies. At the beginning of 1947, just before the Truman Doctrine was made public, East-West tensions seemed to ease somewhat following the completion of the Big Three peace treaties with Germany's former puppet states, Bulgaria, Hungary, and Rumania. The Republicans, led by such economy-in-government advocates as Robert Taft, controlled Congress. The Taft wing of the party was suspicious not only of costly foreign aid programs but also of aggressive foreign policies in general that were sponsored by the administration.

A series of events, plus the deep division over foreign policy in the Republican party, played a vital role in undermining potentially powerful opposition to the containment doctrine. These developments included Russian pressure on Iran and Turkey in 1946, the Soviet Union's chronic obstructionism in the UN's Security Council, the crisis atmosphere surrounding the eastern Mediterranean in early 1947, the Communist coup in Czechoslovakia in 1948, the Berlin blockade of 1948–49, the fall of Nationalist China in 1949, the Russian explosion of an atomic bomb in 1949, and the mounting fear of a Communist conspiracy in the United States. These events provided the Truman administration with several dramatic issues, cleared the way for the announcement of the containment policy, and contributed mightily to the emergence of a cold war consensus. Truman's startling electoral victory in 1948 also strengthened the emerging American consensus on foreign policy. The administration, frustrated in its domestic policies, made skillful use of foreign policy to increase its support during the campaign, and such alarming developments as the Czech coup and the Berlin blockade enhanced its credibility. Fundamentally, containment can be seen as a series of attempts to deal with the consequences of World War II. Forced by expediency to cooperate with the Russians during the war, U.S. leaders soon accepted the idea that it would be necessary, in John L. Gaddis's words, "to prevent the Soviet Union from using the power and position it won as a result of that conflict to reshape the postwar international order."

The national consensus that emerged by 1949 was one of the most remarkable aspects—and manifestations—of the revolution in American foreign policy in the 1940s. Even so, there were limits to this consensus. It did not extend to China and the Far East. Also, the bipartisanship of the late 1940s began to break down by 1950, as Republicans mounted an attack on the Democratic administration's foreign policies. In 1950, for example, Senator Taft and former president Herbert Hoover strongly indicted the Truman administration for its plans to use American ground troops in Europe, for its neglect of the Western Hemisphere, and for the heavy financial burden of its foreign programs. Other critics, including George Kennan and Walter Lippmann, were deploring what they regarded as the excessive moralism and legalism of United States policy makers.

Despite such criticisms, the broad agreement on the policies adopted to contain the expansion of Russian communism continued after the end of Democratic control in 1952. The consensus did not break down until the bitter divisions over the war in Vietnam brought a reassessment of American policy in the late 1960s. In the long interim the radical transformation that had occurred in American attitudes and policies soon after the war largely determined the nation's role in international affairs.

SUGGESTIONS FOR FURTHER READING

The best general works on the American side of the cold war are John W. Spanier, *American Foreign Policy since World War II* (7th ed., 1977); Walter LaFeber, *America, Russia, and the Cold War, 1945–1984* (5th ed., 1985); and Stephen E. Ambrose, *Rise to Globalism: American Foreign Policy Since 1938* (4th rev. ed., 1985). The first of these is favorable in its evaluation of containment; the latter two are more critical. A newer work, Bernard A. Weisberger's *Cold War, Cold Peace: The United States and Russia Since 1945* (1984) offers a stimulating and balanced interpretation. Ralph B. Levering, *The Cold War, 1945–1972* (1982), is a good introduction to the diplomacy of the cold war. Other useful general studies include Norman A. Graebner, *Cold War Diplomacy: American Foreign Policy, 1945–1960* (1962); Louis J. Halle, *The Cold War as History* (1967); Seyom Brown, *The Faces of Power: Constancy and Change in United States Foreign Policy from Truman to Johnson* (1968); Adam B. Ulam, *The Rivals: America and Russia since World War II* (1971); Richard J. Barnet, *The Giants: Russia and America* (1977); and Thomas G. Paterson, *On Every Front: The Making of the Cold War* (1979). Robert A. Divine, *Since 1945: Politics and Diplomacy in Recent American History* (3rd ed., 1985), concentrates on reform initiatives at home and the cold war abroad.

John Lewis Gaddis's *The United States and the Origins of the Cold War, 1941–1947* (1972) is the most authoritative treatment of the genesis of the cold war. The same author's *Strategies of Containment: A Critical Appraisal of Postwar American National Security Policy* (1982) is a thoughtful evaluation of U.S. policies through the 1970s. Other important books on this theme include John L. Snell, *Wartime Origins of the East-West Dilemma over Germany* (1959); Herbert Feis, *From Trust to Terror: The Onset of the Cold War, 1945–1950* (1970); Lynn Etheridge Davis, *The Cold War Begins: Soviet-American Conflict over Eastern Europe* (1974); Daniel Yergin, *A Shattered Peace: The Origins of the Cold War and the National Security State* (1977); Bruce Robellet Kuniholm, *The Origins of the Cold War in the Near East: Great Power Conflict and Diplomacy in Iran, Turkey, and Greece* (1980); and Lawrence S. Wittner, *American Intervention in Greece, 1943–1949* (1982). Economic factors are analyzed in George C. Herring, Jr., *Aid to Russia, 1941–1946: Strategy, Diplomacy, the Origins of the Cold War* (1973), and Thomas G. Paterson, *Soviet-American Confrontation: Postwar Reconstruction and the Origins of the Cold War* (1973). For differing interpretations of the role of the atomic bomb in U.S. diplomacy, see Gar Alperovitz, *Atomic Diplomacy: Hiroshima and Potsdam* (1965); Martin J. Sherwin, *A World Destroyed: The Atomic Bomb and the Grand Alliance* (1975); and Gregg Herken, *The Winning Weapon: The Atomic Bomb in the Cold War, 1945–1950* (1980). Among the significant revisionist studies are William Appleman Williams, *The Tragedy of American Diplomacy* (2nd rev. ed., 1972); David Horowitz, *The Free World Colossus: A Critique of American Foreign Policy in the Cold War* (rev. ed., 1971); Diane Shaver Clemens, *Yalta* (1970); and Joyce Kolko and Gabriel Kolko, *The Limits of Power: The World and United States Foreign Policy, 1945–1954* (1972). Critical evaluations of cold war revisionism are made by Robert W. Tucker, *The Radical Left and American Foreign Policy* (1971), and Robert James Maddox, *The New Left and the Origins of the Cold War* (1973). Several revisionist essays are included in Barton J. Bernstein (ed.), *Politics and Policies of the Truman Administration* (1970).

Lloyd C. Gardner presents a series of enlightening biographical studies in *Architects of Illusion: Men and Ideas in American Foreign Policy, 1941–1949* (1970). Four of the postwar secretaries of state are considered in Norman A. Graebner (ed.), *An Uncertain Tradition: American Secretaries of State in the Twentieth Century* (1961). One of these leaders is treated at greater length by Robert L. Messer, *The End of an Alliance: James F. Byrnes, Roosevelt, Truman, and the Origins of the Cold War* (1982). For the views of several key actors in the drama of recent U.S. foreign policy, see Dean Acheson, *Present at the Creation: My Years in the State Department* (1969), and George F. Kennan, *Memoirs, 1925–1950* (1967), two of the best firsthand accounts. Arthur H. Vandenberg, Jr. (ed.), *The Private Papers of Senator Vandenberg* (1952), and Harry S Truman, *Memoirs* (2 vols., 1955–1956), are also illuminating. An invaluable introduction to the scholarship on the Truman years is provided by Richard S. Kirkendall (ed.), *The Truman Period as a Research Field: A Reappraisal, 1972* (1974), and an earlier edition of the same work published in 1967.

The German problem in the early postwar period is dealt with in John Gimbel, *The American Occupation of Germany: Politics and the Military, 1945–1949* (1968); Lucius D. Clay, *Decision in Germany* (1950); and W. Phillips Davison, *The Berlin Blockade: A Study in Cold War Politics* (1958). Joseph M. Jones, *The Fifteen Weeks (February 21–June 5, 1947)* (1955), is an absorbing if uncritical account of the formulation of the Truman Doctrine and the Marshall Plan. The best book on the latter is Harry B. Price's *The Marshall Plan and Its Meaning* (1955). For NATO, see Robert Endicott Osgood, *N.A.T.O.: The Entangling Alliance* (1962); Timothy P. Ireland, *Creating the Entangling Alliance: The Origins of the North Atlantic Treaty Organization* (1981); and Lawrence S. Kaplan and Robert W. Clawson (eds.), *NATO After Thirty Years* (1981). Theodore H. White, *Fire in the Ashes: Europe in Mid-Century* (1953), throws light on the recovery of Western Europe.

CHAPTER THREE

Harry Truman
and the Politics
of Stalemate

THE POSTWAR SCENE that started unfolding in the United States in the autumn of 1945 promised to be very different from the prewar period, and many Americans anticipated a marked change in politics. It was difficult to conceive of national politics without Franklin Roosevelt, so vital and all-encompassing had been his influence on the political culture; yet it seemed clear that one era had ended and another was beginning in American politics. The new era, it was widely assumed, would be one of Republican dominance, and most people hoped that it would also be a time of relaxation and normality after the long years of national emergency and crisis. These hopes were soon frustrated. The postwar period was dominated by confusion, political division, and pressing problems related to such issues as demobilization, inflation, the role of organized labor, and civil rights, not to mention the unaccustomed pressures of foreign problems.

FDR AND THE LIBERAL TRADITION

Politics in the United States was transformed in the Age of Franklin D. Roosevelt. The thirty-second president dominated the political culture of his day as had none of his predecessors. He established an extraordinary identification with the mass of voters, fashioned strong organizational support, and helped bring about a fundamental realignment in the political system. Roosevelt made the Democratic party an instrument of progressive change, and he was the major contributor to a new liberal tradition of social reform and international involvement. His legacy was destined to have a profound influence on the course of American politics in the postwar period.

The 1930s had witnessed the coming of political age of the urban minorities, the emergence of organized labor as a powerful factor in politics, the shift of a majority of black voters into the Democratic column, and the development of strong loyalties to Roosevelt and the Democratic party on the part of millions of white-collar workers and middle-class Americans. The results of this political revolution were spectacular. FDR had been elected president four times, and the Democrats had ended the one-party domination that had long prevailed in many parts of New England, the Midwest, and the Far West and had won control of both houses of Congress in every election since 1930.

But all of this had changed—or appeared on the verge of changing—by the end of World War II. Bereft of the magnetic and compelling Roosevelt, the Democrats appeared to be leaderless and confused. Harry S Truman, the new president, seemed woefully unprepared to assume the mantle of Roosevelt's leadership. The Democrats, moreover, had been in power a long time, were badly divided along ideological lines, and faced the inevitable discontents and irritations that accumulated with lengthy tenure. A conservative coalition, led by southern Democrats and midwestern Republicans, had emerged in Congress in 1937, and while Roosevelt's foreign policies and war programs had served to unite the party in later years, the coalition asserted itself effectively on many domestic issues. There was also another discouraging prospect. The Democratic administration in Washington was confronted in the postwar period with the threat of rampant inflation rather than severe depression and deflation as in the 1930s. The politics of inflation, unlike the politics of depression, made it difficult to attract and retain the support of major interest groups.

Although the Republicans were themselves divided, they were united in their determination to recapture control of the national government, which they confidently expected to do by winning the midterm elections of 1946 and the presidential election two years later. The unanswered question was: How durable was the Roosevelt coalition?

The Rise of Harry S Truman

The symbol of the Democrats' declining fortunes in the aftermath of the war and the natural target of Republican attacks was Harry Truman, the thirty-third president of the United States. Succeeding to the presidency on April 12, 1945, Truman was immediately faced with a multitude of perplexing problems and momentous decisions, including the use of the atomic bomb, the most effective approach to demobilization and reconversion, and the question of how best to deal with the Soviet Union. No American president had ever encountered greater pressures and strains in time of peace. As Louis W. Koenig has written, "For virtually eight years of as troublous a time as our country and our world have known, a President of the United States arose seven mornings a week to a frame of things in which most news from every front was foreordained to be bad news and in which the unwelcome surprise, the unforeseen setback, had become routine, chronic emergency a way of life, and the conquest of dismay a permanent and indispensable habit of mind."

Truman was born on May 8, 1884, in Lamar, Missouri, a small town in the western part of the state. The son of a farmer and horse trader, and the descendant of forebears from Virginia and Kentucky, young Truman grew up in and around Independence. After being graduated from high school in 1901 and failing because of poor eyesight to secure an appointment to West Point, he worked at a variety of jobs, including farming. His National Guard unit was sent to France in 1918, and he served courageously as an artillery officer on the Alsatian front. This military experience was important in Truman's development, for it brought him an opportunity to demonstrate his capacity for leadership, and it gave him a sense of command. After the war the Missourian married Elizabeth Virginia Wallace, a childhood sweetheart, and with an army friend started a retail men's clothing store in Kansas City. The postwar recession caused the business to fail in 1922.

After his business failed, Truman turned to politics. His friendship with the brother of Thomas J. Pendergast, a powerful Democratic politician in Kansas City, helped him win a position as county judge. Truman's gregarious and down-to-earth personality enhanced his appeal as a politician. In the late 1920s and early 1930s he served as the top administrative official of Jackson County. He proved to be a hard-working and conscientious county officer. In 1934 Judge Truman secured the endorsement of the Pendergast machine in a bid for a U.S. Senate seat, and he was elected in the Democratic sweep of that year. Though much of his political education came from his involvement with an urban Democratic machine and he was sometimes referred to as the "Senator from Pendergast," he was a consistent if rather undistinguished supporter of the New Deal.

World War II made Truman a national figure. His concern about the large amount of waste in defense programs and the neglect of small business in the awarding of war contracts led him to propose an inquiry into defense spending. He was given the responsibility of conducting this investigation, and during the years 1941–1944 the so-called Truman Committee became known as a guardian of the public interest. Truman also made an impression on Franklin Roosevelt and other party leaders, and they turned to him as a compromise candidate for the vice-presidency in 1944 when it became apparent that neither Vice President Henry Wallace nor presidential assistant James F. Byrnes would prove acceptable to a majority of the delegates at the Democratic National Convention. Truman was a border-state senator, he had a liberal voting record, and he was on good terms with all segments of the party, including southern congressmen.

Harry Truman seemed in many ways to be an ordinary man, a small-town, middle-class American. He was a friendly, direct, and practical man, unpretentious, sincere, and uncomplicated. Devoted to his family, he liked the simple things of life—a visit with friends, an occasional drink, and a little poker with the boys. He played the piano and liked to read history. Bespectacled and scholarly in appearance, he spoke in a voice that was flat and monotonous. As Truman himself once said, "I look just like any other fifty people you meet in the street." Truman could be petty and pugnacious, he sometimes acted impulsively, and he was not above name-calling in public. A fierce partisan, he tended to accept Democrats as he found them, and his unswerving loyalty to friends did not always serve him well. But he also possessed many excellent and unusual qualities. He worked hard and studied diligently. While somewhat awed by the enormous responsibilities that confronted him in the White House, he never doubted his ability to handle them. Truman displayed courage and boldness in the presidency, and he soon demonstrated a capacity for making decisions. A sign on his desk read: "The buck stops here." He also had, in Louis Koenig's words, "a gift of simplification, a knack of seeing issues divested of complication and irrelevancy and of stating them in plain, blunt terms."

During his eighty-two days as vice president, Truman had little contact with Franklin Roosevelt and almost no tutelage from the White House. That fact no doubt helps explain a certain confusion and vagueness as to direction in the first part of his administration. Conservatives hoped that the new president's moderate views would bring him into their camp. But Truman did not commit himself to the conservatives' cause. In fact, he did just the opposite. In a comprehensive message to Congress on September 6, 1945, only three weeks after V-J Day, he revealed his progressive inclinations and expressed a determination to add to the structure of New Deal reforms. He presented a twenty-one point reform program. Among his recommendations were the extension of economic controls in the postwar period, an increase in the minimum wage from 40 to 65 cents an hour, extension of the social security system, a full-employment program, more slum clearance and public housing projects, a public works program, regional development of "the natural resources of our great river valleys," reorganization of the executive branch of the federal government, and establishment of a permanent Fair Employment Practices Commission. Soon afterward, Truman recommended the national control of atomic energy, a national health insurance system, federal aid to education, and U.S. approval of the St. Lawrence Seaway.

Although Truman had put himself on record as favoring a broad program of domestic reform, few of his recommendations were approved during the next two years, except for the Employment Act and Atomic Energy Act of 1946. He seemed to desire a continuation of the New Deal but also the maintenance of harmonious relations with Congress, now in a conservative mood and clearly determined to assert its independence of executive restraint. A series of labor crises and the losing struggle to control prices and maintain economic stability dominated the domestic scene in 1945 and 1946. The president also experienced a succession of personal difficulties with executive subordinates, leading to the resignation of such men as Harold L. Ickes and Henry Wallace, and helping to alienate many liberals from the administration. Then, in November 1946, the resurgent Republicans captured control of Congress.

Truman's administration in late 1946 seemed to have run aground after months of drift and vacillation. Harry Truman, people were saying, was certainly no Franklin Roosevelt! His leadership appeared to be designed to promote a politics of stalemate. Truman himself, Samuel Lubell observed in 1952 in *The Future of American Politics*, was "a product of political deadlock." Lubell pictured Truman as "the man who bought time," as a leader whose role was "to raise all issues but to settle none." While this harsh judgment contains a good deal of truth, it is not the whole truth. It does not adequately take into account the turbulent times, the bitter partisanship, and the conflicting pressures of the early postwar years.

THE EIGHTIETH CONGRESS, 1947–48

Republican leaders interpreted their thumping congressional victory in 1946 as a repudiation of Democratic reformism, and they turned with alacrity to the task of reducing taxes, passing legislation to control labor unions, and freeing business from governmental restraints. If Senator Arthur Vandenberg was the most influential Republican spokesman on foreign affairs, Senator Robert Taft was the most powerful party leader in the domestic arena. The son of William Howard Taft, the younger Taft had come to the Senate in 1939, contended for his party's presidential nomination in 1940 and 1944, and in 1947 headed the Republican policy committee. A man of ability, integrity, and intelligence, the Ohio senator was frequently referred to as "Mr. Republican." Although he was willing to support federal programs to develop public housing and to aid education, he was basically a conservative, a spokesman for economic conservatism. "We have got to break with the corrupting idea that we can legislate prosperity, legislate equality, legislate opportunity," he declared.

After the Republicans organized the new Congress, which convened in January 1947, they immediately moved to secure further relief from the high wartime taxes. Federal taxes had already been cut twice since the end of the war, and President Truman warned that additional reductions would only pour more fuel on the fiery inflation then raging. But Congress would not be deterred. In June it passed a tax bill that provided proportionately greater relief to those in high income brackets than to people with lower incomes. Truman vetoed this measure, asserting that it would bring about the "very recession we seek to avoid." A few weeks later the president vetoed a second tax reduction bill with provisions very much like the one passed in June. A third tax cut, providing for a $4.8 billion reduction, was finally passed over Truman's veto, becoming the Revenue Act of April 1948. Although the lawmakers approved an anti-inflation bill in the fall of 1947, they were unwilling to give the president any real power to enforce it.

The most important domestic statute enacted during the Eightieth Congress was the controversial Taft-Hartley Act of 1947. The Republicans were determined to curb the power of organized labor, and under the circumstances it was probably inevitable that some kind of labor-control law would be passed. The Wagner Act of 1935, the basic labor policy statute, had long been criticized in some quarters as one-sided and unfair to employers. Wartime labor strife had led to the imposition of restrictions on labor unions by the Smith-Connally War Labor Disputes Act of 1943. The long series of strikes following the war, as well as John L. Lewis's contemptuous defiance of the government during the war and again in 1946, brought mounting public pressure for congressional action. Congress responded by passing the Case bill in 1946, only to have President Truman veto it on the ground that its various restraints were "punitive." When the Eightieth Congress convened, a large number of regulatory bills were introduced, including one with severe restraints presented by Fred L. Hartley, Jr., of New Jersey, the chairman of the House Committee on Education and Labor. The Hartley bill was rushed through the lower house and passed on April 17 by a large majority. Action in the Senate was led by Taft, chairman of the Labor and Public Welfare Committee. Under his direction, a more carefully drafted and less vindictive labor bill was formulated and eventually adopted, after additional compromises, by both houses in June. The measure outlawed the closed shop; prohibited several "unfair" labor practices by unions, including jurisdictional strikes and secondary boycotts; permitted employers to sue unions for breaking contracts; forbade campaign contributions by labor unions; required loyalty oaths from union officers; and authorized the issuance of injunctions to halt strikes, and "cooling-off" periods for as long as eighty days in strikes that threatened to create a national emergency.

Sponsors of the Taft-Hartley bill described it as "the first step toward an official discouragement" of a trend that had "permitted and encouraged" labor "to grow into a monster supergovernment." Truman responded with a sharp veto on June 20. He charged that the strike procedures provided in the bill were impractical, that the measure was biased against labor, and that it would "reverse the basic direction of our national labor policy." The Republicans, with notable help from southern Democrats, swiftly overrode the veto— by a vote of 331 to 83 in the House and 68 to 25 in the Senate. In practice the Taft-Hartley Act proved less harmful to labor's interests than its opponents had feared. Yet it hurt weak unions in some industries, made organizing more difficult, and encouraged many states to enact stronger "right-to-work" laws. Union leaders denounced Taft-Hartley as a "slave labor law," and with its passage they rallied their forces behind the Truman administration.

While the Truman administration scored a series of foreign policy triumphs, the president and his congressional opponents fought one battle after another in 1947 and 1948. Truman, with an eye on the election of 1948, repeatedly urged Congress to pass a broad range of social welfare measures. But Congress largely ignored the chief executive's recommendations for the extension of New Deal social welfare provisions in such fields as housing, education, medical care, and social security. The legislators refused to enact strong price controls, forced the adoption of tax reductions that favored the well-to-do, and reduced appropriations for agricultural programs and reclamation. General appropriations were constantly reduced from the administration's budget requests. "This Congress," observed T. R. B., the *New Republic* columnist, "brought back an atmosphere you had forgotten or never thought possible. . . . Victories fought and won years ago were suddenly in doubt. Everything was debatable again." Truman's vetoes appeared to confirm this point; he issued more than sixty in 1947 and 1948.

Truman renewed and sharpened his demands for domestic reforms in early 1948. Among his recommendations was a group of civil rights measures. But the administration got little from Congress. Rent controls were extended for another year, a severely limited housing program was approved, and an agricultural bill was passed providing for a continuation of price supports at 90 percent of parity through 1949 and thereafter on a flexible basis. Congress also extended the Reciprocal Trade Agreements Act, though for only one year rather than the three recommended by the president. In addition, the lawmakers authorized the creation of a commission on the reorganization of the executive branch of the government. Truman appointed Herbert Hoover to head this inquiry, and after an extensive study the Hoover Commission in 1949 issued eighteen comprehensive reports, recommending the consolidation and streamlining of numerous executive departments and agencies. Many of these recommendations were put into effect during Truman's second term.[1] Congress followed Truman's recommendation in passing a new Presidential Succession Act, placing the speaker of the House and the president pro tempore of the Senate ahead of the members of the Cabinet in the line of presidential succession after the vice president. And Congress adopted, in 1947, the Twenty-second Amendment to the Constitution, limiting the president's tenure to two terms. It was ratified by the requisite number of states in 1951.

The Republican-controlled Congress won most of the battles over domestic issues in 1947 and 1948. But in opposing Taft-Hartley and the conservatism of the Eightieth Congress, Truman developed a sense of purpose and the image of a fighter for the people. He put himself and his party in position to challenge the Republicans in the campaign of 1948.

THE ELECTION OF 1948

As the presidential campaign of 1948 got under way, the Democratic party was badly split. Henry Wallace, around whom critics of the Truman administration's cold war policies were rallying, had announced his intention of running for president on an independent ticket. The president's strong advocacy of a civil rights program had spurred a group of southern governors to begin laying plans for a regional opposition movement against the national Democratic party. Truman's popularity in all parts of the country had dropped to a low level. "People are restless, dissatisfied, fearful," one administration member explained. "They want someone who can 'take over' and solve everything." A new liberal organization known as Americans for Democratic Action (ADA) wanted to dump Truman and nominate a more attractive standard-bearer in 1948.

Although Truman had earlier given some thought to the possibility of stepping aside in favor of the universally admired General Dwight D. Eisenhower, he had decided by the end of 1947 to run in his own right. He announced his decision publicly on March 8, 1948. Truman's various reform proposals during the early months of 1948 were designed to provide him with a coherent program and a tactical advantage over his Republican opponents in the forthcoming campaign. Moreover, Clark Clifford, the president's special counsel, and other administration officials had begun to develop a strategy for the next presidential campaign soon after the disastrous congressional elections of 1946. In a confidential memorandum to Truman on November 19, 1947, Clifford summed up the views that had been developed within the administration on "the politics of 1948." He advised the president to stake out a liberal position in dealing with the next session of Congress, to exploit his conflicts with his congressional opponents, and to move forward in the field of civil rights. He should consider the South "safely Democratic."

The Republican National Convention was held in Philadelphia beginning on June 21. The front-runner in the contest for the presidential nomination was Governor Thomas E. Dewey, who in late May had won an impressive primary victory in Oregon over Harold E. Stassen, the former governor of Minnesota. Senator Taft was also an aspirant for the honor, and party regulars seemed to prefer him to Dewey; but the senator's isolationist record, outspoken conservatism, and unexciting campaign style made him a less attractive possibility than the internationalist and progressive New York governor. The delegates unanimously nominated Dewey on the third ballot and selected Governor Earl Warren of California as the vice-presidential nominee. The platform, to the chagrin of some extreme conservatives, was a moderate document which, by implication at least, accepted the main features of Roosevelt's New Deal and Truman's foreign policy.

Three weeks later the Democrats convened in Philadelphia to choose their national ticket. The convention was steeped in gloom. A movement by the ADA, labor leaders, and city bosses to draft General Eisenhower had failed shortly before the convention when Eisenhower unequivocally rejected the overtures made to him.

Thus the nomination went to Truman almost by default, although Senator Richard B. Russell of Georgia received most of the southern delegates' votes. Senator Alben W. Barkley of Kentucky, whose old-fashioned keynote address had roused the convention out of its lethargy, was made the vice-presidential nominee. The platform praised the Truman administration's international policies and called for the enactment of most of the president's progressive recommendations. The forthright endorsement of civil rights was made only after a bitter floor fight in which the young mayor of Minneapolis, Hubert H. Humphrey, and other northern liberals demanded that the rather vague plank proposed by the administration be strengthened. "I say the time has come to walk out of the shadow of states' rights and into the sunlight of human rights," declared Humphrey.

President Truman brought the Democratic delegates to life when he appeared before them at two o'clock in the morning to deliver his acceptance speech. "Senator Barkley and I will win this election," he cried. As the climax to his fighting address, Truman announced that he was calling the Eightieth Congress—the worst Congress in American history, he asserted—into special session on July 26, the day turnips are planted in Missouri. He wanted to give the Republicans a chance to carry out their campaign pledges immediately, explained the president, and thus enable the voters to "decide on the record." The Republicans accused Truman of resorting to petty politics. The "turnip Congress" remained in session for almost two weeks, but it accomplished nothing of importance, which was what Truman expected.

Meanwhile, however, the Democratic party seemed to be splitting apart as a result of insurgency on the right and the left. A revolt by southern Democrats, which had been brewing for months, was precipitated by the action of the party's national convention in Philadelphia and the dramatic walkout of the Mississippi and Alabama delegates. A conference of the southern rebels met in Birmingham on July 17. The bolters proceeded to organize the States' Rights Democratic party, to nominate Governor J. Strom Thurmond of South Carolina for president and Governor Fielding L. Wright of Mississippi as his running mate, and to draft a platform that emphasized state rights and opposition to the Democratic party's civil rights proposals. The Dixiecrats, as they were soon dubbed, conducted a vigorous campaign during the following months in an effort to unite the South against the regular Democratic ticket. Since they controlled the Democratic party machinery in several states, they were able to place their electors on the ballot as the regular Democrats. The States' Righters hoped to prevent either of the major parties from obtaining a majority in the electoral college, thus throwing the election into the House of Representatives where they might become the deciding factor.

In some respects the threat to the Democratic ticket from the left appeared even more ominous. At the end of 1947, Henry Wallace had announced his willingness to run for president on a third-party ticket sponsored by the Progressive Citizens of America. Many radicals and disgruntled liberals were expected to support Wallace in demanding a more conciliatory approach to the Russians and a domestic program described by the former vice president as "progressive capitalism." Representatives of the Wallace movement met in Philadelphia on July 23 to launch their campaign. They organized the Progressive party, nominated Wallace and Senator Glen Taylor of Idaho as their standard-bearers, and drafted a platform that blamed the Truman administration for the cold war, condemned its containment policies, and urged a variety of domestic reforms, including the nationalization of basic industries and equal treatment of all minority groups. Although some old-time New Dealers and a wide assortment of radicals took part in organizing the new party, it was apparent that Communists were extremely active in its campaign. Even so, the Wallace movement seemed to pose a formidable challenge to the Democrats in the key northern states.

President Truman's chances of winning the election looked hopeless. Many Democratic leaders had a defeatist attitude, the party was disorganized, and it badly needed money. The Republicans, meanwhile, were conducting an efficient and well-financed campaign. Traveling in his "Victory Special" train, Governor Dewey toured the country, talking confidently and a bit smugly about efficiency and good government. He emphasized the need for an administration that would promote national unity and the cause of peace. Dewey's magisterial campaign, avoiding specifics somewhat in the manner of Franklin Roosevelt's approach in 1932, seemed calculated to ensure a Republican victory. But it made the GOP nominee appear rather remote to the voters—a machine with a cellophane cover, in the opinion of one contemporary. Near the end of the campaign, some of Dewey's advisers expressed concern over the damage Truman might do between election day and January 20, which prompted one reporter to ask ironically: "How long is Dewey going to tolerate Truman's interference in the government?"

Nevertheless, the Democrats under Truman's leadership breathed life into their own campaign. The president's decision to convene the "turnip Congress" revealed an important part of his campaign strategy. He would make the Eightieth Congress rather than the more progressive Dewey his principal target, blaming the Republicans in Congress for the failure of his anti-inflation recommendations, his civil rights proposals, and such social welfare measures as additional public housing and an increase in the minimum wage. "I'm going to fight hard," Truman told Senator Barkley at the outset of the campaign. "I'm going to give them hell." And fight hard he

"Give-'em-hell Harry" (*National Park Service photograph, courtesy Harry S. Truman Library*)

did! Acting as if he expected to win, the president made one of the most strenuous campaigns in our modern history. He traveled 22,000 miles, mostly by train, gave 271 speeches, and was heard directly by approximately 12 million Americans. Speaking extemporaneously at "whistle-stops" across the country, where his friendliness and warmth of personality came through, Truman hammered away at the record of what he called the "do-nothing, good-for-nothing" Eightieth Congress, charging it with the responsibility for high prices and rents, for the housing shortage, and for cutting back on such programs as conservation and reclamation. The crowds that gathered to hear the president grew in size, and people increasingly voiced admiration for his plucky fight in the face of apparent defeat.

In his homely but hard-hitting remarks, Truman pictured the Republicans as the party of "privilege, pride, and plunder," a party with little interest in the common people. Truman's attack on Republican Toryism was shrewdly intended to hold most of the old New Deal coalition together. Making an intense appeal to normally Democratic elements, he urged a resumption of the New Deal on a broad front and warned the various interest groups not to risk losing the benefits of the Democratic reforms of the past fifteen years.

Despite Truman's gallant fight, most informed observers agreed that he would lose the election. All of the leading polls, political analysts, and important newspapers predicted a Dewey victory. After checking with its correspondents, the *New York Times* concluded that Dewey would receive 305 electoral votes to Truman's 105. *Life* magazine carried the New York governor's picture on its cover the week before the election, describing him as the "next President." And in a banner headline on the night of the election, the *Chicago Daily Tribune* announced that "DEWEY DEFEATS TRUMAN!"

The election results surprised almost everyone, and Truman's sensational victory has to be characterized as one of the most extraordinary in American history. The outcome revealed that the public opinion polls had failed to detect a swing to President Truman late in the campaign. The Democratic success also suggested that the political experts had underestimated the extent to which the party of Roosevelt and Truman had become the normal majority party in the United States. In an election marked by a low voter turnout, Truman received 24,105,812 popular votes (49.5 percent) and 303 electoral votes to Dewey's 21,970,065 (45.1 percent) and 189. Thurmond received 1,169,021 popular votes and carried four southern states (with 39 electoral votes), while Wallace had a popular vote of 1,157,172 and won no electoral votes. The Democrats

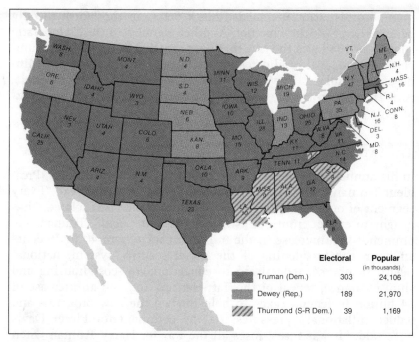

		Electoral	Popular (in thousands)
	Truman (Dem.)	303	24,106
	Dewey (Rep.)	189	21,970
	Thurmond (S-R Dem.)	39	1,169

The Election of 1948

recaptured both houses of Congress, gaining 75 seats in the House of Representatives and 9 in the Senate. They won 20 of the 32 gubernatorial contests. Dewey carried 16 states, most of which were in New England, the Middle Atlantic region, and the Plains belt.

In the immediate aftermath of Truman's surprising victory, George Gallup, the well-known pollster, admitted, "I just don't know what happened." Whatever the explanation, liberals were jubilant. The *New Republic* exuberantly declared that "nothing less than a new era of reform has been demanded by America." Basically, Truman's triumph resulted from his success in maintaining the old Democratic coalition. He ran well among labor voters, ethnic groups, and farmers. "In a sense," observes historian Eugene H. Roseboom, "Roosevelt won his greatest victory after his death." The country was at peace, the economy was doing well, and a consensus had emerged on national policy in the cold war. Ironically, the Progressive party and the Dixiecrat movement probably ensured Truman's election. The Wallace party, by attracting Communists and other radicals, removed the taint of their support from the Democrats. The States' Righters failed to bring about the defection of the entire South, and by undertaking a racist campaign against the Truman administration, persuaded black voters in the North to rally behind the president's banner. Another element in the Democratic success of 1948 was the fact that the party had a considerable number of strong local candidates, including Hubert Humphrey in Minnesota and Adlai E. Stevenson, who was elected governor of Illinois. And Truman's own role must not be overlooked, for he was doubtless his party's greatest campaign asset.

THE FAIR DEAL, 1949–1952

In his annual State of the Union message on January 5, 1949, President Truman outlined what came to be called the Fair Deal. "Every segment of our population and every individual," he declared, "has a right to expect from our Government a *fair deal.*" Truman recommended an increase in the minimum wage from 40 to 75 cents an hour, the broadening of the social security system, national health insurance, federal aid to education, low-cost housing and slum clearance, repeal of the Taft-Hartley Act, and an increase of $4 billion in federal taxes to help finance the new programs and reduce inflationary pressures. As the commentator Elmer Davis once said, "It was roses, roses all the way for Harry Truman when he rode in the bright sunshine to be inaugurated. But a good deal of the rest of the way . . . was poison ivy."

Although the Democrats controlled Congress throughout Truman's second administration, the president's legislative proposals were subjected to continual congressional assault and subterfuge. Congress refused to vote higher taxes or to authorize the price controls Truman had urged. It would not repeal the Taft-Hartley Act. It rejected the administration's new approach to the problem of agricultural subsidies and turned down its recommendations for the extension of the Tennessee Valley Authority concept to the Missouri River and other river valleys. The Eighty-first Congress defeated Truman's national health insurance plan, disapproved his proposal for the establishment of a new Department of Welfare with Cabinet rank, failed to pass legislation to provide federal aid to education, and filibustered to death a Federal Employment Practices Commission (FEPC) bill.

Truman's legislative setbacks cannot be entirely attributed to the opposition of congressional conservatives, though they were a potent influence in the failure of many administration measures. Truman's reform efforts did not receive the impetus of the great public enthusiasm that had sustained the early New Deal. In fact, the Fair Deal precipitated a round of violent controversies and attacks in the press and on the platform, leading many contemporaries to con-

"Everybody hang on back in the trailer." Cartoonist Dowling on the Fair Deal *(Courtesy Harry S. Truman Library)*

clude that Americans were too confused and divided to know what they wanted or needed. Truman himself was unable to stimulate broad public support for his reform program. He usually thought it necessary to give priority to his administration's international objectives. The recession of 1949 caused many members of Congress to doubt the wisdom of a tax increase or other domestic reforms. The growing obsession with the question of Communist subversion hurt the administration's Fair Deal programs, and the Korean War consumed the attention and energy of the president and Congress after June 1950.

As the Eighty-first Congress began its work in January 1949, Truman had high hopes for the repeal of the Taft-Hartley Act. Senator

Taft was willing to make some concessions, and the administration might have obtained a compromise measure revising some provisions of the 1947 law. But the administration was not enthusiastic about such a compromise, and one that got through the Senate bogged down in the House of Representatives. The administration's health insurance plan called for prepaid medical, dental, and hospital care to be financed by employee and employer contributions through a payroll tax and government subsidies. The American Medical Association conducted a frenzied lobbying and advertising campaign against the proposed legislation, which it condemned as "nationalized, bureaucratic, governmental or socialized medical care." Congress bowed before this onslaught. The president was no more fortunate with his recommendation for federal aid to education. Although the Senate passed a bill appropriating $300 million to the states for the support of education, this measure died in the House as a result of the Protestant-Catholic conflict over whether federal aid should go to private and parochial schools as well as to public institutions.

On the agricultural front, the administration in April 1949 presented the Brannan Plan, named for Secretary of Agriculture Charles F. Brannan. This proposal sought to maintain a "farm income standard" comparable to that of the previous decade, to hold food prices at reasonable levels, and to reduce the government's storage expenses if possible. The plan would have retained high fixed support prices for basic commodities. The novel feature of the scheme was the recommendation that the prices of perishable commodities be determined by the free market, with the government compensating producers for the difference between the market price and a price considered fair by the Department of Agriculture. Critics, including the major farm organizations, charged that the plan would cost too much and would lead to the regimentation of American farmers. Congress refused to pass the proposed legislation. Only the heavy demands for food and fiber at home and abroad—demands underwritten by the Marshall Plan and the Korean War—prevented an acute agricultural problem from emerging before the 1950s.

President Truman's worst defeat came in his fight for civil rights legislation. During his second administration, Truman repeatedly tried to get Congress to establish a permanent FEPC, to enact anti-lynching and anti-poll tax laws, and to give legislative sanction to the other recommendations contained in the 1947 report of his Commission on Civil Rights. Southern Democrats, with strong Republican assistance, stymied all these efforts. In 1949 a bipartisan group of congressional reformers had some success in weakening the House Rules Committee, which had long been a bottleneck for civil rights measures, but it failed to modify the cloture rule that permitted filibusters in the Senate. Two efforts to invoke cloture by civil rights advocates failed in 1950. A "voluntary" FEPC bill and a measure to grant suffrage and self-government to residents of the District of Columbia did pass the House, only to be killed in the Senate. Truman had to resort to executive action in order to make any immediate headway in the civil rights struggle. He issued executive orders in 1948 seeking to end discrimination and segregation in the armed forces and in government departments. He established a special committee in 1951 to bar the awarding of defense contracts to companies practicing discrimination. He strengthened the civil rights section of the Justice Department, named the first black man to a federal judgeship, and appointed another as governor of the Virgin Islands. Truman was the first president in modern times to proclaim the equality of blacks, to assail discrimination and violence against them, and to identify his office with the broad objectives of the civil rights movement.

The Eighty-second Congress, elected in 1950, proved even less cooperative than the Eighty-first in responding to Truman's legislative proposals. Although the Democrats retained nominal control of both houses, the conservative coalition was stronger in 1951 and 1952 than it had been in the previous Congress. Exploiting the fears and frustrations connected with the Korean War, internal subversion, and corruption in government, the Republicans made a good showing in the midterm elections; they gained 28 House seats, 5 Senate seats, and 7 governorships.

Republican charges that corruption was rampant in the Truman administration served the interests of the president's opponents in other ways than the ballot box; they helped destroy any lingering hopes Truman had for his unfinished program of social reform. The "mess in Washington" never involved Truman personally, but there was enough evidence of "five percenters"—expediters who sold actual or pretended influence with government officials—and of irregularities in various governmental agencies to lend some credence to the charges. Truman's military aide, General Harry H. Vaughan, was shown to have been given a $520 deep-freeze unit under somewhat cloudy circumstances, while the wife of a Reconstruction Finance Corporation (RFC) official was the beneficiary, for practically nothing, of a $9,540 mink coat. Irregularities in the Internal Revenue Service forced the resignation of several officials and the overhaul of the agency. The RFC was also reorganized. Truman had apparently lost control of public opinion, and one Gallup poll gave him an approval rating of only 23 percent.

It would be a mistake, however, to say that the Fair Deal was a complete failure. In 1950 Congress increased the social security benefits by an average of 80 percent, extended the system's coverage to an additional 10.5 million people, and liberalized many federal-state public assistance programs. It raised the minimum wage to 75 cents an hour, extended rent controls, and gave the chief executive some powers to deal with the problem of inflation. The National Housing Act of 1949, passed with the help of Senator Taft, authorized the construction of 810,000 subsidized low-income housing units over the next six years, as well as grants for slum clearance and rural housing. Congress also increased appropriations for power development and reclamation in the West, for the TVA, and for the Farmers' Home Administration, which was carrying on some of the work of the Farm Security Administration. While Congress rejected Truman's national health insurance plan, it did pass the Hill-Burton Act, which authorized matching federal and state grants for the construction of public and nonprofit hospitals and clinics. In 1950 it set up the National Science Foundation. And at Truman's insistence, Congress in the same year passed the Displaced Persons Act. This statute increased the number of such persons to be admitted to 415,000 over the next three years and remedied some of the defects the president had complained about in earlier legislation. Nevertheless, the politics of stalemate continued, reflecting the powerful conservative coalition in Congress, the internal conflict within the majority party, and the ambivalence of the public mood.

"The Truman Administration established no radically new programs," as Richard O. Davies points out, "but it performed remarkably well in updating and expanding existing programs and, especially, in serving to assimilate the New Deal into American life." If Harry Truman's record as a social reformer represented an extension of New Deal concepts rather than the inauguration of new programs, the thirty-third president's domestic leadership was nonetheless far more significant than most of his contemporaries supposed. Truman not only successfully defended and strengthened the New Deal, but his administration also established the agenda that would reach fruition in the social reforms of the 1960s. He was one of the architects of a liberal persuasion that went beyond the New Deal. This new liberalism, as Alonzo L. Hamby has shown, envisioned an ever-expanding capitalist economy reinforced by Keynesian fiscal policies and extensive social welfare programs. Positioning itself in the "vital center," it was more concerned with inflation than depression, emphasized the importance of civil rights, and assumed a critical attitude toward the Soviet Union.

Truman's reputation brightened with the passage of time, and he eventually became something of a folk hero. People admired him, the historian John Lukacs suggests, because he was viewed as "a man of the older American type: outspoken, courageous, loyal to his friends, solidly rooted in his mid-American past, and *real*—a self-crafted piece of solid wood, not a molded plastic piece." Today, the Missourian's place in history seems secure. Scholarly polls have consistently ranked him as "near great," eighth among all U.S. presidents.

NOTE

1. The Reorganization Act of June 1949 authorized the president to submit plans of reorganization which would become automatically effective unless Congress specifically disapproved.

SUGGESTIONS FOR FURTHER READING

Samuel Lubell's classic book, *The Future of American Politics* (3d ed. rev., 1965), offers a provocative analysis of Franklin D. Roosevelt's political revolution, of the voting coalition he brought together, and of how, "after twenty years of victories, the coalition became deadlocked within itself." Important aspects of the political scene in the United States since the New Deal are described in Herbert Parmet, *The Democrats: The Years after FDR* (1976); William E. Leuchtenburg, *In the Shadow of FDR: From Harry Truman to Ronald Reagan* (1983); and Alonzo L. Hamby, *Liberalism and Its Challengers*, cited in chapter 1. Hamby's *Beyond the New Deal: Harry S. Truman and American Liberalism* (1973) is a valuable study of the relationship between Truman and postwar liberalism.

The range and character of the historiography of the Truman years are revealed in two volumes edited by Richard S. Kirkendall: *The Truman Period as a Research Field* (1967) and *The Truman Period as a Research Field: A Reappraisal, 1972* (1974). Truman himself still awaits a first-rate biography. Jonathan Daniels, *The Man of Independence* (1950), throws light on Truman's early life. Alfred Steinberg, *The Man from Missouri: The Life and Times of Harry S. Truman* (1962), is a sympathetic treatment that makes little use of the voluminous materials in the Truman Library. Margaret Truman's *Harry S. Truman* (1972) is a useful personal account. The best scholarly history of Truman's presidency is Donald R. McCoy, *The Presidency of Harry S. Truman* (1984). The most comprehensive study of the Truman administration is the two-volume work by Robert J. Donovan: *Conflict and Crisis* (1977) and *Tumultuous Years* (1982). These volumes by an outstanding journalist are informative but not very interpretive. Another large study, Harold F. Gosnell's *Truman's Crises* (1980), has a number of shortcomings, although it is helpful in understanding Truman's career before 1944. Cabell Phillips, *The Truman Presidency: The History of a Triumphant Succession* (1966), is a useful overall account. Critical perspectives are provided by Bert Cochran, *Harry S. Truman and the Crisis Presidency* (1973), and Barton J. Bernstein (ed.), *Politics and Policies of the Truman Administration* (1970).

Public Papers of the Presidents of the United States (1961–   ) is an invaluable source for the addresses, public statements, and press conferences of U.S. presidents beginning with Truman. Eight volumes are devoted to the Truman administration. For Truman's views, see also his *Memoirs* (2 vols., 1955–56); Merle Miller, *Plain Speaking: An Oral Biography of Harry S. Truman* (1974); and Robert H. Ferrell (ed.), *Off the Record: The Private Papers of Harry S. Truman* (1980). Louis W. Koenig, *The Truman Administration: Its Principles and Practice* (1956), and Barton J. Bernstein and Allen J. Matusow (eds.), *The Truman Administration: A Documentary History* (1966), are useful documentary works.

Susan M. Hartmann, *Truman and the 80th Congress* (1971), is an informative study. David B. Truman, *The Congressional Party: A Case Study* (1959), examines the workings of the Eighty-first Congress. James T. Patterson's *Mr. Republican: A Biography of Robert A. Taft* (1972) is an important study of a key figure.

Richard S. Kirkendall has written an excellent essay, "Election of 1948," in Arthur M. Schlesinger, Jr., and Fred L. Israel (eds.), *History of American Presidential Elections, 1789–1968* (1971), vol. IV. This work, which contains selected contemporary documents, is also useful for the national elections of 1952 through 1968. Other books on the 1948 election include Irwin Ross, *The Loneliest Campaign: The Truman Victory of 1948* (1968); Jules Abels, *Out of the Jaws of Victory* (1959); Alexander Heard, *A Two-Party South?* (1952); Robert A. Garson, *The Democratic Party and the Politics of Sectionalism, 1941–1948* (1974); Karl M. Schmidt, *Henry A. Wallace: Quixotic Crusade, 1948* (1960); Norman D. Markowitz, *The Rise and Fall of the People's Century: Henry A. Wallace and American Liberalism, 1941–1948* (1973); and Allen Yarnell, *Democrats and Progressives: The 1948 Presidential Election as a Test of Postwar Liberalism* (1974). Clifton Brock's *Americans for Democratic Action* (1962) deals with a significant element in postwar politics.

Many of the scholarly monographs devoted to the Truman period are concerned with the Fair Deal and other aspects of domestic politics. Among the more impressive of these studies are Allen J. Matusow, *Farm Policies and Politics in the Truman Years* (1967); Richard O. Davies, *Housing Reform during the Truman Administration* (1966); Richard M. Dalfiume, *Desegregation of the U.S. Armed Forces: Fighting on Two Fronts, 1939–1953* (1969); William Berman, *The Politics of Civil Rights in the Truman Administration* (1970); and Donald R. McCoy and Richard T. Ruetten, *Quest and Response: Minority Rights and the Truman Administration* (1973). For the labor scene and labor policy, see R. Alton Lee, *Truman and Taft-Hartley: A Question of Mandate* (1966); Arthur F. McClure, *The Truman Administration and the Problems of Postwar Labor, 1945–1948* (1969); Harry Alvin Millis and Emily Clark Brown, *From the Wagner Act to Taft-Hartley: A Study of National Labor Policy and Labor Relations* (1950); and Bert Cochran, *Labor and Communism: The Conflict That Shaped American Unions* (1977). Other political questions are considered in William H. Moore, *The Kefauver Committee and the Politics of Crime, 1950–52* (1974); Monte M. Poen, *Harry S. Truman versus the Medical Lobby: The Genesis of Medicare* (1979); and Andrew J. Dunar, *The Truman Scandals and the Politics of Morality* (1984). Fiscal and economic policies are reviewed in A. E. Holmans, *United States Fiscal Policy, 1945–1959* (1961), and Edward S. Flash, Jr., *Economic Advice and Presidential Leadership: The Council of Economic Advisers* (1965).

CHAPTER FOUR

The Korean War and the Politics of Loyalty

IN ITS EARLY STAGES the cold war between the United States and the Soviet Union was centered in the eastern Mediterranean and Europe, and the American containment policy, while worldwide in its implications, was largely confined to Europe. But the conflict soon shifted to the Far East, and the outbreak of the Korean War in June 1950 precipitated a major change in American Far Eastern policy. The fall of Nationalist China and the beginning of the Korean War, moreover, unleashed a wave of anti-Communist hysteria within the United States. The stage was thus set for the extraordinary rise to power of Senator Joseph R. McCarthy, the frustration of the hapless Truman administration, and the election of Dwight D. Eisenhower as president in 1952.

AMERICAN DILEMMA IN THE FAR EAST

World War II stimulated the growth of nationalist sentiment throughout Asia and encouraged anti-imperialist revolutions that brought about the rapid dismantling of the old British, French, and Dutch hegemonies. In China and Indochina these national movements were led by Communists. At the end of the war, American leaders were not altogether antagonistic toward the new nationalism in Asia, but they acquiesced in the plans of their Western allies to resume control of their Far Eastern holdings in the postwar period. The United States constructed one defense against the postwar revolution in East Asia by undertaking the destruction and reconstruction of the old Japan. Under General MacArthur's direction a new constitution was adopted, a parliamentary system introduced, agrarian reforms carried out, and a variety of other progressive changes completed. The reconstruction of Japan gave the United States its most favorable position in the Far East following the war.

On the mainland of East Asia the key country was China, whose political independence and territorial integrity had been American objectives for almost half a century. During the war U.S. leaders tried to elevate China to the status of a great power. They helped persuade Stalin to sign a treaty of alliance and friendship with China, recognizing the Nationalist government rather than the Communist forces under Mao Tse-tung. But the fact was that China was deeply divided, and Chiang Kai-shek's Kuomintang party was too corrupt, inefficient, and dictatorial to unify the country. Hoping to head off a civil war and effect a coalition government, President Truman dispatched General George C. Marshall to China in December 1945. Marshall secured a cease-fire and other tentative agreements, but neither side wanted to give up its major political objectives, and no settlement could be reached.

The Nationalists and the Communists were soon locked in an all-out military struggle. At first the Nationalists appeared to have the advantage, since they held the most territory, had the larger army, and were better equipped than their adversaries. But Chiang's government had alienated the great majority of the populace, including business people and intellectuals. When General Albert C. Wedemeyer visited China in the summer of 1947 to report on the situation for General Marshall, who was now secretary of state, he was dismayed at the political and military ineptitude of the Kuomintang. The Nationalist armies were soon in retreat everywhere, and by early 1949 Chiang had lost half of his troops and 80 percent of the equipment given him by the United States. Before the end of 1949, he fled with the remnants of his army to the island of Taiwan (Formosa). Meanwhile, in September 1949, Mao Tse-tung announced the formation of the People's Republic of China, with its capital at Peking.

With the breakdown of Nationalist control, the Truman administration faced the task of explaining the failure of its China policy. This was not an easy undertaking, for there had long been a group of "Asia-firsters" in the United States who believed that their government had neglected its interests and obligations in Asia, first by giving priority to the defeat of Hitler in the early 1940s, and later in concentrating its energies on the defense of Europe in the cold war. On August 5, 1949, with the collapse of Nationalist authority clearly imminent, the State Department issued a lengthy White Paper that sought to explain American policy in China. The United States had extended over $2 billion in grants and credits to the Kuomintang—representing far greater resources than those available to the Chinese Communists—and the Nationalists' failure, the document contended, was the result of a great internal change within China, a genuine revolution, over which Americans had no control. The United States could have attempted a "full-scale intervention" with troops, Secretary of State Dean Acheson remarked, but it "would have been resented by the mass of the Chinese people, would have diametrically reversed our historic policy, and would have been condemned by the American people."

During the winter of 1949–50, the Truman administration's foreign policy received one blow after another. The "loss" of Nationalist China and a divisive debate over NATO had apparently destroyed bipartisanship. The Russians had exploded an atomic bomb, and early in 1950 a Sino-Soviet pact had been concluded between the two Communist powers. The United States had begun to negotiate a peace treaty with Japan, but there was growing uneasiness and open hostility among the Japanese because of the American desire to retain military bases on the islands. At about this time the National Security Council was completing its reassessment of U.S. foreign and defense policies; NSC 68 forecast "an indefinite period of tension and danger" and urged the United States to undertake "a bold and massive program" to meet the Soviet challenge. A new challenge came in June 1950 when North Korean troops crossed the 38th parallel and began an invasion of the Republic of South Korea.

THE KOREAN WAR, 1950–1952

Korea—the "Hermit Kingdom"—had been dominated by Japan during most of the twentieth century. At a conference in Cairo in 1943, Allied leaders promised the Koreans their freedom "in due course." Russian troops moved into the northern part of the peninsula just before the Japanese surrender in August 1945, and a short time later American soldiers occupied South Korea. It was decided rather arbitrarily that the occupation zones would be divided at the 38th parallel, and it was assumed that an independent Korean government would eventually take over throughout the peninsula. But that was not to be, for with the beginning of the cold war, the division of Korea became permanent.

In late 1947 the United States took the Korean question to the United Nations Assembly, requesting that body to sponsor free elections throughout Korea. United Nations representatives were denied entry into North Korea, but elections were held under UN auspices in South Korea. The Russians proceeded to establish a Communist "people's government" and to train and equip a strong army in North Korea. In South Korea the American military government aligned itself with conservative elements and on occasion resorted to repressive measures that alienated many people. It also gave support to a reactionary leader named Syngman Rhee, who was elected president following the adoption of a republican constitution in 1948. In 1949 American and Russian troops were withdrawn from their respective zones. Meanwhile, there were frequent border clashes between the two Koreas, neither of which recognized the legitimacy of the other's government.

Communist leaders probably thought there was a good chance that the United States would not come to South Korea's defense. American leaders had defined the nation's line of defense in the western Pacific without including Korea. In the calculation of Russian leaders, the unification of Korea under their control might intimidate Japan, where the United States hoped to retain military bases and to anchor its Far Eastern security system. A Korea united under the USSR might also serve to undermine the role of Mao Tsetung as an exemplar of nationalist revolutions in Asia, a matter of concern to the masters of the Kremlin even that early. Nevertheless, North Korea's assault on June 25, 1950, brought a decisive response from the United States. President Truman, with the concurrence of his advisers, immediately instructed General MacArthur to furnish arms and supplies to the hard-pressed South Koreans. The Truman administration also moved swiftly to bring the matter before the United Nations. In an emergency session on the afternoon of June 25, the Security Council adopted a resolution by a vote of 9 to 0 condemning the invasion and demanding the withdrawal of North Korean troops from South Korea.[1]

The North Korean advance could not be halted by the South Koreans, and within three days the invaders had captured the capital city of Seoul. Truman began to send American air and naval forces into the fray. "The attack upon the Republic of Korea," he declared, "makes it plain beyond all doubt that the international Communist movement is prepared to use armed invasion to conquer independent nations." On June 27 the UN Security Council, with the Soviet delegate still absent, adopted by a vote of 7 to 1 an American-sponsored resolution calling on member nations to provide all necessary assistance to the Republic of Korea. Three days later Truman made the difficult decision to send two divisions of American ground troops from Japan to Korea. He also authorized a naval blockade of North Korea. Soon afterward the Security Council recognized the United States as the leader of the UN forces in Korea, and Truman named General MacArthur to head the defending army. While these developments took place, the nation rallied behind the president's decision to resist the North Korean aggression.

American forces assault a hill in Korea (*U.S. Army photograph*)

Truman had acted "with a magnificent courage and terse decision," declared the *New York Herald Tribune* in a front-page editorial.

For a time the South Korean situation looked hopeless. The North Korean army advanced down the peninsula for almost six weeks, overrunning most of the south and pushing the Republic of Korea and U.S. Eighth Army soldiers to a perimeter around the southern port of Pusan. There the defenders finally held their ground, their position strengthened by heavy reinforcements and crucial support from American air operations. On September 15 MacArthur launched a brilliant amphibious operation with a successful landing at Inchon near the western end of the 38th parallel. At the same time the UN forces broke out of the Pusan encirclement and began a drive northward. A large number of North Korean soldiers were trapped, over half of them were soon captured or killed, and the rest were driven out of South Korea. Seoul was recaptured on September 26, and MacArthur's men were soon at the 38th parallel.

Having driven the Communist invaders out of South Korea, the UN forces had to make a tough decision: should they undertake an invasion of the north? Would such action bring the Chinese Communists into the war? Should American objectives be reconsidered? President Truman first approved military operations north of the 38th degree of latitude on September 11, unless there was, as he later wrote, "indication or threat of entry of Soviet or Chinese Communist elements in force." The UN General Assembly also gave its approval.

MacArthur's forces crossed the 38th parallel on October 7 and began a rapid advance up the peninsula. By the end of the month they were within fifty miles of the Yalu River, the boundary between North Korea and Manchuria. Although the Truman administration did not believe the Chinese would intervene in the Korean War, it wanted to make sure that air strikes were confined to the Korean peninsula. This concern was a major reason for Truman's famous conference in mid-October with MacArthur on Wake Island. The general assured Truman repeatedly "that the Korean conflict was over and that there was little possibility of the Chinese coming in." MacArthur soon began what he thought would be the final great offensive of the war.

By the time Truman left Wake Island on his long flight back to Washington, however, the first military units of the Chinese "volunteers" were crossing the Yalu into Korea. Mao Tse-tung and his associates had evidently decided that a reunited Korea under American control would be intolerable—a powerful opponent at China's very doorstep. But the large-scale Chinese intervention did not come until after MacArthur had commenced his last great offensive. On November 26, thirty-three Chinese divisions hit the middle of the UN line. MacArthur's armies had advanced along two widely separated routes, which left the center wide open. The Communists exploited this mistake, forced the UN soldiers into a retreat, and within two weeks had isolated MacArthur's units into three bridgeheads. The Chinese and North Koreans quickly cleared most of the northern peninsula, sent MacArthur's forces reeling across the 38th parallel, and once more forced the abandonment of Seoul.

The month of December in 1950 was a grim time for Americans. U.S. and South Korean military units suffered a series of humiliating defeats. The UN soldiers during the cruel winter of 1950–51 not only faced a ferocious enemy, equipped with Russian tanks and aircraft, but also had to cope with bitter cold, numerous storms, and an exceedingly rugged terrain. The situation in Washington was jittery, and talk of another world war swept the country. General MacArthur importuned Washington for permission to bomb "the privileged sanctuary of the adjacent Manchurian border." President

The Korean War, 1950–1953

Truman and his advisers considered MacArthur's proposals too risky. They were acutely aware of the Soviet Union's obligation to China under the mutual security pact of February 1950. They were afraid of getting trapped in a large land war in China and of precipitating a global war in the Far East.

In January 1951 the U.S. Eighth Army, under the command of General Matthew B. Ridgway, finally halted the Communist advance in South Korea. The UN forces slowly resumed the offensive, and by March they had reoccupied Seoul and reached the 38th parallel once more. As General MacArthur's men moved northward, the question of crossing the parallel was again raised. With the Republic of Korea largely cleared of Communist troops, President Truman and many United Nations spokesmen believed the time was ripe for a negotiated settlement. MacArthur was informed by Washington on March 20 that Truman was about to seek a settlement of the war through diplomatic means. At this point the general openly challenged the president. On March 24 MacArthur defiantly threatened mainland China with an attack. In Truman's opinion, this threat killed any hope of an early truce. In a letter to Representative Joseph W. Martin, which the congressman read in the House of Representatives on April 5, MacArthur expressed his views freely and vigorously. He wanted to unify Korea, unleash Chiang for an attack on mainland China, and fight communism in Asia rather than in Europe.

Truman could no longer brook such insubordination, and on April 10 he relieved MacArthur of his command, replacing him with General Ridgway. The general's dismissal created a furor such as the country had not experienced since the controversy over Roosevelt's court reorganization bill in 1937. The White House received a flood of vituperative letters and telegrams—more than 27,000 within twelve days. Flags were flown at half-mast in Massachusetts and Ohio, Truman was burned in effigy in towns across the country, and several state legislatures condemned him for his "irresponsible and capricious action." Republican leaders in Washington urged a congressional investigation and talked of impeaching the president. A Gallup poll showed that the public favored MacArthur over Truman by a margin of 69 to 29 percent.

In a few days Douglas MacArthur flew into San Francisco and began a triumphal tour of the United States. He was accorded great ovations. In a moment of high drama he appeared before a joint session of Congress on April 19. "I address you," the general began, "with neither rancor nor bitterness in the fading twilight of my life, with but one purpose in mind: To serve my country." MacArthur described the frustration and humiliation he had suffered in trying to win a war in Korea under the restrictions imposed by his Washington superiors. He rejected the concept of limited war. His views were endorsed by such prominent Republicans as Robert Taft and Herbert Hoover, and the controversy that swirled around his dismissal whipped up the GOP assault on Truman and Acheson. But the reaction to the MacArthur affair went beyond politics. It revealed the dissatisfaction with containment as a strategic concept in the conduct of American foreign policy. Containment ran counter to the nation's historical approach to international conflict, to the American expectation of quick solutions and total victories in foreign disputes and wars.

A joint Senate committee under the chairmanship of Senator Richard B. Russell held extensive hearings on the MacArthur case

Marine tanks and South Koreans direct North Korean prisoners to nearest stockade (*Defense Department photograph [Marine Corps] by SSgt. John Babyak, Jr.*)

between May 3 and June 25, 1951. MacArthur presented his case, but so did the Truman administration, whose position began to elicit more public understanding and backing as the hearings continued. Many Americans, probably a majority of them, came to agree with the administration's contention that Europe was the crucial theater in the cold war and that it would be a terrible mistake for the United States to become involved in a full-scale war with China in Asia. General Omar N. Bradley, speaking as chairman of the Joint Chiefs of Staff, put the administration's case succinctly when he stated that MacArthur's approach would "involve us in the wrong war, at the wrong place, at the wrong time, and with the wrong enemy." MacArthur's challenge did not reverse American policy in the Far East, but it did cause the administration to adopt a more inflexible posture toward Peking—nonrecognition became an established policy—and to increase its aid to the Chinese Nationalists on Taiwan.

By the spring of 1951, the Korean conflict had become deadlocked. In April and May the American forces and their UN allies repulsed two major Communist offensives, with the enemy suffering heavy losses. The United Nations had branded China as an aggressor in February 1951, and on May 18 the United States secured UN approval of an embargo against the shipment of munitions and critical war materials to China. Still, the military action had bogged down in the general vicinity of the 38th parallel. When the Soviet delegate to the UN suggested in June 1951 that an armistice be arranged, with mutual withdrawal of the two sides behind the 38th parallel, Washington welcomed the move. Leaders of the opposing forces began discussions looking toward an armistice on July 10, only to have them break down two days later. They were continued in an on-again, off-again fashion during the rest of the year. A truce was held up because of disagreement over an exact boundary and the disposition of the prisoners of war.

The Korean War was the first war ever fought by a world peace organization with an international army. Technically, the war was "a police action by the United Nations." But its consequences—for Korea and for the United States—were profound. Sixteen nations eventually sent military units to Korea or provided other assistance to the UN forces there. The United States, however, bore the burden of the war, along with the South Koreans. It provided half of the ground forces, 86 percent of the naval power, and 93 percent of the air power. American losses numbered 54,246 dead and 103,284 wounded, and the monetary costs climbed into the billions of dollars. At home, the Korean intervention brought the passage of the Defense Production Act of August 1950, authorizing new economic controls. Rigid price controls and rationing were not necessary, but taxes were increased and efforts were made to prevent price increases and large wage hikes. In December 1950, following the Chinese intervention in the war, President Truman declared a state of national emergency and outlined a vast new mobilization program.

A sharp increase in American military preparedness and an extension of containment were set in motion by the Korean conflict. In the second half of 1950, while the United States was fighting in Korea to contain the Communist expansion in Asia, the nation's defense budget was tripled and its armed forces were greatly enlarged. At the same time, the United States was aiding Chiang on Taiwan and the French in Indochina. American leaders also committed themselves to the rearming of West Germany and to the stationing of four divisions of their own troops in Western Europe. Meanwhile, they were working hard to develop the hydrogen bomb. "Because of these American initiatives," Walter LaFeber observes, "the six months between June and December 1950 rank among the most important of the Cold War era." During the next year, the

United States completed a treaty with Japan that allowed it to retain military bases in the islands. Mutual defense treaties were negotiated with Australia, New Zealand, and the Philippines, NATO was strengthened, and additional American bases were acquired in various parts of the world. When Truman left office early in 1953, containment had been institutionalized in East Asia, it had undergone a process of militarization, and NSC 68 was rapidly being implemented.

INTERNAL SECURITY AND THE POLITICS OF FEAR

By the time the shooting war began in Korea in mid–1950, the American people had succumbed to an irrational fear of disloyalty and subversion within the United States, and this outbreak of distrust and hysteria was to last until about 1954. Many factors were involved in the development of America's second Red Scare:[2] the exigencies and setbacks of the cold war, the Truman administration's loyalty program, a series of sensational spy cases, the Korean War, the Republican party's desperate search for a viable issue to use against the Democrats, and the emergence of a remarkable demagogue. During the late forties and early fifties, suspicion destroyed habitual trust, and guilt-by-association tactics damaged the lives and reputations of many men and women. In the quest for security, teachers were required to sign loyalty oaths, the courts and Congress assumed a harshly punitive attitude toward Communists, and liberals and reformers of every kind were criticized. A large number of states passed legislation denying public employment to individuals who advocated violent overthrow of the government or belonged to suspect organizations, while others adopted Communist-control laws.

Following World War II the Federal Bureau of Investigation began the first comprehensive scrutiny of government workers, and the federal departments undertook their own loyalty checks. In November 1946 the president created the Temporary Commission on Employee Loyalty to study the whole question, and its major recommendations were embodied in Truman's Executive Order No. 9835 on March 21, 1947. This order instituted a thorough investigation of all federal civil servants. The administration's loyalty inquest, while thorough, was conducted with procedural safeguards and provision for nonjudicial review. More than four million individuals were eventually checked. Charges were brought against 9,077 employees, some of whom resigned; the government dismissed 379 people, not as spies but as security risks.

In 1948 the Truman administration began the prosecution of the top Communist party leaders under the Smith Act of 1940. After the Supreme Court upheld the conviction of the Communist leaders, the government proceeded to prosecute dozens of lesser figures in the party. The administration's actions and rhetoric doubtless helped develop the framework for the extravagant anticommunism of later years.

The first public awareness of Russian wartime espionage came well before the introduction of Truman's loyalty program. Early in 1945 FBI agents discovered a large number of classified State Department documents when they raided the offices of *Amerasia*, a small left-wing magazine specializing in Far Eastern affairs. The following year, in February 1946, it was disclosed by a Canadian Royal Commission that several local spy rings had given the Russians military information and atomic secrets during the war. Meanwhile, the House Un-American Activities Committee (HUAC) was engaged in a search for subversives. Two of the witnesses who appeared before HUAC in the summer of 1948 provided information that led to one of the most bizarre and sensational cases in American history. Elizabeth Bentley and Whittaker Chambers—both former Communists—described the existence of two independent espionage rings operating in Washington for the Soviet Union in the 1930s.

Chambers, a senior editor of *Time* magazine, identified Alger Hiss, the highly respected president of the Carnegie Endowment for International Peace and a former State Department official, as a member of a Communist cell in Washington during the thirties. Later in the fall of 1948 Chambers broadened his charges, asserting that Hiss had given him copies of State Department documents to be turned over to Soviet agents. To prove his charges, Chambers escorted government agents to his farm at Westminster, Maryland, where he removed microfilm copies from a hollowed-out pumpkin! He claimed that the documents had been given to him by Hiss in 1938. Hiss, appearing before a federal grand jury in New York, denied that he had ever given State Department documents to Chambers or to anyone else. But the grand jury indicted him on two counts of perjury; the statute of limitations prevented him from being tried for treason. The trial began in May 1949 and ended six weeks later in a hung jury. A second trial was concluded in late January 1950, with Hiss being found guilty and sentenced to five years in prison.

Many liberals felt that Alger Hiss was being persecuted by a vindictive congressional investigating committee, and some men in high places, like Dean Acheson, refused to turn their backs on him. For others, the Hiss case confirmed their darkest fears and suspicions. Representative Richard M. Nixon of California, one of the most aggressive HUAC members in the whole affair, described the case as "the most treasonable conspiracy in American history." To many people who had long suspected the liberalism of Roosevelt and Truman, Hiss had become the symbol of all that had gone wrong in the United States and the world. And if Hiss was guilty of subversion, why not others like him?

The espionage in which Hiss was implicated occurred before the war, but other cases soon produced evidence of Communist infiltration in more recent years. In March 1949 a young New Yorker named Judith Coplon, a former political analyst in the Department of Justice, was arrested with her Russian lover on the charge of stealing classified documents for Soviet agents.[3] The case of Dr. Klaus Fuchs, revealed to the public in early February 1950, was much more important. Fuchs, a German-born scientist employed in the British nuclear energy establishment, had worked at Los Alamos, New Mexico, during the war on the development of the first atomic bomb. When arrested by the British, he confessed to transmitting important atomic secrets to the Russians between 1942 and 1947. The story Fuchs told led to the arrest of Harry Gold, an accomplice in the United States, and four other Americans: Julius and Ethel Rosenberg, Morton Sobell, and David Greenglass. They were all charged with passing atomic secrets to the Russians during and after the war. They were tried and convicted in 1951. The Rosenbergs were sentenced to death and were executed in June 1953.

Hiss and Fuchs and the Rosenbergs seemed to explain many of the disappointments and setbacks the United States had suffered since the war. At a time when the president was asking Congress to vote billions of dollars to halt the Communist expansion in Europe and Asia, how else could one explain the fall of China, the loss of America's atomic monopoly, and the inability to win the war in Korea? Disloyalty, subversion, and trickery at home—by intellectuals, left-wingers, and New Deal internationalists—must be at the root of the nation's difficulties. As Senator Homer Capehart of Indiana exclaimed, "How much more are we going to have to take? Fuchs and Acheson and Hiss and hydrogen bombs threatening outside and New Dealers eating away the vitals of the nation. In the name of Heaven, is this the best America can do?"

Men like Capehart had earlier tried to cope with the threat of internal subversion by adopting strong antisubversive legislation. They had been denied a new law in 1948, when President Truman successfully vetoed the Mundt-Nixon bill. But the shocking developments of 1949, the rising tide of anticommunism, and the sensational charges made by Republican congressmen smoothed the path for the McCarran Internal Security Act of September 1950, which was passed overwhelmingly over Truman's veto. The Mc-Carran Act required Communist and Communist-front organizations to register with the attorney general, made them publish periodic financial statements and other reports, and forbade Communists to work in defense plants or to use American passports. The new law broadened the definition of espionage and sabotage, extended the statute of limitations for prosecution, and made it illegal to *conspire* to perform any act that would "substantially contribute" to the establishment of a totalitarian government in the United States. In the McCarran-Walter Act, which was passed over Truman's veto in 1952, Congress provided for the screening of undesirables seeking entry into the United States and struck at communism through various exclusion and registration clauses.[4]

One of the consequences of the heightened public concern over internal security in the United States was the Republican party's exploitation of the issue. Many Republicans were predisposed to seize hold of this issue because of the long-time conservative hostility toward the New Deal. Thus "a politics of revenge" was promoted by groups that linked antipathy toward communism with strong dislike of New Deal and Fair Deal liberalism. The Truman administration's containment policy, its comprehensive loyalty program, and the defection of Henry Wallace shielded the Democrats from a Republican attack invoking the Communist issue in the campaign of 1948. But the loss of that election left the Republicans frustrated and embittered, and the events of 1949 and 1950 brought them finally to the employment of anticommunism as a principal weapon in their political war against the Democrats.

The man most successful in demonstrating the political possibilities of the Communist issue was a first-term senator from Wisconsin named Joseph R. McCarthy. A lawyer and former circuit judge, McCarthy had narrowly defeated Senator Robert M. La Follette, Jr., in the Republican primary of 1946 and had gone on to defeat his Democratic opponent in the November election. The Wisconsin senator violated the Senate's rules and customs from the beginning of his tenure, spouted immoderate contentions, and engaged in questionable dealings with lobbyists for certain vested interests. He had displeased powerful senators from both parties, lost his only major committee assignment, and was worried about his chances of reelection in 1952. At this point, while casting about for an issue—any issue—that would revive his political fortunes, he adopted the anti-Communist tactic.

McCarthy first came to the attention of the American public as a result of a speech he made to the Republican Women's Club of Wheeling, West Virginia, on February 9, 1950. Asserting that the United States had been the greatest power in the world on V-J Day, he explained that the country's strength had been diminished "because of the traitorous actions of those who have been treated so well by this Nation." McCarthy's precise words on that occasion will probably never be known, but according to the radio and newspaper journalists who followed his rough draft, he held up a sheaf of papers and shouted: "I have here in my hand a list of 205—a list of names that were made known to the Secretary of State as being members of the Communist Party and who nevertheless are still working and shaping policy in the State Department." The senator was hard to pin down, but his charges were swiftly carried by the media from one end of the country to the other.

Back in Washington the Democrats sought to deal with McCarthy by having a subcommittee of the Senate Foreign Relations Committee make a thorough investigation of his accusations. The subcommittee, under the chairmanship of Senator Millard E. Tydings of Maryland, began a series of extensive hearings on March 8, 1950. McCarthy soon stated that he would rest his case on his contention that Professor Owen Lattimore of Johns Hopkins University, a Far Eastern expert who had served as a consultant to the State Department on several occasions, was the "top Russian espionage agent" in the United States. Lattimore denied under oath that he was a Communist or a "follower of the communist line." When he was later indicted for perjury, his case was thrown out by the court. The Tydings committee reported in July 1950; its Democratic majority called the McCarthy charges "a fraud and a hoax" on the Senate and on the American people.

Most Republicans in Congress defended McCarthy. Many GOP members echoed the then-current phrase, "I don't like some of McCarthy's methods but his goal is good." McCarthyism, Robert Griffith remarks, "was shorthand for the issue of 'communism-in-government,' a preeminently Republican issue which served as the cutting edge of the party's drive for power." This was borne out in the congressional elections of 1950, when the Republicans invoked the subversive theme with a vengeance. In California, for example, Richard M. Nixon was elected to the Senate by exploiting McCarthyite issues. McCarthy became the most popular campaigner for his party and probably contributed to the defeat of Senator Tydings in Maryland and Governor Chester Bowles in Connecticut. The Wisconsin senator exploited the social strains of the time and became a powerful articulator of simple answers to complex and baffling questions arising from the cold war. While McCarthy was fundamentally a product of the anti-Communist consensus that existed before 1950, he was a talented demagogue who skillfully manipulated the media and built up a network of informers within the government itself.

The Korean War also strengthened McCarthy by refueling anti-Communist extremism, and in the early fifties his influence increased spectacularly. He fought off all efforts in the Senate to restrain him, and throughout 1951 added his reckless voice to the China inquest and continually sought to discredit the Truman administration. His accusations and innuendos resulted in a long succession of charges and countercharges. Few public figures in American history have matched McCarthy's intemperate and vituperative attacks on his adversaries. He denounced all the "egg-sucking phony liberals" whose "pitiful squealing . . . would hold sacrosanct those Communists and queers" who had sold China into "atheistic slavery," and he committed himself to driving out the "prancing mimics of the Moscow party line in the State Department."

McCarthy was not the only practitioner of McCarthyism; he was joined by many Republican politicians and some powerful anti-Communist Democrats. But the Wisconsin senator was the star of the show. He dominated the channels of mass communications. He intimidated government officials and private citizens, and while many Washington politicians deplored his methods, few of them would openly challenge him at the height of his power. By 1953 McCarthy was given credit for having won almost a dozen Republican Senate elections, and a "myth of political invincibility" had grown up about him. This estimate was exaggerated, but unquestionably McCarthy was an influential force in American politics.

"I LIKE IKE": THE ELECTION OF 1952

The frustration and rancor that spread through American society during the final years of Harry Truman's presidency brightened Republican prospects in the election of 1952. Truman's popularity ebbed sharply, and in the public mind his administration was associated with a wide assortment of national setbacks and threatening problems: the involvement in Korea, Chinese aggression, internal communism, corruption in government, high taxes, and inflation. Republican leaders were determined not to let electoral success slip from their grasp as they had done in 1948, and that determination was one reason for the most vigorous intraparty struggle the GOP had experienced in a generation.

Eisenhower campaigning in 1952 (*United Press International*)

This fight over the Republican nomination in 1952 reflected a division in the party that had existed for many years. The more conservative faction championed Senator Taft, who had announced his candidacy in October 1951. Strongly supported by the regular party leaders and business interests of the Midwest, the conservative wing urged a real alternative to the Democrats. The liberal-internationalist wing of the Republican party, which was strongest in the East and in the Far West, viewed Taft's position on foreign and domestic questions with suspicion, and men like Governor Dewey doubted that he could win if nominated. Liberal Republicans pinned their hopes on General Dwight Eisenhower, then on leave from the presidency of Columbia University to serve as supreme commander of the NATO forces in Europe. A draft-Eisenhower movement began to take shape by the late summer of 1951, and in January 1952 the general finally agreed to accept the nomination if it were offered to him. He seems to have been motivated in part by a desire to save his party and the country from the policies of Taft and McCarthy.

Eisenhower won the New Hampshire primary in March and later was victorious in several other primaries. Meanwhile, Taft was campaigning hard and obtaining a large number of delegate commitments, especially in the Middle West and the South. As the pre-convention campaign proceeded, Eisenhower's spokesmen charged that the Taft-controlled state organizations in the southern states were disqualifying pro-Eisenhower delegates chosen by local and state conventions. By the time the Republican National Convention opened in Chicago on July 7, Taft probably had a slight lead over Eisenhower in the number of committed delegates, although it was clear to most observers that the general was far more popular than the senator with rank-and-file Republicans.

When the convention began, the Eisenhower forces succeeded in passing by a vote of 658 to 548 the so-called Fair Play Amendment, which provided that the contested delegates seated by the national committee during the previous week could not vote on the credentials of other delegates. This victory foreshadowed Eisenhower's nomination, for the Eisenhower delegations challenging the regular slates in Texas, Georgia, and Louisiana were later seated by convention vote, and the general was nominated on the first ballot. Senator Richard Nixon was selected for the vice-presidential nomination. The Republican platform was strongly critical of the Democratic administration, charging that in seven years it had "squandered the unprecedented power and prestige which were ours at the close of World War II" and that it had "lost the peace so dearly earned" by the war.

There were several aspirants for the Democratic nomination, but most of them were handicapped at first by uncertainty over President Truman's possible candidacy. This was not true of Senator Estes Kefauver of Tennessee, who had won a Senate seat in 1948 by defeating the machine of Edward H. Crump of Memphis. Kefauver had attracted national attention as chairman of a special Senate sub-committee created to investigate interstate crime. But he was not popular with the big-city Democratic bosses because his investigations had disclosed links between organized crime and local politics. Nor was he acceptable to Truman, whose administration, he declared, should be doing more to clean up corruption in government. The Tennessee senator entered the March 11 New Hampshire Democratic primary and to the surprise of the nation defeated the president in the preferential vote. This shocking development no doubt hastened Truman's announcement that he would not himself be a candidate for reelection, an announcement he made on March 29 at a Jefferson-Jackson Day dinner in Washington. In order to stop Kefauver, who went on to win a series of other primaries, Truman turned to Adlai E. Stevenson, who had made a fine record as governor of Illinois. When Stevenson insisted that he had no interest in running for president, Truman and other party leaders endorsed seventy-four-year-old Alben Barkley, who eventually retired from the race because of opposition from several labor leaders.

At the Democratic National Convention, also held in Chicago that year, party leaders again sought to persuade Governor Stevenson to seek the nomination, and he reluctantly agreed. Although Kefauver led on the first two ballots, his brave fight was unavailing against the power and influence of the administration and other Democratic leaders. Stevenson was nominated on the third ballot, and Senator John J. Sparkman of Alabama, one of the architects of a compromise civil rights plank designed to prevent a southern bolt, was chosen as his running mate. The platform committed the party to the repeal of the Taft-Hartley Act, maintenance of high price supports for agriculture, and continuation of the Fair Deal. Under the theme of "peace with honor," the assembled Democrats endorsed American intervention in Korea and praised the Truman administration's foreign policies.

The Republican campaign did not get off to a fast start, since General Eisenhower was rather fumbling and uninspiring in his early speeches. In September Eisenhower's "great crusade" began to pick up momentum. The GOP candidate began to stress the formula Senator Karl E. Mundt called K_1C_2: Korea, communism, and corruption in government. Eisenhower pledged his support to all Republican candidates, including extreme conservatives and such rabid anti-Communists as Senator McCarthy. He made a special effort to assuage the bitterness of the Taft faction, arranging a special conference with the senator in New York City on September 12. As a result of that meeting the two Republican leaders reached an agreement on the importance of fiscal responsibility in the conduct of the national government, the need to reduce federal expenditures and balance the budget, and the necessity of defending "liberty against creeping socialism."

The Republicans had a popular candidate, they were united in supporting him, and their campaign was abundantly financed. Republican strategists made extensive use of television, which assumed importance for the first time in a presidential campaign, and they used the advertising and public relations techniques of Madison Avenue to give their candidates a good "image." Party campaigners, including McCarthy and Nixon, did not neglect the Communist issue. They spoke scornfully of the "egghead" support that Stevenson was receiving. As the campaign developed, Eisenhower began to emphasize the Korean War. He described the negotiations as a "swindle," a "Soviet trap" designed to enable the North Koreans to renew their strength. At Detroit on October 24 the general made a sensational announcement. If elected, he declared, "I shall go to Korea," to seek an early and honorable end to the war.

The Eisenhower campaign ran into real trouble only once—the dramatic episode of the secret Nixon fund. On September 18 it was disclosed that Senator Nixon, the GOP vice-presidential nominee, had benefited from a private fund of about $18,000 contributed by California businessmen. Eisenhower, who had said that his administration would be as "clean as a hound's tooth," was in a dilemma. Some of the general's advisers urged him to remove Nixon from the ticket, but Eisenhower hesitated. Meanwhile, Nixon fought back, presenting his case to the people in a national television broadcast on September 23. The speech was melodramatic but effective. The senator emphasized his own relatively limited personal assets, noted that his wife, Pat, "doesn't have a mink coat," and about his cocker spaniel, Checkers—a gift from a Texan who had heard that his children wanted a dog—vowed that "regardless of what they say about it, we're going to keep it." The response was all that Nixon could have wished; nearly 200,000 telegrams poured into the party's national committee urging Nixon's retention on the ticket. Eisenhower accepted this verdict.

In the meantime, the Democrats had launched their campaign. Stevenson quickly emerged as something of a television personality—articulate, thoughtful, and witty. He had a special way with words. He assured his audiences that "if the Republicans will stop telling lies about us, we will stop telling the truth about them." It was clear to Stevenson that in some respects the Truman administration would be a liability to his campaign, and he sought, with only limited success, to establish his independence of Truman. The Democratic nominee laid out his position in a series of extraordinary addresses during the campaign. Basically he continued the New Deal-Fair Deal line.

Both major parties waged vigorous and comprehensive campaigns. The Democrats, remembering the miracle of 1948, hoped the voters would respond to their campaign slogan that Americans had "never had it so good." But the election returns dashed their hopes. Eisenhower won 33,824,351 popular votes (55.4 percent) to Stevenson's 27,314,987 (44.4 percent) in the heaviest turnout since 1908. The electoral vote was 442 to 89, with the Democratic ticket carrying only nine southern and border states.

The defections from the Democratic coalition were numerous, including southerners, Catholics, certain ethnic groups, and even low-income voters. In the South, where Governor James F. Byrnes of South Carolina and Governor Allan F. Shivers of Texas actively supported Eisenhower and Nixon, the Republican ticket obtained 48.9 percent of the popular vote and carried Virginia, Florida, Tennessee, Texas, and Oklahoma. Almost one-fourth of Eisenhower's total vote came from people who had voted for Truman in 1948, and many new voters cast their ballots for the Republicans. Blacks were the only group that gave Stevenson as high a percentage of its vote as it had given Truman four years earlier. Yet the election was preeminently a personal victory for Dwight Eisenhower; he ran an astonishing 19 percent ahead of other GOP candidates in 1952. Only the general's immense popularity enabled the Republicans to win control of Congress. The Republicans gained 22 House seats—just 3 more than the 218 needed to give them control—and only 1 Senate seat, just enough to make it possible for them to organize that body. In spite of preferring the Republican presidential candidate, it was clear that a majority of the voters still thought of themselves as Democrats. Nevertheless, after twenty years of Democratic control, the Republicans were moving back to 1600 Pennsylvania Avenue and also to supremacy on Capitol Hill.

NOTES

1. Jacob Malik, the Russian delegate, was absent when the Security Council met on June 25. He was absent because the Russians had been boycotting the UN in protest against the failure of the international organization to admit the People's Republic of China earlier in the year. Had Malik been present on the 25th, he could have exercised the veto to prevent UN action in Korea.

2. The first Red Scare in 1919–20 was characterized by an outbreak of intolerance and mob violence directed at bolshevism and ideological nonconformity.

3. Miss Coplon was tried and convicted in two separate cases in 1949 and 1950, but she escaped imprisonment when her convictions were overturned on appeal because of technicalities. The government declined to prosecute her again.

4. The McCarran-Walter Act was primarily designed to provide an up-to-date codification of the nation's immigration laws. It repealed the notorious clauses excluding Orientals from the United States but retained the quota system.

SUGGESTIONS FOR FURTHER READING

For the complicated situation in China during and after World War II and American efforts to deal with it, see Herbert Feis, *The China Tangle: The American Effort in China from Pearl Harbor to the Marshall Mission* (1953); Tang Tsou, *America's Failure in China, 1941–1950* (1963); Akira Iriye, *The Cold War in Asia* (1974); Lewis M. Purifoy, *Harry Truman's China Policy: McCarthyism and the Diplomacy of Hysteria, 1947–1951* (1976); Dorothy Borg and Waldo Heinrichs (eds.), *Uncertain Years: Chinese-*

American Relations, 1947–1950 (1980); William Whitney Stueck, Jr., *The Road to Confrontation: American Policy toward China and Korea, 1947– 1950* (1981); Robert M. Blum, *Drawing the Line: The Origin of the American Containment Policy in East Asia* (1982); and Nancy Bernkopf Tucker, *Patterns in the Dust: Chinese-American Relations and the Recognition Controversy, 1949–1950* (1983). Ambrose's *Rise to Globalism* and La-Feber's *America, Russia, and the Cold War,* cited earlier, provide challenging perspectives. The effects of international developments on domestic politics are analyzed by H. Bradford Westerfield, *Foreign Policy and Party Politics: Pearl Harbor to Korea* (1955), and Ross Y. Koen, *The China Lobby in American Politics* (1974). Goldman's *The Crucial Decade,* mentioned in chapter 1, is a breezy treatment of the domestic scene and public attitudes.

Glenn D. Paige, *The Korean Decision* (1968), is a detailed account of decision making between June 24 and June 30, 1950. Bruce Cumings, *The Origins of the Korean War . . . 1945–1947* (1981), is excellent. See also the useful collection of essays edited by Cumings, *Child of Conflict: The Korean-American Relationship, 1943–1953* (1983). The best book on the Korean War is David Rees, *Korea: The Limited War* (1964), but also see Frank Baldwin (ed.), *Without Parallel* (1974); Francis H. Heller (ed.), *The Korean War: A 25-Year Perspective* (1977); and Burton I. Kaufman, *The Korean War: Challenges in Crisis, Credibility, and Command* (1986). Allen S. Whiting's *China Crosses the Yalu: The Decision to Enter the Korean War* (1960) throws light on an important aspect of the war. Joyce Kolko and Gabriel Kolko, *The Limits of Power: The World and United States Foreign Policy, 1945–1954* (1972), contains a critical treatment of the Korean conflict and raises a number of provocative questions about U.S. involvement. John W. Spanier's *The Truman-MacArthur Controversy and the Korean War* (rev. ed., 1965) is a valuable study, stressing the concept of "limited war." For partisan implications, see Ronald J. Caridi, *The Korean War and American Politics: The Republican Party as a Case Study* (1968). An aspect of U.S. mobilization for the war is dealt with by Maeva Marcus, *Truman and the Steel Seizure Case: The Limits of Presidential Power* (1977).

Several good studies have been completed on the internal security problem and anti-Communist hysteria at mid-century. Earl Latham, *The Communist Controversy in Washington: From the New Deal to McCarthy* (1966), provides a full discussion of the rising Communist issue, which is explained in terms of a conservative drive for power. The role of HUAC is considered in Walter Goodman, *The Committee: The Extraordinary Career of the House Committee on Un-American Activities* (1968). Alan D. Harper, *The Politics of Loyalty: The White House and the Communist Issue, 1946–1952* (1969), is a balanced treatment of the Truman administration's loyalty program and its response to the anti-Communist issue. Much more critical of the Truman administration are Athan Theoharis, *Seeds of Repression: Harry S. Truman and the Origins of McCarthyism* (1971), and Richard M. Freeland, *The Truman Doctrine and the Origins of McCarthyism: Foreign Policy, Domestic Politics, and Internal Security, 1946– 1948* (1972). David Caute's *The Great Fear: The Anti-Communist Purge under Truman and Eisenhower* (1978) is also critical. Michal R. Belknap, *Cold War Political Justice: The Smith Act, the Communist Party, and American Civil Liberties* (1977), and Stanley I. Kutler, *The American Inquisition: Justice and Injustice in the Cold War* (1982), are illuminating. Other perspectives are offered by Allen Weinstein, *Perjury: The Hiss-*

Chambers Case (1978), and Victor S. Navasky, *Naming Names* (1980), the latter on HUAC. For the Communists' outlook, see Joseph Starobin, *American Communism in Crisis, 1943–1957* (1972), and Vivian Gornick, *The Romance of American Communism* (1977).

Two major biographies of Joseph R. McCarthy have recently appeared: Thomas C. Reeves, *The Life and Times of Joe McCarthy* (1982), and David Oshinsky, *A Conspiracy So Immense: The World of Joe McCarthy* (1983). An older book, Richard H. Rovere's *Senator Joe McCarthy* (1959), contains a revealing appraisal of McCarthy's character. Robert Griffith's prize-winning *The Politics of Fear: Joseph R. McCarthy and the Senate* (1970) focuses on the senatorial stage upon which the Wisconsin senator operated. Other specialized studies include Richard M. Fried, *Men Against McCarthy* (1976), and Michael O'Brien, *McCarthy and McCarthyism in Wisconsin* (1980). Robert Griffith and Athan Theoharis (eds.), *The Specter: Original Essays on the Cold War and the Origins of McCarthyism* (1974), is useful for McCarthyism and American institutions. Particular institutions are dealt with in David M. Oshinsky, *Senator Joseph McCarthy and the American Labor Movement* (1976); Donald F. Crosby, *God, Church, and Flag: Senator Joseph R. McCarthy and the Catholic Church, 1950–1957* (1978); and Edwin R. Bayley, *Joe McCarthy and the Press* (1981). Daniel Bell (ed.), *The New American Right* (1955, rev. ed. 1964 entitled *The Radical Right*), explains McCarthyism in terms of "status politics" and mass irrationality. Michael Paul Rogin, *The Intellectuals and McCarthy: The Radical Specter* (1967), challenges this interpretation.

For the election of 1952, see Stephen E. Ambrose, *Eisenhower: Soldier, General of the Army, President-Elect, 1890–1952* (1983); Bert Cochran, *Adlai Stevenson: Patrician among the Politicians* (1969); John Bartlow Martin, *Adlai Stevenson and the World* (1977); Samuel Lubell, *The Revolt of the Moderates* (1956); Joseph Bruce Gorman, *Kefauver: A Political Biography* (1971); and Patterson, *Mr. Republican: A Biography of Robert A. Taft*, previously cited.

CHAPTER FIVE

Eisenhower and the Politics of Moderation

DWIGHT DAVID EISENHOWER, the nation's thirty-fourth president, suited the 1950s singularly well. Coming to office at a time of confusion, division, and bitterness, the immensely popular "Ike" rendered the decade's politics less acrimonious, eased the accumulated tensions of a generation of crisis, and helped to restore a sense of national unity. The new president's moderate Republicanism and restrained approach to government appealed to millions of Americans who had grown weary of great public enterprises and social conflict. The purposes and style of the Eisenhower administration blended comfortably into a national mood of complacency, well-being, and self-indulgence.

Eisenhower's two terms in the White House contained their full share of setbacks and unexpected difficulties, including two serious illnesses the president suffered in 1955 and 1956. Many of the general's early supporters were disappointed by the results of his executive leadership, in some cases because the administration did not challenge the New Deal, in others because it did not undertake fresh programs and a more venturesome course in domestic affairs. Yet there were some notable accomplishments during Eisenhower's presidency, and there can be no doubt that he greatly influenced the course of our recent history. Richard Rovere has suggested that, in part because he was a Republican, Eisenhower was able to do "many of the things that needed doing and that could not have been done by a Democratic administration." Thus he liquidated the Korean War without being labeled an appeaser, and his administration helped to establish the New Deal as an enduring feature of our national government.

EISENHOWER AND THE NEW ADMINISTRATION

Dwight D. Eisenhower's long years of military service gave him a unique background among twentieth-century presidents. Born in 1890 at Denison, Texas, into an economically pressed family of Pennsylvania Dutch descent, he spent his boyhood in Abilene, Kansas, which was still something of a frontier town at the turn of the century. In some ways, Ike never left home, for his world would always retain the traditional American values and virtues he had assimilated as a boy in Abilene. In other respects, however, his world soon broadened. He received an appointment to West Point and was graduated from the military academy in 1915. After serving as an officer in the tank training program at Camp Colt during World War I, he held a variety of assignments at army posts and service schools during the next two decades and served as an aide to General MacArthur for several years. He came to know his way around Washington and learned to deal with politicians and with the press. He distinguished himself in army maneuvers held in Louisiana in 1941 and was subsequently assigned to the war plans division of the War Department. General Marshall soon recommended Eisenhower to command American forces in Europe, and he served as commander of the Allied invasion of North Africa, Sicily, and Italy. He was then selected as the supreme commander of the Allied forces in Europe, and in that role he directed the momentous invasion of France and the subsequent conquest of Germany. He emerged from the war as a five-star general and an authentic military hero.

The general had demonstrated a remarkable talent for leadership. His military success had come not as a result of genius as a strategist or brilliance as a field commander, but basically as a result of his unusual personal qualities and his capacity as a coordinator and conciliator. He was, the historian Robert Griffith suggests, "a product of the organizational revolution that had transformed American life in the twentieth century, a member of the new managerial class that led the nation's great public and private bureaucracies." He knew how to direct large projects, was willing to shoulder vast responsibilities, and was familiar with the operation of modern bureaucracies. Eisenhower was also at home in the realm of international relations, and he was firmly committed to a policy of internationalism.

In other ways, however, he was ill-equipped for the task of presidential leadership. His civilian experience before 1952 was severely limited, he was not well acquainted with the way in which the political system worked in the United States, and he was unfamiliar with the problems and complexities of American society. His ideas, embodying such basic values as self-reliance and faith in free enterprise, while widely shared by his fellow Americans, tended to be cast in the simplistic and somewhat romantic mold of an earlier day. Still, he took ideas seriously, was a quick learner, and communicated easily. The new president was also a man of great warmth, personal charm, and becoming modesty. He liked people and expected them to like him. As Arthur Krock of the *New York Times* wrote in 1957:

> His manner is genial; his ways and reflexes are kindly. His bearing is soldierly, yet his well-tailored civilian clothes never seem out of character. His smile is attractively pensive, his frequent grin is infectious, his laughter ready and hearty. He fairly radiates "goodness," simple faith and the honorable, industrious background of his heritage.

Eisenhower's view of the presidency differed sharply from that of his immediate predecessors. He had no taste for the ordinary ways of the politician: the rough-and-tumble of active partisanship, the haggling over matters of patronage, and the involvement in the details of government. This "least partisan president," as the former New Dealer Rexford G. Tugwell called him, seemed to stand above the political battles, to preside over his administration rather than to be actively involved in it. Especially at first, before the death of Senator Taft, on whom he relied, in the summer of 1953, he approached Congress with great deference. Eisenhower seemed to desire a less active role than Roosevelt and Truman, to be more respectful of the separation of powers, and to prefer working quietly behind the scene. Yet his concept of the presidency was expansive, especially in foreign affairs, and he saw it as an office of vital moral leadership. Disliking controversy, he stressed persuasion, patience, moderation, and flexibility. He also relied heavily upon a carefully organized staff and departmental system. Sherman Adams, the former governor of New Hampshire, became the "assistant to the president." His task was to direct a staff in serving as a clearinghouse on policy.

While Adams shielded Eisenhower from many troublesome details and, as a trusted assistant, supervised important governmental functions in the White House, the members of the Cabinet also assumed larger roles in the operation of the executive branch. The most prominent Cabinet official was Secretary of State John Foster Dulles. The second most influential department head was Secretary of the Treasury George M. Humphrey, an Ohio industrialist and financier. "In cabinet meetings I always wait for George Humphrey to speak," Eisenhower once said, because "I know . . . he will say just what I am thinking." Another businessman, Charles E. Wilson, president of the General Motors Corporation, was appointed secretary of defense. Ezra Taft Benson of Utah, a farm marketing specialist and an apostle of the Mormon Church, became secretary of agriculture. The other departments were also headed by businessmen or Republican politicians, except for the department of labor, which was headed by Martin P. Durkin, a Democrat, a Catholic, and the president of the United Association of Journeyman Plumbers and Steamfitters. According to one wit, the new Cabinet contained "eight millionaires and a plumber." The new president had, in fact, surrounded himself with business executives, financiers, and corporate lawyers.

Too much federal intervention, Eisenhower had warned before his nomination, would turn "the American dream into an American nightmare." He was determined to reverse the growth of big government. He intended to balance the federal budget, remove as many economic controls as possible, and prevent the government from becoming further involved in business. He also hoped to heal the sharp division in the Republican party, to curb its strong isolationist tendencies, and to modernize it in certain other respects. At a more fundamental level he wanted to promote social harmony, stability, and consensus.

THE EISENHOWER POLICIES

Dwight Eisenhower's concept of a limited role for the federal government in the economic life of the nation, a concept he labeled "dynamic conservatism," was quickly put into effect by the new administration. The president and his advisers cut back on the recommended expenditures in the Truman budget for foreign aid and military equipment. Some 200,000 civilian workers were removed from the federal payroll during Eisenhower's first term. The administration ended most of the Korean War controls over rents, wages, and prices. The Reconstruction Finance Corporation was allowed to expire in 1953, and efforts were made to sell or close down government establishments that competed with private enterprise. Commissions were formed, conferences were held, and orders were issued to wipe out duplication, increase efficiency, and reduce expenditures throughout the government service.

The economic conservatism of the administration was manifested in other ways as well. Presidential appointments soon weakened several of the independent regulatory commissions. The new chairman of the Federal Trade Commission had spent his entire career defending corporate clients before the FTC. Secretary of

Commerce Sinclair E. Weeks, a Massachusetts manufacturer, had scarcely taken office before he fired Dr. Allen Astin as head of the Bureau of Standards for not being mindful of the "business point of view." The furor that resulted caused Weeks to restore Astin to his position. When a measure was introduced in Congress in the spring of 1955 to have the government provide Dr. Jonas Salk's polio vaccine free to American children, Secretary of Health, Education, and Welfare Oveta Culp Hobby strongly opposed it on the ground that it would lead to "socialized medicine" by the "back door." Eisenhower himself took a firm stand against so-called socialized-medicine proposals, and he spoke out against medical insurance amendments to social security bills. Cooperation between government and business was also evident in the administration's antitrust policy, which was characterized by frequent use of prefiling conferences, consent decrees, and premerger clearances.

Republican candidates had promised in 1952, as in earlier campaigns, to undo the "excesses" of the Roosevelt and Truman administrations: to balance the budget, reduce federal spending, cut taxes, check inflation, and restore an "unregulated" economy. Nevertheless, Eisenhower's proposed budget for the fiscal year 1953–54 contained a deficit of $5.5 billion (a considerable improvement over the $9.9 billion projected by the Truman administration). This so shocked Senator Taft, when he learned of it in a conference with the president, that he exclaimed with great emotion, "You're taking us down the same road Truman traveled." The administration finally managed, with the ending of the Korean War, to pare the deficit down to $3.1 billion. But the next fiscal year ended with a deficit of over $4 billion, and Eisenhower was able to avoid deficits in only three of his eight years in office. By 1956 the administration's nondefense expenditures were higher than those under Truman, and Eisenhower's proposed budget of $71.8 billion for fiscal 1957–58 set a peacetime record. The expenditures for national defense, foreign aid, and social welfare along with such annual outlays as farm subsidies constituted a major portion of the budget and could not easily be reduced. When the economy experienced trouble, as it did in 1954 and 1958, it seemed wise to resort to the fiscal remedies provided by the New Deal and the Fair Deal.

The administration's agricultural policies provide a graphic illustration of this point. Eisenhower and Secretary of Agriculture Benson, a vigorous advocate of private enterprise on the farm, hoped to minimize the government's role in the agricultural economy and at the same time contribute to the solution of the "farm problem," which involved huge annual surpluses, a continuing decline in total net agricultural income, and a steady drop in the farmer's share of the retail cost of his product. Benson talked about restoring the "free market" to agriculture. He was convinced that the rigid price-support system caused farmers to overproduce, thus driving prices down and forcing the government to assume an increasingly heavy burden of subsidies. The administration managed, after a heated congressional struggle, to get the principle of flexible supports incorporated into the Agricultural Act of January 1954. The statute authorized price support on basic farm commodities ranging from 82.5 to 90 percent of parity for 1955 and from 75 to 90 percent for 1956 and subsequent years. But surpluses continued to pile up and government costs continued to mount.

Another approach was then tried. This was the "soil bank" scheme, for which Congress appropriated funds in 1956. Under this New Deal–type program farmers who agreed to cut their acreage below their normal allotments or to commit a portion of their land to soil conservation rather than the production of cash crops would receive government payments for participating in the acreage reserve and conservation reserve programs. Although more than 12 million acres were soon put into the soil bank, the farm problem remained as intractable as ever. Concentrating on their best land and employing scientific methods and the new chemical fertilizers, farmers were able to produce as much on fewer acres as they had in previous years. By 1958 the federal government was spending more than ever on its agricultural programs. Eisenhower and Benson were unable to redirect the course of national farm policy.

The dimensions of Eisenhower's "dynamic conservatism" were fully revealed in the administration's proposals in the areas of natural resources and the production of electrical power. An early indication of Eisenhower's approach came in the disposition of tidelands oil—the rich offshore oil deposits claimed by California and the Gulf states. President Truman had twice vetoed measures designed to turn these rights over to the claimant states, and the Supreme Court, in 1947 and 1950, had decided that the federal government had "paramount rights" to the offshore lands. Eisenhower pledged his support to the states during the campaign of 1952, and as president he promoted the adoption of the Submerged Lands Act of May 1953. This law invalidated earlier arrangements and granted the states title to the coastal lands within their "historic" boundaries.

Near the end of his first administration, Eisenhower supported a congressional amendment to the Natural Gas Act of 1938 that would have exempted gas companies from regulation by the Federal Power Commission. Administration spokesmen argued that this action would stimulate gas production and the expansion of gas distribution facilities. Just before the bill was passed, Senator Francis P. Case of South Dakota learned that an oil company had contributed $2,500 to his campaign for reelection, evidently expecting him to vote for the exemption amendment. Case returned the money and voted against the bill, and in the wake of all the resulting publicity, the president decided to veto the measure.

Eisenhower regarded federal control of electrical power as a menace to private enterprise, as a danger to local autonomy, and as "a threat deadly to our liberties." He wanted to replace "exclusive dependence on Federal bureaucracy" with "a partnership of state and local communities, private citizens, and the Federal Government, all working together." In some cases, the administration conceded, the federal government had to take the major part in river development projects. Thus Eisenhower agreed to large federal expenditures for the construction of hydroelectric, irrigation, and other water supply facilities on the upper Colorado River. He also supported the St. Lawrence Seaway, signing a measure in 1954 that created a self-financed public corporation to finance, construct, and develop the American portion of the long waterway connecting the Atlantic Ocean and the Great Lakes.

In many other cases, the Eisenhower administration worked hard to curtail federal involvement in stream development and power projects. Eisenhower cut the budget of several federal power projects and abandoned certain undertakings already approved by Congress. The administration strongly opposed a Democratic plan, carried over from the Truman period, for the federal construction of a high multipurpose dam and hydroelectric plant in Hell's Canyon along the Snake River. Eisenhower and Secretary of the Interior Douglas McKay endorsed the proposed construction of three smaller dams by private concerns, and the Federal Power Commission eventually granted the Idaho Power Company a license for this purpose. Republicans were then able to beat back a movement in Congress to authorize the building of a high dam by the federal government. Eisenhower also won some concessions for his partnership approach in the Atomic Energy Act of 1954, which authorized the operation of new atomic energy plants by private companies.

Although the president referred to the Tennessee Valley Authority (TVA) as an example of "creeping socialism," he did not attack the agency directly. Opposing the TVA's request for funds to build a new steam generating plant to serve the power needs of the Memphis area, Eisenhower and his advisers sponsored a proposal for the private construction of a steam generating plant in West Memphis, Arkansas, which would contract with the Atomic Energy Commission (AEC) to feed its power into the TVA system, thus enabling the Authority to meet its obligations to the AEC and to serve the needs of Memphis. The new plant would be built and operated by a syn-

President Eisenhower and Secretary of State Dulles (*National Park Service, Washington, D.C.*)

dicate headed by Edgar H. Dixon of Middle South Utilities, Inc., and Eugene A. Yates of the Southern Company. Despite the opposition of the TVA board of directors and many political leaders in the Tennessee Valley, the AEC, following Eisenhower's wishes, signed a long-term contract with the Dixon-Yates combine on October 5, 1954. The terms were extremely generous to the private utilities.

Albert Gore of Tennessee and several other Democratic senators sought unsuccessfully in 1954 to secure congressional action against the Dixon-Yates scheme, and the issue was used against the Republicans in the midterm elections of that year. But Dixon-Yates did not become vulnerable until Senator Lister D. Hill of Alabama charged, in February 1955, that a "conflict of interest" had been involved in the negotiation of the contract. It was eventually revealed that Adolphe H. Wenzell, an officer of a Boston investment firm scheduled to finance the Dixon-Yates project, had earlier served as a consultant to the Bureau of the Budget and had advised the government to sign the contract. This disclosure proved acutely embarrassing to Eisenhower, who decided to cancel the contract with the utilities in July 1955, after Memphis had conveniently announced its intention to build its own power plant.[1]

Eisenhower accepted the necessity for some social welfare programs, and like Truman, he had difficulty in securing congressional approval of his social and economic proposals, modest as they were. His successes in the domestic arena owed a good deal to Democratic support, and in some ways the Republican president got along better with opposition members of Congress than with members of his own party. A series of amendments broadened the social security system, including an act in 1954 that extended the system's coverage to include millions of workers and self-employed people. The minimum wage was raised in 1956 from 75 cents to a dollar an hour. The Refugee Relief Act of 1953 provided for the admission to the United States of more than 200,000 refugees and displaced persons. The administration continued the liberal trade policies begun during the New Deal. It supported the Federal Aid Highway Act of 1956, under which a 41,000-mile interstate highway system was launched, largely at federal expense. Eisenhower also endorsed a modest proposal for federal aid to the states for public education.

Despite its business orientation and its conservative rhetoric, the Eisenhower administration adopted most of the policies of its opposition; it supported the welfare state that had developed by mid-century and used federal power to manage the economy. Americans could no longer use "the governmental processes that were applicable in 1890," Eisenhower declared in April 1957. "We have got to adapt the great principles of the Constitution to the inescapable industrial and economic conditions of our time, and make certain that . . . our people participate in the progress of our economy." In practice, however, the thirty-fourth president's reluctance to increase the budget and to raise taxes limited his support of social welfare programs.

THE CLIMAX OF MCCARTHYISM

Many observers assumed that the election of a Republican president would cause Joseph McCarthy and other vociferous anti-Communists to lose influence and fade from the headlines. But McCarthyism did not disappear. The administration was zealous in its own search for subversives in government, broadening the definition of "security risk" to include behavior quite unrelated to disloyalty. Almost 3,000 such "security risks" were dismissed from government positions in 1953 and 1954, although none of them were charged with subversion or were brought to trial in a court of law. The most publicized security case was that of J. Robert Oppenheimer, who had played a major role in the development of the atomic bomb during World War II. President Eisenhower, following the initiative of Chairman Lewis L. Strauss of the Atomic Energy Commission, directed officials in late 1953 to place "a blank wall between Oppenheimer and all Government secrets." The FBI had prepared a report that detailed the scientist's prewar associations with Communists, and the president acted against him because of alleged "fundamental defects in his character." Oppenheimer was exonerated several years later.

It was soon apparent that the administration's security program and anti-Communist activities did not satisfy Joe McCarthy. Senator Taft had hoped, in organizing the upper house in the Republican-controlled Eighty-third Congress, to sidetrack McCarthy by giving the chairmanship of the Senate Internal Security Committee to the colorless William E. Jenner. McCarthy was made chairman of the Senate Government Operations Committee, and he also assumed the chairmanship of that committee's Permanent Subcommittee on Investigations. The Wisconsin senator quickly asserted the subcommittee's claims to at least a share of the jurisdiction over the campaign against communism in government. He loudly objected to Eisenhower's appointment of Charles E. Bohlen as ambassador to the Soviet Union, charging that Bohlen, a career diplomat who had been at the Yalta conference, was "Acheson's architect of disaster." In March 1953 McCarthy announced that he had "negotiated" an agreement with Greek shipowners to stop all trade with mainland China and North Korea. McCarthy's subcommittee carried out a search for Communists in the Voice of America program, demoralizing the staff of that agency in the process. Two of the senator's assistants, chief counsel Roy M. Cohn and "consultant" G. David Schine, made a whirlwind trip to Western Europe in the spring of 1953, searching for "subversive" literature in the libraries of the American Information Service. The State Department also issued a new directive banning from American information activities all "books, music, paintings, and the like . . . of any Communists, fellow travelers, et cetera." Throughout 1953 and the first part of 1954 McCarthy made one wild charge after another, dramatically announced numerous "disclosures" of Communist infiltration, and conducted a series of widely publicized investigations.

Eisenhower refused to be drawn into a direct confrontation with McCarthy, and the administration went out of its way to please him. Thus R. W. Scott McLeod, a McCarthyite, was made security officer for the State Department, and Secretary Dulles allowed McCarthy a strong voice in the department's personnel policy. Eisenhower was privately contemptuous of McCarthy, but he was quoted as saying, "I will not get in the gutter with that guy." In any case, Eisenhower thought the best way to deal with McCarthy was to ignore him. This was not always possible, and on occasion, as in the book-burning controversy that erupted in the summer of 1953 in the wake of McCarthy's attacks on the overseas information program, the president spoke out against McCarthyism. He did so reluctantly and gingerly, however, and his administration appeared to vacillate between appeasing and opposing the Red-hunting senator.

The McCarthy committee's investigation of alleged subversion among scientists working for the Army Signal Corps center at Fort Monmouth, New Jersey, led the senator, in February 1954, to launch a direct attack upon the Army. A New York dentist named Irving Peress, who had been inducted into military service in 1952, subsequently refused to sign an Army loyalty certificate. When called before the McCarthy committee, he had invoked the Fifth Amendment. The Army had then released Peress, giving him an honorable discharge. McCarthy was incensed. He brought General Ralph W. Zwicker before his committee to explain what had happened. Conceding that the Army had mishandled the case, Zwicker promised to see that it did not happen again. But under orders from his superiors, the general would not reveal the names of those persons who had processed Peress's release. McCarthy proceeded to browbeat and humiliate Zwicker, accusing him of being "ignorant," of "shielding Communist conspirators," and of being "a disgrace to the uniform." Secretary of the Army Robert T. Stevens, under strong pressure from the Pentagon, defended Zwicker and ordered him and other officers not to testify further before the McCarthy committee.

When a meeting between Stevens and McCarthy resulted in a "memorandum of agreement" between the two, it was widely regarded as an administration surrender to the high-riding senator. But McCarthy had finally overreached himself. On March 11, 1954, the administration counterattacked. The Army charged that McCarthy and Cohn had persistently and flagrantly sought preferential treatment for Private David Schine after his induction into the armed forces. The senator from Wisconsin met this challenge by making forty-six charges against the Army. To investigate these charges and countercharges, the Permanent Subcommittee on Investigations voted to make its own inquest, with Senator Karl Mundt temporarily replacing McCarthy as chairman.

The committee began its inquiry on April 22, and for the next five weeks its proceedings were followed as closely as a dramatic production by a nationwide television audience. McCarthy himself was the center of the hearings. He bullied and harangued Secretary Stevens for thirteen days. He was constantly interrupting witnesses, making insinuating comments and veiled threats, and shouting "point of order, Mr. Chairman." Some members of the committee,

"The Grand Inquisitor" during the Army-McCarthy
hearings (*The Bettmann Archive*)

such as Senator Stuart Symington of Missouri, stood up to him, and
Joseph N. Welch, the counsel for the Army, was more than a match
for the Wisconsin senator in most of their verbal encounters. The
hearings revealed McCarthy to millions of Americans as uncouth,
brutal, unscrupulous, and contemptuous of decent men. Technically, neither McCarthy nor the Army won in the committee hearings, but in reality the senator lost; for the inquiry contributed
greatly to his own self-destruction. A Gallup poll revealed, at the
end of the hearings, that McCarthy's standing had dropped to an
approval rate of 35 percent, while the opposition to him had risen
to 49 percent. He had become a liability to the Republican party.

Finally, the Senate bestirred itself to deal with McCarthy. On June
11, 1954, Ralph Flanders, an elderly Republican from Vermont, introduced Senate Resolution 261, calling for McCarthy's removal
from the chairmanship of the Committee on Government Opera-

tions and its Permanent Subcommittee on Investigations. Flanders later changed the resolution to one of censure. A struggle over the resolution followed, but eventually the senators agreed to have the matter considered by a select committee of six members headed by Arthur V. Watkins, a respected Republican from Utah.

The Watkins committee considered five general categories of charges against McCarthy. The Wisconsin senator testified at length in his own behalf. In September the committee adopted a unanimous report which recommended that McCarthy be censured on two counts. The Senate slowly moved to consider the censure report in the fall of 1954, and after a good deal of debate and maneuvering the first vote was taken on December 1. All efforts to head off censure by McCarthy's defenders were defeated, and on March 2, 1955, the upper house voted by a margin of 67 to 22 to condemn McCarthy on two counts: for contempt and abuse of the Subcommittee on Privileges and Elections in 1952, and for contempt and abuse of the Senate and its select committee in 1954. McCarthy's decline was rapid thereafter. Long before he died in May 1957, at the age of forty-nine, he had become just another member of the Senate, a man of some lingering notoriety but no longer a figure of any real consequence.

In retrospect it is clear that Americans were regaining their sense of proportion and becoming less obsessed with anti-Communist apprehensions by the time the Senate voted to censure Joe McCarthy. Tensions began to ease with the signing of an armistice in the Korean War in July 1953. The Democratic victory in the midterm congressional races of 1954, which cost McCarthy and other Republican congressmen their chairmanships, may also have contributed to the decline of McCarthyism. By the mid–1950s the Supreme Court was moving in a more liberal direction in dealing with cases involving civil liberties. The Court held in several cases that congressional investigating committees had violated the constitutional rights of witnesses. It curtailed the scope of the administration's security program, overturned the convictions of Communists, and ruled that the State Department could not deny passports to citizens on arbitrary grounds. But even though McCarthyism had passed from the scene, the manifestations of intolerance, the suspicion of radicalism and unorthodoxy, and the coercive pressures for conformity were still much in evidence. Communists continued to be identified as the embodiment of evil. In 1954 congressional Democrats, including many liberals, sought to demonstrate their patriotism by instigating passage of the Communist Control Act, which in effect made the rapidly declining Communist party illegal.

CHANGE AND CONTINUITY IN NATIONAL POLITICS

Dwight Eisenhower's venture into politics and the "crusade" he began in 1952 were inspired in part by his strong desire to unify and revitalize the Republican party, which would be the instrument for the adoption of new and badly needed national policies. Yet Eisenhower's "modern Republicanism" encountered hard going almost from the beginning, and his success as a party leader was limited. His vision of a new and more purposeful Republican party was never clearly elaborated. Many Republican members of Congress and other influential party members who welcomed Ike's triumphs at the polls were strongly opposed to many of his foreign and domestic proposals. Eisenhower sought to demonstrate his effectiveness as a party leader by vigorously campaigning for the election of a new Republican Congress in the midterm elections of 1954, but the results were disappointing. The Democrats recaptured control of Congress by a margin of one vote in the Senate and twenty-nine in the House.

Even so, by the middle of 1955 Eisenhower could afford to be optimistic about the progress and prospects of his administration. The new Democratic Congress had proved surprisingly cooperative, the economy was once more booming, and the president had apparently achieved notable success at the summit conference held in Geneva during the summer. But the administration's optimism was suddenly shattered on September 24, 1955, when the president suffered a heart attack while vacationing in Denver. The nation held its breath as his doctors, including the eminent Boston cardiologist Paul Dudley White, attended him at the Lowry Air Force Base's Fitzsimons Hospital. Press secretary James C. Hagerty kept the news media fully informed of the president's medical condition during the next several weeks. But there were no complications, and in mid-November he was moved to his Gettysburg farm, where he assumed an increasing portion of his normal executive duties. During earlier weeks Vice President Nixon had presided over meetings of the Cabinet, and the efficient White House staff had continued to function smoothly.

Although Eisenhower had not, prior to his illness, indicated whether he would run for a second term, he came under mounting pressure to do so as his convalescence progressed. The president was cautious, however, postponing a final decision and talking often about his desire to retire to a quieter life at his Gettysburg farm. Meanwhile, his message to Congress in January 1956 hardly sounded like that of a leader contemplating early retirement; it was a comprehensive and generally progressive set of recommendations for the building of "an ever-stronger, ever-better America." In mid-February 1956, Eisenhower's doctors reported, after a thorough examination of the president, that he would be able to "carry on an active life for another five to ten years" in view of his "good recovery." Two weeks later Ike announced, in a nationwide television address, that he would accept renomination.

Eisenhower's renomination was now only a formality to be completed by the party's national convention, which would be held in August 1956. But before that meeting there was another moment of shock and dismay involving the president's health. He underwent a serious operation on June 9 for ileitis (an intestinal obstruction), but his recovery was rapid, and any doubts about his ability to campaign in 1956 were soon removed. He was quickly renominated when the Republican delegates convened in San Francisco. Richard Nixon was renominated for vice president, although Eisenhower had been somewhat slow in endorsing him for the position. The "stop Nixon" movement launched on July 25 by Harold E. Stassen, Eisenhower's adviser on disarmament, suffered an ignominious collapse.

In the meantime, the Democrats had held their convention in Chicago in early August, following a long and hard-fought struggle between Adlai Stevenson and Estes Kefauver for a nomination that appeared, for a time following Eisenhower's heart attack, to be worth a good deal more than it had in 1952. The Tennessee senator, employing a folksy campaign style and prodigious energy, made a fast start early in the year by winning the New Hampshire and Minnesota primaries. Stevenson also conducted a strenuous campaign, attracting broad support from party regulars and capturing important Democratic primaries in Oregon, Florida, and California. Stevenson's lead was so great by summer that Kefauver withdrew on July 16, endorsing the former Illinois governor for the nomination. This left Governor W. Averell Harriman of New York as Stevenson's only challenger, and despite former president Truman's last-minute endorsement of Harriman, Stevenson was easily nominated on the first ballot at the convention in Chicago. In a surprise move, Stevenson asked the delegates themselves to select the party's vice-presidential nominee. A spirited contest resulted between Senator Kefauver and Senator John F. Kennedy of Massachusetts, with the Tennessean winning a narrow victory on the second ballot.

The presidential campaign of 1956 was a dull and uninspiring affair. Democratic speakers found it difficult to combat Republican boasts of having brought peace, prosperity, and unity at home. The Republican party, the president asserted in his acceptance speech, "is again the rallying point for Americans of all callings, ages, races and incomes," and the millions of "I Like Ike" buttons seemed to bear him out. Unlike 1952, Eisenhower spoke mainly in lofty terms ("leave the yelling to the opposition," he advised).

Stevenson tried hard to develop a distinctive program that would build on his party's liberal heritage. But he seemed less convincing, less buoyant, less sparkling than he had in the campaign of 1952. Nothing seemed to work for the Democrats. Stevenson accused Eisenhower of being "a part-time leader," thereby referring indirectly to his health, only to have Ike's doctors report late in the campaign that the president was in "excellent health." Eisenhower easily countered Stevenson's pledge to end the military draft and create a volunteer defense corps. When the Democratic presidential nominee talked about the dangers of radioactive fallout and promised to stop all U.S. testing of nuclear weapons, Republican leaders contended that such a course would be impractical and that it would endanger national defense. The Hungarian uprising and the Suez crisis, occurring just before the election, appeared to enhance the experienced Eisenhower's position in the minds of many Americans. Although the administration seemed somewhat vulnerable on such issues as the farm question, the high cost of living, and its handling of natural resources, the president showed signs of adding support in many new quarters, including black voters.

Eisenhower won by a landslide. His plurality was more than 9 million votes (out of 62 million cast), and he received 457 electoral votes to Stevenson's 73. The Democratic ticket carried only seven states—Missouri and six southern states. Democratic support among black voters dropped to 61 percent and among Catholics to 51 percent. Eisenhower did well everywhere, even in the South, and he captured such Democratic strongholds as Chicago and Jersey City. Yet Eisenhower's victory was an anomalous one. The Democrats won Congress—49 to 47 in the Senate and 234 to 201 in the House—making Eisenhower the first president since Zachary Taylor in 1849 to begin a term with both houses of Congress in the hands of the opposing party.

Republican congressional fortunes would decline even further in the midterm elections of 1958. Eisenhower was still held in the public's affection, but talk of a "lack of leadership" was heard more often as his second administration unfolded. New problems and perplexities had begun to confront him early in his second term, including a scandal involving presidential assistant Sherman Adams.[2] Although a White House manifesto contended that if a new Democratic Congress were elected in 1958, "we are certain to go down the left lane which leads inseparably to socialism," the voters paid little heed to such warnings; they gave the Democrats their most thoroughgoing triumph since the election of 1936. The Democrats would control the next Congress by margins of 64 to 34 in the Senate and 282 to 154 in the House. The election of 1958 brought many new faces to Washington, including quite a number of young and progressive congressmen, but the Eighty-sixth Congress would not venture far from the middle-of-the-road programs recommended by the administration.

President Eisenhower dominated the national political scene in the 1950s. He shattered the Democratic majority in presidential elections. He appealed to the new white-collar elements, to the residents of the mushrooming suburbs, to the growing number of independent voters. He was able to exploit the great economic and social changes taking place in the southern states, whose political solidarity his candidacy disrupted in 1952 and 1956. Nevertheless, Eisenhower proved unable to transfer his own popularity to other Republican candidates; that is, he was unable to create a new majority coalition to replace the one he had broken up. The Republican right wing presented a formidable barrier to the modernization of the party. Eisenhower's own political ideas—his belief in free enterprise and rugged individualism, in balanced budgets, and in governmental noninterference—had led him to the Republican party, but it was heavily freighted with reactionary and bitterly frustrated elements bent on overcoming Democratic control through a politics of revenge.

New sources of Democratic strength also contributed to Republican setbacks. The Democrats became more competitive at the state and local levels through a kind of delayed realignment, which political scientist James L. Sundquist has called "aftershocks of the New Deal earthquake." A new and more attractive Democratic leadership began to emerge in such states as North Dakota, Minnesota, Wisconsin, Iowa, Michigan, Pennsylvania, Vermont, Maine, California, and Oregon, a leadership that was active and liberal and that had a program. Another reason for Democratic vitality was the revival of liberalism in the second half of the 1950s. Following the election of 1956, Paul Butler, the Democratic national chairman, helped form an advisory council in order to give the party a more liberal and progressive program than that provided by congressional leaders between presidential campaigns. This body reflected the new Democratic liberalism, which gave special attention to civil liberties, civil rights, and the need for greater economic growth. A liberal program began to take shape, as it had in 1948 and 1949, and it embodied national solutions to such problems as education, health care, and economic development.

SECOND TERM: PROBLEMS AND PORTENTS

The second Eisenhower term was far more troubled and in some ways considerably less successful than the first. A series of controversies over administration budget requests, school desegregation, national defense, and welfare policies, in addition to new international crises, marked Eisenhower's final years in the White House. The Eisenhower equilibrium broke down. The economy went into a severe recession in the latter part of 1957 and continued weak during most of 1958, and a long steel strike in the summer and fall of 1959 helped disrupt the recovery that began in late 1958. Eisenhower's principal advisers changed in his second term: Humphrey and Wilson left the Cabinet in 1957, Adams resigned in September 1958, and Dulles had to retire because of illness in the spring of 1959. The president experienced another serious illness himself when he suffered a stroke on November 25, 1957. Although he was pronounced "completely recovered" on March 1, 1958, his leadership appeared to become less steady and effective. In the late 1950s, as the pressure mounted for greater federal involvement in such areas as education, public works, and civil rights, Eisenhower's domestic policies seemed increasingly inadequate.

One of the issues that came to the fore early in Eisenhower's second administration was the enforcement of the federal courts' desegregation orders. A series of cases initiated by the National Association for the Advancement of Colored People culminated in the historic decision of *Brown* v. *Board of Education of Topeka* (1954), in which a unanimous Supreme Court struck down the "separate but equal" doctrine in public facilities that had been enunciated in 1896 in *Plessy* v. *Ferguson*. Resistance soon developed in the southern states, and in September 1957 Governor Orval E. Faubus of Arkansas confronted the president with a constitutional crisis by ordering the National Guard to prevent black students from attending a Little Rock high school. After a federal court had decreed the removal of the National Guardsmen and angry demonstrators made it impossible for the black children to attend the school, Eisenhower ordered federal troops sent into Little Rock to enforce the court's order. "Mob rule," the president said when he dispatched the troops to Little Rock, "cannot be allowed to override the decisions of our courts." Eisenhower, however, had done little to encourage compliance with the federal courts' desegregation decrees or to help make Americans sensitive to their legal and moral implications. He considered the *Brown* decision a mistake and seemed to feel that action in this field by the courts or Congress would only create discord and thus slow progress. In civil rights he preferred to act

The Little Rock school crisis (*The Bettmann Archive*)

administratively, with as little publicity as possible. The Eisenhower administration proved incapable of moving beyond symbolism to an open confrontation with racial inequalities in areas like basic human services, employment, and housing. Eisenhower did lend his support, however, to the modest civil rights legislation of 1957 and 1960, which sought to prevent interference with the right to vote.

The record of the Eighty-fifth Congress (1957–58) was one of moderate achievement—a compromise between the "mildly conservative" president and the "mildly liberal" congressional leadership of Lyndon B. Johnson and Sam Rayburn. Several issues relating to national defense received attention during the second session of this Congress. President Eisenhower worked hard and successfully to secure the passage of a military reorganization bill in 1958, and Congress established the civilian-controlled National Aeronautics and Space Administration. Although the administration gave greater priority to the development of new, complex defense systems than to the development of space technology, a succession of space probes was carried out following the launching of the first successful American satellite, *Explorer I*, from Cape Canaveral on January 31, 1958.

The administration's major accomplishment in the field of education in 1958 was the National Defense Education Act, which included a provision for $295 million in loans to needy college students. The same Congress also passed the Alaskan statehood bill; emergency housing and highway construction legislation to help combat the recession; the Transportation Act of 1958, designed to resuscitate the failing railroads; a low-support farm bill with few controls and generally in line with administration recommendations; and an unprecedented four-year extension of the chief executive's power to negotiate reciprocal trade agreements. A $280 million area redevelopment bill providing loans for new industries in economically depressed regions was vetoed by the president, who wanted a measure requiring more local responsibility.

Eisenhower seemed to become more active in seeking the realization of his objectives during his last two years in office. Following the Democratic congressional victory of 1958, he set himself to prevent the large appropriations for domestic programs urged by liberal Democrats. He made greater use of the veto and, employing press conferences and public appeals, tried to dramatize the issue of "lavish spending." Thus he was able, with the powerful assistance of the conservative coalition in Congress, to frustrate such Democratic proposals as a comprehensive program of aid for school construction and teachers' salaries, a higher minimum wage, and increased medical care for the aged under social security. But during 1960 liberals discovered a new issue on which to base their demands for more extensive social welfare legislation: the need for a rapid rate of growth in the national economy. Meanwhile, there was increasing evidence of partisan divisions between the executive and legislative branches. A $750 million pay increase for federal employees was passed over the president's veto, and the Democrats, anticipating success in the approaching elections, refused to approve a measure creating a large number of badly needed new federal judgeships.

The Eisenhower administration was identified with the enactment of some significant legislation in the Eighty-sixth Congress (1959–60). Perhaps the best example on the domestic side was the relatively conservative revision of the Taft-Hartley Act completed in 1959. Hearings held in 1957 by a select Senate committee had revealed widespread racketeering and corruption in the International Brotherhood of Teamsters and other unions. In 1958 the Senate passed a mild anticorruption bill sponsored by Senator John F. Kennedy, but it died in the House of Representatives. During the closing days of the 1959 session, Congress passed a stronger measure, which became the Landrum-Griffin Act. The law contained a number of anticorruption features, and it increased the Taft-Hartley Act's limits on boycotts and picketing. In another act of 1959, Congress established the Labor Pension Reporting Service to compel unions to publish an accounting of the pension and welfare funds under their control.

In a critical assessment written in November 1958, journalist William V. Shannon said of President Eisenhower's administration, "No national problem, whether it be education, housing, urban revitalization, agriculture, or inflation, will have been advanced importantly toward solution nor its dimensions significantly altered." Other critics have pointed to Eisenhower's failures in dealing with McCarthy and the black revolution and to his inability to reform the Republican party. Even so, the Eisenhower years brought a period of relative calm to American politics. Eisenhower's leadership brought a grudging acceptance of the New Deal by most Republicans, and it moved the GOP to a more moderate position on international questions. In retrospect the general appears to have been a shrewd moderate who was more forceful, purposeful, and in command than early interpreters believed.

NOTES

1. In 1959 Congress passed the TVA Revenue Bond Act. This self-financing law permitted the Tennessee Valley Authority to sell its own

bonds up to a maximum of $750 million (later increased) and to finance new power facilities from both power revenues and bond sales. The act also included a territorial limitation, designed to prevent any future expansion of the area served by the agency.

2. A House of Representatives committee discovered, during the summer of 1958, that Adams had apparently sought to influence the Securities and Exchange Commission and the Federal Trade Commission in the interest of Bernard Goldfine, a wealthy Boston textile producer and long-time friend of the presidential assistant. Adams had accepted several gifts from Goldfine, including an expensive vicuna overcoat. Adams denied any wrongdoing, though he conceded that he might have made mistakes in "judgment." Eisenhower defended Adams's "personal and official integrity," but the latter soon resigned. As for Goldfine, he was eventually tried and convicted for income tax irregularities.

SUGGESTIONS FOR FURTHER READING

The best place to begin a study of the Eisenhower administration is Herbert S. Parmet, *Eisenhower and the American Crusades* (1972), the first scholarly assessment; Charles C. Alexander, *Holding the Line: The Eisenhower Era, 1952–1961* (1975), a balanced and perceptive treatment; and Robert F. Burk, *Dwight D. Eisenhower: Hero & Politician* (1986), a trenchant biographical appraisal. Elmo Richardson, *The Presidency of Dwight D. Eisenhower* (1979), is also useful. The second volume of Stephen E. Ambrose's biography, *Eisenhower: The President, 1952–1969* (1984), is of central importance. Peter Lyon's *Eisenhower: Portrait of the Hero* (1974) is especially helpful for the general's early years. For Eisenhower's own views, see his comprehensive but rather bland narrative of events, *The White House Years: Mandate for Change, 1953–1956* (1963), and *The White House Years: Waging Peace, 1956–1961* (1965). The thirty-fourth president's thinking is also revealed in Robert H. Ferrell (ed.), *The Eisenhower Diaries* (1981). One should also consult Robert L. Branyan and Lawrence H. Larsen (eds.), *The Eisenhower Administration, 1953–1961: A Documentary History* (2 vols., 1971), and Dean Albertson (ed.), *Eisenhower as President* (1963), a useful collection of contemporary appraisals.

Several of Eisenhower's advisers have written personal accounts. Among the best of these are Arthur Larson, *Eisenhower: The President Nobody Knew* (1968), a favorable but perceptive interpretation; Emmet John Hughes, *The Ordeal of Power: A Political Memoir of the Eisenhower Years* (1963), by a man who gradually became disillusioned with the administration; and Sherman Adams, *Firsthand Report: The Story of the Eisenhower Administration* (1961), a straightforward account. Garry Wills, *Nixon Agonistes* (1970), contains a revealing evaluation of the Eisenhower-Nixon relationship.

Several scholarly books are devoted to Eisenhower's domestic policies and programs. Gary W. Reichard, *The Reaffirmation of Republicanism: Eisenhower and the Eighty-third Congress* (1975), is a valuable study of Eisenhower's relations with his first Congress. Aaron B. Wildavsky deals with the first of the Eisenhower administration's "scandals" in *Dixon-Yates: A Study in Power Politics* (1962). Other conflicts of interest are discussed by David A. Frier, *Conflict of Interest in the Eisenhower Administration* (1969). Two other important developments are treated in Ernest R. Bartley, *The Tidelands Oil Controversy: A Legal and Historical Analysis* (1953), and William R. Willoughby, *The St. Lawrence Waterway: A Study in Politics and Diplomacy* (1961). Robert Fredrick Burk, *The Eisenhower Administration and Black Civil Rights* (1984), is a solid study. But also see Foster R. Dulles, *The Civil Rights Commission, 1957–1965* (1968). James L. Sundquist, *Politics and Policy: The Eisenhower, Kennedy, and Johnson Years* (1968), analyzes domestic legislation. For the climax of McCarthyism and the downfall of its most visible exemplar, see the works cited in chapter 4.

For presidential leadership during this period, see Richard E. Neustadt, *Presidential Power: The Politics of Leadership* (1960), and Fred I. Greenstein, *The Hidden-Hand Presidency: Eisenhower as Leader* (1982). The latter is a revisionist study that portrays Eisenhower as an active and skilled politician who "hid his hand" to achieve his political goals. Aspects of national politics during the Eisenhower years are considered by James L. Sundquist, *Dynamics of the Party System: Alignment and Realignment of Political Parties in the United States* (rev. ed., 1983); Everett Carll Ladd, Jr., with Charles D. Hadley, *Transformations of the American Party System: Political Coalitions from the New Deal to the 1970s* (2nd ed., 1978); V. O. Key, Jr., with the assistance of Milton C. Cummings, Jr., *The Responsible Electorate: Rationality in Presidential Voting, 1936–1960* (1966); and Martin, *Adlai Stevenson and the World*, cited earlier.

CHAPTER SIX

Strategies of Containment during the Eisenhower Years

THE MAJOR THEME in world affairs during the 1950s continued to be the cold war and the wide-ranging efforts of the Soviet Union and the United States to counter each other's moves and to win the support of other nations. By the time the new Republican administration took over in January 1953, the Russians had achieved a rough parity with the United States in atomic weapons. They had also developed long-range aircraft capable of delivering nuclear weapons to targets in the Western Hemisphere. This meant that the two superpowers had established what one contemporary aptly described as a "nuclear balance of terror."

Many Americans expected President Eisenhower to adopt a bold new approach that would turn back the advances of international communism, and they were encouraged in their expectations by the brave rhetoric of Republican spokesmen. Eisenhower had run on a platform that attacked "the negative, futile and immoral policy of containment," and John Foster Dulles had denounced the Truman-Acheson approach as "treadmill policies which, at best, might perhaps keep us in the same place until we drop exhausted." The new president, like his secretary of state, believed in "personal" diplomacy, and the next eight years were to witness many summit meetings and other high-level international conferences. But administration leaders, while continuing to advertise new departures in foreign relations, soon discovered their freedom of action circumscribed by a variety of stubborn realities. In practice they continued the containment policies of the Truman years, relying on military strength, collective security, regional alliances, and foreign aid.

RHETORIC AND REALITY IN FOREIGN POLICY

John Foster Dulles was a dominant figure in the conduct of the Eisenhower diplomacy. A prominent Presbyterian layman, Dulles had almost a sense of predestination about his role as secretary of state; his family background, long experience in foreign affairs, abundant energy, and supreme confidence surely encouraged such a feeling. While Dulles shared Eisenhower's broad internationalist outlook, he was even more passionately committed to the reform of U.S. foreign policies than his chief. He believed that Americans were losing the cold war because their policies were static and materialistic. The nation needed to reassert its traditional moral mission and identify itself with the universal longing for peace. Eisenhower and Dulles were sensitive to the deep division in the Republican party on international issues, and their espousal of the "reform" movement in foreign policy was no doubt intended in part as a means of reassuring the Taft coalition. It also reflected the administration's need to find ways of differentiating its policy objectives from those of the Democrats while following the same basic lines.

The Eisenhower administration proclaimed a "new look" in its management of national defense and foreign affairs, and for a time there was an appearance of novel approaches and techniques. One example was the doctrine of "liberation," which was to apply to the captive people behind the Iron Curtain. Another was the effort to revamp national defense policy in order to get what Secretary of Defense Charles Wilson called a "bigger bang for the buck"—cutting expenditures for conventional warfare and relying on air power and nuclear weapons. In resisting localized Communist aggression, the United States would employ as a first line of defense American-equipped and -trained indigenous troops. The new defense strategy rested heavily on nuclear deterrence, on what Dulles described as "the deterrent of massive retaliatory power." According to the secretary, it would "depend primarily upon a great capacity to retaliate, instantly, by means and at places of our own choosing." The "new look" also featured the art of "brinkmanship." In an interview published in *Life* magazine on January 16, 1956, Dulles spoke of his approach to foreign affairs:

> The ability to get to the verge of war without getting into the war is the necessary art. If you cannot master it, you inevitably get into wars. If you try to run away from it, if you are scared to go to the brink, you are lost. We've had to look it square in the face—on the question of enlarging the Korean War, on the question of getting into the Indo-China war, on the question of Formosa. We walked to the brink and we looked it in the face.

On January 7, 1953, two weeks before Eisenhower entered the White House, Senator John W. Bricker, a Republican from Ohio, introduced a resolution proposing a constitutional amendment that would render the provisions of treaties conflicting with the Constitution null and void, would require that any treaty, to become effective as internal law in the United States, must have supporting legislation "which would be valid in the absence of a treaty," and would empower Congress "to regulate all executive and other agreements with any foreign power or international organization." The Bricker amendment had powerful support from such organizations as the American Bar Association. Eisenhower and Dulles tried for almost a year to work out a compromise. This proved impossible, and the president eventually declared that he was "unalterably" opposed to the Bricker resolution in its existing form. By curtailing executive autonomy in the area of foreign relations, Eisenhower argued, Bricker's proposal would take away the maneuvering room the president must have in foreign affairs. The amendment was finally defeated on February 26, 1954, but in one form it had come within a single vote of securing the necessary two-thirds majority.

One aspect of the administration's new design in foreign relations was its plan to carry out extensive reforms in the military establishment. President Eisenhower and Secretary Wilson rejected the premise of NSC 68 that the United States could spend up to 20 percent of its gross national product on arms. Defense expenditures were reduced in both fiscal 1954 and 1955, in part as a result of the ending of the Korean War. The ground forces were diminished by one-third between 1953 and 1955, and the size of the Army was cut from about 1,500,000 in 1953 to 873,000 in 1960. The Navy also suffered some reductions in this period.

Eisenhower gave a good deal of time to the task of modernizing the military establishment. The Defense Reorganization Acts of 1953 and 1958 were meant to coordinate and centralize the vast enterprises of the Department of Defense. The administration sought to replace an obsolescent military apparatus with "highly mobile naval, air, and amphibious units" in combat readiness, prepared to strike quickly, and in some cases equipped with tactical atomic weapons. But the new defense policies resulted in reliance on strategic air power and nuclear weapons, for this course seemed to promise maximum destruction at minimum cost. The whole approach was epitomized by the doctrine of "massive retaliation" enunciated by Dulles in January 1954.

Another powerful influence in shaping the Eisenhower administration's foreign policies was developments abroad, particularly within the Communist bloc. After the death of Joseph Stalin in March 1953, Russian leaders soon began to make peace overtures to the United States. In 1955 they agreed to a definite peace treaty for Austria and took part in a widely acclaimed summit meeting in Geneva. They began to talk about the desirability of "peaceful co-existence." By the mid–1950s the Soviet system in Eastern Europe was becoming less monolithic; first Poland and then other Russian satellites won a degree of control over their own affairs.

THE EUROPEAN FOCUS

Despite the spread of the cold war to all parts of the globe, the most important theater for American policy makers continued to be Europe. By 1953 the North Atlantic Treaty Organization (NATO) had provided an integrated command system for Western Europe, and the United States had contributed large stockpiles of weapons and equipment for the alliance's military needs. But NATO's troop strength was far below the projected levels, and the European members of the organization appeared reluctant to undertake large-scale rearmament when the United States was concentrating its energies on the Korean War. Then, in the spring of 1952, France, Italy, the Benelux countries, and West Germany signed treaties for the establishment of the European Defense Community (EDC), which American leaders regarded as a means of implementing and bolstering NATO.

The European Defense Community quickly encountered opposition, especially from the French, who began to have second thoughts about the proposed rearmament of Germany and were disturbed by the specter of foreign control over France's internal affairs. While the French delayed, Secretary Dulles did his best to bring them into line, threatening in late 1953 an "agonizing reappraisal" of American policy toward Europe. The problem of strengthening NATO, however, was more fundamental than French recalcitrance. The Soviet peace offensive encouraged a more relaxed atmosphere in Western Europe, while the growing fear of a thermonuclear holocaust simultaneously raised doubts among Europeans about the real benefits of NATO. In August 1954 the French Assembly finally acted, decisively defeating a resolution to ratify the EDC.

American leaders were stunned and keenly disappointed. But it was Britain and not the United States that rescued the situation. Prime Minister Anthony Eden took the leadership during the following weeks in arranging a compromise that was formally approved in Paris in October 1954. Using the Brussels Pact of 1948, Eden and other Western European leaders created an alliance to be called the Western European Union. The arrangement ended the Allies' military occupation of West Germany except for a small garrison in West Berlin, restored sovereignty to the Federal Republic of Germany, and provided for West Germany's admission to NATO in 1955. The Russian response to these developments was the Warsaw Pact of May 1955, which bound the East European satellites to the USSR in a tight military alliance.

Meanwhile, however, other developments were encouraging new approaches in the relations between the two superpowers. The truce in Korea and a compromise peace in Vietnam in 1954 contributed to the relaxation of international tensions. Following the Soviet Union's explosion of a hydrogen bomb in August 1953, President Eisenhower had turned to the question of renewing international efforts to control atomic energy. In an address to the United Nations on December 8, he dramatically proposed that the major scientific nations of the world jointly contribute to a UN pool of atomic power to be used solely for peaceful purposes. Nothing came of this "atoms for peace" proposal, but it was soon apparent that the American allies in Western Europe, fearing atomic devastation in case of war between the United States and the Soviet Union, welcomed the prospect of a détente between the rival powers. In mid-May 1955 the Foreign Ministers Conference was finally able, after years of controversy and delay, to agree upon an Austrian peace treaty. The treaty signed in Vienna ended the four-power occupation of Austria and created an independent, neutral state.

Plans for a summit meeting were worked out in the spring of 1955, and the top leaders of the Soviet Union, the United States, Great Britain, and France opened the conference in Geneva on July 18. Eisenhower quickly sounded a note of hope and goodwill by urging a new approach to the problem of German unification, free communication between East and West, peaceful use of atomic power, and some practical contributions to disarmament. The warmth of Eisenhower's personality made a tremendous impact on the conference. At one point he turned to Premier Nikolai Bulganin and declared, "The United States will never take part in an aggressive war." To which Bulganin responded, "Mr. President, we believe that statement." It was this atmosphere that produced the "spirit of Geneva."

But when it came to more concrete matters, the summit made little or no progress. In the case of Germany, the United States demanded free elections and suggested that a reunited Germany be given the right to join NATO. Russia advocated a general European security pact that would include the withdrawal of all foreign troops from Germany. Neither side would retreat from its basic position. As Walter LaFeber has written, "The United States had successfully armed and tied West Germany to the Western alliance, while at the same time pushing on the Soviets the blame for blocking reunification through free elections." The Americans did present a new disarmament scheme at Geneva—an "open-skies" plan calling for the exchange of information on each nation's military facilities and allowing planes to photograph each nation's territory to prevent any possible surprise attack. The Soviet leaders rejected the plan on the ground that it would infringe Russia's territorial sovereignty.

Still, the early optimism of the Geneva meeting did not disappear completely. Certain developments within the Soviet Union helped sustain the thaw in the cold war. For one thing, the new Soviet leaders accelerated their de-Stalinization campaign. At the Twentieth Communist Party Congress, held in Moscow in February 1956, Nikita S. Khrushchev denounced Stalin and his use of terror. While still critical of capitalist states, he declared that "war is not a fatalistic inevitability."

Later developments in 1956, however, provided little comfort to those people who hoped for a Soviet-American rapprochement. In October, after Polish Communists had succeeded in easing the grip of Soviet control somewhat, Hungarians staged an uprising against Russian domination. But 200,000 Soviet soldiers and hundreds of tanks soon swept into Hungary, and the revolt was ruthlessly put down. Eisenhower made no move to intervene. Meanwhile, Russian leaders aggressively challenged the Western nations in a new Middle East crisis. These events seemed to reveal the illusory nature of the administration's doctrine of "liberation." They also dispelled whatever remained of the "spirit of Geneva." Meanwhile, Eisenhower and Dulles were confronted by new challenges in the Far East.

THE PROGRESS OF CONTAINMENT IN THE FAR EAST

The Eisenhower administration's Far Eastern diplomacy was in considerable part an inheritance from, and a natural outgrowth of, the Truman period, as was evident in such policies as the nonrecognition of the People's Republic of China, the support of Nationalist China, the strong commitment to the defense of South Korea, and the aid given to the French in Indochina. But the determination by Eisenhower and Dulles to go beyond the Truman-Acheson policies in Asia was also a corollary of their broader indictment of the Truman administration's handling of foreign affairs and a concession to the extreme nationalist, Asia-oriented right wing of the Republican party. Thus when Eisenhower announced, soon after entering the White House, that the U.S. Seventh Fleet would "no longer be em ployed to shield Communist China,"[1] he was suggesting that the doctrine of "liberation" might be applied in the Far East.

The administration's first diplomatic problem in the Far East was the ending of the Korean War. In mid-December 1952, after returning from Korea, Eisenhower had warned that unless the war could be brought to an end quickly, the United States might retaliate "under circumstances of our own choosing." During its first months in office, the Eisenhower administration not only "unleashed" Chiang Kai-shek, but also hinted that if the war continued, the United States would bomb Chinese bases, blockade the mainland of China, and use tactical atomic weapons. For whatever reason, the Communists indicated their willingness to resume the Korean truce talks in the early spring of 1953, and on July 27 of that year an armistice was finally signed. It provided for a cease-fire, for a demilitarized zone that coincided with the military line and generally followed the 38th parallel, and for a possible conference within three months to consider the withdrawal of all foreign forces from the peninsula and "the peaceful settlement of the Korean question." The Korean War was over at last, but a permanent settlement failed to emerge in the aftermath of the armistice. Instead, Korea was divided, like Germany, into Communist and non-Communist states.

By the early months of 1954, the focus of the American containment policy in Asia had shifted to Indochina, where French colonialism had encountered mounting resistance following World War II. A strong nationalist movement had developed in Vietnam, led by Ho Chi Minh, a longtime Communist and professional revolutionary. War in Vietnam had dragged on for years, with the resistance forces employing Mao Tse-tung's doctrines of peasant guerrilla warfare. The Chinese Communists, having overcome Chiang's forces, had recognized Ho's Vietminh early in 1950 and began to send it arms. The United States, shocked over the "loss" of China and increasingly obsessed with a determination to contain the Communists in the Far East, had begun to provide the French in Indochina with military and economic supplies in the spring of 1950. The war went badly for the French, however, and by 1954 they were on the verge of military collapse. Thousands of their best troops were surrounded in a military garrison at Dien Bien Phu, an ill-advised defensive site near the Laotian and Chinese borders. On March 20, 1954, the French chief of staff arrived in Washington to plead for American intervention.

Eisenhower and his advisers were fully aware of the implications of a French defeat in the Indochinese war. As the president warned in early April, "You have a row of dominoes set up, you knock over the first one, and what will happen to the last one is that it will go over very quickly. So you have the beginning of a disintegration that would have the most profound influence." Dulles was convinced that the United States could not permit the loss of Vietnam to the Communists, and he joined Admiral Arthur W. Radford, chairman of the Joint Chiefs of Staff, in urging that Congress be requested to pass a resolution authorizing an air strike to save Dien Bien Phu. Other leaders suggested a more cautious approach. Public opinion also proved to be critical of such a venture, and British leaders, in spite of American appeals, would not endorse any kind of joint support of the French. In the end Eisenhower decided against intervention. Although the doctrine of massive retaliation logically called for an attack on mainland China, the United States followed a course the London *Economist* described as "vociferous inaction."

Dien Bien Phu fell on May 7, and the French, facing the prospect of further military losses in other parts of Indochina and domestic disenchantment with the war, gave up the struggle and accepted a compromise, which was signed at Geneva on July 20 and 21, 1954. The Geneva Agreements provided for a cease-fire in Vietnam, recognized the independence of Laos and Cambodia, and divided Vietnam along the 17th parallel, with the Communists under Ho Chi Minh in control in the north, and the French puppet emperor Bao Dai and his new prime minister, Ngo Dinh Diem, dominant in the south. One provision stipulated that internationally supervised elections to determine the reunification of Vietnam would be held in 1956. Although the major powers, including mainland China, worked out the Geneva Accords, the United States was not a formal party to the arrangement. Yet when South Vietnam refused to take part in the elections called for at Geneva, the United States supported the Saigon regime.

The United States moved to strengthen its Far Eastern position in other ways. Secretary Dulles took the lead in creating the Southeast Asia Collective Defense Treaty, which was signed in Manila on September 8, 1954, by representatives of the United States, Britain, France, Australia, New Zealand, Pakistan, Thailand, and the Philippines. The Southeast Asia Treaty Organization (SEATO) would, if any of its members were threatened with armed aggression, "meet in order to agree on the measures which should be taken for common defense." In a separate protocol the SEATO allies later agreed to defend the independence of South Vietnam, Laos, and Cambodia. Dulles praised SEATO as a vital part of the American defense system in the Far East—an Asian counterpart of NATO—but the two alliances were not very analogous. SEATO had no armed forces of its own and possessed no permanent command structure or standing military organization.

Another area in which the U.S. policy of containment in the Far East collided with the aims of mainland China was Taiwan. The question of the two Chinas persisted from the beginning to the end of the Eisenhower administration, and the malignant character of the Chinese Communists became an *idée fixe* in American thought. The immediate area of confrontation between the United States and mainland China was not Taiwan and the nearby Pescadores Islands, however, but the small offshore islands of Quemoy, Matsu, and the Tachens, which were also occupied by Nationalist forces. In September 1954 the Chinese Communists began to bombard Quemoy and Matsu, apparently as a prelude to assaulting them. Near the end of 1954 the United States signed a mutual defense treaty with the Nationalist government, pledging itself to defend Taiwan and the Pescadores and to station American land, naval, and air forces "in and about" the area. The Communists soon began to move into the Tachen Islands, causing the evacuation of the Nationalist forces with U.S. assistance. On January 24, 1955, Eisenhower went before Congress to request authority for the use of U.S. forces in protecting the Nationalists. Congress responded swiftly by passing a joint resolution on January 28, authorizing the president to use whatever means he considered appropriate to defend Taiwan and the Pescadores, as well as "such related positions and territories" as he found necessary. A war scare followed, but the crisis gradually eased when the attackers relented in their bombardment of the islands.

In August 1958 the Communists resumed their heavy shelling of the offshore islands, and the United States was faced with another crisis in the Far East. Secretary Dulles declared that the joint congressional resolution of 1955 might apply to Quemoy and Matsu, and he implied that the United States would defend the islands if they were invaded. Meanwhile, a powerful American striking force was assembled in the Taiwan area, and U.S. naval units escorted supply carriers to the beleaguered Nationalist outposts. It was a time of enormous tension, when many observers fearfully anticipated the outbreak of Sino-American hostilities. The administration then appeared to adopt a more moderate position, and Dulles hinted that the offshore islands might be demilitarized and even abandoned by Chiang if the Communist attacks were ended. The bombardment was reduced, and the acute crisis slowly passed, though the status of Quemoy and Matsu remained uncertain through the remainder of the Eisenhower presidency.

The Eisenhower administration had decided soon after the signing of the Geneva Accords in the summer of 1954 to supply aid to the anti-Communist government in South Vietnam. Between 1955 and 1961, the United States would provide Vietnam with more than a billion dollars in economic and military assistance. Early in 1956 the U.S. Military Assistance and Advisory Group (MAAG) assumed from the French full responsibility for training the Vietnamese army. The United States was undertaking an experiment in nation-building. Eisenhower and Dulles committed themselves to creating a nation that would halt the Communist expansion in Southeast Asia and serve as a proving ground for democracy in the Far East.

Although American leaders suggested the desirability of introducing certain domestic reforms in South Vietnam, Prime Minister Ngo Dinh Diem followed his own course. He eliminated Bao Dai in 1955 and made himself president. He refused to permit the general elections scheduled for 1956, and his government became increasingly repressive. Diem's Communist opponents occasionally resorted to terrorism, but North Vietnam did not publicly announce a war of liberation against the south until 1960. At the end of that year the National Liberation Front of South Vietnam (NLF) was established, and within a short time men and supplies were being sent from North Vietnam to the Vietcong, as the NLF was called.

The American position in the Far East was little if any better at the end of the decade than it had been in 1953. To be sure, the Eisenhower administration had ended the Korean War, and a settlement of sorts had been brought to that troubled peninsula. But the focus of the containment policy had shifted to Indochina, where, in spite of large amounts of U.S. aid, conditions were perilous and prospects for non-Communist states were uncertain. The Chinese Nationalists still survived on Taiwan—thanks to American power—but the illusions surrounding their reconquest of the mainland had long since disappeared. While SEATO gave the United States a defensive alliance in Asia, it was little more than a paper organization. At the same time, Americans were increasingly identified as imperialists in the minds of anticolonialists in the Far East.

THE MIDDLE EAST, LATIN AMERICA, AND THE THIRD WORLD

The cold war was altered in several respects during the years after 1953, but none was more dramatic than the growing involvement of the underdeveloped countries of the world. By the mid-1950s the cold war had moved from Europe and the Far East to the Middle East, a vast and strategic area embracing some twelve countries and stretching from the Dardanelles to the Caspian Sea and from Egypt to the Gulf of Oman. Long dominated by Western colonialism, this "bridge of three continents" contained the richest oil resources in the world along with masses of desperately poor people, a feudalistic society, and backward and unstable governments. An upsurge of nationalism and independence movements had swept over the Middle East following World War II, and by mid-century the populations of the various states were infused with an ardent Arab nationalism, a strong hatred of colonialism, and a fierce hostility toward the Jewish state of Israel.

Egypt's emergence as the leader of the Arab nations and the eager champion of Arab nationalism complicated Western diplomacy in the Middle East. A revolution led by young, nationalistic army officers had deposed the inefficient and corrupt regime of King Farouk in 1953 and resulted in the establishment of an Egyptian republic. General Gamal Abdel Nasser, who had quickly become the head of the revolution, became the premier of the new republic. Nasser set about improving the internal conditions of his country and uniting the Arab nations. In October 1954 he completed an agreement with Britain providing for the withdrawal of British troops from the Suez Canal within twenty months. Nasser secured economic aid from the United States and the Soviet Union. He signed an arms agreement with Czechoslovakia and formed a close military alliance with Syria, Yemen, and Saudi Arabia. He proposed the construction of a huge dam at Aswan, on the upper Nile River, to increase the nation's arable land and encourage its industrialization and economic growth.

In 1955 American leaders indicated their willingness to provide Nasser with a substantial part of the funds needed to construct the Aswan Dam. The United States also moved to create the equivalent of NATO and SEATO in the Middle East, although the United States would not formally be a member of this alliance. In February 1955 Secretary Dulles was instrumental in bringing Turkey and Iraq into a defensive alliance, which was soon broadened to include Great Britain, Iran, and Pakistan. In effect, the NATO line had been extended from Turkey to India. This Baghdad Pact was very upsetting to Nasser, who viewed it as an effort to split the Muslim world and as a means of enhancing the influence of Iraq as a rival of Egypt for Arab leadership in the Middle East.

Meanwhile, the recurrent truce violations and border clashes between Egypt and Israel finally resulted in a large-scale Israeli raid in February 1955 on the Egyptian territory of Gaza. The success of this attack spurred Nasser's determination to strengthen Egypt's armed forces, and after the signing of the Baghdad Pact, he found Russian leaders quite willing to supply him with arms. The Egyptian leader also intimated that the Soviet Union might finance the building of the Aswan Dam on more favorable terms than the Western powers. In the spring of 1956 Egypt withdrew its diplomatic recognition of Nationalist China and extended recognition to the People's Republic of China. These actions no doubt influenced Dulles's abrupt announcement, in July 1956, that the United States had decided not to advance funds for the Aswan Dam.

Nasser responded to this rebuff within a week by nationalizing the Suez Canal on July 26, 1956. The British and French protested Nasser's seizure of the canal, but a compromise resolution in the United Nations that would have satisfied the European allies was blocked in the Security Council by a Russian veto. Eisenhower and Dulles stated publicly that the United States would not be a party to armed intervention in settling the Middle Eastern crisis. Nevertheless, there was a small war in the fall of 1956. Israel, provoked by the repeated conflicts along its border with Egypt, convinced of the desirability of a preventive war against the Egyptians, and probably secretly encouraged by the British and French, suddenly attacked Egypt. The Israeli forces drove swiftly across the Sinai Peninsula, scattering a much larger Egyptian army and approaching the canal within a few days. Meantime, the British and French, after issuing an ultimatum to the two sides to stop the fighting on the ground that the conflict was endangering the operation of the canal, moved against the Egyptians themselves on October 31. Egyptian forces managed to obstruct the canal with sunken ships, however, and Syrian saboteurs succeeded in cutting British oil pipelines from Iraq, thus making the Western nations dependent on the United States for petroleum.

The Anglo-French intervention came as a surprise to the Eisenhower administration, which was preoccupied with the approaching national election. Angry and embarrassed over their allies' action, the Americans strongly endorsed the cease-fire resolution overwhelmingly passed by the UN General Assembly on November 2. Three days later the UN agreed to create an international emergency force to "secure and supervise the cessation of hostilities." The speedy arrival of the UN emergency force permitted the invaders to withdraw with a modicum of dignity, but no one could doubt the extent of the Anglo-French setback. Their prestige and influence in the region had been dealt a devastating blow. Nor was that all. The Suez crisis had separated and almost shattered the Western alliance. And to add to the irony, it was the Soviet Union rather than the United States that received most of the credit among Arab nations for the peaceful settlement of the conflict.

On January 5, 1957, President Eisenhower asked Congress for authority to counter the threat of Communist infiltration in the

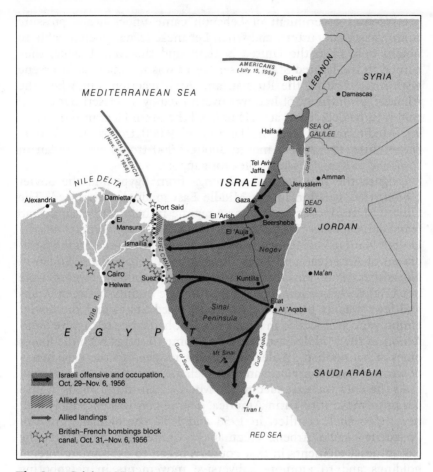

The Suez Crisis, 1956

Middle East. Two months later Congress passed a joint resolution approving the extension of economic and military aid to any nation in the area "requesting assistance against armed aggression from any country controlled by international communism." The success of this Eisenhower Doctrine in halting Soviet penetration of the region was limited, but it was used as a pretext for U.S. intervention in Middle East affairs during the years that followed.

When King Hussein of Jordan was confronted by an anti-Western revolt in the spring of 1957, Eisenhower sent the Sixth Fleet to the eastern Mediterranean and provided Hussein with $20 million in American aid. Hussein's government managed to survive the crisis. More severe crises developed as Nasser's influence and intrigue spread throughout the Middle East. In the late spring of 1958 the pro-Western government of Lebanon came under heavy pressure from Nasser supporters, and when Lebanese leaders were unable to obtain help from the United Nations and the Arab League, they turned to the United States. Eisenhower was reluctant to intervene with force, fearing the Russian and Arab reaction, but when the friendly government of Iraq was overturned by a Nasserite revolt in mid-July, he decided to act. He ordered the Sixth Fleet into the eastern Mediterranean and the landing of 9,000 troops in Lebanon. Meanwhile, the British moved about 3,000 troops into Jordan in response to King Hussein's plea for support.

Despite the protests and warnings from Egypt and the Soviet Union, the situation in the Middle East gradually improved. The United States recognized the new regime in Iraq, thus easing Arab fears considerably. Dag Hammarskjold, secretary general of the United Nations, helped work out arrangements that led to the withdrawal of American and British troops from Lebanon and Jordan in November 1958. Prospects for long-range stability, however, were not bright. Nasser remained powerful. The enmity between Arabs and Jews was as bitter as ever. The United States and the Soviet Union were still locked in a cold war that had come to involve every nation in the Middle East. Unable to come to terms with the forces of Arab nationalism, American leaders resorted to the expediency of wooing reactionary monarchies such as Saudi Arabia.

As the cold war extended to the Middle East in the 1950s, it also began to move into Latin America. The region was extremely vulnerable to such conflict. In 1953 and 1954 the radical regime of President Jacobo Arbenz Guzman of Guatemala, encouraged by Communist elements in that country, began to expropriate foreign holdings and to promote subversive movements in neighboring states. This threatened to give the Communists their first foothold in the Western Hemisphere. Secretary Dulles sought to deal with this threat through diplomatic channels, persuading the Tenth Inter-American Conference, meeting in Caracas in March 1954, to condemn "any dominion or control of the political institutions of any American state by the international Communist movement." This did not stop Guatemalan leaders, who obtained a shipment of military equipment from Czechoslovakia in May and in early June proclaimed martial law, claiming that a foreign plot sought to overturn the government. The United States had supplied weapons to Honduras and Nicaragua, and the Central Intelligence Agency engineered a successful invasion of the country by Guatemalan exiles.[2] Arbenz appealed to the United Nations, where Russia sparked a bitter debate, and a call for an end to hostilities was approved by the Security Council. But the Council deferred action. Arbenz soon fled to Czechoslovakia, and a strong anti-Communist government came to power in Guatemala.

Evidence of deteriorating U.S.–Latin American relations was dramatically revealed in the spring of 1958 when Vice President Nixon and his wife undertook an eighteen-day goodwill tour of leading South American countries. They were met with popular demonstrations and mobs, evidently organized by Communists and other enemies of "Yankee imperialism." Some changes in American policies had been made by this time, and others were gradually initiated. In 1955 the United States had agreed to a liberalization of its treaty with Panama. U.S. leaders promoted regional free-trade agreements in Latin America and backed an international program to stabilize the price of coffee. They agreed in the late fifties to supply almost half the capital for a new billion-dollar Inter-American Bank to make development loans. Eisenhower visited South America in 1960. "We are not saints," he said in Santiago, Chile. "We know we make mistakes, but our heart is in the right place."

Near the end of the Eisenhower period, a perplexing situation developed in Cuba. When the repressive regime of Fulgencio Batista was overthrown and a new government headed by Fidel Castro took control on January 1, 1959, public opinion in the United States was highly favorable toward the change. It soon became evident, however, that Prime Minister Castro was no ordinary liberal. He undertook an extensive program of agrarian reform and began to confiscate foreign assets, including over one billion dollars of American holdings. In February 1960 Castro signed a five-year trading agreement with the Soviet Union, and he soon extended diplomatic recognition to the People's Republic of China.

The United States had tried unsuccessfully in the late summer of 1959 to isolate and restrain Cuba with diplomatic pressure exerted through the inter-American foreign ministers. In May 1960 Washington ended all economic aid to Cuba, and in July of that year the president, on the recommendation of Congress, virtually ended the import of Cuban sugar. When the West Indian nation complained of American action to the UN Security Council, Russia's Khrushchev could not refrain from a shrill denunciation of the United States, warning that "Soviet artillerymen can support Cuba with rocket fire" if the United States attacked the island. In the fall of 1960 the Unites States imposed an embargo on all exports to Cuba except food and medicine and began a naval patrol in the Caribbean to stop any possible invasion of Nicaragua and Guatemala by Castro's forces.

It became apparent in the 1950s that there were three large groups of nations in the world: the Western bloc, the Communist bloc, and a growing number of neutral states. The Bandung Conference of 1955 was an indication of the increasing importance of the Third World of nonaligned nations. While that conference mounted a vehement attack on colonialism, its most significant action was its formulation of the doctrine of "neutralism," an affirmation that much of Asia and Africa would not ally itself with either side in the cold war and that its major goal was to liberate the underdeveloped nations of the world from dependence upon the economically advanced powers.

Neutralism spread from Asia to the Middle East and Africa. The outbreak of the Algerian revolt against French control in late 1954 posed a problem for the United States, which was not unsympathetic with the rebel cause but was anxious to maintain good relations with its Western ally. Neutralism was not always possible, and the superpowers' struggle for the support of the newly independent states of sub-Saharan Africa soon brought the cold war to that vast region. The first major international crisis did not come until 1960, however, when a confusing and chaotic upheaval began in the Congo. The trouble started after the Congo became independent of Belgium. The complex developments that followed included the return of Belgian military units, the outbreak of civil war, the involvement of the Soviet Union and other Communist nations in the struggle, American support of an anti-Communist faction, and eventually UN intervention in the form of an international peace force.

NEW CONTROVERSIES IN EUROPE

The thaw in the cold war that was manifest during much of Eisenhower's first term in the White House had clearly succumbed to a new freeze well before the president's second inauguration. The "spirit of Geneva" had disappeared in the face of the integration of West Germany into the North Atlantic Treaty Organization, the failure to reach agreement on the German problem, and the inability of the superpowers to work out a mutually acceptable formula for the limitation and control of armaments. Rivalry between the United States and the USSR for the allegiance of the emerging nations of Asia and Africa also indicated the resurgence of East-West friction.

The comfortable assumption most Americans held about U.S. military superiority over the Soviet Union was suddenly upset in the late summer and fall of 1957. The Russians announced in August that they had successfully tested an intercontinental ballistic missile (ICBM). On October 4 they launched the first man-made earth satellite—*Sputnik* ("traveling companion" in Russian), a 184-pound vehicle. A month later they launched *Sputnik II*, six times heavier than *Sputnik I* and carrying aboard a live dog. During the next few years the Russians made other spectacular ventures into space. The Soviet Union also possessed the most powerful army in the world, it was developing a navy second only to that of the United States, and its submarine fleet was unexcelled by any other nation's.

News of Russia's sensational accomplishments in the development of long-range missiles and the launching of powerful satellites into space coincided with its diplomatic gains in the Middle East and its growing intransigence in the on-again, off-again disarmament negotiations. Many U.S. military spokesmen and political leaders urged a concentrated effort to overtake the Russians, but the Eisenhower administration did not immediately surrender to the advocates of a huge increase in military spending. Nor was the public altogether prepared to undertake yet another forward leap in the arms race. A *New Yorker* cartoon in September 1957, poking fun at a much-publicized Ford Motor Company flop, showed a middle-aged, middle-class woman saying to her husband, "It's a great week for everybody. The Russians have the intercontinental ballistic missile, and we have the Edsel."

Torn between its commitment to economy and the pressure for greater military preparedness, the administration followed a middle course in the years after 1957. Military expenditures for missiles and other new devices were increased, although not as much as many critics wanted. The United States fired its first ICBM (the Atlas) in the autumn of 1958, and by 1960 each branch of the armed forces had designed and put into operation a wide variety of missiles.

The threat of a terrible nuclear conflict haunted the minds of people everywhere. The Joint Congressional Committee on Atomic Energy reported in August 1959 that an attack on this country might well kill 50 million people and seriously injure an additional 20 million, while destroying or making uninhabitable half of all the nation's dwellings. By 1958 disarmament talks had begun to focus on the possibility of formulating an agreement to halt the testing of nuclear weapons, a proposal Prime Minister Jawaharlal Nehru of India had urged as early as 1954. Recognizing an opportunity for a propaganda coup, Soviet leaders announced in March 1958 a unilateral suspension of nuclear testing. The United States countered with a proposal for joint technical studies of feasible means to detect violations of such a test ban, and in August Washington and London suggested a one-year moratorium on testing. Negotiations for a more permanent disarmament settlement were resumed in Geneva at the end of October, but in spite of the hundreds of sessions held during the next two years, no agreement could be reached. Meanwhile, however, the three nuclear powers voluntarily adhered to the cessation of tests begun in 1958.[3]

Germany continued to be an incendiary issue in East-West relations. The United States had followed the twofold policy of urging the reunification of the two Germanies through free elections and the rearmament of West Germany. The Russians had urged German reunification under various guises but had adamantly opposed free elections, while linking the settlement of the German question to a general European security arrangement, including the withdrawal of American forces. Soviet leaders were especially concerned about the status of West Berlin, which not only provided the Western powers with a ready source of intelligence concerning the Communist world, but also served as an avenue of escape for East Germans, some three million of whom had fled to the West since 1945. Furthermore, the contrast between the prosperous and brightly lighted western zones of Berlin and the depressed and drab eastern part of the city was a constant reminder to Germans and Russians alike of the economic recovery and vitality of West Germany and its allies.

In November 1958 Khrushchev suddenly announced a six-month deadline for a settlement of the West Berlin question; if an agreement was not reached by May 27, 1959, he threatened to sign a separate peace treaty with East Germany and relinquish to it the control of Berlin. Another nerve-tingling crisis now enveloped the cold war antagonists. But the Western allies took a firm stand in the face of this Russian harassment. The Berlin crisis subsided during the early months of 1959, and the Russians began to reveal their interest in another summit meeting. In September 1959 the ebullient Khrushchev made a two-week tour of the United States that culminated in a visit with President Eisenhower at his Camp David retreat in Maryland. During the meeting the Soviet premier canceled his Berlin ultimatum, while Eisenhower conceded that the troublesome question of West Berlin should be resolved in the near future. Later in the year, Eisenhower and other Western leaders agreed to invite Khrushchev to a top-level conference in May 1960.

A few days before the bilateral summit was to convene in Paris, the Soviet Union announced that an American plane had been shot down over Russia on May 1. The United States indicated that the aircraft was a weather plane that had wandered off course. Soviet leaders then revealed that the American plane had been downed 1,200 miles inside Russia, that the aircraft was a high-level photo-

Eisenhower and Khrushchev at Camp David, September 1959 (*U.S. Naval Photo Center, Washington, D.C.*)

reconnaissance plane (it was later learned that the airplane was flying from Pakistan to Norway), and that the pilot had conceded the "spy" character of his mission. Khrushchev bitterly attacked the United States for its "aggressive acts," denounced Eisenhower, demanded an apology for the invasion of Soviet territorial sovereignty, and threatened to destroy those "accomplices" in Europe that provided bases for the U-2 flights. Acutely embarrassed, Eisenhower now admitted the validity of Khrushchev's accusations; he described the U-2 flights, which had been going on since 1956, as "a distasteful but vital necessity."[4]

It is clear that Khrushchev used the U-2 incident as a pretext to destroy a meeting that he no longer wanted. He was under pressure in the Kremlin, and his caustic public statements on the Berlin situation during the weeks before the summit suggested the difficulties that would have attended the Paris negotiations. American prestige did suffer as a result of the incident. Khrushchev announced that Eisenhower's scheduled visit to the USSR later in the year must be canceled, and he soon made it clear that no serious negotiations would be undertaken with the United States until the advent of a new presidential administration.

Not all American problems in Europe during the second Eisenhower administration were the result of Soviet opposition and diplomatic initiatives. The U.S. decision to provide West Germany with tactical nuclear weapons disturbed some members of NATO, and as the missile rivalry intensified, there were sharp differences between the United States and other Western powers. Meanwhile, General Charles de Gaulle, who came to power in France in 1958, proposed a radically new approach to the control of NATO—a three-power directorate of the United States, Britain, and France.

Despite Eisenhower's dedicated search for peace during the last years of his presidency, he found it an elusive goal. He made three goodwill trips between December 1959 and the summer of 1960— the first to India, the Middle East, and southern Europe; the second to Latin America; and the third to the Far East. "Our basic aspiration," he declared on one of these tours, "is to search out methods by which peace in the world can be assured with justice for everybody." Ironically, the last six months of Eisenhower's administration were among the most trying of his eight years in the White House: the Paris summit was a fiasco, the long-continued disarmament negotiations at Geneva soon broke up, his trip to Japan had to be canceled, a new crisis developed in the Congo, and the Communists appeared to have found in Cuba an ally only a few miles from United States soil.

In a farewell address delivered on the eve of his retirement from the White House, Dwight Eisenhower warned against the military-industrial complex—against the "conjunction of an immense military establishment and a large arms industry." It was a prescient warning, in view of the swollen defense budgets of the postwar period, the close ties that linked the nation's industrial society and the military, and the enormous power concentrated in the Pentagon and the giant corporations that dominated the business of defense procurement. The military-industrial complex included, in addition to military and business leaders, members of Congress eager to secure defense contracts for their districts, universities and new institutions like the Rand Corporation interested in research funds, veterans' groups, labor organizations, and cities dependent on defense expenditures. The complex was, in reality, a vast, loosely organized pressure group working for an active foreign policy based on military power.

Despite their rhetorical flourishes, Eisenhower and Dulles eventually adopted, with slight modification, the very policies they had criticized in the hands of their predecessors. Accepting the basic assumptions of the Truman administration, they supported and even extended its cold war commitments and objectives. Still, Eisenhower was a prudent chief executive in dealing with foreign and military affairs. He resisted an arms buildup and was skeptical of military adventurism; and he kept the United States from involvement in another war. He left office as one of the nation's most popular presidents, and in recent years a flowering revisionism among scholars has elevated his reputation from one of mediocrity to a standing well above average.

NOTES

1. When North Korea attacked South Korea in June 1950, President Truman had placed the Seventh Fleet between Taiwan and the mainland, not to "shield" Communist China, but to prevent any possible conflict in that area. The fleet had remained there during the remainder of Truman's tenure as president.

2. The CIA, under Director Allen Dulles, assumed great importance during the Eisenhower administration. Few restraints were placed on the agency by Congress, and the president allowed an increase in its clandestine operations. In August 1953, for instance, it was instrumental in the overthrow of Premier Mohammed Mossadegh of Iran, who was succeeded by a more pliable leader. Mossadegh had nationalized his country's oil fields and seemed to be moving closer to the Tudeh, Iran's Communist party.

3. Great Britain was the third nation to develop a nuclear bomb, having exploded a hydrogen bomb in 1957. France began to develop such a bomb in the late 1950s and successfully tested it in 1960.

4. The pilot of the U-2 plane, Francis Gary Powers, was subsequently tried by the Russians and convicted of espionage. He served almost two years in a Russian prison before being exchanged in February 1962 for Colonel Rudolf Abel, a Russian who had been convicted of espionage in the United States in 1957.

SUGGESTIONS FOR FURTHER READING

Volume 2 of Stephen Ambrose's biography, *Eisenhower: The President*, contains a fresh and authoritative treatment of the thirty-fourth president's foreign policies. Robert A. Divine, *Eisenhower and the Cold War* (1981), is a useful and sympathetic examination of the Eisenhower policies. Gaddis, *Strategies of Containment*, referred to earlier, is thoughtful and balanced in dealing with developments in the 1950s. The foreign policies of Eisenhower's first administration are critically examined by Norman A. Graebner in *The New Isolationism: A Study in Politics and Foreign Policy since 1950* (1956). Ambrose's *Rise to Globalism* and the general works by LaFeber, Parmet, and Spanier cited in earlier chapters are also helpful. For the contributions of John Foster Dulles, see Louis L. Gerson, *John Foster Dulles* (1967), and Townsend Hoopes, *The Devil and John Foster Dulles* (1973), the latter being the more critical and interpretive. Valuable information is contained in the annual volumes of *The United States in World Affairs*, prepared for the Council on Foreign Relations.

The Eisenhower defense policies are discussed by Samuel P. Huntington, *The Common Defense: Strategic Programs in National Politics* (1961); Richard A. Aliano, *American Defense Policy from Eisenhower to Kennedy* (1975); and Douglas Kinnard, *President Eisenhower and Strategy Management* (1977). Seymour Melman, *Pentagon Capitalism: The Political Economy of War* (1970), throws light on the military-industrial complex.

American involvement in various parts of the world during this period is the subject of many illuminating books. James L. Richardson, *Germany and the Atlantic Alliance: The Interaction of Strategy and Politics* (1966), is a good treatment of the remilitarization of West Germany. Another aspect of the conflict over Germany is dealt with by John Mander, *Berlin, Hostage for the West* (1962), and Jack M. Schick, *The Berlin Crisis, 1958–1962* (1971). Robert A. Divine examines the debate over fallout and the movement for a nuclear test ban treaty in *Blowing on the Wind: The Nuclear Test Ban Debate, 1954–1960* (1978). Davis Wise and Thomas B. Ross have written a revealing journalistic account entitled *The U-2 Affair* (1962).

Among the useful books on U.S. involvement in the Far East during the 1950s are Fred Green, *U.S. Policy and the Security of Asia* (1968); Ellen J. Hammer, *The Struggle for Indo-China, 1940–1955* (1966); and Stanley D. Bachrack, *The Committee of One Million: The "China Lobby" and U.S. Policy, 1953–1971* (1976). For the early phases of the struggle over Vietnam, see Melvin Gurtov, *The First Vietnam Crisis: Chinese Communist Strategy and United States Involvement, 1953–1954* (1967); Robert F. Randle, *Geneva 1954* (1969); and George C. Herring, *America's Longest War: The United States and Vietnam, 1950–1975* (2nd ed., 1986).

Hugh Thomas, *Suez* (1967), is a good account of the Middle East crisis of 1956. Herman Finer, *Dulles over Suez: The Theory and Practice of His Diplomacy* (1964), is very critical of Dulles's role. Robert W. Stookey, *America and the Arab States: An Uneasy Encounter* (1975), and Steven L. Spiegel, *The Other Arab-Israeli Conflict: Making America's Middle East Policy From Truman to Reagan* (1985), are useful for Middle East affairs in the 1950s. For the United States and Cuba, see Theodore Draper, *Castro's Revolution: Myths and Realities* (1962).

CHAPTER SEVEN

The Triumph of American Capitalism

EMERGING FROM the depression that racked the nation in the pre–World War II years, the United States entered the greatest and most sustained period of prosperity in its history. Although the passage from war to peace proved difficult, the economy did not revert to the hard times of the 1930s. Instead, Americans enjoyed an almost uninterrupted boom that raised production figures, incomes, and standards of living to heights thought incredible a short time earlier. Despite several recessions, the gross national product, in constant dollars, increased more than twice the rate of the population growth. By 1960 the GNP had reached $500 billion, and within little more than another decade it had climbed to the trillion-dollar level. By 1980 it had reached $2.6 trillion. "It became clear to all the world," the economist Harold G. Vatter has written, "that the United States economy after mid-century was capable of producing enough to provide every man, woman, and child with a minimum-comfort level of living."

ECONOMIC TRENDS

The economy came through the difficult shoals of the immediate postwar period in surprisingly good condition. The sharp cutbacks in federal spending—from an annual rate of $91 billion during the first quarter of 1945 to a rate of $26 billion a year later—were only moderately depressing in their effect on the national economy. Inflation became a serious problem in 1946 and 1947, complicated in part by the failure of Congress and the president to impose adequate controls. But citizens and public officials alike seemed to have confidence in the capacity of the "built-in stabilizers" such as unemployment benefits and discretionary action by government to counter downward economic movements. The economy did lose its buoyancy in the fall of 1948, by which time the heavy postwar consumer demand had largely been satisfied and inventories had been built up. Unemployment eventually rose to 7.6 percent of the total labor force and the nation entered a recession.

Recovery from the 1949 recession was well under way when the outbreak of the Korean War triggered a new boom, which reached its peak in the second quarter of 1953. A substantial reduction in military spending, accompanying President Eisenhower's ending of the war in Korea, and a slowdown in retail sales were factors in bringing on another recession, in the fall of 1953. The Eisenhower administration, having abandoned most of the emergency controls surviving from the Truman government, also contributed to the economic stringency by resorting to a tight-money policy in trying to contain inflation. Nevertheless, the new administration's faith in the ability of the economy to right itself seemed to be justified when a brisk recovery from the recession began in the autumn of 1954. The upturn was encouraged by a tax cut in 1954.

Economic life flourished during the mid-1950s. Demand slackened in 1956 but not enough to halt overall business expansion. The economy weakened during the latter part of 1957, however, and the country entered the worst recession it had experienced since World War II. The slump resulted from a marked decrease in business investment in plants and equipment as well as cutbacks in defense spending and a drop in net exports. The 1957–58 recession differed from its two predecessors in that prices continued to rise while production dropped, employment fell off, and consumer spending remained static. Production moved upward in the fall of 1958, though unemployment hovered around 6 percent at the end of the year. The economic stabilizers helped to cushion the impact of the downturn, and the easy credit policy adopted by the Federal Reserve Board encouraged better times.

Early in 1960 the economy faltered again, and the situation worsened during the rest of the year. Eisenhower's fiscal and monetary policies played a part in what has been called the "year of the hidden recession," while consumer credit and bank loans shrank in the face of high interest rates and a reduced money supply. By the beginning of 1961, factory output had declined, unemployment stood at almost 7 percent, and steel mills operated at only 50 percent of capacity. The recession "bottomed out" in February 1961, and during the administration of John F. Kennedy the economy improved under the stimulus of expansionary fiscal and monetary policies.

But joblessness continued to mar the recovery. Kennedy proposed various solutions—including a large tax reduction—to solve the problems of an inadequate growth rate and too much unemployment.

The economic expansion that began early in Kennedy's term increased during the administration of Lyndon B. Johnson and continued month after month. The prosperous years between 1962 and 1968 represented the longest unbroken peacetime economic prosperity in American history. The real rate of economic growth during the 1960s was around 5 percent a year, and the level of inflation was held to about 1 percent annually during the first half of the decade. The unemployment rate fluctuated between 3 and 5 percent during most of the decade. A bold tax cut in 1964, a liberal monetary policy, the Johnson administration's large domestic expenditures, and the increasing costs of the Vietnam War all contributed to the economic dynamism of the mid-1960s. But Johnson and his advisers made the mistake of assuming that the administration's expensive social reform programs and the increasing appropriations for the war in Southeast Asia could be financed without additional taxes. The result was mounting inflation and growing concern about the economy.

Richard M. Nixon, who became president in January 1969, was determined to slow the inflation. He wanted to restrict the government's intervention in the economy, to reduce the federal budget, and to have the Federal Reserve System tighten the money supply. Efforts to achieve these objectives helped to precipitate a recession. The real gross national product declined in 1970 for the first time since 1958, the stock market dropped over 300 points by mid-1970, and unemployment reached 6 percent by the end of the year. Yet prices kept climbing. Nixon then abruptly shifted from a restrictive to an expansionary fiscal strategy, calling for massive deficit spending to restore full production and employment. The economy continued to be sluggish in 1971, while unemployment remained high and prices kept going up. The administration eventually resorted to more stringent controls, but after some recovery in 1972, economic conditions worsened.

Inflation, accompanied by a drop in the growth of productivity, plagued the economy throughout the 1970s and into the 1980s. Whereas the general price level had risen at an annual rate of only 2.2 percent between 1948 and 1968, it rose at an annual rate of 6.6 percent during the years 1968–1980. Meanwhile, unemployment had become a major problem, federal budget deficits grew larger, and the nation was confronted with adverse trade balances. Although inflation, which reached double-digit heights during the administration of Jimmy Carter, slowed after Ronald Reagan entered the White House, the United States found itself in a full-fledged recession by early 1982. Recovery took hold in 1983, and a sustained period of good times followed. But this economic vitality was attended by a number of worrisome problems, including high rates of unemployment, unparalleled budget deficits, and large trade deficits.

Despite the economy's instability and its uneven distribution of earnings and profits, Americans enjoyed an era of extraordinary affluence during the postwar period. The civilian labor force grew from 54 million workers in 1945 to 111 million in 1983. While unemployment during the 1930s ranged between 15 and 25 percent of all workers, the average unemployment rate during the 1950s was 4.6 percent. Corporate profits rose from $33 billion in 1963 to $229 billion in 1978. Per capita income, in constant dollars, went up from $1,350 in 1945 to $1,824 in 1960 to over $2,000 in 1970. Median family income in current dollars increased from $5,660 in 1959 to $19,917 in 1979.

All levels of American society have increased their incomes since the 1930s, but the relative positions of the various income segments have changed little. The percentage of aggregate income received by the top 5 percent of American families declined from 25.7 in 1940 to 15.8 in 1983. On the other hand, the 20 percent of the population receiving the least income consistently obtained about 5 percent of the national income during the postwar years. Indeed, prosperity was far from being universal in America, social mobility was limited, and for a goodly number of people, opportunity was nonexistent.

Share of Aggregate Income before Taxes Received by Each Fifth of Families, 1947–1983 (Percent)

Income rank	1947	1950	1960	1966	1972	1983
Total families	100.0	100.0	100.0	100.0	100.0	100.0
Lowest fifth	5.1	4.5	4.8	5.6	5.4	4.7
Second fifth	11.8	11.9	12.2	12.4	11.9	11.1
Third fifth	16.7	17.4	17.8	17.8	17.5	17.1
Fourth fifth	23.2	23.6	24.0	23.8	23.9	24.4
Highest fifth	43.3	42.7	41.3	40.5	41.4	42.7
Top 5 percent	17.5	17.3	15.9	15.6	15.9	15.8

Sources: *Economic Report of the President, 1974* (Washington, 1974), p. 140; U.S. Bureau of the Census, *Statistical Abstract of the United States, 1985* (Washington, D.C., 1984), p. 448.

THE MIRACLE OF PRODUCTION

So expansive was the American economy that the output of goods and services doubled and then redoubled during the twenty-five years after 1945. World War II revivified the nation's industrial and business system, created a huge backlog of consumer demand and purchasing power, and left the United States as the dominant economic power in the world. Prosperity in the years that followed was also promoted by the growth of population, the vital role government had come to play in the nation's economic life, and the increase in production resulting from technological innovations. The federal government's enormous military budgets (they reached $50 billion a year in the early 1960s), its foreign aid programs, and its far-reaching social welfare programs constituted a profoundly important element in the national economy. The expenditures of federal, state, and local governments after the mid-1950s made up about one-fifth of all purchases in the private sector, dwarfing those of any other "industry." Federal support for research and development (R&D) spurted ahead in the late fifties, following *Sputnik*, and by the mid-sixties it had reached $15 billion a year—two-thirds of the total national expenditures for R&D. Increasing horsepower per worker, use of the mass-production system, application of the principles of scientific management, and growing reliance on scientific and technological research all contributed to the increase in productivity.

Theoretical knowledge provided the foundation for a vast increase in technological and scientific expertise. One manifestation of this "knowledge revolution" was automation, the talisman of the new productivity in the 1950s. Simply put, automation involved the use of machines to operate other machines. It meant "the introduction of self-regulating devices into the industrial sequence through the feedback principle whereby electronic sensing devices automatically pass information back to earlier parts of the processing machine, correcting for tool wear or other items of control."[1] The result was increased production and output per employee-hour, improved quality and uniformity of products, and more efficient management and greater speed in decision making. Automation not only affected industrial work in factories but also rapidly transformed many jobs in office, administrative, and service occupations. The trend toward automation was given impetus by the invention and commercial production of the electronic digital computer. First developed in 1944 and rapidly perfected in the 1950s, the computer was perhaps the most far-reaching and significant of the nation's postwar technological achievements.

Computers were introduced commercially in the 1950s to process data. Their capacity for analysis, synthesis, and memory soon led to other uses. They transformed the manufacturing and processing of many products and revolutionized numerous business operations. By 1970 the number of computers in the United States had increased to an estimated 100,000. The declining price and expanded memory of the newer models combined to put these devices in the hands of millions of individuals and small businesses. More than 6 million personal and home computers were sold in the United States in 1983 alone. By that time, computer technology had begun to affect almost every facet of American life. But its greatest impact has been in the workplace. Computers now design products, control the flow of materials on production lines, and operate robots that paint cars and weld metal. Even more significant, perhaps, has been their acceleration of growth in the service area—the banks, insurers, utilities, and other businesses that make up half of the U.S. economy. Meanwhile, education has been reshaped by the computer, which has also become a household tool. People are using it, one journalist noted, "to play games, prepare tax returns, monitor investments, write résumés, and trace their family trees." Indeed, the computer has come to symbolize a nation moving from an industrial to a scientific society, a society characterized by computerized information and telecommunications and by a technology ranging from the laser to nuclear power and robotics.

Another trend in postwar production was the decline of some old industries, including coal, textiles, and public transportation. After 1945, they became less important in the overall configuration of American business. Other mature industries expanded in the postwar period—sometimes in spectacular fashion, as in the case of automobiles, sometimes at a slow but steady rate, as was true of steel. One of the traditional industries that played an important part in the peacetime prosperity was housing, which usually represented at least 20 percent of all private investment. Construction of all kinds boomed in the postwar years, but the growth of residential housing, held back for a decade and a half by depression and war (the value of all U.S. housing was less in 1945 than in 1929), enjoyed a phenomenal advance in the new era. Government support, through G.I. loans, the Federal Housing Administration, and public housing appropriations, augmented the large investments from private sources to create a great housing boom in the 1950s. During some years, over a million new units were constructed.

Automobiles, another mature industry, continued to be crucially important to the well-being of the national economy. The industry went through a temporary time of rebuilding immediately after the war, but it soon entered a flush period that surpassed even the 1920s. Factory sales of cars and trucks averaged almost 7 million a year in the fifties, and in the peak year of 1955 over 9 million cars, trucks, and buses were sold. Dominated by General Motors, Ford, and Chrysler, the industry made use of a type of product innovation known as "dynamic obsolescence" or "planned obsolescence," in which new models featuring ever-more powerful engines and an endless array of frills were emphasized. The advent of the small car—the so-called compact—from abroad in the mid-1950s brought a sharp jump in the importation of Volkswagens and other foreign brands, and American producers belatedly introduced their own compacts. The auto industry sustained a vast network of enterprises: automobile dealerships, garages, filling stations, a giant highway system, and the manufacture of tires and other accessories, in addition to a multitude of services catering to the motoring public such as motels and drive-in restaurants.

Chemicals became one of the most spectacularly successful of the nation's industries after World War II. Chemicals and petrochemicals encompassed many subgroups, having great variety and manifesting divergent trends. Du Pont, Monsanto, Dow, and other large corporations produced a large number of synthetic materials, drugs, and detergents. The industrial chemicals market grew at an annual rate of 10 percent between 1947 and 1960. Profits were enormous.

The extraordinary increase in the consumption of electrical power in the United States in the 1940s and 1950s both reflected and contributed to the growth of three industrial giants: electrical power utilities and the related electrical machinery and equipment industry, the electrical appliance industry, and electronics. Growing at a rate of 15 percent a year, electronics had become the nation's fifth largest industry by 1960, exceeded only by automobiles, steel, aircraft, and chemicals. One major category of the industry included such products as computers, testing and measuring equipment, industrial control equipment, microwave communications systems, television sets, radios, phonographs, tape recorders, and high-fidelity components. The use of transistors rather than vacuum tubes in radios, television sets, and other electronic devices eliminated time-consuming and bulky hand-wiring. Transistors, followed by miniaturization encouraged by space vehicle research in the 1960s, contributed to the far-reaching electronics revolution in the 1970s and 1980s.

Other relatively new arrivals as important components of the U.S. economy included the aircraft and air transport industries. The shift to jet propulsion in commercial aviation boosted the industry in the 1950s, while the development and production of missiles in the late fifties and early sixties resulted in some retrenchment in the manufacture of aircraft. A related area that grew swiftly in the 1960s was the space industry. Metals like aluminum also developed rapidly in the postwar era, as did fuel industries such as natural gas.

Nuclear power, an energy source of great potential importance, developed more slowly. Its commercialization was fostered by the Atomic Energy Act of 1954, the Eisenhower administration's Atoms-for-Peace proposal, and the generous aid of government funds. Doubt about the economic feasibility of the new industry hindered its growth for several years, but the advantages of large, electricity-generating nuclear plants had apparently been established by the late 1960s. Then a major environmental controversy, stimulated by mounting concern over health and safety risks, checked the progress of nuclear power during the 1970s. In the mid-1980s the industry began to recover. Over eighty nuclear plants were in operation by that time, accounting for about 20 percent of the electricity produced in the United States (but only 4 percent of the country's total energy consumption).

One of the notable features of the economic scene during the years after 1945 was the way in which the new industrial and business developments contributed to the transformation of several regions. The expansive forces that promoted these regional changes varied. The aircraft industry, for instance, spurred the rapid development of the Pacific Coast economy during the 1940s and 1950s. Government expenditures for defense and space programs played an important role in the economic growth of such states as California, Texas, Massachusetts, and Ohio. The economy of the South was stimulated during the war by a large infusion of federal money. The southern region benefited in the contest for new industry because of its abundant land and water, its supplies of electrical power and other fuels, and its favorable tax policies.

The most dramatic economic growth in the postwar period took place in the Pacific Coast states and particularly in California, where a distinctive style of life furnished one of the incentives for westward migration. By 1963 California had surpassed New York as the wealthiest and most populous state in the Union; it was first in both industrial and agricultural production. The most spectacular southern development occurred in Texas, where a giant petrochemical industry grew up in a complex of Gulf Coast cities. New growth industries such as instruments and aircraft construction also contributed to the Texas boom. The rapid growth of Florida was scarcely less impressive, and that state's economic life flourished on the basis of tourism, citrus fruits, and the space industry. The Great Lakes and Middle West regions, long the country's agricultural and industrial heartland, basically held their position in the national economy—no mean feat in itself. Some other leading industrial and business centers, such as Pennsylvania, faced serious stagnation in certain industrial lines. Much of New England fought a rearguard action to prevent a lag in economic growth as compared with other parts of the country. Large depressed areas such as Appalachia, as well as numerous centers of declining industries and hundreds of depopulated counties and small towns throughout the country, failed to participate directly in the economic expansion.

Agricultural productivity following the Second World War was even greater than that of industry. A revolution swept over American farms. One feature of this revolution was the rapid mechanization of farm operations: larger tractors and bigger and better machines for preparing the soil, planting, cultivating, and harvesting came into use. The agricultural transformation was also furthered by the genetic research of plant and animal breeders; by the use of chemical fertilizers and of insecticides, fungicides, and herbicides; and by increasing specialization of production and greater emphasis on modern management. As Gilbert C. Fite writes, "Technology, science, and modern management, assisted by government policies,

Changes in Farming: 1950–1983

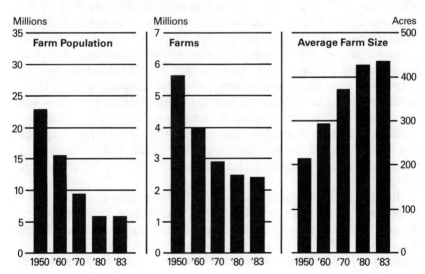

Source: U.S. Bureau of the Census, *Statistical Abstract of the United States, 1985* (Washington, D.C., 1984), p. 628.

were rapidly creating a new agriculture." In the meantime, the trend toward larger and more efficient farms became increasingly pronounced. There were 1.7 million fewer American farmers in 1959 than at the beginning of that decade, and the number of farms in the United States declined from 4 million in 1960 to 2.3 million in the mid-1980s. The production of huge surpluses and a cost-price squeeze resulting from mounting operating costs and falling agricultural prices during many years encouraged the shift toward highly organized and highly capitalized farm units. These developments have placed great pressure on poor and marginal farmers. Indeed, the celebrated family farm clearly faces extinction, even though millions of poor rural inhabitants continue to hang on to the only livelihood most of them have ever known.

STRUCTURE AND COMPETITION

No aspect of the American economy was more prominent than the continuing trend toward large-scale corporate enterprise. The growing concentration of economic power in the United States went far beyond the combination movement at the turn of the century and the big holding companies and business consolidations that marked the 1920s. By the 1950s and 1960s giant corporations dominated almost every area of the nation's business, and a few hundred large concerns exerted a preponderant influence on the economy as a whole. In 1960, 600 corporations had annual earnings of over $10 million. These 600 companies made up only .5 percent of all U.S. corporations, but they accounted for 53 percent of total corporate income. The emerging supercorporations were national and even international in operation, bureaucratic in organization, and increasingly diversified in the range of their products and services. Small business enterprise did not disappear, but its role grew less significant in the economy. In 1958 there were some 5 million individually owned businesses outside of farming, mining, and fishing in the United States, but 85 percent of all employed persons were working for someone else—as compared with 36 percent in 1900.

Oligopoly, or the dominance of an industry or business by a few large firms, became the rule. Three automobile companies produced 95 percent of the new cars manufactured in the United States, three aluminum companies produced 90 percent of all the aluminum, and three radio and television networks monopolized the nation's airwaves. Bank deposits increased fourfold between 1940 and 1960, but the number of banks declined by over a thousand during the two decades, and branch banking became increas-

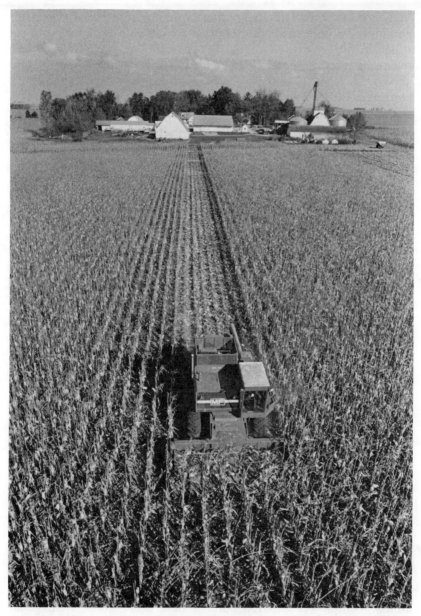

Harvesting the corn crop on an Iowa farm. The machine cuts and shells six rows of corn at a time (*USDA photo*)

ingly common. In aircraft production in the mid-1950s, ten firms employed 94 percent of the total labor force in the industry; in petroleum, fifteen firms employed 86 percent; in steel, thirteen corporations hired 85 percent; in office machinery, four concerns employed 71 percent; and in electrical machinery, six employed 50 percent of all workers.

The trend toward bigness in the U.S. economy was encouraged by hundreds of mergers every year. Holding-company pyramids came into vogue again, and a new form of consolidated firm emerged: the conglomerate, which brought together under one financially powerful management several companies whose products were frequently quite unrelated to one another. The goal of the conglomerate was to minimize risks and maximize profits through industrial and mercantile diversification. By the end of the 1960s, conglomerates made up over 90 percent of U.S. mergers. Combinations and acquisitions were a widely chosen alternative to the creation of new capacity and additional output, which might have been attended by price reductions. Acquisitions were also accelerated by tax deductions available to the acquiring companies. The new technology contributed to the further growth of industrial concentration, since the costs of research, retooling, and development in an age of faster-than-sound transport, atomic power, and intercontinental missiles were simply prohibitive for smaller firms. During the years 1950–1961, the 500 largest American corporations merged with and absorbed no fewer than 3,404 smaller companies in a wide variety of production and distribution areas.

Big business in the United States tended to become "multinational" as well as diversified. Indeed, multinational corporations flowered in the postwar period, and American firms led the trend in that direction. Huge international corporations such as General Motors, International Business Machines, Eastman Kodak, and Exxon had extensive operations in foreign countries. In the early 1970s the International Telephone and Telegraph Company, to take a striking example, employed over half a million people in ninety-three countries and owned more than 330 subsidiary corporations around the world.

Ownership and management in the large corporation were now almost completely separate, and a new professional managerial class, possessing enormous power, directed the great business units. Since most of the new capital for the operation of the supercorporations was generated internally from profits and depreciation accounts, the large concerns no longer were very dependent upon banks, insurance companies, and individual investors. At the same time, these large bureaucracies were sensitive to the conditions and morale of their employees. Because most of them competed in a broad consumers' market, they were increasingly concerned about their "public image" and very attentive to the requirements of public relations. They sought long-run security in a variety of ways, including diversification through product innovation or merger. After the war, the historian Alfred D. Chandler writes, "nearly all the major oil and rubber companies began producing petrochemicals, rubber chemicals, plastics, and many sorts of synthetics; and the automobile companies began turning out tractors, farm equipment, marine engines, and other non-automotive products." With the strategy of diversification came a new decentralized structure in large-scale business.

Economic concentration clearly led to a decline in traditional competition, increased the incidence of so-called administered prices, and made for instability in the economy. Nevertheless, a good deal of competition continued to exist in some sectors of the nation's economy, including construction, mining, services, and trades, where a large number of producers or service units prevailed. Some authorities pointed out, moreover, that competition was widely evident in quality, product design, and advertising. John Kenneth Galbraith, in *American Capitalism: The Concept of Countervailing Power* (1952), argued that the long trend toward concentration of industrial enterprise in the hands of a few firms had created "not only strong sellers . . . but also strong buyers." In this system of countervailing power, according to Galbraith, "one large bloc is offset by the growth of another group in an effort to prevent its own exploitation." Adolf A. Berle contended, in *The 20th Century Capitalist Revolution* (1954), that the managerial revolution had divorced property from power and helped to create a responsible "people's capitalism," in which economic power was controlled by "the operation of the public consensus" and "an equipoise of strong organizations."

The record of the federal government's antitrust suits since 1945 reveals its recurrent attempts to halt the trend toward ever-greater economic concentration. In a case against the Aluminum Company of America, decided in 1945, the government secured the dissolution of the corporation. The following year, in a suit against three giant tobacco companies for conspiring to control the price of leaf tobacco and cigarettes, the government won another important decision. Significantly, the Supreme Court in this case declared that monopoly consisted as much in the possession of power to suppress competition and raise prices as in the commission of unlawful acts. The Celler-Kefauver Act of 1950, an amendment to the Clayton Antitrust Act of 1914, made it illegal for a corporation to acquire in whole or part the assets of another corporation if the effect would be to lessen competition. The Justice Department, under this authority, initiated a number of successful suits to prevent mergers or acquisitions in the milk, steel, paper, and sugar industries. In one of the most famous court actions of the postwar period, Du Pont was forced to divest itself of its 23 percent stock interest in General Motors.

Americans were shocked in 1960 when twenty-nine leading electrical equipment companies and forty-four of their officers were brought to trial for conspiring to rig bids and fix prices on $1.75 billion worth of equipment sold between 1955 and 1959. The government won the case, and the guilty firms were fined a total of $1.9 million. In a series of decisions during the immediate postwar years, the Supreme Court invalidated the notorious basing-point pricing system, which had long been used in such industries as steel and cement to avoid price competition.[2] The courts in other decisions opened patents to more liberal licensing arrangements, prohibited tying contracts, required the sale rather than the mere leasing of equipment, and in general assured greater access to technological knowledge. In the mid-1970s the Justice Department filed an antitrust suit against AT&T that led to the signing of a divestiture agreement early in 1982. Although the agreement broke the Bell System into eight independent corporations, it was not immediately clear how divestiture would affect consumers.

None of the postwar administrations in Washington pursued a determined antitrust policy, and the government's occasional successes in the courts did little to counter the increasing concentration in the economy. Critics of the big corporations seemed more concerned with the social implications of corporate power than with its economic consequences. Thus William H. Whyte's widely read book, *The Organization Man* (1956), emphasized the malign effects of big-business bureaucracy. He lamented the way in which it smothered individuality and caused the new businessman to abandon the "Protestant ethic" and assume the "social ethic."

There was still much talk in America about "free enterprise," and Washington lawmakers were not unresponsive to the precarious position of many small businessmen. The House of Representatives set up a Small Business Committee as early as 1941, and the Senate created its own Select Committee on Small Business in 1950. The Small Business Administration was established in the fifties to absorb the remaining functions of the Reconstruction Finance Corporation and the Small Defense Plants Administration and to render aid "to small business concerns, including financial, procurement and technical assistance."

If the power of the federal government was used in some instances to protect small businesses, it was exercised in many other cases actually to foster the growth of oligopoly. World War II encouraged this development, for it ushered in a new era of government-business cooperation, and it allowed the great corporations to enhance their market position in preparation for peacetime operation. Congress strengthened the monopolistic principle of resale price maintenance in the McGuire Act of 1952.[3] The Reed-Bulwinkle Act, also passed in 1952, exempted railroads from public approval of agreements relating to "rates, fares, classifications, divisions, allowances or charges." The government gave its approval in 1968 to a merger of the Pennsylvania and New York Central Railroads.

The link between government and business was most conspicuously manifested in the defense and space programs. A community of interest developed between the Pentagon and the giant corporations that received the bulk of the procurement funds, and the defense contractors were frequently able to avoid competition or to secure payments for billion dollar cost overruns, as in the case of Lockheed's C-5 transport plane. Early in 1969 some 2,072 retired military officers of high rank were employed by one hundred of the major defense contractors. In 1966 a single firm—General Dynamics—received government contracts totaling $2.2 billion. Lockheed, the recipient of $2 billion in defense contracts in 1968, faced bankruptcy in 1971. But Congress came to its aid, authorizing a $250 million loan to rescue the company. One scholar has used the term "military Keynesianism" in referring to the economic effects of U.S. defense expenditures. In 1958, for instance, the military purchased virtually all of the nation's ordnance production, 94 percent of its aircraft, 61 percent of its ships and boats, and 21 percent of its electronic equipment.

PATTERNS OF TRADE AND DISTRIBUTION

The domestic commerce and foreign trade of the United States in the postwar years revealed the extent to which the economy had shifted to a mass-consumption base at home and how dominant the nation had become in the international sphere as the world's industrial and financial center. The domestic market seemed to be almost insatiable, and it was sustained year in and year out by accumulated savings and rising incomes, large annual crops of new babies, a vast network of credit, new technology, huge government expenditures, and enormous advertising outlays. The country's preeminent position in the world economy reflected its importance as a market for goods and as a source of goods and savings.

In the new "affluent society," the business world was drawn as if by a magnet to the needs and desires of the consumer. The American consumer, the historian George E. Mowry remarks, was "daily cajoled by advertising, frequently consulted as to his wishes by market surveys, and his future inclinations to buy or not to buy [were] intently studied by research organizations." A marginal decline in the consumer's purchasing expectations, Mowry noted, "was often enough to curtail inventories and cause the stock market to waver." The consumer orientation was evident in the growing importance of the service industries and trades. By the late 1950s the service industries employed more than half of all U.S. wage-earners, an indication of the nation's shift from an industrial to a "post-industrial" economy. Expenditures for services had risen by 1983 to 50 percent of all consumer spending (the figure for 1950 was 36.9 percent), as compared with 13 percent for durable and 37 percent for nondurable goods.

The consumer market not only spread into all manner of personal services but also came to encompass an endless array of durable goods: television sets, stereos, tape recorders, dishwashers, home freezers, boats, sporting goods, and so on, not to mention new houses and new automobiles. By 1958, 96 percent of the nation's families owned refrigerators, 89 percent had washing machines, and 81 percent had acquired television sets. The "youth market" developed rapidly in the 1960s, with a host of its own special products. Americans spent increasing amounts of money for entertainment, recreation, and travel. The commercialization of athletics proceeded apace, as was strikingly illustrated in the rise of televised sports. This far-flung consumer culture spawned a variety of institutions, such as gourmet food stores, art centers, record stores, and pet shops. At the same time, the older trend toward larger retail stores continued in the form of chain stores, department stores, and mail-order houses. New marketing techniques brought a wider range of attractive goods. The most impressive new type of store in the retail area was the supermarket, whose spacious and glistening rows of well-displayed merchandise included virtually any item the customer might fancy. Accompanying the new consumerism was the growth of an "underground economy," involving illegal goods and services like bookmaking, illegal drugs, and prostitution.

Economic prosperity had become dependent in considerable degree upon the creation of what John Kenneth Galbraith called a "synthesis of desire"—the contrived creation of demand—in which advertising played an indispensable part. Advertising in such traditional media as newspapers and periodicals enjoyed a substantial increase, but the most spectacular new medium for this purpose was television. One development in this field was the popularization of depth psychology (that is, the study of the unconscious mind) and the use of motivational research in an effort to discover what would have a favorable effect on the consumer's ego and libido. The public relations expert became a prominent figure in the postwar business world, and every corporation of any size had its own public relations department, where such schemes as "press junkets" and newsworthy activities were conceived. Frederic Wakeman's popular novel, *The Hucksters*, drew public attention to the existence and influence of the advertising business—"Madison Avenue"—and alerted many readers to the cynicism of some advertising methods. Another writer suggested that "the giant corporation, in alliance with the most efficacious advertising medium ever invented, the television screen, has done more than anything else to establish our present habits of consumption and thus to a great extent set the style and pattern of our lives."[4]

The flourishing business involving consumer goods and services was stimulated by the ready availability of credit. Total private debts in the United States increased from $73 billion to $196 billion during the 1950s. Consumer credit at the end of 1963 amounted to almost $70 billion, eight or ten times what it had been in 1945. Credit was available for nearly every kind of purchase, and consumer buying was facilitated by checking accounts, credit cards, home mortgages, auto loans, installment buying, and finance companies. The credit card, valid throughout much of the world, became a symbol of U.S. affluence and consumerism. Meanwhile, a whole new industry had emerged, based on the need to investigate, report, and maintain records on the credit rating of individuals.

While a large number of Americans customarily spent more than they earned, many others were able to save money. Personal savings contributed directly to the impressive growth after 1945 of life insurance companies, savings and loan associations, mutual savings banks, investment companies, and credit companies, in addition to commercial banks. An enormous increase took place in private pension funds—from a total of $11 billion in 1950 to $44 billion in 1959 and to $453 billion in 1980. The stock market also reflected the mounting volume of savings and investments in the United States. There were at least 20 million individual stockholders in 1965, in contrast to only 6.5 million in 1952. Some so-called growth stocks, such as IBM, doubled their assets every four or five years beginning in the late 1940s and were traded at 60 to 70 times their earnings in the 1960s.

American leaders worked to reduce international economic barriers during and after the war. They pursued a liberal tariff policy, especially during the years 1946–1950, entering into the General Agreement on Tariffs and Trade (GATT) in 1947–48 and extending the reciprocal trade program every few years. Making use of the GATT formula, the United States and other major trading nations achieved substantial tariff reductions in six rounds of negotiations between 1948 and 1967. The United States also contributed to the internationalization of foreign lending. It took the lead in 1944 in creating the International Monetary Fund, to avoid drastic fluctuations in exchange rates and competitive currency devaluations following the war, and the International Bank for Reconstruction and Development, to provide long-term investment funds to Europe and less developed countries.

The United States was a leading supplier of goods and services, accounting in 1961 for nearly one-fourth of the total world exports of manufactures and for almost one-third of the world exports of capital goods. It also exported large amounts of military equipment and many agricultural goods, especially cotton, wheat, tobacco, soybeans, and poultry. The Marshall Plan and other foreign aid programs were obviously designed with an eye to the support of U.S. economic interests overseas. Foreign trade and investment were likewise promoted through liberal tax policies and such agencies as the International Cooperation Administration, established in 1948. In the mid-1960s foreign markets accounted for 29 percent of IBM's business, 40 percent of Coca Cola's, and 45 percent of Caterpillar Tractor's. Eleven of the top twelve American industrial corporations had foreign sales exceeding $1 billion in 1970.

American corporations and citizens in the postwar era made large investments abroad. These investments totaled more than $12 billion in Europe alone by the mid-1960s. Direct U.S. private investment abroad rose from $11.8 billion in 1950 to $54.6 billion in 1966, with an additional $32 billion in portfolio holdings in the latter year. By 1963 U.S. firms controlled over half of the British automobile industry, 40 percent of the German petroleum industry, and 40 percent of the French telegraph, telephone, electronics, and statistical equipment business. One estimate fixed the gross value of products manufactured by American companies abroad in 1967 at over $100 billion.

Reversing a longtime trend, the United States after 1945 became a major importer of industrial and consumer goods. Americans were increasingly attracted to the efficient, low-priced cars, cameras, stereo equipment, and other products from countries like Germany and Japan. The United States had also become more dependent on foreign raw materials such as iron ore, bauxite, and crude oil. In addition to payments for imports, the United States had spent almost $100 billion in economic and military aid to other countries by the late 1960s. Large foreign investments also affected the balance of payments adversely, as did American travel abroad, interest on foreign investments in the United States, foreign transportation, and the like. As the deficits mounted in America's balance of payments, the U.S. position in the world economy began to be affected. The gold drain from the United States became a chronic problem after 1958, and the possibility of a dollar crisis grew steadily larger. The crisis came in 1971, forcing the Nixon administration to devalue the dollar.

In the 1980s the weak performance of the United States in the international economy provoked a new sense of urgency among Americans. The most obvious evidence of this weakness was the country's growing foreign trade deficit, which rose sharply after 1980, climbing to more than $60 billion in 1983, to $102 billion in 1984, and to about $120 billion in 1985. The strength of the American economy, combined with high interest rates, created a favorable climate at home, attracting a substantial inflow of foreign capital. The dollar rose rapidly against foreign currencies, placing American goods at a disadvantage in world markets and stimulating U.S. imports. Meanwhile, foreign competitors became more aggressive exporters of manufactured and agricultural products, while American producers seemed to lose their superiority in heavy industry and other areas. The United States found it difficult to compete with Japan, for example, in the production and sale of such items as video recorders, semiconductor chips, robots, and computer parts. This brought heightened pressure for protectionist legislation and restrictive agreements. Accelerating foreign investments in the United States represented another aspect of the international economy. Foreign direct investment in the United States increased tenfold between 1970 and 1984, reaching $135 billion in the latter year (as compared with an American investment abroad of $226 billion).

THE WORKER'S WORLD

One manifestation of the sustained prosperity in postwar America was the general security enjoyed by most workers. The civilian labor force expanded enormously, from 57.5 million workers in 1946 to 82.7 million in 1970 and to 111.5 million in 1983. Labor's share of the national income rose appreciably. Average nonagricultural weekly earnings increased from $45.58 in 1947 to almost $120.00 in 1970; real weekly earnings of factory workers went up 50 percent between 1945 and 1970. Organized labor, having grown to maturity, assumed a place of great power in the economy. American workers increasingly took on a bourgeois appearance.

The composition of the working force underwent great change in the postwar era. The number of farmers declined steadily and by 1960 made up only 8.5 percent of the nation's workers. At some point in the fifties, the number of persons engaged in goods-producing activities dropped below 50 percent of all civilian labor, and by 1960 the blue-collar percentage of all workers had fallen to 45, as compared to 59 in 1929. The great increase in employment occurred in the ranks of white-collar workers, including business and personal services, finance, distribution, education, and government. An important aspect of this white-collar domination was the accelerated movement of women into positions of gainful employment. Between 1940 and 1960, approximately 9.4 million women joined the labor force as against only 7.5 million men. During the same years the percentage of married women working outside the home doubled, and by 1970 about half of all married women were gainfully employed. In the 1960s two out of every three clerical workers were women (only one out of four had been in 1900). Women began for the first time to enter such fields as finance, public relations, and computer programming. Nevertheless, American women achieved only a token presence in many occupations and

Trends in the Labor Force: 1950–1983

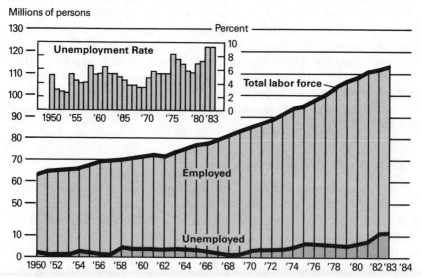

Source: U.S. Bureau of the Census, *Statistical Abstract of the United States, 1985* (Washington, D.C., 1984), p. 386.

professions, and they continued to suffer discrimination in pay, promotions, and recognition.

Organized labor, moving ahead on the basis of the great expansion of the New Deal years and World War II, made impressive progress, particularly during the first postwar decade. The number of union members in the United States climbed from 14.7 million in 1945 to 18 million (about 35 percent of total nonagricultural employment) in the mid-1950s. Having secured legal safeguards to ensure its right to organize and bargain collectively, labor enjoyed great success in gaining its specific economic objectives. It was also a power center in the nation's politics. By mid-century the American Federation of Labor (AFL) and the Congress of Industrial Organizations (CIO) were prepared to cooperate in their efforts to advance labor's interests in Congress, and they took an active part in national political campaigns. After the merger of the two organizations, the AFL-CIO established a new Committee on Political Education (COPE), and in later years the giant federation became a major component of the Democratic coalition.

Labor-management relations became far less antagonistic and much more orderly than they had been in the 1930s. The 116-day steel strike of 1959 demonstrated how disruptive national strikes in vital industries could be, but in general the relationship between labor and management had become peaceful and stable. Most unions and corporations negotiated mutually acceptable contracts, without strikes or with only brief work stoppages. A key factor in labor's cooperative attitude was the fact that workers won so many benefits in the new era. The scope of labor-management negotiations came to include a wide range of "fringe benefits," among which were pension plans, paid vacations and holidays, sickness and hospitalization benefits, and supplementary unemployment insurance.

An important new feature of the corporate environment was the long-term labor contract, which became common in most of the large industries. The practice of "pattern settlements" also spread, whereby wage agreements in certain big industries like automobiles and electrical manufacturing were followed in other industries. General Motors and the United Automobile Workers agreed as early as 1948 to an "escalator clause" in a new contract, tying wages to the cost of living, and similar arrangements were soon included in most leading contracts. Growing use was made of what was termed the "annual improvement factor," through which a portion of the gains from improved productivity was transferred to the wage earner each year. Another innovation was the "package settlement" that combined a cost-of-living adjustment with so many cents per hour for fringe benefits, to which was frequently added a separate productivity increment.

Still another example of labor progress was the merger, in December 1955, of the AFL and CIO into one great federation. Although the differences and the rivalry between the two national organizations had been acute in the thirties and forties, the situation changed considerably during the first decade after the war. The Taft-Hartley Act of 1947 tended to unify labor against the common enemy, and the old industrial-versus-craft distinction was no longer a significant source of friction. The new AFL-CIO brought the great majority of American unionists into one organization, with George Meany of the AFL as president and the dynamic Walter P. Reuther of the CIO as senior vice president. But it soon became evident that the merger had not solved the problems of jurisdictional rivalry and internal friction.

Nor did the AFL-CIO show much initiative in trying to bring in unorganized workers. While union bureaucracy increased and organized labor became more centralized, the movement lost its old militancy. Trade unionism in the 1950s seemed to be hardening, to be growing stodgy and conservative. As the historian David Brody has written, "Its ideas lacked freshness, its policies popular appeal. Age crept up even on those new style leaders like Walter Reuther, who were raised in the great upheaval of the thirties." Organized labor began to experience a relative decline in the late 1950s, and between 1954 and 1962 it actually lost more than a million members. Labor's relative decline continued in later years.

Massive structural changes in employment were a major factor in organized labor's loss of vitality. Technological changes sharply reduced the available jobs in many areas where unions were traditionally strong. Between 1947 and 1961, for example, approximately two-thirds of the jobs in bituminous coal mining disappeared, two-fifths of those in railroading, and almost one-fifth of those in steel, copper, and aluminum production. Containerization, to take another example, revolutionized the loading and unloading of ships, drastically reducing the need for dockside labor. Increasingly after mid-century, new jobs in the labor market were being created in such areas as sales, services, and government rather than manufacturing, where some older industries were declining and automation was taking its toll of workers. The white-collar sector was difficult to organize, having a traditional aversion to unionization. Labor organizations faced still other difficulties, including powerful opposition from many employers, the hostility of local authorities and the absence of a union tradition in the South and Southwest, where much of the new economic expansion occurred, and a number of strong political barriers. The Taft-Hartley Act, with its list of "unfair labor practices," reduced union power in several respects. A wave of state right-to-work laws was enacted at about the same time, striking at the union shop and tending to favor nonunion workers.

Behind the legislatures and the courts was a public that had become more and more critical of organized labor's "excesses." Many people disliked the union encouragement of "featherbedding"—the retention of useless positions. Basically, however, a large number of Americans, perhaps even a majority, had begun to feel that big labor had grown too powerful and irresponsible. This attitude was broadened and reinforced by congressional revelations in the late 1950s. Early in 1957 a special Senate committee under the chairmanship of John L. McClellan of Arkansas launched an extensive investigation of corruption and other "improper activities" in the labor and management fields. The McClellan committee found evidence of widespread bribery, graft, misuse of union funds and expense accounts by labor leaders, racketeering, corrupt practices, and undemocratic internal politics in many unions. The publicity resulting from this inquest led to the passage of the Landrum-Griffin Act of 1959[5] and spurred the more responsible labor leaders to set about putting their own house in order.

Few developments in the postwar period were more disturbing to labor than the rapid progress of automation. The continuing mechanization of industries such as coal mining, steel, longshoring, and certain of the mass production lines drastically reduced the employment in those areas. Automation alone eliminated an estimated 1.5 million blue-collar workers between 1953 and 1959. When new machinery and technological advances forced middle-aged and older workers out of jobs, it was frequently impossible for them to find substitute employment or to secure the training and expertise necessary for more sophisticated work. School dropouts and young people from disadvantaged groups were doubly handicapped, for many of them were financially unable or insufficiently motivated to acquire much education and training, and without such preparation they stood no chance in the competition for good jobs.

The unfavorable situation confronting organized labor was reversed for time in the middle and late 1960s as a result of the buoyant economy and the expansive policies of President Lyndon B. Johnson. As the "blue-collar blues" momentarily became less resounding, the labor movement began to attract new groups of workers such as retail clerks, teachers, and government employees. Teachers, nurses, social-service professionals, and a variety of public servants began to join labor unions and to engage in strikes, sometimes to the dismay of the public. White-collar workers became the most rapidly growing part of the labor movement. Union membership among state and local government workers tripled between 1968 and 1978, increasing from 764,000 to 2.4 million members. Another 2.4 million public workers belonged to employee associations, which in practice behaved much like trade unions. One element in the expansion of organized white-collar workers was the growing number of women in the labor movement. During the two decades between 1958 and 1978, for example, the number of women in unions doubled, rising from 3.3 million to 6.6 million.

Despite these gains, organized labor's relative decline continued in the 1970s and 1980s. Between 1974 and 1978 alone, unions in manufacturing lost more than a million members. By 1980 the most thoroughly organized sectors of the economy—basic manufacturing, mining, transport, and the skilled crafts—made up only 34 percent of all employees, the smallest proportion in half a century. The AFL-CIO had fewer members than at the time of its formation a quarter-century earlier. The economic and political trends of the late 1970s and early 1980s exacerbated the situation that faced organized labor. The economy performed erratically, unemployment worsened, industries like automobiles, steel, rubber, and petrochemicals encountered increasing competition from foreign producers, and management began to demand "givebacks" from workers and unions. Meanwhile, a breakdown was apparently occurring in "patterned bargaining," in which an entire industry customarily bargained with labor. State and local government reduced public employment and resisted union claims. The political climate became more conservative. Nevertheless, organized labor is an established institution in America, with over 23 million members and about a fourth of all nonagricultural workers in the early 1980s. But it is clear that the labor movement is on the defensive. The movement has lost its momentum, is facing job losses in many of the older industries, and is unable to attract workers in the "growth industries," where employers have resorted to a "new welfare capitalism" as a means of making unions less attractive to their employees.

One industry that clearly had a surplus of labor in the postwar era was agriculture, in which production increased as the number of workers declined. The total number of farm workers dropped from 10.3 million in 1946 to 7 million in 1960 and to only 3.7 million in 1980. The federal government's expensive price support system principally aided large commercial farmers. According to the *Economic Report of the President* in 1959, "More than 2.5 million farmers—whose annual sales are less that $2,500 and who produce each year only about 9 percent of our marketed farm products—receive only very small supplements, or none at all, to their incomes from Government expenditures for price support." Unable to expand and modernize their operations, many of the smaller and poorer farmers dropped out of agriculture after 1945. The industrialization of some poor agricultural regions, such as parts of the South, enabled some of these disadvantaged farmers to find a more productive life in the towns and cities. But a goodly number of small farmers held on, continuing to eke out a subsistence on the land. In 1968 at least one-fifth of the nation's farm families received less than $5,000 a year from farming. Even more discouraging was the tragic plight of about 200,000 migrant farm workers, who provided much of the seasonal labor for the orchards and truck farms of California and other areas specializing in the production of fruits and vegetables. The low wages, inadequate housing, and social deprivation suffered by these workers and their families represented a status little better than peasantry.

The great majority of Americans were more fortunate. They had jobs and, equally important, opportunities for new jobs and occupational advancement. They shared in the postwar prosperity. Millions of men and women, moreover, used their jobs and professions as escalators not only to a higher standard of living but also to a social status within the nation's dynamic middle class.

NOTES

1. Harold G. Vatter, *The U.S. Economy in the 1950's: An Economic History* (1963), p. 11.
2. The "Pittsburgh-plus" system illustrates the way in which the basing-point price arrangement operated. Under this scheme of administered prices, buyers of steel in Atlanta had to pay the equivalent of freight charges on steel from Pittsburgh to Atlanta, even though the steel was produced in Birmingham, a relatively short distance away.
3. This legislation, an amendment to the Federal Trade Commission Act, authorized the continued exemption from antitrust prosecution of resale price maintenance; it permitted individual firms to prevent the resale of a branded item below a minimum price.
4. John Brooks, *The Great Leap: The Past Twenty-five Years in America* (1966), p. 46.
5. This measure sought to provide greater protection for individual union members and closer government supervision of union activities.

SUGGESTIONS FOR FURTHER READING

There is no adequate economic history of the period since 1945, but Harold G. Vatter's *The U.S. Economy in the 1950's: An Economic History* (1963) provides an authoritative treatment of one decade. Ralph E. Freeman (ed.), *Postwar Economic Trends in the United States* (1960), is useful for the early years after 1945. Various aspects of the U.S. economy are dealt with in Michael Gort, *Diversification and Integration in American Industry* (1962); Robert T. Averitt, *The Dual Economy: The Dynamics of American Industry Structure* (1968); Emma Rothschild, *Paradise Lost: The Decline of the Auto-Industrial Age* (1973); John B. Rae, *Climb to Greatness: The American Aircraft Industry, 1920–1960* (1968); and Lawrence J. White, *The Automobile Industry since 1945* (1971). On the economic transformation of the South, see Thomas D. Clark, *The Emerging South* (2nd ed., 1968), and James G. Maddox and associates, *The Advancing South: Manpower Prospects and Problems* (1967). Martin Feldstein (ed.), *The American Economy in Transition* (1980), is a collection of valuable essays on changes in the national economy between mid-century and the late 1970s. Jack Blicksilver (ed.), *Views on U.S. Economic and Business History: Molding the Mixed Economy* (1985), is a good anthology with several illuminating selections on the period since 1945.

The distribution of income and wealth in the postwar period is analyzed by Robert J. Lampman, *The Share of Top Wealth-Holders in National Wealth, 1922–1956* (1962); Gabriel Kolko, *Wealth and Power in America: An Analysis of Social Class and Income Distribution* (1962); and Herman P. Miller, *Rich Man, Poor Man* (1964). Bernard D. Nossiter explodes several myths concerning the economy in *The Mythmakers: An Essay on Power and Wealth* (1964). Robert Heilbroner takes a critical view of the economy's prospects in *The Limits of American Capitalism* (1966).

Thomas C. Cochran's *American Business in the Twentieth Century* (1972) is a thoughtful synthesis of modern U.S. business history. See also Morton S. Baratz, *The American Business System in Transition* (1970). The role of the corporation is treated in Richard J. Barber, *The American Corporation: Its Power, Its Money, Its Politics* (1970); Robert Sobel, *The Age of Giant Corporations: A Microeconomic History of American Business, 1914–1984* (1984); and Morton Mintz and Jerry S. Cohen, *America, Inc.: Who Owns and Operates the United States* (1971). An important aspect of the relationship between government and business is critically explored in Walter Adams and Horace M. Gray, *Monopoly in America: The Government as Promoter* (1955). Adolf A. Berle, *Power without Property: A New Development in American Political Economy* (1959), identifies some of the newer tendencies in the American economy. Three of John Kenneth Galbraith's books are important for an understanding of recent U.S. economic developments: *American Capitalism: The Concept of Countervailing Power* (1952); *The Affluent Society* (1958); and *The New Industrial State* (1967). For the economic implications of research and technology, see Leonard S. Silk, *The Research Revolution* (1960); Walter Buckingham, *Automation: Its Impact on Business and People* (1963); and Daniel Bell, *The Coming of Post-Industrial Society* (1973). David F. Noble, *Forces of Production: A Social History of Industrial Automation* (1984), is an interesting study of the process of technological development, concentrating on the postwar period.

Herbert Stein's *The Fiscal Revolution in America* (1969) is a valuable study of the "new economics" and of postwar fiscal policies. Also useful in this connection are A. E. Holmans, *United States Fiscal Policy, 1945–1959: Its Contribution to Economic Stability* (1961); Hobart Rowen, *The Free*

Enterprisers: Kennedy, Johnson, and the Business Establishment (1964); Jim F. Heath, *John F. Kennedy and the Business Community* (1969); and Herbert Stein, *Presidential Economics: The Making of Economic Policy from Roosevelt to Reagan and Beyond* (1984). The influence of Keynesian economics is suggested by Robert Lekachman, *The Age of Keynes* (1966), and Robert M. Collins, *The Business Response to Keynes, 1929–1964* (1981). David P. Calleo's *The Imperious Economy* (1982) is a perceptive examination of U.S. economic and foreign policy in the 1960s and 1970s.

The postwar labor situation is considered by Joel Seidman, *American Labor from Defense to Reconversion* (1953), and Millis and Brown, *From the Wagner Act to Taft-Hartley*, cited in chapter 3. James R. Green's *The World of the Worker: Labor in Twentieth-Century America* (1980) includes a brief and trenchant treatment of the labor scene since 1945. For the relationship between communism and the labor movement, see Bert Cochran, *Labor and Communism: The Conflict That Shaped American Unions* 1977), and Harvey Levenstein, *Communism, Anticommunism, and the CIO* (1981). Workers, rather than institutions of labor, are considered by Robert Blauner, *Alienation and Freedom* (1964); Richard Sennett and Jonathan Cobb, *The Hidden Injuries of Class* (1972); Studs Terkel, *Working* (1972); and William Kornblum, *Blue-Collar Community* (1974). Other aspects of the labor scene are dealt with in John Hutchinson, *The Imperfect Union: A History of Corruption in American Trade Unions* (1970); Frank Cormier and William J. Eaton, *Reuther* (1970); Walter Sheridan, *The Fall and Rise of Jimmy Hoffa* (1972); and Juanita M. Kreps, *Women and the American Economy: A Look to the 1980s* (1976).

Gilbert C. Fite's *American Farmers: The New Minority* (1981) is a splendid general history that emphasizes the postwar period. Fite's *Cotton Fields No More: Southern Agriculture, 1865–1980* (1984) is illuminating on the postwar South. John L. Shover, *First Majority—Last Minority: The Transforming of Rural Life in America* (1976), throws light on the agricultural revolution of the recent period. The best treatment of agricultural policy is by Willard W. Cochrane and Mary E. Ryan, *American Farm Policy, 1948–1973* (1976). But also see Marion Clawson, *Policy Directions for U.S. Agriculture* (1968), and Luther Tweeten, *Foundations of Farm Policy* (1970). The modern farm situation is discussed in Lauren Soth, *An Embarrassment of Plenty: Agriculture in Affluent America* (1965), and Ewell Paul Roy, *Exploring Agribusiness* (1967).

CHAPTER EIGHT

The Emergence
of a New
Social Order

THE SOCIAL ORDER in recent America has undergone profound change, despite the fact that traditional social patterns have continued to hold sway. The enormous growth of the economy and the pervasive influence of technology accelerated the pace of social change in the postwar years. In certain respects, American society became more homogeneous, more stable, more conservative, and less divided by geography and national origin. Yet it also experienced conflict, fragmentation, and insecurity, and Americans continued to be divided by distinctions of class, race, and ethnicity.

POSTWAR DEMOGRAPHIC TRENDS

If American society continued to be mobile and dynamic in the postwar era, it was also extraordinarily expansive. The population increased from 139.9 million in 1945 to 151.3 million in 1950. During the 1950s the total population grew by more than 24 million people, a remarkable growth rate of 18.5 percent in that decade. The 200 million mark was passed in 1967, and the total number of Americans had increased to 237 million by 1984. An important factor in this growth was a reversal of the declining birthrate of the prewar period. The birthrate, which stood at 19.4 per thousand in 1940, rose to 23.3 in 1946, to 25.8 in 1947, and to 25 or above during the years 1951–1957. The rate began to drop in the late fifties, and it fell still further in later years as Americans became more concerned about environmental problems at home and soaring population in much of the rest of the world. The birthrate stood at 15.9 in 1980.

The marrying age for men and women dropped at the end of the war, as millions of G.I.'s came home and as thousands of Rosie the Riveters left the war plants. The "nesting" phase of the postwar period had begun, and from 1947 to about 1960 the United States enjoyed the greatest "baby boom" in its modern history. In 1947 there were 3.5 million births, a jump of 800,000 in one year, and the number of new babies increased with every change of the calendar, reaching 4.3 million in 1960. The baby boom of the forties and fifties had a telling effect upon the age distribution of the American people. In 1970 there were twice as many fourteen-year-olds as there were people forty years of age.

The population was growing older as well as younger. The death rate declined from 10.8 per thousand in 1940 to 9.5 per thousand in 1970 and to 8.6 in 1981. Almost 12 percent of all Americans were sixty-five or older in the mid-1980s, as compared with 8.1 percent in 1950 and only 4.1 percent in 1900. In 1960 for every 100 children under the age of five, there were only 81 persons aged sixty-five or over. By 1980, for every 100 children there were 156 senior citizens. As longevity continued to rise, the male-female ratio among older adults also widened. The life expectancy of boys born in 1980 was 69.8 years, compared with 77.5 years for girls. At birth there are

Birth and Death Rates: 1960–1983

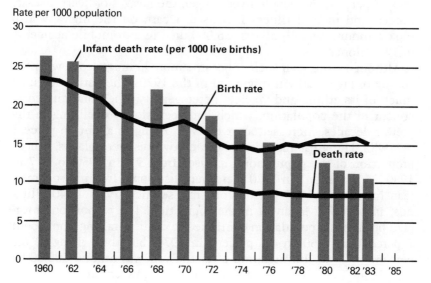

Source: U.S. Bureau of the Census, *Statistical Abstract of the United States, 1985* (Washington, D.C., 1984), p. 54.

about 105 males to every 100 females, but by age nineteen the ratio is about even. By age sixty-five, however, there are only 68 men to every 100 women.

By the early 1980s, life expectancy at birth in the United States had risen to more than seventy-four years—an increase of 9.6 years for males and of 12.7 years for females since 1940. Better diets made possible by the higher standard of living in the postwar period contributed to this improvement in the health of the American people. But the most important factor was the spectacular progress in medical science. Many dreaded diseases, including diphtheria, typhoid fever, and poliomyelitis, were virtually eliminated. Syphilis and tuberculosis in the early 1960s caused only one-tenth as many deaths per hundred thousand people as in 1939. Infection-fighting drugs made possible tremendous advances against bacteria and virus disease: penicillin during World War II, streptomycin in 1945, and in the following years aureomycin and other antibiotics, the Salk and Sabin vaccines, cortisone, oral antidiabetic drugs, and an array of tranquilizing agents. Great advances were also made in the reduction of infant mortality, in the perfection of heart surgery, in the techniques of organ transplants, and in the development of psychiatry. Increasing evidence that death and certain serious diseases were associated with the heavy use of tobacco encouraged nearly 8 million Americans to quit smoking between 1965 and 1970, during which time the incidence of cigarette smoking declined from 41.6 to 36.7 percent. As people lived longer, the ravages of heart disease, cancer, and mental illness increased. Death on the highway also took a mounting toll; almost 55,000 died in automobile accidents in 1971 alone.

Although American society became more homogeneous with the ending of large-scale immigration in the 1920s, the nation retained much of its ethnic and "racial" heterogeneity. The nonwhite component of the population, which had been slowly declining in the prewar decades, increased after the war, rising to about 16 percent by 1980. The great majority of the nonwhites were blacks, whose proportion of the population increased from 9.9 in 1950 to 11.7 in 1980 (26.5 million). In 1980 there were also some 1.4 million American Indians, 806,027 persons of Chinese ancestry, 774,640 Filipinos, and 700,747 Japanese in the population. The proportion of foreign born in the population continued to decline, falling from about 7 percent in 1950 to 4.7 percent in 1970, but then rising to 6.2 percent in 1980. Immigration after the war was around 300,000 a year, including thousands of "war brides" from Germany, Japan, and other occupied countries and several hundred thousand "displaced persons" admitted by special act of Congress. A great many Puerto

Ricans, who were not technically immigrants, also poured into New York's Spanish Harlem and other urban ghettos. By 1980 Puerto Ricans and others of Hispanic background in the United States numbered over 14.6 million, or about 6.5 percent of the total population.

Americans had always been characterized as a people on the move, and in the postwar years the open road beckoned them as never before. In the age of the automobile, the jet airliner, and the expense account, people traveled constantly for business and pleasure. One out of every five Americans changed his or her place of residence each year. Among the more notable aspects of this geographic mobility was the continued movement of people from the farm to the town and city. Over two-fifths of the counties in the

Selected Statistics, 1945–1980

	1945	1950	1960	1970	1980
Population (millions)	140.5	152.3	180.7	205.1	227.7
Percentage urban	58.6	64.0	69.9	73.5	73.7
Percentage rural	41.4	36.0	30.1	26.5	26.3
Percentage nonwhite	10.0	10.5	11.0	12.5	16.8*
Birthrate (per 1,000 population)	20.4	24.1	23.7	18.4	15.9
Life expectancy					
White	66.8	69.1	70.6	71.7	74.4
Nonwhite	57.7	60.8	63.6	64.6	69.5
High school graduates (percent of population with 4 years of high school or more)	24.5†	34.3	41.1	52.3	66.5
Labor union members (millions)	14.8	15.0	18.1	21.8	22.8
Gross national product (billions, in current dollars)	212.0	285.0	504.0	993.0	2,632.0
Motor vehicle registrations (millions)	31.0	49.2	73.9	108.4	155.7
Advertising expenditures (billions of dollars)	2.9	5.7	11.9	19.6	53.6
Military personnel on active duty (millions)	12.1	2.4	2.5	2.9	2.0

*The sharp increase in percentage nonwhite between 1970 and 1980 is largely attributable to the fact that only 55.6 percent of persons of Spanish descent identified themselves as "white" in 1980, as compared with 93.3 percent who did so in 1970. Most of those who relocated themselves on the race and nationality list chose the category "other," which was apparently their way of saying that their Spanish origin was their full identity.

†Figure for 1940.

Sources: *Historical Statistics of the United States, Colonial Times to 1957; Digest of Educational Statistics, 1970; Statistical Abstract of the United States, 1973;* and *Statistical Abstract of the United States, 1985.*

The Shifting Population, 1980–1985

SOUTH

+737,000
from Northeast

+1.1 million
from North Central

+60,000
from West

WEST

+234,000
from Northeast

+475,000
from North Central

−60,000
to South

NORTH CENTRAL

+50,000
from Northeast

−1.1 million
to South

−475,000
to West

NORTHEAST

−50,000
to North Central

−737,000
to South

−234,000
to West

Source: *New York Times*, November 30, 1985.

United States lost population during the 1960s, and a net out-migration was the experience of about 70 percent of all counties during that decade. As the rural population declined, the nation became increasingly urbanized: 58.9 percent in 1945, 69.9 percent in 1960, and 73.7 percent in 1980. But the most striking feature of the nation's postwar pattern of urbanization was the extraordinary growth of the suburbs.

A regional redistribution of population has also taken place since the early 1940s. The rapid movement of blacks out of the South, a phenomenon that began during World War I, was accelerated during and after World War II. The number of blacks living outside of the southern states increased from 3 million in 1940 to over 7 million in 1960 and to 12.4 million in 1980. Today more than 45 percent of all American blacks live in non-southern states. Some regions grew much more rapidly than others in the postwar period. The population of the Pacific Coast, for example, increased 40.2 percent in the 1950s and that of the Mountain States 35.1 percent in the same decade. During the 1960s the population of the Northeast, by contrast, increased only 9.7 percent and that of the North Central region 9.6 percent, while the percentage gain in the South was 14.2 and that of the West 24.1. The population of the South rose by 20 percent and that of the West by 24 percent during the 1970s, while the Northeast had little measurable growth in the same period.

The massive redistribution of population in the period following the war blurred the old regional identities in the United States; yet regionalism persisted and in some respects found new expression as a result of demographic trends and economic developments. The growing importance of the service sector of the economy and the emergence of new "footloose" industries in search of locations with climatic, scenic, and recreational advantages contributed to the regional pattern of growth. The rapid influx of people into these areas and the dynamic quality of their economies combined with a distinctive life-style to give some of them a peculiar kind of regional character. At the same time, the most clearly identified section in modern America—the South—lost some of its homogeneity and apartness.

CITY AND SUBURB

If regionalism became less important as a distinguishing feature of American life, urbanization became a much more powerful force in the nation's social order. Three-fourths of the American people now live in what the Census Bureau calls Standard Metropolitan Statistical Areas (SMSAs), that is, cities of 50,000 or more people and the surrounding county or counties economically integrated with the city. The number of SMSAs increased from 168 in 1950 to 284 in 1980, and during this period the "metropolitan" portion of the population rose from 56.1 percent to 74.8 percent. The most spectacular example of metropolitan growth was the supercity, or "megalopolis"—great concentrations or clusters of cities so closely situated as to constitute one enormous urban area. The region from Boston to Washington formed one of these "conurbations," and by the 1970s there were ten or twelve others, such as the area stretching from San Francisco and Oakland south to San Jose. It was truly the age of the Metro-American.

Most large American cities after World War II were hard hit by the separation between the central city and the mushrooming suburbs that surrounded them. A mighty exodus from the inner cities to the peripheral areas was soon under way, with the middle class leading the way. Fourteen of the fifteen U.S. cities with more than a million inhabitants actually lost population during the 1950s. Of 13 million dwelling units erected in nonfarm areas between 1946 and 1958, 85 percent were constructed outside the central cities. The suburban trend reflected the great increase that was simultaneously taking place in social mobility. Much of the young, active, and better-educated population left the old parts of the metropolis for the new suburbia. The development of suburbia involved not only the attraction of open and unsettled country, where badly needed homes could be bought or built at reasonable cost, but also a flight from the encroachment of blacks and other newcomers in the old city. Still other factors encouraged the growth of the postwar suburbs: the role of housing developers and speculators, the mortgage policies of federal agencies like the Federal Housing Administration (FHA), the use of the automobile as a major means of transportation, the construction of new highways and freeways, the use of assembly-line construction with standardized materials, and the trend toward the decentralization of business operations.

Some of the suburban developments were mushroom communities that were built almost overnight. One of the best-known builders and merchandisers of new homes in bulk was William Levitt, whose firm built and sold 17,500 homes in Levittown, Long Island, in the postwar years, using mass production methods. Other Levittowns were constructed in Pennsylvania and New Jersey. The first batch of 16,000 houses on 1,100 streets "cut through acreage where but a few months ago local farmers raised only spinach." Penn Kimball described the new Levittown in the *New York Times Magazine:*

Starting from scratch, the Levitts will have converted eight square miles of open farm country into a densely populated community of 70,000. Paved streets, sewer lines, school sites, baseball diamonds, shopping center, parking lots, new railroad station, factory sidings, churches, trunk arteries, newspapers, garden clubs, swimming pools, doctors, dentists and town hall—all conceived in advance, all previously planned in one of the most colossal acts ever of mortal creation.

As a rule the rapidly growing suburbs were neither planned nor controlled. They sprang up randomly in the outlying areas, often unlovely settlements comprising rows of identical houses in the middle of small lots. The suburban sprawl scattered residential developments over large areas, since single-family houses took up much more room than multiple-family dwellings. People usually drove to work—alone or in car pools—and housewives were forced to drive wherever they went and were constantly chauffeuring their children from one activity to another. During the 1950s several sociologists and novelists criticized the life-styles and attitudes of the suburbanites, citing their bourgeois smugness and conformity, the pressures on the commuting father, the child-centered and mother-dominated homes, and the social shortcomings of the suburbs. Criticism of suburban life was summed up in books such as John Keats, *The Crack in the Picture Window* (1957), Richard and Katherine Gordon, *The Split-Level Trap* (1961), and William H. Whyte, *The Organization Man* (1956).

Whatever one thought of the new suburbia, the flight from the inner city continued and the urbanization of the outlying areas went on apace. Suburban institutions such as schools, churches, civic organizations, shopping centers, and organized "culture" groups flourished. By 1960 there were 3,840 suburban shopping centers. In time, moreover, some of the defects of unattractive suburbs were remedied. Trees and shrubs were planted, houses were repaired and enlarged, and even the tract housing usually escaped the fate of becoming new slums. No matter how ordinary their houses or how stultifying their lives may have seemed, most suburban dwellers did have more room, better living accommodations, more fresh air, and more independence than they would have had in the old parts of the metropolis. The suburbs themselves varied, of course, and while they tended to be internally homogeneous, they were typically differentiated along social and economic lines—a circumstance that would create serious obstacles to the development of areawide governments or planning authorities. Although ethnic attachments became more tenuous in the suburbs, suburbanization encouraged the growth of a racially segmented society.

The decay and disorganization in the great cities grew progressively worse as the middle class continued to move out, as the cost of social services mounted, as the tax base shrank, and as crime grew worse. Many of the commercial and cultural institutions also left the central areas. In the early 1970s many cities were reporting the abandonment of houses, despite a housing shortage. In a typical case a speculator would purchase an old house, make a few repairs, and sell it to a low-income family at an inflated price under a mortgage guaranteed by the FHA. Shortly after moving in, the family would find the property in need of extensive repair. Since the new owners were often unable to make such repairs and since they had only a small equity in the property, they would move out, with the house going to the FHA at a substantial loss to the government.

Suburban growth tended to lock nonwhite and poor people into the urban ghettos and in effect to create two cultures. On the other hand, the report of the Advisory Commission on Intergovernmental Relations in the mid-1960s concluded that "in the small and medium sized metropolitan areas outside the Northeast some elements of both high and low socioeconomic status tend to be equally important in both central cities and suburbs, while other low status characteristics predominate in the suburbs and some high status characteristics are more important in the central city." Some big cities became "black" cities. Washington, D.C., was 60 percent black by the early 1970s, while Newark, Gary, Richmond, and Atlanta had a black majority by that time. The terrible conditions in the ghettos and the ethnic concentrations in the nation's large cities were of central importance in the great riots in Watts, Detroit, Newark, and other places in the 1960s. Most metropolitan authorities tried to deal with the urban blight by bulldozing the slums away and building huge high-rise apartments. Critics like Jane Jacobs, in *The Death and Life of Great American Cities* (1961), and Martin Anderson, in *The Federal Bulldozer* (1964), spoke out against the wholesale destruction of neighborhoods and of architectural treasures, called attention to the profit motive that inspired many of the projects, and protested the instrumental role of the federal government in such "urban reform."

Still, notable efforts were made to arrest the decay of the inner city and to rejuvenate the metropolis. Urban renewal was usually the focus of these efforts, and in city after city new skylines arose comprising office buildings, apartment complexes, public housing, and downtown shopping centers. Some attempts were made to retain and restore old buildings that were still basically sound, although new functional but uninspiring buildings too often replaced the old elegant structures. In an effort to eliminate the perennial traffic problem, most cities constructed huge freeways and hundreds of parking lots. A few cities, including San Francisco and Atlanta, laid plans in the 1960s for elaborate new rapid transit systems. There was also evidence of a cultural revival in many American cities. A new breed of mayors appeared, better educated, more sophisticated, and more dedicated to improving the city than the average prewar mayor. In some cases cities made genuine progress. Pittsburgh, for instance, achieved marked success under the leadership of Mayor David Lawrence and an urban reform coalition. The city's central business district was revitalized, and its accomplishments in such activities as housing renewal and pollution control were impressive. Other cities, including Miami, Florida, and Nashville, Tennessee, combined overlapping county and municipal governments by creating new metropolitan systems.

In an environment of "urban catacombs and suburban cellblocks," a few bold spirits dreamed of constructing entirely new cities. A scattering of "new towns," somewhat reminiscent of the Greenbelt towns of the New Deal period, appeared in the 1960s. Perhaps the best-known of these communities is Reston, Virginia, near Washington, D.C. Reston, which was officially opened in December 1965, is an imaginative arrangement of several neighborhoods of clustered "town houses," situated on plazas that are grouped around an artificial lake and open on acres of wooded and terraced land. The houses are reached by walkways inaccessible to automobiles, and the shops and other community facilities are all within easy walking distance.

The small town has not disappeared from the contemporary scene. The census of 1970 identified almost 21,000 incorporated and unincorporated places, only some 7,000 of which were classified as urban. More than half of the country's nonmetropolitan municipalities grew during each of the first three postwar decades. The President's Commission on Population and the American Future reported in the early 1970s that, when asked where they would prefer to live, Americans showed pronounced preferences for small towns and rural areas. Nevertheless, the traditional community based on local attachments, a particular place, and a web of personal relationships has declined. The small town and countryside were steadily being absorbed into a broader national framework. "Rural America's energy," historian Thomas E. Williams has written, "was being consumed in trying to adapt the latest technological and scientific innovations affecting its economy and culture, and in struggling to maintain enough of the trappings of a modern consumer society to hold its young."

CLASS AND STATUS IN POSTWAR AMERICA

The long period of prosperity that began in the early 1940s enabled most Americans to make steady advances in occupational status, income, and standard of living. They appeared to be achieving the "new goals of human happiness and well-being" Franklin Roosevelt had spoken of in his Economic Bill of Rights message of 1944. Many observers echoed former TVA director David E. Lilienthal's statement in the early 1950s that "one finds the physical benefits of our society distributed widely, to almost everyone, with scant regard to status, class, or origin of the individual." In the piping good times of the postwar era, Americans began to feel an exhilarating sense of new possibilities—for better jobs, higher incomes, business ventures, opportunities to enter college or professional school, and changes in social status. The new affluence, it seemed, was boosting occupational and social mobility, stimulating movement up the ladder of wealth and status, and thus reordering the nation's social classes. Many social commentators concluded that income in the United States was becoming better distributed and that the hardening of class distinctions during the previous half-century was being reversed.

Although the benefits of prosperity were widely shared in American society after 1945, a decided concentration of wealth at the top continued, though at a slightly reduced level. Studies of stratification in postwar America showed the presence of marked differentials in wealth and income and in social participation, authority and power, education, health, safety, and legal protection. While lacking an established aristocracy, the United States possessed a discernible upper class, set apart not only by income and wealth but also by position, elegant life-style, membership in exclusive clubs, patronage of private schools, extensive travel, and, in some older regions, connection with old, locally prominent families.

The extent to which political and economic power was monopolized in the postwar period has been a matter of considerable disagreement among social commentators and scholars. It was argued by many political scientists and other social analysts that a "pluralist" system had emerged in the United States, despite the trend toward economic concentration, bureaucracy, and centralized administration. Power in this system was dispersed among numerous voluntary associations, or "veto groups," which balanced each other in a rough equilibrium. Other analysts contended that power was concentrated in the hands of economic and social elites. The sociologist C. Wright Mills asserted in *The Power Elite* (1956) that most people in the American political system were powerless and that a complex elite of political, business, and military leaders ruled the country. Mills stressed elite domination rather than class conflict, but in the 1960s several other writers began to emphasize class differentials and tensions in explaining the concentration of wealth and power in the United States.

Organized blue-collar workers made dramatic gains in economic security and well-being in the years following the war, and some observers even contended that the working class in the United States was becoming indistinguishable from the middle class. This was a myth. While there was substantial working-class social mobility in this period, the most impressive economic and social leveling was the broadening of the middle class. The steady increase in per-capita income, the vast changes in the structure of employment, and the great expansion in the number of college graduates all helped swell the ranks of the middle class.

If the middle register of the American social order was expanding, it also appeared to be increasingly homogenized. Americans, especially the white-collar employee and the suburban dweller, seemed to conform not only in dress, food, and housing, but even in their ideas. Novels such as Sloan Wilson's *The Man in the Gray Flannel Suit* (1956) and sociological studies like C. Wright Mills's *White Collar: The American Middle Classes* (1951) called attention to the loss of individualism, the stuffiness, and the mindless materialism that characterized contemporary middle-class living. The psychologist Erich Fromm, for instance, wrote of the prevalence of individuals with a "marketing orientation," who wanted to avoid having to make choices and eagerly accepted values imposed by the group. Social scientist David Riesman noted how the consumer-oriented economy reinforced the old American tendency to conform to the tastes and attitudes of one's neighbors. Riesman suggested, in *The Lonely Crowd: A Study of the Changing American Character* (1950), that the national character had changed from an "inner-directed" type, responding to a sort of internal gyroscope, to an "other-directed" personality, basically attuned to the mass values of his neighbors.

The greatest split within the middle class was that between its white-collar and blue-collar elements. Millions of industrial workers had become, by any objective measure, members of the middle class, and many skilled workers now earned more than office workers, schoolteachers, and people in the service trades. Yet the entry of skilled and semiskilled workers into the economic middle class did not lead to wholesale adoption of middle-class manners and tastes—of middle-class values and attitudes, social life, methods of rearing children, social roles, and the like. Reporting in 1964 on the results of a study of working-class married couples, the sociologist Mirra Komarovsky wrote, "From all appearances, the working-class style of life—its values, attitudes, institutions—remains in many respects quite distinct from the dominant . . . patterns of contemporary American society."

In the late 1950s, social critics began to point out the persistence of poverty in the United States. But poverty was not "discovered" in the postwar era until the early 1960s. One of the writers who publicized its existence was Michael Harrington, whose popular *The Other America: Poverty in the United States* was published in 1962. Harrington argued that too much had been made of the country's affluence, since, by his count, something like one-fourth of all Americans were living in poverty (which the federal government defined then as a family income below $3,000 a year). As Harrington said, poverty in America "is a culture, an institution, a way of life." By 1969 the number of citizens below the poverty line had declined to 12.1 percent, and it remained at that general level during the 1970s. The poverty rate began to increase in 1980, reaching 15.2 percent in 1983.

The government's definition of poverty was extremely narrow, and in many respects it was a highly arbitrary and unrealistic means of dividing the poor and the nonpoor. A great many people remained barely above the poverty level, although they were frequently somewhat better off than they had been a generation earlier. The economist Leon Keyserling called such people the "deprived Americans." They stood above the poverty line but fell short of the minimum requirements for "a modestly comfortable level of living." In 1964 Keyserling estimated the number of such deprived persons (those with family incomes between $3,500 and $4,500 a year) at 77 million. They included manual laborers, laundry workers, clerks, and many similar low-paid people. While lacking income, moreover, they were expected to provide their families with the amenities that advertising, television, and national folklore had long proclaimed to be middle-class custom.

Yet the absence of militant class consciousness on the part of Americans is striking. At least three-fourths of U.S. adults label themselves as middle class. There is some evidence to support such a generous characterization. Education during the last four decades has been a powerful vehicle of social equality. The treatment of minority and ethnic groups has improved. Some old vestiges of social inequality, such as high society and the servant class, have disappeared. The nation's consumer culture has become pervasive. Americans look, dress, and act more alike than ever before.

RACE AND ETHNICITY

American society in 1945 was divided along racial and ethnic lines as well as by class distinctions. Despite regional variations, the color line was a fact of life everywhere in terms of economic subordination, legal insecurity, and social inferiority. The elaborate structure of Jim Crow proscription was intact throughout the South, and blacks in all parts of the country were the daily victims of social prejudice and discriminatory treatment in employment, housing, and education. Nevertheless, World War II had a notable effect upon American blacks, giving them new experiences, new skills, and new confidence in themselves. The ideological conflict between the United States and the Communist powers caused U.S. policymakers to become more sensitive to the status of Afro-Americans and other minority groups at home. At the same time, the emergence of new nations from colonialism in Asia and Africa, under the direction of nonwhite leaders, had a profound influence upon blacks in the United States. Things were changing—even in the South. Following the Supreme Court's invalidation of the white primary in 1944, Negroes began to take part in that crucially important part of the electoral process in the one-party South. Another kind of change occurred in New York in 1947 when a talented baseball player named Jackie Robinson joined the Brooklyn Dodgers and thus became the first black to play in the major leagues.

The major manifestations of these new currents came in the arena of national politics and were dramatized in the civil rights program sponsored by the Truman administration. In the 1950s the Supreme Court became the main instrument for reform in race relations, and its decisions sparked the civil rights movement during that decade. The momentous school desegregation decision, *Brown v. Board of Education*, was handed down on May 17, 1954. Speaking for a unanimous court, Chief Justice Earl Warren declared that "in the field of public education the doctrine of 'separate but equal' has no place." It would be hard to exaggerate the influence of the *Brown* decision as a dynamic factor in the development of the modern civil rights movement.

Although the progress of school desegregation in the southern region was slow in the late 1950s, the civil rights movement entered a new phase during the second half of the decade, in response both to the *Brown* decision and to the development of new leaders, new organizations, and new tactics that went beyond the NAACP approach of challenging Jim Crow laws in the courts. The starting point of this black protest was the simple, unpremeditated act of a forty-three-year-old Negro seamstress in Montgomery, Alabama, named Rosa Parks. Tired after a hard day's work, Mrs. Parks on December 1, 1955, suddenly decided she would not surrender her bus seat to a white person. She was promptly arrested. The response of the black community could scarcely have been predicted. Under the leadership of the Montgomery Improvement Association, the city's blacks rallied overwhelmingly to support a crippling boycott of the local bus system. The boycott was maintained for almost a year and ended in an impressive victory for blacks after the federal courts invalidated the Alabama segregation laws. The Montgomery bus boycott was a portent of things to come. Its church meetings, singing of old religious hymns, frequent reference to American ideals, nonviolent tactics, and black unity and discipline would be characteristic of the "movement" during the years ahead.

The leader of the Montgomery Improvement Association was an eloquent young Baptist minister named Martin Luther King, Jr. The son of a successful Atlanta preacher and a doctoral graduate of Boston University in theology, King developed during the long months of the Montgomery struggle a program of nonviolent resistance. It was based on the evangelical Christianity in which he had been nurtured and on Mahatma Gandhi's Satyagraha philosophy, to which King had been attracted for some time. King would use "nonviolent direct action" to provoke crisis and "creative tension," which would force the white community to confront its racism. "If we are arrested every day, if we are exploited every day, if we are trampled over every day," the young minister declared at one of the Montgomery mass meetings, "don't ever let anyone pull you so low as to hate them. We must use the weapon of love. We must have compassion and understanding for those who hate us." In 1957 King organized the Southern Christian Leadership Conference, with headquarters in Atlanta, and the influence of his leadership soon spread throughout the South.

Black protest took still another turn on February 1, 1960, when four students from North Carolina Agricultural and Technical College, an all-Negro institution in Greensboro, took seats at a Woolworth lunch counter and refused to move when they were denied service. This new tactic, based on King's nonviolent ethic, quickly caught on; the result was a wave of sit-ins at lunch counters and restaurants, "kneel-ins" at churches, and other challenges to segregated facilities in the South. The sit-ins also produced a new civil rights group, the Student Nonviolent Coordinating Committee (SNCC), and during the next year over 50,000 people were involved in demonstrations in about one hundred cities. SNCC, according to the historian Howard Zinn, "became the militant arm of the civil-rights movement for the next four years." In the spring of 1961 the Congress of Racial Equality (CORE) sponsored "freedom rides" through the South to challenge the continued segregation of interstate buses and terminals.

By the summer of 1963 the equal rights movement had almost reached flood tide. School desegregation had, to some degree at least, breached the defenses even of Mississippi and Alabama. Protests and demonstrations, often accompanied by white retaliatory beatings and bombings, flickered over the South like heat lightning. In April 1963 Martin Luther King led a giant demonstration in Birmingham to protest the city's segregated businesses and institutions. Millions of Americans saw what happened on their television screens when the Birmingham police, under the notorious segregationist T. Eugene "Bull" Connor, turned on the black demonstrators with clubs, police dogs, and high-pressure water hoses. A different kind of demonstration took place in Washington, D.C., on August 28, 1963, when over 200,000 black and white marchers gathered before the Lincoln Memorial in a dramatic gesture of protest against the federal government's long indifference to the plight of black people in America. Dr. King's eloquent address—his inspiring dream of racial equality and brotherhood some day—was a fitting climax to this stirring demonstration. Meanwhile, the work at the grass-roots level continued. SNCC, for example, initiated voter registration drives in Mississippi in 1962 and 1963, and joined other equal rights organizations in planning a great "Mississippi Summer" in 1964.

Ironically, the legal and political progress of the early 1960s served to heighten black expectations that all too often were not realized, leading to greater frustration in the black community. Nothing revealed the growing mood of frustration, bitterness, and anger among blacks more dramatically than the explosion of ghetto riots between 1964 and 1967. These uprisings were largely unplanned, unorganized, and unscheduled, but much of the violence that attended them was directed at such symbols of white power as the police and white-owned businesses. The four-year period of ghetto rebellions began in New York's Harlem in July 1964, with an outburst of arson, looting, and attacks on whites. But it was the following summer's riot in Watts, a black community in Los Angeles, that first aroused the country to the danger of large-scale ghetto violence. Watts erupted five days after President Johnson signed the Voting Rights Act of 1965, and it resulted in the deaths of 34 people, in the arrest of almost 4,000 persons, and in an estimated $35 million in property losses. In the midst of the riot there were cries of "burn, baby, burn" and "kill whitey." The climax came in 1967,

Martin Luther King, Jr., addresses throng from Lincoln Memorial in August 1963 (*Wide World Photos*)

when forty-one major outbreaks occurred, including terrible riots in Newark and Detroit. Joseph Boskin, a historian who has studied the revolt of the urban ghettos, concludes that "the revolts of the mid-1960s—more than the nonviolent movement of Dr. Martin Luther King and the extraordinarily powerful civil rights movement of the early 1960s—directed attention to the anguished plights of millions of Negroes, Puerto Ricans, and Mexican-Americans living in the urban centers of the country."

The ghetto riots were also related to an accelerating shift in the direction and control of the equal rights movement—from interracial collaboration to black domination. The white liberal response to racism seemed to many young blacks to be inadequate, paternalistic, and even hypocritical. "White liberal," as August Meier and Elliott M. Rudwick observe, thus joined "black bourgeoisie" and "Uncle Tom" as "an epithet of opprobrium in the vocabulary of many Negro militants." As the radicalization of the civil rights movement proceeded, as its more militant spokesmen began to emphasize the economic, housing, and educational inequalities oppressing the masses, the demands for "Freedom Now!" became more strident. Dr. King, the most charismatic leader of the civil rights crusade during its nonviolent phase, faced a growing challenge from more militant black leaders. It was this challenge, in part at least, that caused King to become steadily more critical of the American war in Vietnam, which was infused with racial implications, and to plan a mighty "poor people's" march on Washington in the spring of 1968.[1] The minister was killed in Memphis before he could lead the Washington march, and his death as much as any other single event of the late 1960s symbolized the end of a reform movement that had already lost its direction, its unity, and much of its momentum.

One expression of the new black militancy was the slogan "black power," which seems to have been used first by Stokely Carmichael in 1966. Carmichael, the chairman of SNCC, asserted that the black masses suffered from both class exploitation and white racism. He and his successor, H. Rap Brown, rapidly became more radical, more hostile toward whites, and more committed to the concept of black power. Some of the more moderate separatists advocated "black capitalism," the creation of industries and retail businesses operated by Negroes. Others, like Carmichael, urged the establishment of separate political parties. A more revolutionary group known as the Black Panther party was organized in Oakland, California, in 1966 by Huey P. Newton and Bobby Seale. Many of the Black Panthers and black ideologues among college students praised revolutionaries like Ernesto "Che" Guevara, subscribed to a Marxist or Maoist theory of class struggle, and supported the alignment of American blacks with Third World peoples. The Black Muslims were still another black nationalist group. The most magnetic Black Muslim leader was Malcolm X, whose influence grew in the sixties despite his break with Elijah Muhammad in 1963 and his assassination in 1965.

The black power movement nourished the growth of racial consciousness, promoted the development of black pride and black culture (including Afro hair styles, soul food, and Afro-American history), and helped complete a revolution in the thinking of black Americans. But it also did much to fragment the movement for racial reform. Most of the older, established civil rights organizations and black leaders, including Martin Luther King and Roy Wilkins, opposed the separatism of the black power program and continued to espouse nonviolent methods, integration, and political and economic reforms. The new black militancy also encouraged a "white backlash" and frightened many white liberals, who interpreted black power to mean black supremacy, reverse racism, and another form of *apartheid*.

Although the United States in the 1970s remained in many fundamental respects a racist society, a profound social upheaval and a great alteration in race relations had occurred during the previous quarter-century. For the first time since Reconstruction, the U.S.

government had used its authority to stamp out racial discrimination and to integrate Afro-Americans into the larger community. While this precipitated a new crisis in federalism, it resulted in the destruction of the legal structure of segregation, discrimination, and political proscription. Jim Crow was legally banished from the South, and by the spring of 1971 all but 76 of the region's 2,700 school districts had at least begun the desegregation of their pupils and teachers. The percentage of American blacks who had completed high school rose from 38 in 1960 to 58 in 1970. By the early 1980s black students accounted for 10 percent of all college enrollments, as compared with only 4.8 percent in 1965. The black presence in politics assumed increasing importance. Meanwhile, the black middle class was expanding. A growing number of blacks were employed as skilled laborers, managers, and white-collar workers. Twenty-eight percent of all black employees were white-collar workers in 1970, as compared with only 10 percent in 1950.

Even so, the situation for most black Americans was far less encouraging than for other minority groups, including those with ethnic identities. World War II had sharpened the sense of ethnic self-awareness in the United States but at the same time had softened ethnic divisions and animosities. Following the war many people with immigrant backgrounds moved up the occupational ladder, entering white-collar employment and the professions, taking advantage of educational opportunities, and steadily improving their economic and social status. These elements were rapidly assimilated, and fewer and fewer of their number thought of themselves as having any national identification other than American, although many people associated their religious faith with the national origins of their parents and grandparents. Americans of recent immigrant stock were, if anything, more intense in their nationalism than older groups, as many of them demonstrated during the period of McCarthyism. Anti-Semitism, which seemed to increase during the war, declined sharply in the years that followed.

In 1965 Congress completed a major reform of the nation's immigration policy. The act of 1965 abolished the quota system and established an annual limitation of 170,000 immigrants, with no more than 20,000 to come from any one country. The act also set an annual limit of 120,000 per year on Western Hemisphere immigration, which had previously been unrestricted. This legislation changed the composition of the immigrant stream. By the early 1970s Asian immigration exceeded that from Europe, and the largest numbers of newcomers were from Mexico, the Philippines, Cuba, and Korea. Many of those granted entry were professionals, since the act of 1965 gave priority to people with specially needed skills. Of the two major groups of new immigrants, the Asian Americans generally enjoyed better living standards than the Spanish-speaking Americans.

The changing character of immigration to the United States after 1965 no doubt contributed to a heightened ethnic awareness on the part of Americans. It sometimes revived declining ethnic communities, as in the case of San Francisco's Chinatown. But the new ethnicity also reflected a substantial increase in the number of native Americans who had become more conscious of their national origins. This was evident in the activities of organizations formed to further ethnic interests, in the popularity of visits to ancestral homelands, and in a burgeoning literature devoted to ethnic themes. In 1972 Congress took note of these developments by passing the Ethnic Heritage Studies Act, described by its supporters as "a new federal effort to legitimize ethnicity and pluralism in America."

One of the consequences of the black revolution was a broader ethnic crisis that involved demands by other submerged groups for entrance into the major institutions of American society. Many of these groups assumed a more militant position in the 1960s, manifested renewed interest in cultural nationalism, and began to advocate brown or yellow or red power. This was the case with Mexican-Americans, who constituted the nation's second largest minority. While composing only 2.3 percent of the national population in 1960, they numbered almost 3.5 million and made up 12 percent of the population in California, Texas, New Mexico, Arizona, and Colorado. By 1980 the Hispanic population of those five states had increased to almost 9 million. The postwar period witnessed continued migration from Mexico to the United States, increasing self-awareness and recognition among the newcomers of the cultural values of the Mexican heritage, some improvement in the social conditions of la raza,[2] and eventually the development of movements by Mexican-Americans for a greater share in the American way of life through an insistence on equality of economic opportunity, education, and full civil rights.

The programs and organizations that sprang up in the 1960s were known collectively as the Chicano movement. It was given direction by a number of new leaders, ranging from moderate advocates of nonviolence to fiery militants. The first Chicano to achieve national recognition was César Chávez of California, who organized the National Farm Workers' Association in 1963. Chávez led a boycott of California grape growers between 1965 and 1969 that forced the producers to recognize the union and to bargain with it. The "Huelga" drive and other strikes of the *obreros* led by Chávez in the vineyards and vegetable fields symbolized and helped mobilize the Chicano revolt. Meanwhile, Reies López Tijerina of New Mexico organized the separatist and millennial *Alianza Federal de Mercedes* (Federal Alliance of Land Grants); Rodolfo "Corky" Gonzales led the Crusade for Justice in Colorado; and José Angel Gutierrez established a new political party in Texas known as *La Renza Unida*. A cultural separatist wing of "La Causa" also emerged, demanding bilingual education in the public schools, Chicano courses, and the like. Gradually Mexican-Americans began to exert greater influence in local and state politics.

The plight of the oldest of all Americans, the Indians, represented a tragic and poignant national wrong. By the early 1970s, over 300,000 "urban" Indians had left the reservations and were living in the nation's cities, often in wretched poverty. Approximately 477,000 Indians remained on the reservations, occupying a kind of no-man's-land, both subject to the guardianship of the Bureau of Indian Affairs (BIA) as a kind of "dependent nation" and excluded from many rights held by other Americans. The reservations lacked industries and good schools, and the Indian unemployment rate was frequently over 50 percent. During the late 1960s and early 1970s Indian protests over the problem of alienated lands and the policies of the BIA mounted, to the accompaniment of renewed interest in an Indian culture and heritage. Books like Vine Deloria's *Custer Died for Your Sins* (1969) deplored the sad condition of the Amerindians. Other works pointed up Indian demands for the retention of a separate culture. The seizure of Alcatraz Island, the capture of Wounded Knee, South Dakota, and the occupation of the BIA offices in Washington, D.C., by Indian militants provided dramatic evidence of yet another minority's rebellion. While the protests were not very fruitful, the Indians did regain some of their ancestral lands, and by the mid-1970s the federal government seemed to recognize that many of them did not want to be assimilated into American society.

Minorities, *U.S. News & World Report* noted in 1984, "are putting their imprint on every aspect of American life." The writer went on to say that "blacks, Japanese, Puerto Ricans, Koreans, West Indians and Chinese Americans mingle in what were once all-white neighborhoods. . . . Sushi bars sit next to taco stands. Oriental and Mexican eateries are among the fastest-growing segments of the restaurant business." These comments reflected a new openness in American society and a wide range of new options available to ethnic and religious groups in the United States. The old melting-pot idea had given way to the concept of ethnic and religious pluralism, to the kind of society Senator Hubert H. Humphrey once described as "a rich tapestry of separate strands woven together." "Out of many, one" was an ideal that Americans had never achieved. But since the end of World War II, the social critic Charles E. Silberman writes, "the gap between ideal and reality has been substantially narrowed, and for some groups almost completely closed, for . . . the United States has become a genuinely multiethnic, multireligious, and, increasingly, a multiracial society."

THE SEARCH FOR COMMUNITY

"Around one's home and the places where one shops and the corridors through which one travels," Professor Richard A. Lamanna has written, "there is for each of us a public sphere wherein our sense of security, self-esteem, and propriety is either reassured or jeopardized by the people and events we encounter." Lamanna also observed that at the very time people were drawing physically closer together and becoming increasingly dependent upon one another, they were "drifting toward an extreme form of individualism and privatization of social behavior which undermines the foundations of communal life." Do Americans value individualism over citizenship? The sociologist Robert N. Bellah has recently suggested that "over time, and especially since World War II, the traditions of atomistic individualism have grown stronger, while the traditions of the individual in society have grown weaker. The sense of cohesive community is lost."

One of the things that tended to cast Americans adrift was the growing instability of the family. Not only has the extended family with deep roots in a particular locality become a victim of modern mobility, but the nuclear family itself has been subjected to heightened strain and has undergone considerable change. On the surface, at least, the late forties and fifties seemed to be a time of well-being for the American family. The baby boom was accompanied by a renewed emphasis on family life, while the "feminine mystique" fostered the creation of competent, happy women devoted to child-rearing. The interest many people displayed in their homes, gardens, and the "do-it-yourself" vogue suggested an extreme preoccupation with the cares and rewards of private life. Nevertheless, the mood of "togetherness" in the 1950s did not altogether conceal a broad uneasiness about the disintegration of the family as an organic and healthy institution.

This vague anxiety was related to a number of significant social forces, including the massive uprooting of Americans during World War II; the accelerating mobility that characterized U.S. life; the increasing size, complexity, and bureaucratization in almost every aspect of economic and social endeavor; and the growth of secularism and the weakening of religious sanctions. Families became decentralized, and the nation's affluence itself encouraged a phenomenon demographers called "uncoupling." Among the disruptive trends in the postwar years were earlier marriages, more births out of wedlock, and an increase in the rate of divorce. Young people and older folk set up separate one-person households in increasing numbers. Relations between parents and children became less and less certain as the youth developed their own values in a rapidly changing society. Juvenile delinquency increased. The training of children was increasingly left to the schools and other outside agencies. The economic system made husband and wife much more independent of each other than was true in earlier periods.

Marriage and the traditional role of housewife became steadily less fulfilling to American women, a tendency that millions of men found difficult to comprehend. All through the 1950s, John Brooks wrote in 1966, "the girls seem to have been sneaking away from diapers and pacifiers to nice, calm, stimulating offices, even though the popular books and magazines of the time did everything possible to make them feel guilty about it." The process picked up speed in the sixties and seventies. By the early 1970s more than half of all married women were working outside the home, a great many because of economic necessity and many others because of their families' middle-class aspirations. Even women with preschool children were working in large numbers. About a third of the women with children under six years of age were working for pay. Meanwhile, women—and men—were increasingly less willing to tolerate an unhappy marriage. Individual costs and benefits assumed greater importance in intimate personal relations, which became more contractual and often more fragile. The combination of more education for women, a greater percentage of women in the labor force, freer attitudes toward sex, and the sway of youth culture seemed likely to alter still further attitudes toward marriage and childbearing in the United States.

Following the war, the voluntary group became more than ever before the primary institution for maintaining American society or reforming it. The ordinary citizen was likely to belong to voluntary associations of several types, and these associational establishments performed substantial cultural, social, civic, and economic functions. There were hundreds of thousands of these private groups—

trade associations and chambers of commerce; agricultural and horticultural federations; labor unions; professional societies; associations of scholars, scientists, engineers, civil servants, and military officers; groups involved in public health and social welfare; athletic associations; leagues of lobbyists; and so forth. Service clubs flourished in the postwar decades as the older fraternal societies and secret orders declined. All of these associations, Rowland Berthoff suggests, "indulged in rituals that were merely symbolic of the social integrity of the group, but more than ever such private organizations carried the weight of the cultural, philanthropic, and even spiritual concerns of American society—of nearly everything that was neither narrowly economic nor technically governmental." At the same time, the voluntary associations have tended to become special-interest groups primarily concerned with defending the rights of their members rather than working for the good of society.

The ethnic protest movements of the 1960s, the insurgency of students and of women, and the development of a counterculture all demonstrated, in one way or another, the search for new forms of community in a swiftly changing society. The search took many different directions. Some people worked hard to revitalize and adapt established institutions like the church. Others launched campaigns to renew their neighborhoods, and the antipoverty programs of the sixties were community-centered endeavors calling for neighborhood participation. The "hippies" who were attracted by the thousands in the mid-1960s to the Haight-Ashbury district of San Francisco and to places like the East Village in New York City were searching for alternative ways of living. The students who attacked established institutions and the military-industrial complex in the late sixties were rebelling against the anonymity of contemporary society and the impersonality and bureaucracy of the huge multiversities. Encounter and sensitivity groups, institutes like Esalen, and rock concerts were widely regarded as new forms of communion.

The emergence of the communal movement provides another example of the revolt against modern urban-industrial society and traditional ideas about community life. The *New York Times*, reporting the results of a survey it had made, estimated in December 1970 that there were at least 2,000 communes in the United States. During the early seventies there were perhaps as many as 3,000 scattered over the country, with possibly 150,000 people involved. Strange and wonderful visitors descended on areas like the mountains of New Mexico in search of "community." The communes were of many types—rural, urban, working, cooperative, and so on—and they varied in population from about 10 to 100 or more

Exodus from a rock music festival, White Lake, New York, August 1969 (*The Bettmann Archive*)

members. Although they frequently rejected modern technology and creature comforts, discarded the nuclear family, and displayed a good deal of anti-intellectualism, they also emphasized many traditional American values such as individualism, local autonomy, self-sufficiency, open space, and nature.

American society remained essentially conservative in the years after 1945, but it was challenged by the upheaval of the 1960s and the Vietnam War, which produced fragmentation, alienation, and confrontation. Nor was that all. Social conflict growing out of racial prejudice, ethnic and minority discrimination, extensive poverty, and the disappearance of older forms of community left its scars. Although people talked about the need for citizen involvement, the complexity of modern society frequently overwhelmed them. A great many Americans no longer thought they could make a difference in a complex society. Still, there was evidence of continuity, stability, and resilience in U.S. society. And there is reason to think that support has grown for a social order based on cultural diversity and mutual respect among many distinctive social groups.

NOTES

1. See pp. 299–300.
2. A term connoting ethnic solidarity and a sense of common destiny.

SUGGESTIONS FOR FURTHER READING

As yet there is no adequate social history of the United States since 1945, but Richard Polenberg, *One Nation Divisible: Class, Race, and Ethnicity in the United States Since 1938* (1980), illuminates the nation's recent society and culture by focusing on significant patterns of division. Two general works, *The Urban Nation, 1920–1980* (rev. ed., 1981), by George E. Mowry and Blaine A. Brownell, and *Another Chance: Postwar America, 1945–1968* (1981), by James Gilbert, are good on many aspects of postwar social life. William Issel, *Social Change in the United States, 1945–1983* (1985), examines the effects of capitalism on American society. Rowland Berthoff's *An Unsettled People: Social Order and Disorder in American History* (1971) provides a perceptive background to the postwar era. Max Lerner's *America as a Civilization: Life and Thought in the United States Today* (1957) is a broad-ranging social commentary useful for the first postwar decade. Social trends continuing into the 1960s are discussed in John Brooks, *The Great Leap: The Past Twenty-five Years in America* (1966), while statistical information for American society at particular points in recent years is contained in Ben J. Wattenberg, *This U.S.A.: An Unexpected Family Portrait of 194,067,296 Americans Drawn from the Census* (1965); E. J. Kahn, Jr., *The American People: The Findings of the 1970 Census* (1974); and Andrew Hacker (ed.), *U/S: A Statistical Portrait of the American People* (1983). Andrew J. Cherlin, *Marriage, Divorce, Remarriage* (1981), is also useful.

For the persistence of regionalism as manifested in the contemporary American South, see John C. McKinney and Edgar T. Thompson (eds.), *The South in Continuity and Change* (1965); John Shelton Reed, *The Enduring South: Subcultural Persistence in Mass Society* (1972); and Charles P. Roland, *The Improbable Era: The South Since World War II* (rev. ed., 1976).

A good place to begin the study of postwar urbanization and metropolitan life is Zane L. Miller's *The Urbanization of Modern America: A Brief History* (1973). See also Blake McKelvey's *The Emergence of Metropolitan America, 1915–1966* (1969) and Sam Bass Warner's *The Urban Wilderness: A History of the American City* (1972). *The Emerging City: Myth and Reality* (1962), by Scott A. Greer, deals with the leadership, governance, and distribution of power in contemporary American cities. Mark I. Gelfand, *A Nation of Cities: The Federal Government and Urban America, 1933–1965* (1975), is a valuable study of national policy. Among the most instructive of the many books on the urban crisis and efforts to revitalize the modern city are Scott A. Greer, *Urban Renewal and American Cities: The Dilemma of Democratic Intervention* (1966); Jeanne R. Lowe, *Cities in a Race with Time: Progress and Poverty in America's Renewing Cities* (1967); and Daniel Patrick Moynihan (ed.), *Toward a National Urban Policy* (1970). Jane Jacobs offers a sharp critique of modern urban culture and the work of urban planners in *The Death and Life of Great American Cities* (1961). Different historical approaches are revealed in Roy Lubove, *Twentieth-*

Century Pittsburgh: Government, Business, and Environmental Change (1969), and Stephen Thernstrom, The Other Bostonians: Poverty and Progress in the American Metropolis, 1880–1970 (1973).

The rapid growth of suburbs following World War II is illuminated by Robert C. Wood, Suburbia: Its People and Their Politics (1958); William M. Dobriner, Class in Suburbia (1963); Herbert J. Gans, The Levittowners: Ways of Life and Politics in a New Suburban Community (1967); Scott Donaldson, The Suburban Myth (1969); and Kenneth T. Jackson, Crabgrass Frontier: The Suburbanization of America (1985). Auguste C. Spectorsky, The Exurbanites (1955), contains a wry description of some inhabitants of the belt just beyond suburbia. Excellent in showing the impact of mass society on village life is Arthur J. Vidich and Joseph Bensman, Small Town in Mass Society: Class, Power, and Religion in a Rural Community (1960). Maurice R. Stein, The Eclipse of Community: An Interpretation of American Studies (1960), is a revealing treatment of several well-known community studies. For the recent commune movement, see Ron E. Roberts, The New Communes: Coming Together in America (1971), and Laurence R. Veysey, The Communal Experience: Anarchist and Mystical Counter Cultures in America (1973).

Several of the dimensions of class and status in recent America are revealed in Peter M. Blau and Otis Dudley Duncan, The American Occupational Structure (1967); Ferdinand Lundberg, The Rich and the Super-Rich: A Study in the Power of Money Today (1968); Richard Parker, The Myth of the Middle Class: Notes on Affluence and Equality (1972); Michael Harrington, The Other America: Poverty in the United States (1962); and Herman P. Miller, Rich Man, Poor Man (1971).

The literature on the civil rights movement and black protest is extensive. Among the best general works are C. Vann Woodward, The Strange Career of Jim Crow (3d rev. ed., 1974); Louis Lomax, The Negro Revolt (1963); Benjamin Muse, The American Negro Revolution: From Nonviolence to Black Power, 1963–1967 (1968); Anthony Lewis, Portrait of a Decade: The Second American Revolution (1964); and Harvard Sitkoff, The Struggle for Black Equality, 1954–1980 (1981). Richard Kluger, Simple Justice: The History of Brown v. Board of Education and Black America's Struggle for Equality (1976), is a splendid account of the school desegregation cases. But see also G. Edward White, Earl Warren: A Public Life (1982), and J. Harvie Wilkinson III, From Brown to Bakke: The Supreme Court and School Integration, 1954–1978 (1979). The reaction of the South in the 1950s is analyzed in Numan V. Bartley, The Rise of Massive Resistance: Race and Politics in the South during the 1950's (1969); Neil R. McMillen, The Citizens' Council: Organized Resistance to the Second Reconstruction, 1954–64 (1971); and Donald R. Matthews and James W. Prothro, Negroes and the New Southern Politics (1966). Steven F. Lawson's Black Ballots: Voting Rights in the South, 1944–1969 (1976) is a good study of the campaigns for voting rights in the South. A different kind of black struggle is recounted by Jules Tygiel, Baseball's Great Experiment: Jackie Robinson and His Legacy (1983).

For Martin Luther King, Jr., see the biographies by David L. Lewis, King: A Critical Biography (2nd ed., 1978), and Stephen B. Oates, Let the Trumpet Sound: The Life of Martin Luther King, Jr. (1982), and King's books Stride Toward Freedom: The Montgomery Story (1958) and Why We Can't Wait (1964). Merrill Proudfoot, Diary of a Sit-in (1962), and William H. Chafe,

Civilities and Civil Rights: Greensboro, North Carolina, and the Black Struggle for Freedom (1980), throw light on black protest. August Meier and Elliott M. Rudwick, *CORE: A Study in the Civil Rights Movement, 1942–1968* (1973), and Clayborne Carson, *In Struggle: SNCC and the Black Awakening of the 1960s* (1981), are good studies of two key organizations. A major campaign in the movement is dealt with in David J. Garrow's *Protest at Selma: Martin Luther King, Jr., and the Voting Rights Act of 1965* (1978) and Charles E. Fager's *Selma, 1965* (1974).

Ethnicity as a factor in postwar America is considered in Milton M. Gordon, *Assimilation in American Life: The Role of Race, Religion, and National Origins* (1964); Nathan Glazer and Daniel Patrick Moynihan, *Beyond the Melting Pot: The Negroes, Puerto Ricans, Jews, Italians, and Irish of New York City* (2nd ed., 1970); and Nathan Glazer, *Ethnic Dilemmas, 1964–1982* (1983). Charles E. Silberman's *A Certain People: American Jews and Their Lives Today* (1985) is a perceptive study of the dramatic changes in the position of Jews in the United States since World War II and a vivid illustration of contemporary American pluralism. For the so-called white ethnics, see Arthur B. Shostak, *Blue-Collar Life* (1969), and Michael Novak, *The Rise of the Unmeltable Ethnics: Politics and Culture in the Seventies* (1972). Other minority groups are described by Matt S. Meier and Feliciano Rivera, *The Chicanos: A History of Mexican Americans* (1972); Peter Matthiessen, *Sal Si Puedes: Cesar Chavez and the New American Revolution* (1973); and Stan Steiner, *The New Indians* (1968).

CHAPTER NINE

The Culture of Affluence and Anxiety

AMERICAN CULTURE was profoundly influenced by the long-sustained prosperity of the postwar period and by the awareness of living under the shadow of a global holocaust. Many traditional values persisted in the new era, while long-time trends like secularization continued and were frequently accelerated. But there were also powerful new forces that affected the nation's culture, including the development of the mass media, particularly television. None of the new trends was more remarkable than the rise of science, which swiftly attained a position of almost universal prestige and popular faith. In the 1960s a much-publicized counterculture began to emerge that savagely attacked established cultural patterns and sought alternative life-styles and values. Meanwhile, the literary scene changed drastically in the quarter-century following the war, reflecting not so much the realities of the evolving American society as the subtle shifts in fundamental assumptions, outlook, and values.

EDUCATION: THE TROUBLED CRUSADE

Education in the United States at the end of the war had the strengths and weaknesses of a highly decentralized, pyramidal system. The nation's schools also faced a number of pressing problems, including a teacher shortage, low salaries, a desperate need for new buildings and equipment, overcrowded colleges and universities, and uncertainty about funding sources. In the absence of broad federal support, there was no effective means of equalizing educational funds, and thousands of small, poorly equipped schools continued to exist. While engaging in a spirited debate over the nature and solution of these problems, Americans set out to expand and improve their schools. This postwar educational expansion rested on the traditional American belief in the social utility of as much education as possible for everyone, a widely shared view that was almost a public creed. There were also more tangible factors in the growth of the schools: continuing prosperity, the broadening middle class, the baby boom, the G.I. Bill of Rights, and the demands of an increasingly complex society in a technological era.

Almost every year witnessed more people in attendance at every level of education. The number of children attending public schools increased from 25 million in 1945 to almost 45 million in 1975. Expenditures for public schools during the 1950s rose from $6 billion to $15 billion a year, and the proportion of the gross national product devoted to education steadily increased. Teachers' salaries enjoyed marked improvement, the average expenditure per pupil went up substantially, the school term was lengthened, and facilities were gradually improved. College and professional-school enrollments boomed. By 1970 almost 60 million students were attending schools in the United States, and the nation's expenditures for education totaled more than $78 billion annually. Three out of every four American youths were completing high school, two out of every five were going to college, and nearly a million persons were earning a college or university degree every year.

During the 1950s the public schools became the subject of widening criticism, much of it by educators. The criticism centered on the charge that the educational system lacked intellectual vitality and discipline, that it emphasized mediocrity at the expense of excellence, and that it promoted athletics and social activities rather than basic academic work. A spate of books and articles challenged the rationale of a "child-centered" school system and pointed out the essential mindlessness of the "life adjustment" doctrine associated with "progressive education." Such books as Albert Lynd's *Quackery in the Public Schools* (1953) and Arthur E. Bestor's *Educational Wastelands* (1953) proclaimed their themes in their titles. Later in the decade James B. Conant, former president of Harvard University, wrote a widely read volume, *The American High School Today* (1959). Conant found fault with the current educational methodology for slighting the teaching of English grammar and composition, for neglecting foreign languages, and for failing to meet the needs of either the brightest or the dullest students.

Russia's spectacular success in launching the two *Sputnik* satellites in the autumn of 1957 had a galvanizing effect upon American thinking about the school system, for it dramatized the apparent superiority of Soviet scientists, highlighted the fact that the USSR spent a larger percentage of its income on education than did the United States, and increased the influence of the critics of the educational system at home. Most people now agreed that the national interest depended upon improvements in the quality of U.S. schools, and the demands for federal action grew more intense. *Sputnik* undoubtedly contributed to the passage of the National Defense Education Act (NDEA) of 1958. This legislation provided loan funds for college students as well as fellowships for advanced study in new and expanded programs. It also sought to strengthen the instruction in mathematics, the sciences, and foreign languages at the elementary and secondary school levels. Federal aid, as well as the grants made by such private foundations as the Fund for the Advancement of Education, encouraged reforms in teacher training methods, better facilities, and new courses in the natural sciences, foreign languages, and other fields. Innovators like Jerome S. Bruner demonstrated novel approaches to learning, and the school curriculum soon began to include the "new math," the "new biology," and so forth.

School Enrollment, by Level of Instruction: 1960–1983

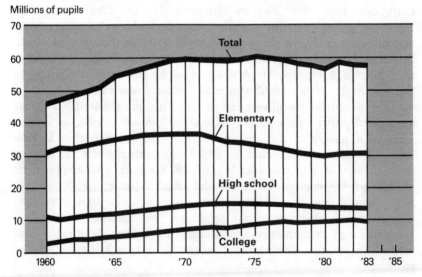

Source: U.S. Bureau of the Census, *Statistical Abstract of the United States, 1985* (Washington, D.C., 1984), p. 127.

Although federal aid to education became an established fact in the 1960s, it was still far too small to solve the financial problems of the schools. In the late sixties and early seventies, city after city rejected bond issues designed to finance the schools, and the courts in California and several other states struck down the heavy reliance on property taxes in educational expenditures. Meanwhile, the performance of the average public school continued to leave much to be desired. The writer Charles E. Silberman, in conducting a three-year investigation of the schools in the late 1960s, found overwhelming evidence of repressive and arbitrary rules, the dehumanizing of learning, and what he called the "killing of dreams and the mutilation of spirits." He was dismayed to discover "what grim, joyless places most American schools are, how oppressive and petty are the rules by which they are governed, how intellectually sterile and aesthetically barren the atmosphere, what an appalling lack of civility obtains on the part of teachers and principals, what contempt they unconsciously display for children as children."

Crisis and reform were recurrent features of the educational scene in the years after 1945. During the 1960s, in an era of curriculum reform and increasing federal involvement, the nation's schools were buffeted by social unrest. Schools and colleges were subjected to new political pressures and found themselves having to deal with new responsibilities such as affirmative action programs and altered mechanisms of governance. Nor did the level of popular esteem and professional criticism give educators much cause for satisfaction. In 1975 the College Entrance Examination Board revealed that scores on the Scholastic Aptitude Test (SAT), taken each year by more than a million high school seniors, had declined steadily since 1964. Several reports over the next few years documented the alarming proportions of the school system's deficiencies. The National Commission on Excellence in Education concluded its report, *A Nation at Risk* (1983), by calling attention to "a rising tide of mediocrity" sweeping American schools. By the early 1980s, education had become a prominent issue in politics, one result of which was a flurry of state legislation and special programs designed to raise educational standards and achieve more effective schools.

The development of higher education after 1945 in the United States was nothing less than spectacular. College and university enrollment more than doubled between 1940 and 1960, climbing to almost 4 million by the latter year and to more than 12 million by 1980. The growth of community and junior colleges, once scorned as "high schools with ashtrays," was especially notable in the 1960s. By 1980 approximately 4.5 million students were attending institutions of this type. Adult education also flourished; by 1984 about 23 million people were involved in continuing education programs. The inundation of the campuses in the postwar years created enormous problems, including the need for more classrooms, dormitories, library facilities, and laboratory equipment. But the needs were somehow met, and state and private support of higher education became steadily more impressive. The federal government also contributed indispensable assistance, first in the form of the G.I. Bill and various foreign exchange programs and later through the NDEA legislation and the education measures of the sixties.

The democratization of higher education, paralleling the growth of the middle class, went a long way to end the old exclusiveness of the nation's colleges. University professors after mid-century were increasingly drawn from new-stock Americans and other new additions to the middle class. With the expansion of higher education, a college degree became a prerequisite for a growing number of occupations. One study found, for example, that almost 60 percent of the big business leaders of 1952 were college graduates, as compared with 30 percent a generation earlier. Meanwhile, the universities became more intimately involved in the larger community: in the social application of their scientific and social science investigations, in their cultural programs, and in big-time football and other athletic events.

Many educational institutions became huge "multiversities"—impersonal, mechanical in approach, bureaucratic. Student demonstrations at the University of California, Berkeley, in 1964 and on many other campuses in later years were, in part at least, protests against enormous classes, a routinized approach to learning, a sterile lecture system, and the neglect of individual student development. The ferment of the 1960s, including the Vietnam War, had a pronounced impact upon colleges and universities. Students seemed to become more socially conscious, and they began to demand a greater voice in the operation of the universities. A student rebellion swept the country during the late 1960s. This movement resulted in greater student involvement in academic decision making, the relaxing of in loco parentis rules, the introduction of new courses, and increased enrollment from minority groups. Still, the student movement did not radically transform American institutions of higher education. As the campus upheavals subsided after 1970, there was mounting concern over the "new depression in higher education," a consequence of the leveling off in the rate of growth of the college-age population and of the economic recession of the Nixon and Ford years.

No aspect of contemporary intellectual progress can compare with the dramatic emergence of science in American life. By 1965 a million Americans held scientific degrees, and the annual output of new science Ph.D.'s was about 8,000. Whereas the federal government spent a paltry $50 million for scientific research and development in 1939, it was allocating approximately $15 billion for such work by the mid-1960s. An incredible proliferation of scientific literature resulted from the publication of hundreds of thousands of scientific papers every year. Employment opportunities continually increased for engineers, scientists, and technicians. The university was central to this "knowledge revolution," which proved to be a major factor in the dynamism of the U.S. economy and in reshaping the nation's society, including its occupational structure.

The great accumulation of significant new scientific knowledge involved basic research, the application of scientific findings to new processes and products, and the commercial development of new technology. Among the more notable developments by American scientists were the advances in nuclear physics, the progress of medical science, the rise of jet air transportation, the spectacular successes in exploring outer space, and the perfection of the electronic computer. Americans won more than their share of the prestigious Nobel Prizes in science and medicine. The effects of science and technology on contemporary America are suggested by John Brooks's device of following a hypothetical man through a hypothetical day:

> We begin with him having slept in an apartment house protected against burglars by a closed television circuit, being awakened by his clock radio as he lies under his thermostat-controlled electric blanket, arising to clean his teeth with his electric toothbrush, putting on his drip-dry shirt and his suit with no-iron pants, crossing the vinyl floor of the kitchen to get the frozen orange juice out of the deep freeze and switch on the automatic coffee-maker; and then, a few minutes later, lighting up the day's first charcoal-filter cigarette.

Scientists in the postwar era were increasingly called upon by government, business, and private organizations for their expertise and assistance in solving problems and formulating policies. Universities became heavily involved in governmental and commercial enterprises. These trends reflected what has been called the "dialogue between science and American society." A conspicuous illustration is afforded by the computer revolution. The writer Otto Friedrich has recently suggested that "the enduring American love affairs with the automobile and the television set are now being transformed into a giddy passion for the personal computer. This passion is partly fad, partly a sense of how life could be made better, partly a gigantic sales campaign."

Whatever its failures and inadequacies, the American educational system was transformed during the decades following the Second World War. As time passed, increasing numbers of children attended school, more attractive and better equipped school buildings appeared, more teachers acquired degrees, classes declined in size, and curricula, methods, and materials became more diversified. The drive to consolidate small schools and school districts was largely successful, bringing some benefits but also making most schools larger, more impersonal, and more bureaucratized. Noteworthy progress was made in the crusade for equal educational opportunity. The gap in the educational attainment between whites and blacks was substantially narrowed. Educational issues during this period moved into the arena of national politics, and the operation of the schools tended to shift from the traditional local-state axis to a state-federal axis. "In the crusade against ignorance," Diane Ravitch observes in concluding her history of American education since 1945, "there have been no easy victories, but no lasting defeats."

THE CHANGING SHAPE OF AMERICAN RELIGION

Religion prospered in the post–World War II era. Church membership increased from 64.5 million (49 percent of the total population) in 1940 to 125 million (64 percent) in 1965 and to 140 million (60 percent) in 1982. Almost all religious bodies added to their membership during this period, the Pentecostal groups, Southern Baptists, and Roman Catholics being especially noteworthy for their rates of growth. By 1972 the membership of the Roman Catholic Church stood at 48.2 million. The various Baptist churches counted 27 million members, the Methodists 13 million, and the Lutherans 8.8 million. Jewish congregations comprised 5.6 million members. Most Americans were prepared, in response to an inquiry of the mid-fifties, to identify themselves in religious terms: 68 percent as Protestants, 23 percent as Catholics, and 4 percent as Jews. Gallup polls taken in 1975 and 1976 indicated that on Sundays 41 percent of the nation's adult population went to church, that 94 percent of those questioned claimed to believe in God, that 69 percent believed in life after death, and that 34 percent had undergone a "born again" experience.

Among the more remarkable aspects of the religious landscape in the early postwar years was the vogue of a "peace-of-mind" religion which seemed to result, in some measure, from the shadow of the bomb, the frustrations of the cold war, and the search for relief from social ills. The "cult of reassurance" was reflected in a rash of inspirational books such as Fulton J. Sheen's *Peace of Soul* (1949) and

Norman Vincent Peale's *The Power of Positive Thinking* (1952), in spectacular films like *The Ten Commandments*, in religious songs like "I Believe" and "The Man Upstairs," and in "Religion in American Life" campaigns which were popular on college campuses. Even theologians seemed to foster the idea that the church's role was, as one scholar has said, "to translate the Gospel into the pieties of contemporary culture." Closely related to these developments was a new interest in revivalism and the extraordinary phenomenon of Billy Graham's mass conversions. Graham, a clean-cut and eloquent young Baptist minister, spoke with passionate sincerity and powerful effect, reasserting fundamentalist doctrine in a modern idiom. Graham led one great crusade after another for Christ, speaking for example to 60,000 people at one time in New York's Yankee Stadium. He also made effective use of radio and television in his popular evangelism.

Religion in America clearly reflected and was part of the popular culture. It was also boosted by politicians, including top leaders in Washington, which led writer William Lee Miller to speak of "piety on the Potomac" in describing the 1950s. President-elect Eisenhower declared in late 1952, for instance, that "our government makes no sense unless it is founded on a deeply felt religious faith—and I don't care what it is!" In 1954 Congress lent its support to the new piety, adding the phrase "under God" to the pledge of allegiance and during the next year making it mandatory that all U.S. currency bear the inscription "In God We Trust." Some contemporaries lamented the fact that all creeds seemed to be submerged in a kind of "civil religion," which might be called the "American Way of Life." The emphasis seemed to be humanistic and secular.

Will Herberg has noted that, fundamentally, one's "ultimate, over-all way of life is one's religion." In *Protestant—Catholic—Jew*, an influential book published in 1955, Herberg suggested that the impressive growth of religion following World War II was part of a search for identity, especially by third-generation Americans in a rapidly changing social order where ethnic and other distinctions seemed to be disappearing. Thus, while the church enabled Americans to maintain some nominal distinctions, it also contributed to the homogenizing of the society. A kind of "national religion" had emerged, based on good fellowship and good works. "By and large," Herberg wrote, "the religion which actually prevails among Americans today has lost much of its authentic Christian (or Jewish) content." Much of the church growth took place in the suburbs, and to a considerable extent the new institutional strength of the churches was a product of suburbia. The expansion of the middle class was particularly significant for American Catholics, whose rapid economic and social advancement ended the class disparity that had previously set them apart from the mainstream Protestants.

At a more fundamental level the return to religion in contemporary America mirrored an alteration in outlook—a decline of optimism, of faith in progress, of confidence in man's ability to play a constructive role in the world. Inspired partly by European theologians, including the Protestant Karl Barth, the Catholic Jacques Maritain, and the Jew Martin Buber, what came to be known as neo-orthodoxy emphasized the need to return to genuine religion and to basic Judaic-Christian values. American theologians like Reinhold Niebuhr and Paul Tillich, while not denying the desirability of social reform, pointed to the inadequacies of the progressive "social gospel." No longer optimistic about the perfectibility of man, they sought to develop modern versions of Calvinism and other old orthodoxies. Their impact in the United States was considerable, and for a while at mid-century neo-orthodoxy became fashionable in certain religious quarters.

More significant in the long run, however, was the new vitality demonstrated by the ecumenical movement in the United States. One manifestation of this movement was the merger of several important Protestant denominations, including two branches of the Society of Friends in 1955, the Congregational Christian Churches and the Evangelical and Reformed Church in 1957, the Methodists and Evangelical United Brethren in 1968, and the final Presbyterian union in 1983. The National Council of the Churches of Christ, the main vehicle for interdenominational cooperation, grew rapidly after its reorganization in 1950. American religious groups also took an active part in the World Council of Churches, which was organized in 1948 and held its Second Assembly in Evanston, Illinois, in 1954. The movement received support from the Vatican as well as from most American Protestant and Jewish leaders.

In spite of these trends, religious division and conflict had by no means disappeared from the American scene. Catholics might be more fully assimilated into the national culture than ever before, but they were still resented and distrusted by many Americans. Organizations like the Protestants and Other Americans United for Separation of Church and State focused their attention on Roman Catholics, as did Paul Blanshard in such books as *American Freedom and Catholic Power* (1949) and *Communism, Democracy, and Catholic Power* (1952). The question of federal aid to education and the possible support of parochial schools became a bitterly divisive issue among U.S. churches, with both sides sometimes resorting to name-calling.

Billy Graham addressing a large crowd in Trafalgar Square, London, April 1954 (*The Library of Congress*)

No development of the postwar period provoked such a storm of protest and anguished condemnation as did the U.S. Supreme Court decision in *Engel* v. *Vitale* (1962), which held that compulsory prayer in public schools was unconstitutional. The House of Representatives Committee on the Judiciary held hearings on the matter, many bills were introduced in Congress to restore prayer in the schools, and one congressman presented Emanuel Celler, the chairman of the committee, with a petition containing 170,000 signatures asking that God be returned to his rightful place in the classroom. The Court's ruling was frequently disregarded, and many schools carried on with prayers as usual, seldom receiving any interference from local officials. In the meantime, another series of Supreme Court decisions, those involving school desegregation and civil rights, resulted in much controversy in religious circles, particularly in the South, where rank-and-file church people tended to divide along racial lines in debating the Court's decrees.

The social gospel was not abandoned by American churches in the postwar years, despite the peace-of-mind emphasis and the somber views of the neo-orthodox. Most churches continued to perform good works in society, but a broader and stronger social reform impulse began to course through U.S. churches in the late 1950s and early 1960s. One example of this involvement of religious bodies in social meliorism was the role of the black church in the equal rights movement and especially the extraordinary leadership of Martin Luther King, Jr., in making the Negro church a powerful lever in the fight for racial justice and equality. White ministers and lay leaders, most notably outside of the South, soon began to take an active part in the struggle for civil rights, integration, and social justice in other areas.

In the 1960s American churches encountered new developments and new controversies. The churches, in part no doubt because of their participation in the social reform movements of the time, seemed to be increasingly inadequate, to be in a state of crisis. Traditional Christian theology was clearly being eroded, existential doctrines were gaining adherents, and a situational ethics was postulating that people should be guided by internal human urges in dealing with a constantly changing and often irrational universe. The sense of crisis in religion contributed to the emergence of the "New Theology," which owed a good deal to the work of Dietrich Bonhoeffer, a German theologian martyred by the Nazis, and John A. T. Robinson, an English bishop. The New Theology emphasized the concept of "immanence," the idea that God dwells in man, as opposed to "transcendence," or the otherness of God. Those who came to be called the "God Is Dead" theologians embodied this distinction in their thinking. Professor Thomas J. J. Altizer of Emory University, who coined the phrase, asserted that Jesus Christ really was the son of God, and that the incarnation and crucifixion had actually occurred. But there had been no resurrection and, in a sense, God had died. Having been transcendent, he became immanent, a part of the universe; thus to Altizer "Christ is the God who remains in the world." The New Theology implied that many of the traditional moral assumptions of Christianity had been destroyed by the evils of modern life. Harvey Cox's widely read *The Secular City* (1965) argued in favor of the new "secularity" with its pragmatic and technological style. Theology, Cox declared, must make religion relevant and responsive to the new forces in society. By the end of the decade Cox and other religious interpreters had embraced what they described as a Theology of Hope.

The religious upheaval of the 1960s was particularly evident among the young, some of whom now believed that mysticism or astrology or magic were more helpful guides to ultimate truth than either science or religion. Yet the dissent of American youth and their counterculture contained a strong appeal to faith. Jesus, whose ministry had stressed love and resistance to unjust institutions, attracted many of the young dissenters, as was evident in the popular musical *Jesus Christ Superstar*. The new supernaturalism was apparent in the antiwar movement, and many of the peace demonstrations in the late sixties were filled with religious symbolism. Some of it was absorbed by the established churches in the form of happenings, rock masses, light shows, and readings from Eastern mystics. The meditation and transcendentalism of Zen Buddhism and other Oriental religions attracted thousands of youthful followers. A movement of "Jesus freaks," who were Bible-oriented but employed the language of the counterculture, began in California and spread to campus areas across the country. Among Americans generally, the fundamentalist religion of Billy Graham, Oral Roberts, and other revivalists elicited an enthusiastic and broad-based response in the late 1960s and early 1970s.

In some ways the nation's Catholics experienced an even more profound upheaval. This eruption was to some extent a consequence of the extraordinary influence of Pope John XXIII, who died in mid-1963. Although this much-loved pope reigned for less than five years, he took the first real steps toward reconciliation with other Christian churches, and he convened the first Vatican Council in several centuries. The Vatican Ecumenical Council (1962–1965) brought a more democratic spirit involving the substitution of modern languages for Latin in the liturgy and greater Catholic participation in ecumenical activities. It recommended the creation of a synod of bishops to consult with the pope in managing the church, adopted a flexible position on birth control, attacked anti-Semitism, condemned nuclear arms, and proposed numerous changes in doctrine and practice.

If the reforms associated with Pope John proved upsetting to many conservative Catholics in the United States, the more traditional policies of his successor, Paul VI, aroused the opposition of numerous liberals and moderates in the American Catholic Church. Thus Pope Paul's long-awaited encyclical on birth control, *Humanae Vitae (Of Human Life)*, reaffirming the church's ban on artificial contraception, was widely challenged and was opposed by a majority of the younger priests. Many Catholics had begun to reassess the Church's position on such questions as divorce, abortion, and the celibacy of the priesthood. The revolution in the American Catholic Church released the energies of individuals and groups for the support of other movements. Priests and nuns took a leading part in the civil rights movement. Father James Groppi's open-housing marches in Milwaukee attracted national attention. Catholic radicals, led by the Fathers Berrigan, were in the vanguard of the peace movement. Well might the *National Review* burst out in the spring of 1965, "What, in the name of God, is going on in the Catholic Church?"

A new surge of religious fervor and revivalism marked the 1970s. Although the phenomenon of the "Jesus freaks" began to lose strength early in the decade, more durable Jesus movements developed in the conservative denominations. Meanwhile, the Pentecostal movement broadened its appeal and grew rapidly. There was also a boom in conservative Protestantism in the form of neo-evangelicalism. By the late 1970s, these fundamentalist groups claimed the loyalty of every third church member in the United States, and some 40 million Americans described themselves as "born again" Christians. The remarkable appeal of evangelical, fundamentalist, and Pentecostal religions was promoted by television personalities and best-selling authors. Out of these movements and conservative political interests came organizations that were often identified as the New Christian Right. One of the most prominent representatives of the New Christian Right was the Reverend Jerry Falwell, a Virginia evangelist and television superstar. Falwell led what he called the "Moral Majority." He worked with other fundamentalist groups and with nonreligious right-wing organizations to register voters, campaign for political candidates like Ronald Reagan, and work to outlaw abortion and restore prayer in the schools.

These movements may have advanced at the expense of "mainline" Protestantism, but the established religious groups retained great vitality in the 1970s and 1980s. Approximately 100 million

Americans remained in the membership of Protestant and Catholic churches. Many Protestant churches underwent a process of spiritual reinvigoration. With ethnic diversity being more highly valued, Roman Catholicism demonstrated a renewed sense of peoplehood. Judaism also experienced a spiritual recovery, an "inward journey" similar to that of other religious groups in the seventies. At the same time, some older causes such as ecumenism lost ground. Yet polls suggested that the American people were eager to be tolerant of each other, and real progress was made in facilitating closer relations between and better understanding among Catholics, Protestants, and Jews.

POPULAR CULTURE

In a society characterized by enormous production, widespread prosperity, and increasing leisure, the stage was set for the emergence of a remarkable cultural democracy. The economy was oriented toward the consumer as never before, and the insatiable demands for middle-class amenities constantly reinforced the mass-production and mass-consumption business system. As technology made more leisure available for the average citizen, it also created the instruments for the use of that leisure in the form of the mass media, especially television, radio, and motion pictures. The boom in mass culture also made the arts, literature, and high culture in general more and more available to ordinary people.

Any realistic characterization of the consumer culture in the United States must stress the sheer volume and variety of items purchased by Americans in their supermarkets, department stores, specialty shops, and shopping malls. An incredible array of products is consumed, which an earlier generation, more circumscribed by the need to buy basic necessities, would have considered unattainable luxuries—art objects, stereo sets, jewelry, exotic foods, wine, camping and boating equipment, swimming pools, outdoor cooking equipment, power tools, and sporting goods, not to mention houses, appliances, and automobiles. Vacation travel has become almost universal, and the motel has become as ubiquitous as the automobile. Teenagers in the affluent society following World War II composed an important part of the new consumerism, with their patronage of television, movies, records and phonograph equipment, and distinctive youth clothes.

The Golden Age of Television! Nothing was more central to mass culture than the small, glittering screen that soon made its way into virtually every American house and apartment. "The most striking thing about the arrival of television on the American scene," John Brooks wrote, "was certainly the almost apocalyptic suddenness with which it became a fully established part of our national life, complete with a huge audience and an established minority opposition, affecting not only all our other communications media and the whole world of our popular arts but also our manners, morals, habits, ways of thinking." Television was almost unknown at the end of the war, and only a few thousand sets had been sold by 1947. But by 1960 there were approximately 45 million sets in operation, and a decade later 96 percent of the country's households had at least one TV set, a growing number of them being equipped to receive transmission in color. By the 1970s television reached more people than all the other media combined. In 1979 there were a thousand commercial TV stations and 140 million receivers.

Almost everyone quickly accepted the idea that television was the *new* medium. Three national networks, dominating the field of mass entertainment, presented numerous programs designed to attract a mass audience. Most of this fare, including the soap operas, westerns, quiz programs, and variety shows, was incredibly vapid and uninspiring. The live coverage of athletic events soon became a TV staple, and by the 1960s television audiences for professional and college football, basketball, and baseball were enormous. There were some holdouts among academics and urban intellectuals, who complained about the superficiality of most programs and the tyranny TV exercised over children, but their reservations did nothing to stem the tidal wave of enthusiasm for the new medium. Still, the low level and trivial character of many of the network programs did provoke criticism, and the revelation of rigged quiz shows, highlighted by the dramatic case of Charles Van Doren in 1959, increased the adverse opinion of TV's performance.[1] In 1961 Newton Minow, the chairman of the Federal Communications Commission, described television programming as "a vast wasteland."

Few people doubted the tremendous potential of television. It seemed to offer great hope, for example, as a means of easing the loneliness and brightening the lives of older people, of slum dwellers, of rural households. No other communications medium could compare with television in its capacity to dramatize individual events, to etch them indelibly into the viewer's mind. Thus it seemed that the whole nation focused its attention on the Kefauver crime hearings, on the quadrennial political conventions beginning with 1952, on the Army-McCarthy hearings, on the events following the assassination of John F. Kennedy, and on the urban riots and peace marches of the 1960s. Daniel J. Boorstin has suggested that "just as the printing press democratized learning, so the television set has democratized experience." TV's impact was protean and undeniably immense. For example, it stimulated a great expansion of professional sports, contributed to the "revolution of rising expectations" among the nation's poor and disadvantaged, and helped nationalize and homogenize American society.

The attack of the critics had some effect, for the networks cautiously began to introduce greater variety into their programming. Some high-caliber classical music, ballet, and drama programs were presented, as well as some excellent documentaries, public affairs forums, and news commentaries. Educational television eventually made a place for itself, and National Educational Television became a real force in the early 1970s, stimulated by a $150 million contribution from the Ford Foundation. In the early 1980s almost 300 public television stations were operating in the United States. Use of television was broadened still further in the 1970s and 1980s. The video revolution was advanced by a series of important government decisions, the expansion of cable television, the launching of communications satellites, and the ready availability to the consumer of videocassette recorders, videodiscs, and home video games.

Television greatly restricted the role of radio, limiting it largely to news and music. Yet, while losing the central place it had enjoyed in the entertainment field during the 1930s and 1940s, radio remained an indispensable medium of popular culture. Radio had two huge constituencies: the millions of Americans on the highway at any given time and the millions of teenagers who listened to it as a source of current popular music. The wisecracking disc jockey became a cultural hero to the younger generation. Improvements resulted from the application of the new electronics to high fidelity and stereophonic sound and from the introduction of frequency modulation (FM). FM stations, of which there were more than 3,600 in early 1984, frequently played classical music and presented cultural programs. Some radio stations provided excellent news reports and commentaries.

With the dramatic growth of television, the movies ceased to dominate the popular culture as they had in the prewar years, and Hollywood's voice became less powerful. Average weekly movie attendance dropped by about half between 1948 and 1958, and many movie theaters were forced out of business. One response by the moviemakers to the box-office decline was the production of high-priced extravaganzas like *The Ten Commandments*, *Exodus*, and *Cleopatra*—the last, a colossal flop. Some Hollywood pictures such as *Dial M for Murder* and *Born Yesterday* achieved a high level of technical excellence, and others, especially such popular musicals as *The Music Man*, *My Fair Lady*, and *The Sound of Music*, proved to be smashing box-office attractions. But great numbers of inferior pictures were made during the fifties. Toward the end of that decade, Hollywood capitulated to television by making available for

The showgirl and the playwright—Marilyn Monroe and her husband Arthur
Miller (*The Bettmann Archive*)

showing on the home screen most of its huge library of films. The
industry soon began to produce motion pictures especially for TV,
and by the mid-sixties Hollywood was once more prospering.

The 1960s brought new vitality to American movies, including
the growing importance of small independent companies. Another
factor was the importation of creative foreign films and their influence on American producers. Some noteworthy movies resulted,
among them being *The Graduate, Patton, M*A*S*H, Dr. Strange-
love, Easy Rider, Midnight Cowboy,* and *Z.* The star system declined, meanwhile, although celebrated performers like Ronald Col-
man, Clark Gable, Bette Davis, Gary Cooper, Spencer Tracy, and
Humphrey Bogart, as well as such younger stars as Elizabeth Taylor,
Marlon Brando, Grace Kelly, William Holden, Gregory Peck, Paul
Newman, Marilyn Monroe, George C. Scott, and Jane Fonda contin-

ued to attract large followings. With the liberalization of obscenity laws, X-rated films became common. Movies became sexier than ever in the mid-1960s. They also featured unprecedented amounts of violence, brutality, and death, as was evident in such popular films as *Bonnie and Clyde, True Grit, A Clockwork Orange,* and *The Godfather.*

Popular music, a major component of contemporary mass culture in the United States, attracted the largest audiences in history through the media of radio, television, recordings, and tapes. Although the more conventional music forms represented by such varied performers as Guy Lombardo, Duke Ellington, Count Basie, and Louis Armstrong remained popular, a new style known as be-bop or modern jazz emerged in the mid-1940s. Looser in rhythm and more advanced in harmony than earlier jazz, it was played by small ensembles mainly for listening rather than dancing. It was best exemplified in the music of the alto saxophonist Charlie Parker and the trumpeter Dizzy Gillespie and in the "smooth jazz" of the Dave Brubeck Quartet. A new urban music identified with the black community and known as rhythm and blues also gained popularity in the late 1940s and early 1950s.

"Rock 'n roll" was a reaction against the prevailing popular music in America. A rhythm-and-blues variant with overtones of country and white gospel music, it erupted in 1954 with Bill Haley's recording of "Rock Around the Clock," which eventually sold 16 million copies. Singers like Chuck Berry, Fats Domino, and Carl Perkins prepared the way for rock 'n roll's tremendous success, but its most popular performer proved to be Elvis Presley, a young white truck driver from Tupelo, Mississippi, with a wild vocal style and a potent combination of country music, gospel, and rhythm and blues. During the "golden era" of rock 'n roll, between 1956 and 1958, Presley had ten number one hit records, including "Heartbreak Hotel," "Don't Be Cruel," "Hound Dog," "All Shook Up," and "Jailhouse Rock." His succession of hit recordings continued during the next decade. Folk music also grew in popularity, especially after it became identified closely with the equal rights movement in the early 1960s. Pete Seeger, Bob Dylan, and Joan Baez attracted large audiences wherever they performed. The rise of country music was nothing less than phenomenal. "Country" was a generic term applied to such musical varieties as "hillbilly," "mountain," "cowboy," "western," and "rockabilly." Nashville, with its Grand Ole Opry, became known as the country-music capital of the United States.

Rock music, which owed a good deal to black music and the new dances, came to dominance in the 1960s. Introduced in England by the Beatles, the Rolling Stones, and other groups, the new rock music was based on the older rock 'n roll, employing a system of intensely amplified electrical guitars and other instruments. The Beatles appeared on Ed Sullivan's Sunday evening TV show in 1964, and thereafter their music quickly became the rage in the United States. During the years that followed, innovators such as Bob Dylan, John Sebastian, the Procol Harum, Paul Butterfield, Janis Joplin, and Frank Zappa elaborated the new music into folk-rock, country-rock, classical motif-rock, blues-rock, and jazz-based rock. Groups like the Who, the Yardbirds, and Led Zeppelin revealed the range of hard-rock sounds. Rock also stimulated new ideas and new forms in other kinds of music. It was an important element in the musicals *Hair* and *Jesus Christ Superstar*.

Meanwhile, Frank Sinatra, who began as a big band singer, became a bobby-soxer idol, and then emerged as the "saloon singer" supreme, continued to perform, surviving the years of changing tastes and cultural upheaval. Sinatra's firm, pure baritone voice made him one of the greatest singers in the history of American popular music. Other stellar performers in the field of popular music included Bing Crosby, Perry Como, and Nat "King" Cole, all of whom recorded extensively and were perennial favorites. The most popular female pop vocalists in the seventies and eighties were Barbra Streisand, Donna Summer, Aretha Franklin, Diana Ross, Olivia Newton-John, and Linda Ronstadt.

The consumer culture in America has been nourished by old as well as new media. Newspapers are still widely read, although the daily papers have been hard hit by rising costs, labor strikes, and increasing competition from radio and television. Newspaper publishing, more than ever, has become a species of big business, and the trend toward consolidation has gone forward steadily. The quality of the newspapers is not very high, except for a few first-rate papers like the *New York Times*, the *Washington Post*, and the *Los Angeles Times*. Most papers have a more or less standardized assortment of features and departments—sports, home furnishings, food, comics, finance, editorial, and the like—and the great emphasis is on the highest possible display of advertising. One interesting new trend that became noticeable in the 1960s was the rapid growth of small-town and suburban newspapers.

Mass media magazines were threatened by the emergence of national television in the 1950s, but many of them enjoyed huge circulations during the first two postwar decades. Henry Luce's *Time* claimed almost 14 million readers in the mid-1960s, while *McCall's* was read by nearly 14 million adult women and *Ladies' Home Journal* by almost 12 million. The *Reader's Digest* was even more successful. Nevertheless, ruinous competition for circulation, chronic management upheavals, and unequal editorial quality contributed to the demise of many famous magazines, among them *Collier's, Saturday Evening Post, Look,* and *Life.* The pulp magazines, including the "romance" periodicals, the comic magazines, and pornographic journals, have continued to prosper. Aside from the pulps, most of the magazines that have seemed to fare best are those aimed at special audiences, periodicals as varied as *National Geographic, Psychology Today, Ebony, Playboy, Esquire,* the *New Yorker,* and numerous hobby and sports publications.

The popular book, in a variety of forms, has been another agent of mass culture in the United States. Boosted by the "paperback revolution," the sale of books more than doubled between 1952 and 1961. By 1966, at least 38,000 titles were available in paperback editions, many of them serious works and even classics. Dr. Benjamin Spock's *Baby and Child Care,* first issued in paperback in 1946, went through 167 printings within ten years and had sold 30 million copies by 1984, making it second only to the Bible as the best-selling book in American history. Books that reached a huge market, however, were often ephemeral, popular fiction like westerns, sexual novels, and detective stories, much of which appealed to the romanticism and nostalgia in the American mind. Thus Harold Robbins's series of sexual novels, beginning with *The Dream Merchants* (1949), enjoyed tremendous success, as did Grace Metalious's sexual epic of a small New England town, *Peyton Place* (1956), and Jacqueline Susann's stories of sexual conquest and ennui among the jet set, *Valley of the Dolls* (1966) and *The Love Machine* (1969). Even more remarkable was the popularity of Mickey Spillane's books, which had sold over 50 million copies by 1969. The spy novel, a detective variant, was widely read by Americans. Ian Fleming's James Bond (Secret Agent 007) adventures proved especially popular in the 1950s and 1960s, and resulted in a series of lucrative movies. The popular book also included humor books, of which 650 titles, with a combined circulation of 100 million a month, were in print in 1953–54.

The possible consequences of America's fantastic consumer culture—its penchant for the cheap and sensational, its homogenizing tendencies, its vulgarization of the older, established culture, and its threat to rigorous standards—evoked stringent criticism from guardians of "high" culture. The offensive was led by a group of New York intellectuals associated with the *Partisan Review* and other magazines; they argued that the more culture spreads, the more it tends to become corrupted and commercialized. Mass culture did not lack for defenders, however. Most of its advocates maintained that the spread of culture was inherently good for the country and would eventually overcome the deleterious effects of such cultural democratization. Marshall McLuhan contended that the old intellectual and aesthetic standards had been made anachronistic by technological innovation, particularly in the electronic media, and that society was being reordered. Content was far less important than the experience of seeing and hearing, according to McLuhan. Others suggested that popularity and validity are not mutually exclusive, and that there have been accomplishments of genuine merit in the popular arts.

A very different challenge to the consumer culture came from the cultural rebellion of the 1960s and the search for an alternative lifestyle by the young radicals of that decade. Like the beatniks of the 1950s, the adherents of the so-called counterculture criticized the values of the consumer society and resisted established social and economic patterns. Skeptical of the nation's vaunted technological achievements, they condemned its unbridled materialism and manipulative social structures. The counterculture assumed various forms: absorption in rock music, adoption of distinctive clothing and hair styles, creation of a new vocabulary, acceptance of a more liberal code of sexual behavior, use of hallucinogenic drugs, and interest in mystical experiences. Although most of the youthful radicals of the late sixties sooner or later rejoined the mainstream culture, they left a significant cultural residue.

ART AND AMERICAN LIFE

The cultural boom that developed in the United States by mid-century extended to the fine arts as well as the popular culture. Not only were more and more Americans financially able to patronize artistic endeavors, but the number of well-educated people with an interest in the arts had reached substantial proportions. Cultural centers, arts councils, and local art museums multiplied. The number of symphony orchestras in the United States more than doubled between 1950 and 1965, and virtually every American city with more than 50,000 inhabitants had such an orchestra. Innumerable chamber music groups, "art" cinema houses, FM radio stations, and community theaters made their appearance.

In spite of the public's heightened interest in the arts and increasing private support of artists, the continuing need for more adequate financial backing eventually resulted in greater governmental involvement at all levels in the promotion of art and culture. Thus in the 1960s New York City completed its Lincoln Center for the Performing Arts, an impressive complex for concerts, opera, ballet, and drama. In 1964 Los Angeles inaugurated its huge music center pavilion, and in 1971 the John F. Kennedy Center for the Performing Arts in Washington, D.C., was opened. In 1965 Congress passed the National Arts and Humanities Act, which provided, among other things, for federal grants-in-aid to groups and individuals concerned with creative and performing arts.

The American response to operatic and other forms of classical music was most noteworthy in its enthusiasm for performing artists. But there were some outstanding American composers of "serious" music, including Aaron Copland, Kurt Weill, Samuel Barber, Vittorio Giannini, Roger Sessions, and Hugo Weisgall. Many universities attracted composers such as Walter Piston and Douglas Moore as permanent residents. The versatile Leonard Bernstein, conductor of the New York Philharmonic Orchestra, produced operas, symphonies, chamber music, and musical comedies.

Ballet enjoyed considerable support in the United States, not only in the widespread interest in famous foreign groups but also in the support of numerous local organizations. The postwar era was also characterized by a good deal of experimentation in architecture. Perhaps the most conspicuous evidence of "modern" architecture was the growing popularity of the so-called international style, which was exemplified in the work of men like Ludwig Mies van der Rohe and in such structures as the Lever Building and the UN Secretariat in New York City. Employing new building materials such as stainless steel, aluminum, and enormous quantities of glass, the international style had the great virtue of simplicity and of sweeping, geometric lines. But all too often the new public and commercial buildings designed in this style were simply glass-walled, rectilinear structures.

If new artistic movements did not often originate in the United States, they seemed to flourish here more exuberantly than in any other country. Stimulated by an expansive economy, U.S. art galleries, art schools, art publications, and private and public foundations provided artists with unprecedented support, instruction, and access to a public hungry for quality and novelty. The greatest artistic renaissance in postwar America occurred in the field of painting. American painters moved away from the realism and socially conscious themes and mood of the 1930s—regionalism in painting, folk art, and the WPA artists' projects—toward abstraction, surrealism, and new art forms. Even the realistically oriented Andrew Wyeth, the single most popular American painter of modern times, considered himself an abstractionist. Like some other realists, his pictures projected a haunting quality of fantasy and dreaminess.

The movement that dominated American art in the postwar period was called "abstract expressionism." Rejecting representational art and traditional symbols of visual communication, the expressionists sought, whatever their particular emphasis, to create a mood or feeling, not a figure as it actually existed. Their great concern was with feeling at the moment paint touched the canvas. These painters were unconcerned with perspective or objects except as they might be used to symbolize powerful life forces. They seemed to paint without plan or precision—with great splashes of color, crude shapes, and gobs of paint slapped or dripped on huge canvases. Much of this work could be characterized as "action painting." As Harold Rosenberg wrote in an essay on the expressionist movement:

> At a certain moment the canvas began to appear to one American painter after another as an arena in which to act—rather than as a space in which to reproduce, re-design, analyze or "express" an object, actual or imagined. What was to go on canvas was not a picture but an event. . . . What matters always is the revelation contained in the act . . . the way the artist organizes his emotional and intellectual energy as if he were in a living situation.

Traditionalists were frequently shocked and offended by the new art, while those without artistic knowledge often found it uninteresting, unintelligible, and chaotic. Yet abstract expressionism mirrored contemporary American society surprisingly well. It reflected the estrangement of the artist from the world of the atomic bomb and embodied a revolt against the materialism and novelty-for-novelty's sake of contemporary mass culture.

The most famous of the abstract expressionists was Jackson Pollock (1912–1956). He laid his huge canvases on the floor, working from four sides, walking around on the canvas, literally in the painting. Pollock produced a number of extraordinary works, such as his *Blue Poles*, notable for its use of brilliant color. Among the other well-known abstract expressionists was Mark Rothko, who painted great pools or vaguely defined planes of color. Franz Kline's paintings consisted of wide black strokes at seemingly random angles on a white background, conveying a generalized sense of modern tension. Great, gaudy slashes of paint characterized the work of Willem de Kooning, who was most famous for "The Women," a series of paintings completed in the early 1950s. There were other talented artists in this mode, which was accepted in the 1950s as the movement that had propelled American art to a leading position in the international avant-garde.

Jackson Pollock's *Echo*, 1951 (*Oil on canvas, 7'7⅞" × 7'2". Collection, The Museum of Modern Art, New York. Acquired through the Lillie P. Bliss Bequest and the Mr. and Mrs. David Rockefeller Fund*)

One of the new directions taken by American painters was "pop art," whose antecedents included the dadaists and such works of Picasso as *Plate with Wafers* (1914). Possessing clearly defined, hard-edged forms, this new art lacked the quality of movement or a sense of duration. Pop artists, painters of the popular and commercial image, seemed to be satirizing the nation's mass-production, consumer-oriented society. Their work contained an element of social realism and a statement about the deteriorating human environment. They painted such mundane objects as soup cans, packing cases, and comic strips. Robert Rauschenberg, one of the new mode's originators, created a successful object work in 1955 which he entitled simply *Bed*. It consisted of a real quilt and pillow on a stretcher, with other designs and objects added. Jasper Johns produced a celebrated work he called *Painted Bronze* (1960), a casting of two Ballantine Ale cans with the labels painted on. Roy Lichtenstein, Andy Warhol, and other free spirits made pop art the vogue during the following few years. Critics such as Hilton Kramer of the *New York Times* charged that these "unserious" painters were offering easy-to-read, cheap thrills in place of the more difficult, less amusing works of modernism.

By the 1970s American viewers were confronted with a variety of artistic movements and styles that was baffling in its diversity. Indeed, the conceptual range of art in the United States had become so great that once-familiar distinctions and terminology no longer applied. Words like "figurative" and "abstract" became meaningless as art took in all reaches of the mind and senses. Writing in 1979, the art historian Joshua C. Taylor suggested that, "with bases from scientific experiments in perception to drug-induced imagery, art represented too wide an exploration of human activity to be encompassed in a single set of terms or aligned in a particular direction."

THE LITERARY IMAGINATION

Unlike the aftermath of World War I, the years following World War II failed to produce a noteworthy literary renaissance in America. Several of the major literary figures of the interwar period continued to be productive in the 1940s and 1950s, including Ernest Hemingway, John Dos Passos, Eugene O'Neill, John Steinbeck, and William Faulkner. Few of these writers, however, added to their earlier reputations, and none was closely identified with any important new development in creative writing. Hemingway produced only two major works after the war, and one of those, *Across the River and into the Trees* (1950), proved a great disappointment. The other was a short novel entitled *The Old Man and the Sea* (1952), a compelling story of individual heroism in the face of relentless adversity. Faulkner, who wrote steadily until his death in 1962, was perhaps the most talented of all modern American writers. He turned out a succession of novels in the postwar period, among them being *Intruder in the Dust* (1948), a Pulitzer Prize winner concerned with race relations. *The Town* (1957) and *The Mansion* (1959) completed his trilogy on the Snopes clan. The human drama that Faulkner unfolded had a southern setting, but his artistic genius transcended regionalism and at its best achieved a powerful universality in its depiction of the contingency and precariousness of the human condition.

A series of war novels published between 1945 and 1952 bridged the country's transition from war to peace. The most widely acclaimed of these novels was Norman Mailer's *The Naked and the Dead* (1948), a work obviously influenced by the examples of Hemingway and Dos Passos. It described the adventures of a combat platoon in the Pacific theater. Many of the war novels focused on the relationship between the individual and the impersonal military machine. Thus Private Prewitt, in James Jones's *From Here to Eternity* (1951), tries to maintain his individuality in the prewar army.

The postwar novel of manners was illustrated in the work of such writers as John O'Hara and John Gould Cozzens, who ably portrayed small-town well-to-do groups; but this literature became steadily less characteristic of the literary scene. The social tragicomedies of John Marquand, usually set against the relatively fixed society of New England, began to seem more parochial. John Cheever, author of *The Wapshot Chronicle* (1957), *The Wapshot Scandal* (1964), *Bullet Park* (1969), and other novels, revealed a vision of everyday life that was anything but normal. Cheever seemed to be less interested in exposing the fatuities and self-deceptions of his suburban New York and Connecticut world than he was in understanding the compromises and the repressions of the "upwardly dispossessed," whose very material success had removed them from all that was genuinely vital in life. As for postwar novelists in general, life seemed to have become too threatening, tenuous, and ambiguous to give social comment in fiction the fixed moral background that traditional storytelling requires. Saul Bellow's character in *Henderson the Rain King* summed up the mood: "Nobody truly occupies a station in life any more. There are displaced persons everywhere."

Novelists and poets turned to the isolated individual experience. Their writings reflected a deep-seated anxiety that the emerging technological society was threatening to destroy the individual entirely. So strong was this sense of alienation—this feeling that people are strangers even to themselves—that the writers found it almost impossible to create order in their imaginary world. Heroes and heroines disappeared from modern fiction, or they assumed absurd dimensions like Yossarian in Joseph Heller's *Catch-22* (1961), or they were simply anti-heroes. The compelling focus became the individual's search for his or her own identity. American fiction also revealed a new preoccupation with the bizarre and grotesque and with satire and black comedy, as was evident in such works as Ken Kesey's *One Flew Over the Cuckoo's Nest* (1962), Thomas Pynchon's *V* (1963), and Kurt Vonnegut's *Slaughterhouse Five* (1969). In *Giles Goat-Boy* (1966), John Barth explored and satirized the human condition by making his hero the offspring of a woman and a computer. John Hawkes, Joyce Carol Oates, and other promising young writers were concerned in their narratives with horror and nightmare.

Many of the new writers departed radically from the conventional format of the American novel. The "beatnik school," including such novelists and poets as Jack Kerouac and Allen Ginsberg, drew a picture of violence, perversion, and madness in their work. Vladimir Nabokov, a Russian émigré writer, produced one of the best fictional portrayals of contemporary America: the novel *Lolita* (1955), the story of an automobile tour of the United States taken by a seedy and depraved refugee scholar and a rudderless and sexy American adolescent. The book is funny and sad, and its evocation of the physical and moral aspects of postwar America is curiously unforgettable. J. D. Salinger, a favorite of high school and college students in the 1950s, was concerned in *Catcher in the Rye* (1951) with the inner rebellion of Holden Caulfield and his search for identification and self-awareness. He examined the same theme in *Franny and Zooey* (1961). A more prolific writer, John Updike, illustrated the use of unconventional form in *The Centaur* (1963), while revealing the modern concern with individual character and the anti-hero in such novels as *Poorhouse Fair* (1959), *Rabbit, Run* (1960), *Couples* (1968), and *Rabbit Redux* (1971).

One of the striking features of the American literary scene after World War II was the emergence of a new group of talented writers from the South. The group included Carson McCullers, Eudora Welty, Walker Percy, Peter Taylor, Reynolds Price, and Elizabeth Spencer, in addition to more established writers such as Robert Penn Warren and Caroline Gordon. Two of the most talented of the new southern authors were William Styron of Virginia and Flannery O'Connor of Georgia. Styron's major books include *Lie Down in Darkness* (1951), *Set This House on Fire* (1960), *The Confessions of Nat Turner* (1967), and *Sophie's Choice* (1975). The first is a powerful depiction of the deteriorating relationship between a girl and her father in the stifling atmosphere of a small southern town. *The Confessions of Nat Turner* is a moving re-creation of the life of the famous slave insurrectionary. O'Connor, who died at an early age in 1964, provides an illustration of southern gothic at its best. Her novels and short stories—*Wise Blood* (1952), *A Good Man Is Hard to Find* (1955), and *The Violent Bear It Away* (1960)—are tragicomic allegories on humanity's fall, redemption, and faith, written from the perspective of a devout Catholic. This second generation of modern southern writers had, as Professor Louis Rubin has observed, a strong awareness of the "inroads of time," a special feeling for landscape and place, a "relish for rhetoric," and an "uninhibited commitment to the full resources of the language both spoken and written."

Some southern writers were black, and the black experience provided the focus for another significant group of postwar novelists and poets. In a sense these authors perpetuated the socially conscious literature of the prewar years, since they were intent upon showing what it was like for a black to live in white America. Yet even they were forced to resort to symbols, and Ralph Ellison, in *The Invisible Man* (1952), the most celebrated Negro novel of the period, adopted an oblique approach in order to suggest how it felt to be a sophisticated and sensitive black man in a white-dominated society. In his book, Ellison used the metaphor of "invisibility" to show that the black person in America was living in the midst of a society that refused to recognize his humanity. The best-known black writer of the 1950s and 1960s was James Baldwin, whose first novel, *Go Tell It on the Mountain* (1953), is about the great Negro migration from the South to the urban slums of the North. As the black revolt intensified, Baldwin spoke out eloquently and sometimes bitterly in support of the drive for racial equality. *The Fire Next Time* (1963), a work of nonfiction, is an anguished and deeply moving indictment of white racism in the United States. Among a number of gifted younger black writers are Ernest Gaines, John A. Williams, and Alice Walker. In *The Third Life of Grange Copeland* (1970), *Meridian* (1976), *The Color Purple* (1982), and other novels, Walker writes in moving language and with profound insight about the inner life and character of black people.

In 1967 Norman Podhoretz, the editor of the Jewish journal *Commentary*, expressed the opinion that Jews were replacing southern writers as "the leading school of novelists." There was unquestionably an outburst of creativity among Jewish writers in the United States in the postwar era. Saul Bellow, Bernard Malamud, Philip Roth, and several other young writers produced novels that dealt with American-Jewish life. Bellow, perhaps the most impressive of the group, in *The Adventures of Augie March* (1953), *Herzog* (1965), and other works not only provided a brilliant commentary on the confusion and sordidness of modern life, but also helped transform the novel from a story to pure expression. It is not clear whether this literature signaled the reawakening of Jewish consciousness or the literary climax of assimilation and the end of Jewish consciousness.

Although Norman Mailer is Jewish, he is not primarily concerned with ethnic and religious consciousness, and his literary imagination has transcended that theme. *Advertisements for Myself* (1959) was evidence that Mailer was developing a literary genre peculiar to himself; the book included essays, doggerel verse, fictional experimentation, and a great deal of self-exposure. In the late 1960s Mailer turned to reporting, a shift also evident in the work of other writers such as Truman Capote, and in a series of nonfictional books he dealt with the Democratic national convention of 1968, the moon landing of 1969, and American involvement in Vietnam. His novel *The Executioner's Song* (1979), an imaginative and exhaustive recreation of a real case in which capital punishment was resumed following its abolition by the Supreme Court, won the Pulitzer Prize. As the critic Richard Poirier has written, "More than anyone else of his time, Mailer is implicated, in every sense of that word, in the way we live now."

American poetry also entered into new directions and showed evidence of considerable vitality in the postwar period. A number of established poets from earlier years such as Robert Frost, Carl Sandburg, Archibald MacLeish, W. H. Auden, Conrad Aiken, E. E. Cummings, Marianne Moore, Wallace Stevens, and William Carlos Williams continued to be productive. Frost, the grand old man of American poetry, became more abstract in his old age. Another of the older poets, Ezra Pound, was declared insane and committed to a hospital in 1946. He continued to write, however, and ironically his *Pisan Cantos*, based on his experiences in an army prison camp in Pisa, won the Library of Congress' Bollingen Award in 1948. The newer poets were preoccupied with psychological and mythological themes, with humanity's alienation, and with its quest for self-identification. Robert Lowell's *Lord Weary's Castle* (1946), for instance, was the exploration of a ruined world. Many of these younger poets demonstrated great technical ability, new and intricate styles, and philosophical subtlety. Among the more impressive of these writers, in addition to Lowell, are John Berryman, Randall Jarrell, Karl Shapiro, Theodore Roethke, Richard Wilbur, Phyllis McGinley, William Meredith, Louis O. Coxe, and James Merrill.

When they thought of the theater, most Americans thought of Broadway and of such famous musicals as *Oklahoma, South Pacific,* and *My Fair Lady.* (The last, based on Bernard Shaw's *Pygmalion,* ran on Broadway for over five years.) But there were also more serious dramas produced in the post–World War II period. Eugene O'Neill, the most famous American playwright, while demonstrating less vitality and originality than in earlier years, wrote four plays after 1945, including *The Iceman Cometh* (1946) and *Long Day's Journey into Night* (1956). Of the newer dramatists, the most prolific was Tennessee Williams, who produced a long series of plays. The best of these—such works as *The Glass Menagerie* (1945), *A Streetcar Named Desire* (1947), and *Cat on a Hot Tin Roof* (1955)—were powerful plays, with great psychological penetration. Arthur Miller, in dramas like *Death of a Salesman* (1948), *The Crucible* (1953), and *A View from the Bridge* (1955), protested against the materialism and conformity of mid-century life, while demonstrating his belief that tragedy was still possible in the modern theater and that its proper hero was the common man and woman. Other talented playwrights included William Inge, Lillian Hellman, and Edward Albee. Inge, whose plays included *Come Back, Little Sheba* (1950), *Picnic* (1953), *Bus Stop* (1955), and *The Dark at the Top of the Stairs* (1957), was the representative American playwright of the 1950s. In *Who's Afraid of Virginia Woolf?* (1960), Albee exposed the illusions that people use to get along in modern life. *Raisin in the Sun* (1959), by a young black playwright named Lorraine Hansberry, is a poignant portrayal of a black family's struggle in an unfriendly white environment. During the years that followed other new playwrights came to the fore, among them Ronald Ribman, Sam Shepard, Jules Feiffer, and Lanford Wilson.

Critics and other informed observers could scarcely deny the fact that American culture was wonderfully dynamic and full of life in the years following 1945. The rest of the world could no longer ignore the cultural dimensions of the western colossus—such of its manifestations as the expressionism of Jackson Pollock, the literature of Faulkner and Mailer, the scientific achievements of U.S. Nobel Prize winners, and the continuing American efforts to develop a workable system of universal education. In that sense, at least, American culture had achieved its independence.

NOTE

1. Van Doren, an assistant professor at Columbia University and member of a well-known literary family, had been a highly successful and widely admired contestant on NBC's program "Twenty-One" in 1956 and 1957. He later admitted that he had been carefully coached, provided with the correct answers to questions, and eventually told to lose to another contestant. Early in 1962 Van Doren was convicted of perjury before a grand jury investigating the case in 1959 and given a suspended sentence.

SUGGESTIONS FOR FURTHER READING

John Brooks, *The Great Leap*, cited earlier, provides a general introduction to the postwar cultural scene. Several chapters in another popular work, Godfrey Hodgson's *America in Our Time* (1976), deal with cultural themes.

William L. O'Neill, *Coming Apart: An Informal History of America in the 1960's* (1971), is a readable introduction to that decade. Morris Dickstein, *Gates of Eden: American Culture in the Sixties* (1977), gives special attention to fiction and rock music in showing the shift in cultural sensibility during the 1960s.

The best history of education in the United States since 1945 is Diane Ravitch, *The Troubled Crusade: American Education, 1945–1980* (1983), especially helpful on the politics of education. For other books on educational developments, see Martin Mayer, *The Schools* (1961); Jonathan Kozol, *Death at an Early Age: The Destruction of the Hearts and Minds of Negro Children in the Boston Public Schools* (1967); and Charles E. Silberman, *Crisis in the Classroom: The Remaking of American Education* (1970). Two books by Ray C. Rist describe day-to-day life in American schools: *The Urban School: A Factory for Failure* (1973), and *The Invisible Children: School Integration in American Society* (1977). On changes in the colleges and universities, see Clark Kerr, *The Uses of the University* (1963), and Christopher Jencks and David Riesman, *The Academic Revolution* (1968). H. L. Nieburg, *In the Name of Science* (1966), throws light on the role of government in scientific research and development. Hugh Davis Graham, *The Uncertain Triumph: Federal Education Policy in the Kennedy and Johnson Years* (1984), is a valuable study.

The main contours of American religious history in the postwar era are outlined in Sidney Mead's *The Lively Experiment: The Shaping of Christianity in America* (1963). More up-to-date treatments can be found in two books by Martin E. Marty, *Pilgrims in Their Own Land* (1984), and *Protestantism in the United States: Righteous Empire* (2nd ed., 1986). Important works on a variety of key religious issues in the recent period are Will Herberg, *Protestant—Catholic—Jew: An Essay in American Religious Sociology* (1955); Murray S. Stedman, Jr., *Religion and Politics in America* (1964); Philip Gleason (ed.), *Contemporary Catholicism in the United States* (1969); William G. McLaughlin and Robert N. Bellah (eds.), *Religion in America* (1968); and David Edwin Harrell, Jr., *White Sects and Black Men in the Recent South* (1971). Harrell's *All Things Are Possible: The Healing & Charismatic Revivals in Modern America* (1975) offers a revealing glimpse into a distinctive world-view and religious subculture.

Russel B. Nye has written a sprightly history of popular culture entitled *The Unembarrassed Muse: The Popular Arts in America* (1970). For other illuminating treatments of mass culture, see Reuel Denney, *The Astonished Muse: Popular Culture in America* (1957); Russell Lynes, *The Tastemakers* (1954); Alvin Toffler, *The Culture Consumers: A Study of Art and Affluence in America* (1964); and Philip Olson (ed.), *America as a Mass Society: Changing Community and Identity* (1963). The following books are useful for particular aspects of popular culture: Richard Griffith and Arthur Mayer, *The Movies* (rev. ed., 1970); Erik Barnouw, *The Image Empire: A History of Broadcasting in the United States* (1970), and *Tube of Plenty: The Evolution of American Television* (1975); G. A. Steiner, *The People Look at Television* (1963); David Marc, *Demographic Vistas: Television in American Culture* (1984); John Rockwell, *Sinatra: An American Classic* (1984); Bill C. Malone, *Country Music U.S.A.: A Fifty-Year History* (rev. ed., 1985); Charlie Gillett, *The Sound of the City: The Rise of Rock and Roll* (rev. and expanded ed., 1983); Jerry Hopkins, *The Rock Story* (1970); Arnold Shaw, *Honkers and Shouters* (1978), an oral history of black music from blues through soul; Nick Tosches, *Unsung Heroes of Rock 'n' Roll* (1984); and Les Daniels and John Peck, *COMIX: A History of Comic Books in America* (1971).

Provocative evaluations of the mass media and mass culture are provided by Dwight Macdonald in *Against the American Grain* (1962); Marshall McLuhan in *Understanding Media: The Extensions of Man* (1964); and Daniel J. Boorstin in *The Image: A Guide to Pseudo-Events in America* (1964). Christopher Lasch's *The Culture of Narcissism: American Life in an Age of Diminishing Expectations* (1979) is a stimulating but thorny description of the culture of competitive individualism, which the author argues has carried Americans to the dead end of a narcissistic preoccupation with the self.

Good historical introductions to the arts in the United States are contained in Oliver W. Larkin, *Art and Life in America* (1949), and Matthew Baigell, *A Concise History of American Painting and Sculpture* (1984). Modern art is discussed by Barbara Rose, *American Art Since 1900* (1967). Architecture is treated by James Fitch, *American Building* (2d ed., 1966), and Ian McCallum, *Architecture U.S.A.* (1959). For mid-century developments in American painting, see Sam Hunter, *Modern American Painting and Sculpture* (1959); Frank O'Hara, *Jackson Pollock* (1959); and Harriet Janis and Rudi Blesh, *De Kooning* (1960). For two other illuminating studies, see Joshua C. Taylor, *The Fine Arts in America* (1981), and Harold Rosenberg, *Discovering the Present: Three Decades in Art, Culture, and Politics* (1985).

The broad expanse of American literature since World War II is surveyed in Ihab Hassan, *Radical Innocence: The Contemporary American Novel* (1961); Leslie Fiedler, *Waiting for the End: The American Literary Scene from Hemingway to Baldwin* (1964); Raymond M. Olderman, *Beyond the Waste Land: A Study of the American Novel in the Nineteen-sixties* (1972); and Alfred Kazin, *Bright Book of Life: American Novelists and Storytellers from Hemingway to Mailer* (1973). For a comprehensive recent appraisal, see Daniel Hoffman (ed.), *Harvard Guide to Contemporary American Writing* (1979). For southern writers see John M. Bradbury, *Renaissance in the South: A Critical History of the Literature, 1920–1960* (1963). The work of recent black writers is assessed by Robert Bone in *The Negro Novel in America* (rev. ed., 1965). Allen Guttmann's *The Jewish Writer in America: Assimilation and the Crisis of Identity* (1971) is important for its historical and sociological perspectives.

CHAPTER TEN

John F. Kennedy
and the American
Mission Abroad

BY 1960 the postwar world appeared to have achieved a kind of fragile stability, and in the United States there were indications that the
next decade would bring some major shifts in the nation's politics.
John Fitzgerald Kennedy, the youngest man ever to be elected to the
presidency, succeeded the elderly Eisenhower, making himself the
spokesman for "a new generation of Americans." Many people were
hopeful that, under Kennedy's leadership, the United States would
not only undertake a more aggressive foreign policy but would turn
resolutely to the solution of the great social problems that had been
neglected or postponed in the 1950s.

THE ELECTION OF A NEW PRESIDENT, 1960

There was a spirited contest for the Democratic nomination in
1960. Four U.S. senators became active candidates: Lyndon B. Johnson of Texas, Hubert H. Humphrey of Minnesota, Stuart Symington
of Missouri, and John F. Kennedy of Massachusetts. Adlai E. Stevenson still had strong support and seemed to be waiting in the wings
for a possible third call. Johnson, who was strong in the South, saw
his best chance in the gratitude and loyalty he had won from virtually all Democratic senators in his skillful role as majority leader.
Kennedy had launched a well-organized drive for the nomination
immediately after the election of 1956, when he first came to national attention as a surprisingly strong contender for his party's
vice-presidential nomination. He was challenged by Humphrey in a
series of primary contests early in 1960. The two key primaries
turned out to be those in Wisconsin and West Virginia. Most ob-

servers thought that Humphrey had an advantage in Wisconsin, which adjoined his home state and seemed to reflect his brand of midwestern liberalism, but Kennedy won a surprising victory there on April 5. The struggle then shifted to West Virginia, where the Massachusetts senator's Catholicism became a major though largely silent issue in the strongly Protestant state. The outcome was a stunning victory for Kennedy by a 61 to 39 percent margin. Humphrey dropped out of the race.

When the Democratic National Convention met in Los Angeles in July, Kennedy was nominated on the first ballot, receiving 806 votes to 409 for Johnson and 86 for Symington. Kennedy's 65,000 miles of travel in two dozen states, his impressive primary victories, and his skillfully organized and well-financed campaign had paid off. Having secured the nomination, the Massachusetts senator moved at once to strengthen the ticket by persuading Senator Johnson to accept the vice-presidential nomination.

Meanwhile, the Republican party managed to avoid the kind of divisive and heated nomination fight the Democrats had gone through. The principal reason for this situation was the powerful position Vice President Richard M. Nixon had established by the late 1950s. The vice president encountered only one significant challenger along the road to his presidential nomination. The challenge came from Nelson A. Rockefeller, who was elected governor of New York in 1958 in a sweeping victory over Averell Harriman. Handsome, hard-driving, and immensely wealthy, the ambitious Rockefeller sought to attract moderate and liberal Republican support as a fresh, exciting alternative to Nixon. But Nixon had far more political experience and know-how than the governor, and he was identified with the popular Ike's presidency and was strongly preferred by most party leaders. In December 1959 Rockefeller withdrew from the hopeless contest.

Nevertheless, in June 1960 Governor Rockefeller challenged the GOP and its platform committee, then at work in Chicago, in effect to repudiate the Eisenhower administration on a long list of national security, civil rights, and social welfare issues. Determined to avoid a bitter platform fight and to hold the party together for the November election, Nixon flew to New York for a secret meeting with Rockefeller. The two men agreed upon a detailed program that reflected the governor's views on domestic and foreign policy. The "Compact of Fifth Avenue" infuriated conservatives like Senator Barry Goldwater, who characterized the agreement as the "Munich of the Republican Party." The Nixon forces managed to effect an acceptance of the main features of the agreement in the national convention, and the vice president was easily nominated on the first ballot. Nixon selected Henry Cabot Lodge, Jr., ambassador to the United Nations, for the vice-presidential nomination.

Although Nixon and Kennedy had convincingly demonstrated mastery over their respective parties, both leaders suffered from potentially telling weaknesses. No one in public life was more patently ambitious than Nixon, who seemed to be a plastic man, without any genuine convictions, constantly manipulating himself in order to appear to better advantage. Kennedy, for all of his attractiveness, was regarded with suspicion in many quarters. He had failed to take a strong position on the issue of McCarthyism; his father, Joseph P. Kennedy, had a mean reputation as a conservative isolationist; and most important, the senator was a member of the Roman Catholic Church. Some cynical observers, Theodore C. Sorensen later recalled, "regarded the 1960 election essentially as a contest between two ruthlessly ambitious young men, both smoothly skilled in politics and public relations, and both possessing more cool reserve than deep emotional convictions."

Kennedy, being in effect the challenger, took the initiative in developing campaign issues. He emphasized the need for positive leadership, public sacrifice, and vigorous action to "get America moving again." He frequently referred to an alleged "missile gap" between the United States and the Soviet Union, challenged the American commitment to defend certain offshore islands in the Formosa Strait, and criticized the administration for its handling of Castro's Cuba. Concentrating on the large industrial states, Kennedy also hammered away at unemployment, the worsening economic slump, and the need to stimulate economic growth.

Nixon, the leader of the minority party, emphasized his own knowledge, experience, and long association with Eisenhower. "The major test to which the people of the country are putting the candidates," he declared, "is which by experience, by background, by judgment, by record . . . can best continue the leadership of Dwight D. Eisenhower and keep the peace without surrender for America and extend freedom throughout the world." A Gallup poll taken immediately after the two conventions gave Nixon a 50 to 44 percent lead over Kennedy, with only 6 percent of those questioned being undecided.

The "Catholic issue" reminded worried Democrats of Al Smith's disastrous campaign in 1928, and it was soon evident that, despite Nixon's refusal to invoke the question, the matter of Kennedy's religion had become the subject of widespread uneasiness as well as scurrilous attacks. In early September a highly publicized Washington convocation of conservative Protestant clergymen accused the Catholic Church of openly intervening in political affairs, and they

Kennedy-Nixon televised debates, 1960 (*Copyright* Washington Post. *Reprinted courtesy of the D.C. Public Library/Imagefinders, Inc.*)

ascribed this and other evils to candidate Kennedy. The Democratic leader decided, as he had done in the West Virginia primary, that he must meet the issue directly. He did so in a bold and dramatic appearance on September 12 before a group of 300 Protestant ministers in Houston. In his frank discussion of his religion he declared:

> I believe in an America where the separation of Church and State is absolute—where no Catholic prelate would tell the President (should he be a Catholic) how to act, and no Protestant minister would tell his parishioners for whom to vote—where no church or church school is granted any public funds or political preference—and where no man is denied public office merely because his religion differs from the President who might appoint him or the people who might elect him.

Kennedy's speech in Houston did not silence anti-Catholic bigots, but it offered reassuring answers to many reasonable questions on the subject.

A series of four television "debates" between the two major candidates gave Kennedy an opportunity to demolish the notion of his youthful inexperience and to force Nixon into the role of defending a passive administration. An estimated 70 million adult Americans viewed the first of the hour-long confrontations on September 26. Most people thought Kennedy appeared to best advantage during the initial encounter. The following three debates were more even, but Kennedy benefited from the favorable impression he had made on millions of viewers. According to a Roper poll, of 4 million voters who were decisively influenced by the debates, 3 million voted for Kennedy.

Nixon's relationship with President Eisenhower was both a source of strength and a continuing problem for the GOP nominee. Although Nixon privately disagreed with the administration's position on a number of issues, he found it necessary to endorse the Eisenhower policies as a whole. Eisenhower's own entry into the campaign was somewhat delayed, but he delivered several hard-hitting speeches in the closing weeks of the contest, attracting great crowds and enthusiastic responses wherever he appeared. Meanwhile, Nixon crammed into those weeks an extraordinarily full traveling and speaking schedule. The Republicans also launched a massive television effort in the final days of the campaign.

In an election that set a record for voter participation (over 10 percent greater than 1956), Kennedy had a popular margin of only 119,450 votes out of 68.8 million cast, although his electoral advantage was 303 to 219.[1] Kennedy carried twelve states by margins of less than 2 percent of the two-party votes, and if 4,500 more voters in Illinois and 28,000 more in Texas had gone against him, he would have lost the election by 2 electoral votes. The Democrats carried

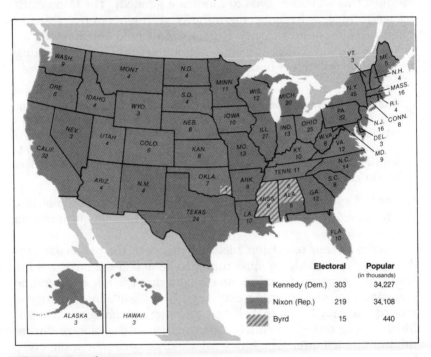

	Electoral	Popular (in thousands)
Kennedy (Dem.)	303	34,227
Nixon (Rep.)	219	34,108
Byrd	15	440

The Election of 1960

Congress handily, however, winning a 65 to 35 majority in the Senate and a 262 to 174 superiority in the House.

The Massachusetts senator's strong showing in the industrial states of the East and Midwest was obviously an indispensable factor in his success, as was the powerful influence of Senator Johnson in the Democratic victories in Texas and several other southern states. The business recession in the fall and Kennedy's focus on economic stagnation undoubtedly hurt the Republicans. Blacks had not initially responded with much enthusiasm to Kennedy's candidacy, but his emphasis on social reform coupled with Nixon's calculated efforts to attract southern whites made the Democratic ticket more appealing to blacks throughout the country. Then, near the end of the campaign, Kennedy and his brother Robert made a dramatic gesture that had a decided impact on black thinking; when Martin Luther King, Jr., was sent to a Georgia prison on a technicality, John Kennedy called Mrs. King to express his concern, while his brother managed soon afterward to secure the black leader's release on bail.

One political scientist has suggested that the Democratic standard-bearer won "in spite of his religion." Kennedy's religious faith brought him some votes from Catholics who had supported Eisenhower, but it hurt him badly in the South and Midwest. An estimated 4.5 million Protestant Democrats who had voted for Stevenson switched to Nixon in 1960. Still, large numbers of Protestants who had supported Eisenhower voted for Kennedy in 1960.

THE KENNEDY APPROACH TO FOREIGN POLICY

The new president devoted most of his moving inaugural address on January 20, 1961, to the challenges that confronted American preeminence in the world. He called upon the nation's citizens to join him in developing new frontiers to achieve greatness. "Let the word go forth from this time and place, to friend and foe alike," he declared, "that the torch has been passed to a new generation of Americans—born in this century, tempered by war, disciplined by a hard and bitter peace, proud of our ancient heritage—and unwilling to witness or permit the slow undoing of those human rights to which this nation has always been committed, and to which we are committed today at home and around the world." The United States must be "the watchman on the walls of world freedom."

John F. Kennedy had come to maturity during the years of Franklin D. Roosevelt's burgeoning internationalism and wartime diplomacy. Born on May 29, 1917, in Brookline, Massachusetts, Kennedy was part of an Irish Catholic family that was rapidly moving up in

John F. Kennedy takes command (*U.S.A. Signal Corps, courtesy John F. Kennedy Library*)

the world as he himself grew up. Someone has described him as "the first of the Irish Brahmins." He was educated in private schools and was graduated with honors from Harvard College in 1940. During the war he served in the Navy and was seriously injured in 1943 when the PT boat he commanded was sunk by a Japanese destroyer off the Solomon Islands. He was elected to the House of Representatives in 1946 and was twice returned to his seat before moving up to the Senate in 1952.

There was a bit of the scholar and the writer in the politician. His senior thesis at Harvard, an examination of the reasons for Britain's refusal to oppose Hitler's challenge in the 1930s, had been published as *Why England Slept* (1940). He wrote a second book during his early Senate tenure while convalescing from a serious operation on his injured back. That work, *Profiles in Courage* (1956), surveyed the careers of several courageous senators who, in times of crisis, stood against the prevailing sentiment of their colleagues and the public. It won the young senator a Pulitzer Prize. Kennedy's intellectual qualities and personal attributes were, in fact, quite extraordinary. His mind was practical, ironic, skeptical, and inexhaustibly curious. He tended toward understatement. When asked on one occasion how he became a wartime hero, Kennedy replied, "It was involuntary. They sank my boat." Kennedy was convinced, as Aida DiPace Donald has written, "that one man in motion could make a difference." He believed that the American presidency required "a vigorous proponent of the national interest," that the White House should be "the vital center of action," and that the president "must be prepared to exercise the fullest powers of his office—all that are specified and some that are not."

In the beginning, Kennedy made few changes in the fundamental U.S. approach to the containment of communism. He bypassed such frequently mentioned possibilities as Adlai E. Stevenson and Senator J. William Fulbright in selecting a secretary of state.[2] Instead, Kennedy chose Dean Rusk, a soft-spoken and urbane southerner who had served as assistant secretary of state for Far Eastern affairs in the Truman administration and, since 1952, as president of the Rockefeller Foundation. Robert S. McNamara took over as Kennedy's secretary of defense. McNamara, who had been president of the Ford Motor Company, was an expert in applying statistical analysis to management problems. Distrusting professional diplomats, Kennedy surrounded himself in the White House with a group of bright young advisers. Several of these aides were academic intellectuals, such as McGeorge Bundy, special assistant for national security affairs, and Arthur M. Schlesinger, Jr., an adviser on Latin American affairs. The new chief executive made little use of Cabinet meetings, dismantled the elaborate National Security

Council structure developed by Eisenhower, and relied on the small, efficient staff directed by Bundy in the White House.

Assuming that United States and Russian thermonuclear power was so awesome as to constitute a "balance of terror" or a "mutual deterrent," Kennedy and McNamara adopted a strategy of "flexible response" in place of the Eisenhower-Dulles doctrine of "massive retaliation." Searching for a wider range of options and greater flexibility in meeting aggression, the administration emphasized a balanced and diversified defense establishment, one that would include not only strategic and tactical nuclear weapons, but also conventional arms and guerrilla forces. The emphasis on a more sophisticated and diversified defense was accompanied by an increase in military expenditures. The defense budget rose by $7 billion during the first year of Kennedy's tenure. The airborne-alert capacity of the Strategic Air Command was extended. The submarine-launched Polaris missile program was accelerated, as were the intercontinental Minutemen (which were launched from underground sites). The Army's combat divisions were increased from eleven to sixteen and modernized in various ways. The tactical wings of the Air Force were expanded from sixteen to twenty-one. The Marine Corps was enlarged. McNamara wanted to build up NATO's ground forces to the long-sought thirty divisions, and while that goal was never reached, about 400,000 American troops were stationed in Europe by 1963.

The strategy of "controlled and flexible response" was conceived as a means of preventing Communist subversion in the Third World and bolstering the American capacity to deter or resist local aggression. Identifying the most dangerous form of Communist expansionism as "wars of national liberation," the Kennedy administration created special forces to help put down aggression by guerrillas and concentrated on developing techniques of counterinsurgency. While expanding and diversifying the defense establishment, the Kennedy team sought to control nuclear forces more closely and thus reduce the chances of accidental war. McNamara opposed the proliferation of nuclear arsenals within the NATO alliance, and the administration canceled plans to provide Britain with a nuclear air-to-ground missile called Skybolt. France's Charles de Gaulle interpreted this decision as further evidence that the United States would not allow its European allies to use nuclear weapons in some future crisis.

Although President Kennedy fully subscribed to the containment policy and shared the conventional American view of communism as a monolithic force, he also realized that the key to world peace was improved relations between the United States and the Soviet

Union. He hoped to relax cold war tensions. While his own public statements were not devoid of militant rhetoric, he abandoned some of the clichés of the cold war, especially in references to the Third World, where he claimed to be willing to accept neutralism and even socialism. In writing his inaugural address, he decided to use the word "adversary" rather than "enemy"—and he continued to make this distinction in later statements. "Let us never negotiate out of fear," he had declared on that January day in 1961, "but let us never fear to negotiate." By taking the lead in strategic weapons and building mobile strike units to suppress wars of national liberation, America would bargain with Russia from strength.

Kennedy thought that important changes should be made in the U.S. approach to Latin America and other underdeveloped areas, whose social problems and revolutions seemed to provide a fertile breeding ground for political extremism and international communism. The administration expanded and reorganized the foreign aid program, reorienting it toward the Third World. It established the Agency for International Development (AID) to manage the aid program. Congress approved the president's proposals for the Development Loan Fund to help underdeveloped countries, the Alliance for Progress to assist Latin America, and U.S. membership in the Organization for Economic Cooperation and Development (OECD), in which Canada and eighteen Western European countries collaborated on improving world trade and helping underdeveloped nations. The most successful of the Kennedy foreign aid programs was the Peace Corps, an idea JFK borrowed from others but pledged himself to during the campaign of 1960. Kennedy announced the formation of the Peace Corps by executive order on March 1, 1961. Congress passed legislation in September 1961 putting the program on a permanent basis and appropriating $30 million for its operation during the first year. During the next few years, Peace Corps volunteers served two-year stints in scores of underdeveloped countries, making significant contributions in such fields as education, sanitation, irrigation, and agriculture. By early 1963, five thousand volunteers were enrolled. The Peace Corps proved to be immensely popular in the United States and brought an overwhelmingly favorable response from other parts of the world.

The first two years of Kennedy's foreign policy were ambiguous. Kennedy brought renewed vigor and innovation to the handling of international relations, and he appealed successfully to the idealism and altruism of his fellow citizens, especially of young people. Yet the globalism of earlier years continued to hold sway, manifesting itself in a dangerous tendency to react indiscriminately to every international crisis without regard to national capability. Twice dur-

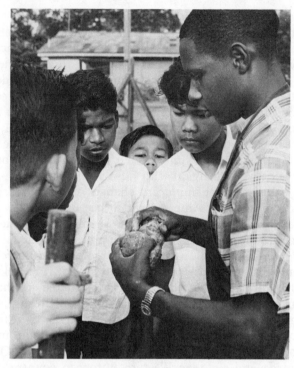

Volunteer Hubert Jones of Dallas, Texas, teaches
industrial arts and agriculture in a boys' school at
Sungei Mangis in Selangor Province, Malaysia (*Peace
Corps photograph*)

ing the first twenty months of its tenure the Kennedy government
was confronted with a crisis that threatened to plunge the world
into nuclear war.

A TROUBLED BEGINNING

One of the problems Kennedy inherited from Eisenhower was Fidel
Castro's revolution in Cuba. As president-elect, Kennedy first
learned of a secret plan, approved by Eisenhower in the spring of
1960, for the invasion of Cuba by anti-Castro refugees. Kennedy's
military advisers endorsed the scheme, and the Central Intelligence
Agency assured him that the attack would succeed. Although Senator William Fulbright and a few others opposed the undertaking
and JFK himself had some qualms about it, the president acquiesced
in the foolhardy venture. Not only was Kennedy basically hostile to
a Cuban revolutionary government like Castro's, but he had criticized the Eisenhower administration during the campaign of 1960

for not being tough enough with Castro. The invasion took place on Cuba's southern coast at *Bahía de Cochinos* (Bay of Pigs) on April 17, 1961. The invading forces included fewer than 1,500 troops who were never able to establish a defensible beachhead along the swampy terrain selected for the operation. Lacking naval and air support, they were quickly pinned down by Castro's military forces. There was no popular uprising, and the invasion was completely crushed within three days.

The whole affair was an appalling and humiliating disaster for the United States and the Kennedy administration. The overconfident CIA had grossly misjudged the situation. The project was poorly planned, the size of the invading force totally inadequate, and the operation filled with tactical blunders and miscalculations. One anti-Castro exile said it was "like learning that Superman is a fairy." Kennedy was badly shaken by this early mishap in foreign policy.[3] The Bay of Pigs adventure brought an increase in Castro's domestic support and strengthened his ties with Russia. It gave Nikita Khrushchev a pretext to bluster and threaten. It outraged many Latin Americans, revived fears of Yankee imperialism in the Southern Hemisphere, and set back Kennedy's promising attempts to identify the United States with anticolonialism. It was a clear violation of American treaty agreements and obligations, not to mention domestic statutes outlawing such activities.

The Bay of Pigs setback encouraged President Kennedy to agree to a meeting with Premier Khrushchev and to test the Russian's mettle. Kennedy and Khrushchev held a series of private meetings in Vienna on June 3 and 4, 1961. They did not get along well. The two leaders did agree to stop the growing conflict in Laos (see pages 233–34), but there was little harmony in their other discussions. Kennedy's position was that efforts to impose communism by force of arms in any country would threaten the balance of power all around the globe. Khrushchev would not agree to stop supporting what he termed "wars of liberation." He was even more militant about Berlin, renewing his demand of the late fifties for an "immediate" peace treaty with Germany and an end to the current four-power occupation of Berlin. The American leader was deeply disturbed by his confrontation with the Soviet premier.

At Vienna Kennedy emphasized his determination to defend West Berlin, but Khrushchev seemed to take these warnings lightly, and he insisted throughout the following summer that the problem of Berlin would have to be resolved before the end of 1961. If the West would not sign a treaty turning Berlin into a "free city," the Soviet Union would sign a separate peace treaty with East Germany, thereby automatically abrogating the right of the Western powers to be in Berlin. The Russians wanted a satisfactory settlement in Germany before the effects of Kennedy's military buildup could be felt. But they were also concerned over another matter—the enormous success of West Berlin as a "showcase of democracy" behind the Iron Curtain. In the late spring of 1961 a thousand refugees a day, including many technicians, skilled workers, and young people, were flocking into West Berlin. The very economic survival of the East German state, to say nothing of its prestige, was involved in this swelling exodus. Fearful of appearing weak, Kennedy was resolved to make the Berlin crisis not only a question of West Berlin's rights, but, in Theodore Sorensen's words, "a question of direct Soviet-American confrontation over a shift in the balance of power."

During the weeks that followed the Vienna conference, Khrushchev heightened the tension over Berlin by increasing his demands for concessions from the Western powers and by strengthening his military posture. Kennedy, bolstered by advice from such stout cold warriors as Dean Acheson, was prepared to engage in a "conflict of wills" with his Russian adversary. By July a war of words and of nerves had developed. On July 25 Kennedy announced that he was speeding up draft calls, extending enlistments, and mobilizing some reserve and National Guard units; he eventually increased the size of the armed forces by 300,000 men. At the same time he requested an additional defense appropriation of $3.25 billion. Congress voted Kennedy's new defense budget by overwhelming majorities. Encouraged in part by a presidential recommendation, a frenzy of fallout-shelter building momentarily swept the country. Then, suddenly, the climax came in Berlin.

Before dawn on August 13, 1961, the East German government closed the border between East and West Berlin, and during the next few days the Communists began constructing an elaborate wall of concrete and barbed wire throughout the city, a barrier that was ultimately extended along the entire western border of East Germany. The Western powers protested sternly but did not use force against the barricade. President Kennedy dispatched a battle force of U.S. troops down the 100-mile autobahn from West Germany through the Communist zone into Berlin as a gesture of defiance and as a test of Soviet intentions. The Communists did not halt this convoy. Kennedy also sent Vice President Johnson and General Lucius D. Clay (the commander of the American forces in Germany during the Berlin blockade of 1948–49) to West Berlin as evidence of continuing American support of the Allied position.

The Berlin crisis finally dissipated in the fall and winter. Khrushchev's wall was a brilliant and dramatic stroke, and it removed a running sore on the Russians' western flank. But the wall was also a confession of Communist frustration and bankruptcy.

THE CUBAN MISSILE CRISIS AND THE TEST BAN TREATY

The most crucial event of the Kennedy years and the most dangerous of all cold war confrontations was the Cuban missile crisis of October 1962. After the Bay of Pigs, Fidel Castro's hostility toward the United States understandably grew. He built up a large army, renewed a trade pact with the Soviet Union early in 1962, and boasted of his Communist ideology. Khrushchev, frustrated in the face of American nuclear superiority, unable to get the Western Allies out of Berlin, and irritated by Chinese criticism of Soviet weakness, sought an opportunity to alter the strategic balance. In the summer of 1962 he decided to make a daring move: to deploy intermediate-range ballistic missiles in Cuba, the first such commitment of nuclear weapons outside of Russia. This Soviet effort was altogether a very large undertaking, involving many months of planning, 175 ships, 6,000 men, and a cost of about three quarters of a billion dollars. The success of this strategem would make the Russian strategic force more credible, weaken the United States in the eyes of its NATO allies, possibly enable Khrushchev to reopen the Berlin negotiations, and undermine the U.S. position in the Americas. Installation of nuclear missiles ninety mile off the U.S. coast would, at the very least, give the "appearance" of Soviet power.

Unfortunately for Khrushchev, he was unable to achieve strategic surprise. U.S. officials were well aware of the heavy movement of Russian military equipment and personnel into Cuba, although they assumed that the USSR was simply ensuring Castro's regime against external attack. When Kennedy learned of the clandestine construction of missile launching sites in Cuba, he began a series of secret meetings with close advisers and NSC members in an atmosphere of utmost tension. Quick action was imperative since additional missiles were on the high seas and the missile sites would become operational within a matter of days. During the lengthy sessions of these top aides and officials, a variety of alternatives were explored, but gradually two possible courses of action came to the fore. One group, including the military spokesmen and Dean Acheson, argued vigorously for a "surgical" air strike against the missile bases, even though such an attack would probably kill Soviet technicians working on the sites. A second group of the president's advisers supported Under Secretary of State George Ball's recommendation that some kind of blockade be instituted against Cuba. This would represent a flexible arrangement that would give the Russians the maximum opportunity to back down without humiliation. Ball's position won the support of Secretary of Defense McNamara and Attorney General Robert F. Kennedy, who became a key figure in the formulation of the American response.

It was the president, however, who dominated the secret meetings and made the ultimate decision. The discovery of the missiles put the administration in a difficult position. A "war party" had already begun to develop in the United States as rumors of Soviet military penetration of Cuba spread. The midterm congressional elections were less than three weeks away, and Republicans could be expected to make the most of any administration weakness in responding to new cold war challenges. Sensitive to any appearance of weakness, Kennedy was resolved to act; but he chose the more moderate course of imposing a blockade instead of an immediate attack on Cuba. At the same time, he decided upon a public confrontation in order to dramatize and reverse Khrushchev's cold war offensive. Having made these critical decisions, Kennedy acted swiftly to put the plan into effect. On October 22, he briefed the Cabinet and congressional leaders, informed the other NATO nations of the situation, and called a meeting of the Organization of American States for the next day. At 7 P.M. he delivered a nationwide television address to the American people.

Kennedy described what had happened and told the country what to expect. The Russian tactic in Cuba, he declared, was "a deliberately provocative and unjustified change in the status quo which cannot be accepted by this country, if our courage and our commitments are ever again to be trusted by either friend or foe." He proclaimed a "strict quarantine"—actually a blockade—on "all offensive military equipment under shipment to Cuba." He issued a stern warning to the Russians and demanded that Khrushchev remove the missiles already in Cuba. Even as the president spoke, the Strategic Air Command was beginning a massive airborne alert, 156 intercontinental ballistic missiles were in combat readiness, a fleet of Polaris submarines was on guard at sea, the Navy was establishing a 2,100-mile ring around Cuba (eventually employing 180 ships), and hundreds of thousands of men were placed in combat readiness.

The world shuddered as the two great powers confronted each other at the brink. Would Soviet missiles "fly" in defense of Cuba, as Khrushchev had previously warned? What would happen when the Russian missile-carrying freighters were intercepted by the

American blockading units? The Soviet Union's immediate reaction was to denounce the U.S. blockade as illegal. But finally, after two of the most anxious days in modern times, the crisis began to ease. A dozen Soviet vessels headed for Cuba suddenly reversed course or were diverted, prompting Secretary Rusk to remark, "We're eyeball to eyeball and I think the other fellow just blinked." Conditions remained dangerous and uncertain, but it was clear that Khrushchev had overplayed his hand.

On October 26 a solution began to emerge. First through an unofficial emissary and then in a long, emotional letter, Khrushchev started backing off. The letter seemed to imply that Russia would

Executive Committee of the National Security Council during the Cuban Missile Crisis (courtesy John F. Kennedy Library)

remove the missile bases if the United States would end its blockade and promise not to invade Cuba. Before the United States could
respond to this offer, a second Soviet message reached Washington
on October 27, offering to dismantle the missile sites in Cuba if the
United States would withdraw its missile bases from Turkey. Faced
with this perplexing situation, American leaders adopted Robert
Kennedy's suggestion that they respond to the first message and
ignore the second. This ingenious expedient worked. The United
States promised not to invade Cuba if the missiles were quickly
withdrawn and if a number of Russian medium-range bombers were
returned to the USSR. The United States also made an oral promise,
delivered by Attorney General Kennedy to Soviet Ambassador An-
atoly Dobrynin, that the American missiles in Turkey would be removed.[4] Khrushchev agreed to this arrangement, and the crisis
ended.

The crisis over Cuban missiles in the autumn of 1962 turned out
better than Kennedy and his advisers had dared to hope. Kennedy,
gaining new confidence, was at last persuaded that his will and
courage were no longer in doubt. He became more moderate and
less strident, at least in dealing with the USSR, and he understood
that the missile withdrawal suggested no universal formula for dealing successfully with the Russians. As for Khrushchev, the missile
crisis tarnished his image in many neutral countries and contributed to his decline within the Soviet bloc.

The missile crisis set the stage for a gradual improvement in
Russo-American relations. The most notable evidence of this relaxation of tensions during the Kennedy administration was the agreement reached in the summer of 1963 to restrict the testing of nuclear weapons. The antecedents of this so-called test ban were
numerous and diverse. They included Kennedy's new confidence
and the more moderate approach he began to employ toward the
Soviet Union. There was also Khrushchev's desperate need to ease
the military pressure on his slumping economy, the possibility that
a diplomatic coup would restore his fading reputation, and the widening rift between Russia and the People's Republic of China. Both
China and France coveted nuclear weapons, and the USSR and the
United States were by no means happy over the prospect of such
nuclear dispersion. Still another consideration was the growing concern over the large amounts of radioactive materials being released
into the atmosphere as a result of nuclear testing, which the Soviet
Union had resumed in the fall of 1961 and the United States in the
spring of the following year.

Disarmament talks had dragged on fruitlessly for years when
Kennedy made the decision, in the spring of 1963, that the United

States would not be the first nation to carry out further atmospheric tests. In a conciliatory address at American University on June 10, 1963, the president disclosed that representatives of Britain, Russia, and the United States would soon meet in Moscow to discuss the question of a nuclear test ban treaty. If the United States and its adversaries could not now end all differences, he declared, "at least we can help make the world safe for diversity. For, in the final analysis, our most basic common link is that we all inhabit this small planet. We all breathe the same air. We all cherish our children's future. And we are all mortal."

To emphasize the importance the administration attached to the Moscow deliberations, Kennedy selected Averell Harriman, perhaps the most experienced and formidable American who had dealt with the Russians, to represent the United States. Harriman proved to be a skillful negotiator, and he had a large part in fashioning the treaty concluded by the three powers on July 25. Although the agreement did not provide for on-site inspection or ban underground testing, it did prohibit all nuclear tests in the atmosphere, in outer space, on land, and under water. The Nuclear Test Ban Treaty was quickly signed by about a hundred other nations, although neither the People's Republic of China nor France ratified it. While the treaty encountered some opposition in the United States, including that of a few scientists like Dr. Edward Teller who were concerned about the maintenance of American nuclear deterrence, the Senate ratified the agreement, under strong administration pressure, on September 24 by a vote of 80 to 19.

The test ban treaty was one of Kennedy's most positive diplomatic achievements. The agreement had a profound impact upon world opinion. It reduced the pollution of the earth's atmosphere by radioactive fallout and offered renewed hope for the negotiated settlement of international conflicts. Yet, ironically, the underground testing clause provided a loophole through which the nuclear arms race was continued and new weapons were later perfected. "The eventual achievement of the atmospheric test ban in 1963," Robert E. Osgood has noted, "was more significant as a symbolic initiative toward détente than as a restriction of arms."

A few weeks after the treaty was signed, Kennedy proposed a joint Soviet-American expedition to the moon. He also approved the sale of $250 million worth of surplus wheat to Russia, which was suffering from a grain shortage. Washington and Moscow soon agreed to the installation of a "hot line" between the White House and the Kremlin. A mild thaw in the cold war had clearly begun, although there was little evidence of progress in the resolution of fundamental differences between the two superpowers.

GLOBAL CONNECTIONS AND THIRD WORLD POLICIES

John F. Kennedy's foreign policies reflected his country's mounting interest during the late fifties and early sixties in the underdeveloped nations or the so-called Third World. Kennedy's concern over these emerging nations, many of which had only recently won their independence and were as yet aligned with neither side in the cold war, stemmed both from his desire to halt the spread of international communism and from his belief that these countries constituted the real arena of competition between the United States and the Soviet Union.[5] The American president understood that the underdeveloped countries desperately needed economic and technical assistance, and he appreciated the desirability of encouraging internal change and social reform in much of the Third World.

Although the United States generally remained aloof from the conflict between the new nations of Africa and their erstwhile European colonizers, it was impossible not to take some part in the Congo, which was plunged into civil war almost as soon as it received its independence from Belgium in 1960. Hoping to avoid a confrontation with the Soviet Union in the Congo, where the Russians were backing one of the contending factions, Kennedy supported the military efforts of the United Nations to suppress the Katanga secession movement led by Moishe Tshombe. The president persuaded Congress to purchase $100 million worth of UN bonds as a means of strengthening United Nations operations, which managed to reunite the country by early 1963. One of the tragedies of the conflict was the death of UN Secretary General Dag Hammarskjold, who died in a plane crash while trying to arrange a settlement in the Congo. His death precipitated a struggle in which the Soviet bloc tried to change the nature of the Secretariat into a "troika," or three-horsed harness arrangement, composed of Communist, Western, and neutralist representatives, each to have a veto. This scheme, which would have rendered the UN utterly powerless, was defeated in November 1961, with strong American help, and U Thant of Burma was chosen as acting secretary general.

Meanwhile, the Kennedy administration was taking a keen interest in Latin America, a region that had long felt neglected by the United States. While Kennedy's Latin American diplomacy was designed to counter Castroism and to win the support of the nations to the south in the cold war, the young chief executive seemed to sense the pressure for social change and the urge for a better life in that vast underdeveloped area. In mid-March 1961, Kennedy urged that a partnership be undertaken between the United States and the several Latin American nations in order "to satisfy the basic needs of the American peoples for homes, work and land, health and schools." The idea was received with enthusiasm in Latin America, and in August 1961, representatives of the OAS meeting in Punta del Este, Uruguay, formulated a blueprint for the Alliance for Progress.

The Act of Punta del Este called for a massive developmental program during the next decade, with the United States agreeing to provide over half of the $20 billion to be obtained outside of Latin America. In return the Latin American nations would make an immense investment of their own, while committing themselves to important land and tax reforms. Although Congress appropriated funds to help inaugurate the new program and every American republic except Cuba joined it, the *Alianza* got off to a poor start. The Alliance seemed to lose some of its urgency following the missile crisis of 1962 and the discovery that Castro's revolution could not be easily exported. Increasing military costs in the United States as well as bureaucratic infighting in Washington and the administration's growing emphasis on military aid as a means of "helping" other people undermined U.S. support of the undertaking. Looking toward liberal and voluntary reforms, the Alliance was unable to reallocate to any significant degree the power and privileges of the wealthy oligarchies that controlled the region. Furthermore, the major revenue-producing properties in Latin America remained in the hands of U.S. corporations, and one of the strings attached to Alliance loans was that such money should be spent on relatively expensive American-made goods. Despite all of its publicity, the Alliance for Progress did little to change the lives of the Latin American masses.

President Kennedy never questioned the need to support American commitments to contain communism in the Far East. One trouble spot was Laos, an isolated mountain country that bordered the People's Republic of China on the north and stretched southward roughly parallel to the divided Vietnam. The pro-Western Laotian government was weak and unstable, and by the beginning of the 1960s it was under increasing attack from the Pathet Lao, a revolutionary movement modeled on Ho Chi Minh's Vietminh. By early 1961 the Communist-assisted Pathet Lao had captured the strategic Plain of Jars and was pushing south along the Vietnam border. In March JFK warned Moscow, Peking, and Hanoi that the United States would not tolerate a Communist takeover in Laos. The president decided against large-scale American intervention, however, and at the urging of Averell Harriman, sought a diplomatic solution that would preclude a Pathet Lao victory, avoid an armed confrontation with the Soviet Union, and establish a "neutral and independent Laos."

A neutralization formula was finally agreed to on July 21, 1962. Although the agreement prevented a superpower confrontation in Laos, the civil war was soon resumed by the Pathet Lao, which received military support from North Vietnam so that the Ho Chi Minh Trail could be kept open as a means of supplying the National Liberation Front in South Vietnam. In May 1962 the United States sent troops into Thailand, which borders Laos on the west, in order to counter gains by the Pathet Lao. Thailand, disturbed over the pending neutralization of Laos, had signed a treaty with the United States in March 1962, permitting the American government to come to the Thais' rescue, even if other SEATO members should object (thereby transforming the multilateral nature of the original SEATO pact). The neutralist government of Prince Souvanna Phouma was still trying to govern Laos at the end of 1963, with the United States continuing its grudging support.

The neutralization of Laos was related to the Kennedy administration's decision to base American defense of Southeast Asia on South Vietnam, whose independence Kennedy supported no less than did Eisenhower. Kennedy's approach to Southeast Asia was no doubt influenced by the inquest over the "loss" of China and the frustrations of the Korean War during the years of McCarthyism, as well as his acceptance of the domino theory. Having accepted defeat at the Bay of Pigs and compromise in Laos, Kennedy was not inclined to give any ground in Vietnam, which represented a fallback position for the United States in Southeast Asia. Yet the influence of North Vietnam was spreading among the South Vietnamese, and the National Liberation Front, or Vietcong, was increasing its attacks on the regime of Ngo Dinh Diem. A Vietcong victory, in the president's view, would lead to Communist control of all Vietnam, prepare the way for Communist success in Cambodia and Laos, and make the situation for the United States and its allies precarious in Thailand, Burma, and other East Asian countries.

Kennedy set about strengthening the Diem regime. At the suggestion of American experts, for example, Diem instituted a counterinsurgency plan (known as the strategic-hamlet program) as a means of securing the countryside and protecting friendly peasants. In the spring of 1961 Kennedy sent Lyndon Johnson to investigate conditions in South Vietnam, and the vice president brought back some ominous impressions. Johnson recommended an increase in U.S. assistance to Diem, whom he brashly characterized as the "Winston Churchill of Asia." In the fall JFK sent another mission to Saigon, headed by General Maxwell D. Taylor and presidential aide Walt Whitman Rostow. They reported that South Vietnam had enough vitality to justify a major U.S. effort, and their recommendations pointed toward great reliance on a military solution. In a later report the Defense Department and the Joint Chiefs of Staff urged the desirability of using American troops if necessary to preserve the Diem government. They estimated the force needed would not exceed six divisions. After returning from Vietnam in June 1962, Secretary McNamara asserted that "every quantitative measurement we have shows we're winning the war."

Vietnam seemed to offer the kind of situation in which the new Kennedy-McNamara flexible defense program could be employed successfully. Special forces like the Green Berets, the Americans assumed, relying heavily on technology and guerrilla warfare, would be able to put down insurrections or revolutions. The Cuban missile crisis probably accelerated U.S. intervention in Vietnam by encouraging the administration to assume that it could manage crisis situations. In any event, Kennedy steadily expanded the American training program in South Vietnam. By early 1962 there were over 4,000 military "advisers" in the country, compared to about 650 when Eisenhower left office. Many Europeans found it difficult to comprehend the choice of South Vietnam as "a proving grounds for democracy." "For you," Charles de Gaulle somberly remarked to Kennedy, "intervention in this region will be an entanglement without end."

Ultimately, American success in Vietnam would rest upon the effectiveness of the Saigon government in resisting the challenge of the National Liberation Front. Although the United States made sporadic efforts to persuade Diem to carry out land reform and other needed domestic changes, the South Vietnam leader showed little interest in such programs. The ruling Catholic minority encountered mounting dissent from the large Buddhist population, and in May 1963 a series of Buddhist protests were brutally suppressed by Diem. Such blatant repression not only played into the hands of the Vietcong but provoked outcries in the United States and eventually undermined the Kennedy administration's confidence in Diem. On November 1, 1963, a military conspiracy, with the acquiescence of Washington, overthrew the Diem regime and assassinated the president and his brother. Unfortunately, however, the new leaders came from the same conservative elements that had produced Diem.

Kennedy and his advisers insisted that the area south of the 17th parallel was vital to U.S. interests and that American success there would contribute to the isolation of the People's Republic of China and halt the Communist expansion in East Asia. "In my opinion,"

Kennedy declared near the end of his life, "for us to withdraw from that effort would mean a collapse not only of South Vietnam but Southeast Asia. So we are going to stay there." By the end of Kennedy's thousand days, there were 16,000 American military men in South Vietnam, and they were more and more involved in the actual fighting there. The chief executive failed to give sufficient weight to the fact that the struggle in Vietnam was in large part a civil war and that the opponents of the pro-Western government in Saigon reflected nationalist sentiment as well as Communist ideology.

President Kennedy's international objectives also included a stronger trans-Atlantic partnership. Through the Grand Design for Europe, JFK hoped to strengthen the unity and effectiveness of the Western alliance. He envisioned a Western Europe united in the Common Market and moving toward political federation, cooperating with the United States and Britain in freer trade agreements that would promote the economic growth of non-Communist countries everywhere. To lend American support to this development, Kennedy persuaded Congress to pass the Trade Expansion Act of 1962, empowering the chief executive to lower tariff barriers in return for trade concessions. On the military front, the Kennedy administration opposed de Gaulle's plan to build an independent French nuclear deterrent. Kennedy wanted the nations of Western Europe to spend more for their own security, and he hoped to broaden NATO's defense options by having them place renewed emphasis on conventional, non-nuclear forces. These proposals met with little favor from his European allies.

The easing of cold war tensions that followed the Cuban missile crisis encouraged European leaders to assert greater independence in their relations with the United States. Thus General de Gaulle prepared a Franco-German treaty of friendship, worked to improve relations with the Warsaw Pact nations, and stepped up the pace of French nuclear development. He withdrew his country's naval forces from NATO and made a bold bid for European independence from American international domination. Early in 1963, in characteristically dramatic fashion, de Gaulle rejected Britain's request for membership in the Common Market, repudiated the U.S.-sponsored Multinational Defense Force (MDF), and declared that France would provide itself with the necessary nuclear defenses. Kennedy soon abandoned the MDF plan, and while he and other American spokesmen continued to talk about a stronger and more unified Europe, it had become clear that many of the NATO countries were no longer willing to follow U.S. leadership unquestioningly.

Perhaps the most distinctive characteristic of Kennedy's foreign policy was its ambiguity. Thus he neutralized Laos but was drawn into ever-greater involvement in Vietnam. If, as McGeorge Bundy has said, Kennedy "rejected the stale rhetoric of the cold war" and if he shifted its direction with the test ban agreement, he remained adamant in his conviction that the United States must meet the Communist challenge all over the world. Even so, the young president demonstrated an ability to learn and to grow in dealing with international problems. His record in foreign affairs was promising in some respects, and had he lived and served a second term in the presidency, there is at least a chance that contemporary American history would have been considerably different.

Notes

1. Senator Harry Flood Byrd of Virginia received 15 electoral votes: 8 from Mississippi, 6 from Alabama, and 1 from Oklahoma. Byrd was not a candidate.
2. Stevenson was appointed ambassador to the United Nations.
3. To secure the return of some 1,100 invaders imprisoned in Cuba, the administration subsequently encouraged private American citizens to raise the $53 million in ransom demanded by Castro and to negotiate the release of the prisoners.
4. Actually, the decision had already been made to remove these missiles, which were regarded as obsolete and no longer of strategic value.
5. Twenty-seven African and Asian countries achieved their independence during Kennedy's brief presidency.

Suggestions for Further Reading

The best biography of John F. Kennedy is Herbert S. Parmet's two-volume study: *Jack: The Struggles of John F. Kennedy* (1980) and *JFK: The Presidency of John F. Kennedy* (1983). For Kennedy's early life and pre-presidential career, see in addition to Parmet's first volume, James Mac-Gregor Burns, *John Kennedy: A Political Profile* (1960), and Joan and Clay Blair, *The Search for J.F.K.* (1976). Henry Fairlie, *The Kennedy Promise: The Politics of Expectation* (1973), presents a caustic view of its subject. Nancy Gager Clinch, *The Kennedy Neurosis* (1973), and Garry Wills, *The Kennedy Imprisonment* (1982), are also critical. Jim F. Heath offers a balanced overview of the Kennedy presidency in *Decade of Disillusionment: The Kennedy-Johnson Years* (1975). A more searching and less favorable evaluation of Kennedy's domestic politics is presented in Allen J. Matusow, *The Unraveling of America: A History of Liberalism in the 1960s* (1984). Bruce Miroff, *Pragmatic Illusions: The Presidential Politics of John F. Kennedy* (1976), is a critical appraisal from a radical perspective. Alonzo L. Hamby's *Liberalism and Its Challengers*, cited in chapter one, contains a thoughtful essay on John and Robert Kennedy in which the two are characterized as "the most magnetic national political leaders of the 1960s." Arthur M. Schlesinger, Jr., *Robert Kennedy and His Times* (1978), is a valuable source for the Kennedy administration as well as a moving biography. Aida DiPace

Donald (ed.), *John F. Kennedy and the New Frontier* (1966), is a useful collection of articles and essays on JFK and his administration.

Two of the most important books on the Kennedy presidency by White House "insiders" are Arthur M. Schlesinger, Jr., *A Thousand Days: John F. Kennedy in the White House* (1965), and Theodore C. Sorensen, *Kennedy* (1965). For the campaign and election of 1960, see the absorbing popular account by Theodore H. White, *The Making of the President, 1960* (1961), and the scholarly work edited by Paul T. David, *The Presidential Election and Transition, 1960–1961* (1961).

Kennedy's foreign policies are treated in the works by Ambrose, LaFeber, and Spanier, cited in chapter two. Roger Hilsman's *To Move a Nation: The Politics of Foreign Policy in the Administration of John F. Kennedy* (1967) is a revealing account by a State Department official. Robert E. Osgood and others put the Kennedy policies in the broad perspective of the 1950s and 1960s in *America and the World: From the Truman Doctrine to Vietnam* (1970). Warren I. Cohen, *Dean Rusk* (1980), is a useful study. The military buildup of 1961–62, the globalism of the Kennedy administration, and other of its policies are criticized by Louise FitzSimons, *The Kennedy Doctrine* (1972), and Richard J. Walton, *Cold War and Counterrevolution: The Foreign Policy of John F. Kennedy* (1972). *The Kennedy Crises: The Press, the Presidency, and Foreign Policy* (1983), by Montague Kern, Patricia W. Levering, and Ralph B. Levering, explores the relationship between Kennedy and the press by examining the foreign-policy crises over Laos, Berlin, Cuba, and Vietnam.

David Green's *The Containment of Latin America: A History of the Myths and Realities of the Good Neighbor Policy* (1971) throws light on U.S. policies in that part of the world. Peter Wyden, *Bay of Pigs* (1979), is a good account of that fiasco. For the missile crisis of 1962, see Elie Abel, *The Missile Crisis* (1966); Robert F. Kennedy, *Thirteen Days: A Memoir of the Cuban Missile Crisis* (1969); Graham T. Allison, *Essence of Decision: Explaining the Cuban Missile Crisis* (1971); Robert A. Divine (ed.), *The Cuban Missile Crisis* (1971); Herbert S. Dinerstein, *The Making of the Missile Crisis* (1975); and David Detzer, *The Brink* (1979). Other aspects of the Cuban problem are dealt with by Theodore Draper, *Castroism, Theory and Practice* (1965), and Ramon Eduardo Ruiz, *Cuba: The Making of a Revolution* (1968). The Alliance for Progress is the subject of William D. Rogers, *The Twilight Struggle: The Alliance for Progress and the Politics of Development in Latin America* (1967), and Jerome Levinson and Juan de Onis, *The Alliance That Lost Its Way: A Critical Report on the Alliance for Progress* (1970).

The American-Soviet conflict over Germany is discussed by Robert M. Slusser, *The Berlin Crisis of 1961* (1973), and Honore Catudal, *Kennedy and the Berlin Wall Crisis* (1980). The nuclear buildup and disarmament efforts are considered in Desmond Ball, *Politics and Force Levels* (1980); Bernard J. Firestone, *The Quest for Nuclear Stability* (1982); and Glen T. Seaborg, *Kennedy, Khrushchev, and the Test Ban* (1982).

In *America's Longest War: The United States and Vietnam, 1950–1975* (2nd ed., 1986), George C. Herring provides a reliable and balanced history of the United States in Vietnam. Another general treatment is provided by George M. Kahin and John W. Lewis, *The United States in Vietnam* (rev. ed., 1969). David Halberstam's *The Best and the Brightest* (1972) illuminates some of the key decisions made during the Kennedy administration. For two other books on Vietnam, see Halberstam, *The Making of a Quagmire* (1965), and Neil Sheehan (ed.), *The Pentagon Papers* (1971).

CHAPTER ELEVEN

New Frontiers
and the Politics
of Reform

WHEN HE accepted his party's presidential nomination in July 1960, John F. Kennedy declared that the New Frontier "is here whether we seek it or not . . . [in the form of] uncharted areas of science and space, unsolved problems of peace and war, unconquered pockets of ignorance and prejudice, unanswered questions of poverty and surplus." During the campaign the young Democratic leader had promised to "get America moving again," at home as well as abroad, and in domestic affairs he was generally comfortable in the mantle of New Deal-Fair Deal reformism. He urged Congress to enact a broad array of proposals ranging from aid to depressed areas and expanded health insurance to larger defense appropriations and foreign assistance. But the record of the Eighty-seventh Congress (1961–62) was not especially impressive, although a few notable measures were enacted. During the third year of his tenure, Kennedy showed definite signs of becoming a bolder and more advanced reformer, and when he left for Dallas in November 1963, he was already planning an ambitious reform program on which to run for reelection in 1964.

JFK AND ECONOMIC PROGRESS

The fourth postwar recession in the United States had not yet ended when Kennedy entered the White House, and during February and March of that winter more men and women were out of work than at any previous time in the postwar period. Kennedy's State of the Union message drew a bleak picture. "We take office," the new president said, "in the wake of seven months of recession, three and one-half years of slack, seven years of diminished economic growth, and nine years of falling farm income." Kennedy declared that his administration did not intend "to stand helplessly by." Among his recommendations to the first session of the Eighty-seventh Congress were measures designed to promote economic recovery and expansion, health care for the elderly, federal aid to schools, conservation and use of natural resources, highway construction, housing and community development, and the strengthening of national defense and foreign aid.

Kennedy's reform proposals did not fare well in 1961; of twenty-three proposed laws he sent to the House of Representatives that year, sixteen were defeated. Nevertheless, the administration could point to some accomplishments by the autumn of 1961 in its efforts to end the recession. The president expanded government expenditures in a variety of ways, tried to stimulate residential construction by lowering interest rates, and dealt adroitly with the balance-of-payments problem. Congress liberalized social security benefits, raised the minimum wage to $1.15 an hour (and authorized a further increase to $1.25 two years later), passed legislation enabling the states temporarily to extend unemployment benefits for an additional thirteen weeks, approved an expanded public works program, and passed a $4.88 billion omnibus housing bill. The most controversial measure adopted was the Area Redevelopment Act, a

Caroline and John dance in the Oval Office (*courtesy John F. Kennedy Library*)

bill strongly supported by Kennedy and twice vetoed by Eisenhower. By the end of 1961 the secretary of labor had designated some 675 areas as "distressed" and thus eligible for federal aid under the law. Meanwhile, the recession had tapered off, in part because of the sharp increase in federal spending, and substantial economic recovery had occurred by late 1961.

The administration's major congressional triumph in 1962 was the Trade Expansion Act, which Kennedy hailed as the most significant advance in U.S. foreign policy "since the passing of the Marshall Plan." Designed to improve the U.S. economy by stimulating competition and trade with the nations of the European Common Market, the act included the largest tariff-cutting power ever granted a president. Congress also enacted the administration's Manpower Retraining bill, which appropriated $435 million over the following three years, if the states would provide a like amount, for the training of the unemployed in new skills. Yet few of Kennedy's proposals came through the Eighty-seventh Congress without limiting amendments. Thus the accelerated Public Works Act of 1962 appropriated $900 million for projects in areas of high unemployment but failed to include JFK's request for standby authority to initiate a $2 billion public works program. The Revenue Act approved during the same session followed the president's recommendation in giving $1 billion in special tax credits to business as a means of encouraging investments in industrial machinery and equipment. But the administration lost the provisions that would have instituted the withholding of income taxes on dividends and interest and curtailed expense-account deductions.

Kennedy's "new approach" to the agricultural problem in the form of tighter production controls was rejected. The president and his secretary of agriculture, Orville L. Freeman, urged the adoption of the "supply management" technique, which was intended to prevent farm products from becoming surplus-storage inventories while keeping farm income up and helping to preserve small farmers. The proposed legislation encountered strong opposition in Congress, particularly from southern Democrats and midwestern Republicans, some of whom cited the notorious case of Billie Sol Estes to buttress their arguments.[1] Although some of the administration's land-use proposals were approved in the Farm Act of 1962, the stringent production controls were defeated and the existing program was continued.

Another of the administration's proposals to the second session of the Eighty-seventh Congress turned out better. This was the president's request for authority to establish a privately owned and financed corporation to administer a communications-satellite system capable of relaying telegraph and telephone messages and television programs throughout the world. Despite the spirited attack on the measure in the Senate led by Paul H. Douglas of Illinois and Estes Kefauver of Tennessee, who labeled the bill a giveaway to the communications industry and urged that the system be owned and controlled by the government, the Communications Satellite Act was approved in 1962. The "Telstar" bill reflected Kennedy's enthusiastic commitment to the United States space program. On May 6, 1961, soon after the Russian cosmonaut Yuri Gagarin had circled the earth in a space vehicle, Commander Alan B. Shepard, Jr., made a 300-mile suborbital flight from Cape Canaveral. During the same month Kennedy urged Congress to commit the United States "to achieving the goal, before this decade is out, of landing a man on the moon and returning him safely to the earth." Congress responded by doubling NASA appropriations in 1962 and again in 1963. Project Apollo soon began to pay off. On February 20, 1962, Lieutenant Colonel John H. Glenn flew around the earth three times in his Mercury space capsule, *Friendship 7*, and landed in the Caribbean on the same afternoon.

One of Kennedy's mounting concerns, as the recession lifted in the second part of 1961, was the danger of inflation. Kennedy and Secretary of Labor Arthur J. Goldberg worked closely in March 1962 with management and labor in the steel industry to avoid a strike and to negotiate a noninflationary labor contract. It was tacitly understood that the steel manufacturers would not raise their prices, but ten days later, on April 10, Roger M. Blough of the United States Steel Corporation informed the president that his company was increasing its prices by about $6 a ton. Five other large firms announced identical increases on the following day. Kennedy, feeling betrayed, denounced the steel companies' action as "a wholly unjustifiable and irresponsible defiance of the public interest." He quickly mobilized the power of the federal government against the offending firms. The Defense Department announced that it would award new contracts only to those companies that refrained from raising prices. The steel executives capitulated within seventy-two hours!

This incident served to increase business distrust of the Kennedy administration, which many businessmen regarded as "antibusiness." When the stock market, on May 28, 1962, experienced its most precipitate drop since the crash of 1929, the setback was attributed in business circles to "lack of confidence" in Kennedy's leadership. Bumper stickers soon appeared with such messages as "I Miss Ike—Hell, I Even Miss Harry." It is true that Kennedy was provoked into attacking the steel companies in 1962. He also fostered Justice Department suits against Chrysler Corporation executives for conflict-of-interest activities and against General Electric and Westinghouse officials for price-fixing conspiracies. On the other hand, there were many indications of Kennedy's economic conservatism, including his backing of AT&T on the Telstar bill, his successful efforts to obtain the Trade Expansion Act, his refusal to move against the oil depletion allowance, and his approval of the merger of Standard Oil of Kentucky and Standard Oil of California. He appointed such businessmen and financiers as C. Douglas Dillon, Luther H. Hodges, and Robert S. McNamara to his Cabinet.

Although the economy had improved, it was still hindered by certain basic underlying problems. Unemployment remained at a disappointing 5.5 percent. The annual increase in the gross national product for the period 1960–1962 was only about 3.6 percent, as compared with a growth rate in Western Europe of from 4 to 6 percent. These trends eventually helped persuade the president to follow the recommendations of Walter W. Heller, chairman of the Council of Economic Advisers, and other liberal economists who were urging a substantial reduction of taxes even in a time of relative prosperity as a means of stimulating growth. Kennedy thus combined the conservatives' desire for a reduction in taxes with the Keynesian faith in the power of fiscal policy. He considered the health of the economy vital not only to a harmonious and workable society at home but also to the success of American foreign policy.

When the new Congress convened in January 1963, Kennedy presented a comprehensive proposal that would result in a reduction in taxes of over $10 billion during a three-year period. While Kennedy set out to win the support of sophisticated businessmen for his tax-cut plan and to educate Americans generally as to the advantages of the "new economics," his proposal encountered criticism from many different directions. Congress was extremely slow in responding to the administration's request, and the House did not pass the bill until late September. In the Senate Harry Flood Byrd and other conservatives prevented a vote on the measure during the first session of the Eighty-eighth Congress.

SOCIAL REFORM—AND LOSING BATTLES

John F. Kennedy came to the presidency by taking advantage of the vague discontents that had begun to spread through American society and by identifying himself with the growing desire for a renewed sense of national purpose, for the restoration of U.S. prestige in the world, and for a more dynamic administration in Washington. Emerging from this orientation were not only the demands for a revitalization of the economy and a stronger and more flexible defense program, but also an increasing concern over the quality of American life and measures to enhance it. Although Kennedy persuaded Congress to enact several of his domestic reform bills, the administration's struggles for its major social welfare plans often proved to be losing battles.

At the outset, the administration moved to eliminate a bottleneck in the House of Representatives by seizing control of the vitally important Rules Committee, where the Republican–southern Democratic coalition was strongest. This committee, under Chairman Howard W. Smith of Virginia, had the power to clear or block the legislative path of all important measures considered in the House. The administration used all of its resources in obtaining the adoption of Speaker Sam Rayburn's resolution to enlarge the committee membership from twelve to fifteen. The liberalization of the Rules Committee made it easier to secure congressional action on such legislation as raising the minimum wage, area redevelopment, housing reform, and unemployment compensation.

But there were other discouraging aspects of the congressional scene for the president and his supporters, one of which was a shift in the party's leadership. In the Senate Lyndon Johnson's leadership role was assumed by the mild-mannered Mike Mansfield of Montana, and when "Mr. Sam" died in November 1961, after serving seventeen years as speaker, he was replaced by the less effective John W. McCormack of Massachusetts. Kennedy himself seemed curiously restrained in his relations with Congress, even when the large Democratic majorities repeatedly failed to enact the administration's principal bills. Always cognizant of his own slender electoral margin in 1960 and with his sights on a more impressive mandate in 1964, Kennedy was no doubt constrained by the absence of a resounding call for social change among the American people.

The president's patience was not inexhaustible, however, and after two years of foot-dragging by a Democratic Congress, he decided to bring his legislative program more directly to the voters. Thus he involved himself actively in the midterm congressional elections of 1962, making many appearances in support of pro-administration Democratic candidates. The results were encouraging for the administration and the Democratic party, which avoided the normal midterm losses, gaining four Senate seats and suffering only nominal losses in the House.

One of the Kennedy administration's disappointing setbacks during the Eighty-seventh Congress was the fate of its ambitious education program. The administration's proposed legislation in 1961 provided for a federal grant of $2.3 billion over a three-year period for school construction and teachers' salaries, plus another $3.3 billion for the support of higher education over a five-year period. After passing the Senate in May, the measure was killed in the House. Catholic leaders insisted that parochial schools should share in the federal aid program, a demand the president opposed, and the resulting controversy played into the hands of the opponents of the proposal. Many southern congressmen were suspicious of federal aid because they viewed it as an instrument, in the hands of aggressive blacks like Representative Adam Clayton Powell, for the advancement of school desegregation. Kennedy's education assistance legislation, which had been broadened to include provisions for combating adult illiteracy and training handicapped children, fared no better in 1962.

The administration was dealt another significant reversal in 1962 when Congress rejected its proposal for the creation of a Cabinet-level Department of Urban and Housing Affairs. The lawmakers also refused to act on the president's recommendation for a federally assisted mass transportation program, and such administration measures as the liberalization of the immigration law, youth employment legislation, general aid to medical schools and medical students, and a bill to assist migrant workers all bogged down in Congress.

Kennedy was no more successful in his fight for the so-called Medicare program. He had cosponsored a federal medical assistance bill while in the Senate, but it had been sidetracked in favor of the Kerr-Mills Act of 1960.[2] As president, JFK presented his recommendations in a special message to Congress in February 1962, and the plan was embodied in the King-Anderson bill. Medicare would provide medical insurance under the Social Security Act for retired workers over sixty-five. As in the case of other retirement benefits, the insurance would be financed by payroll deductions.

The American Medical Association led a powerful attack on the health insurance bill, characterizing it as "socialized medicine." The various health insurance firms also lobbied against the proposed law. Most Republicans and many southern Democrats in Congress contended that Medicare would be too expensive, that it would exclude millions of people not covered by social security, and that the Kerr-Mills Act was adequate for the nation's needs. The administration marshaled all of its forces for the battle in 1962, and the president spoke out against the critics of the bill, on one occasion addressing a rally of senior citizens in Madison Square Garden. With the measure mired in the House Ways and Means Committee and facing the implacable opposition of Harry Byrd in the Senate Finance Committee, Kennedy persuaded the Democratic leadership in the upper house to attach a slightly amended form of the legislation to a depressed-area appropriation bill, hoping by this stratagem to bypass Byrd's committee, secure Senate passage, and force the House to act. But a motion to table the Medicare rider carried by a vote of 52 to 48.

Though defeated on Medicare, the Kennedy administration could point to some modest legislative accomplishments in the medical field. The administration urged the enactment of stronger drug control legislation, in part because of the revelations growing out of an investigation of the drug industry in 1959 by Senator Kefauver's Antitrust and Monopoly Subcommittee. The regulatory bill made little congressional headway in 1961, but during the following year it suddenly began to receive greater support as a result of national concern over the thalidomide scandal. It was shown that thalidomide, a European-manufactured tranquilizer, when taken by pregnant women, caused many babies to be born with deformities. The Drug Industry Act of October 1962 gave more powers to the Food and Drug Administration, while establishing additional safeguards in the manufacture, marketing, and prescribing of drugs. In 1963 Congress approved, in response to Kennedy's recommendation, a $329 million fund to be expended over the next four years for research and treatment of mental illness and mental retardation.

Most of the thirty-fifth president's domestic reforms—federal aid to housing, liberalization of social security, expanded public works, a higher minimum wage, increased federal aid to education—represented extensions of the New Deal and the Fair Deal. Still, Kennedy grew as a social reformer during his three years in the presidency, and under his leadership critical beginnings were made in such fields as area redevelopment, manpower training, and ways of dealing with water and air pollution. His boldest domestic proposals, including federal programs for education and medical care, were defeated, but those lost battles helped smooth the way for the social reforms of his successor. During his last year in office, Kennedy began to call for an "unconditional war on poverty in America."

KENNEDY AND THE CIVIL RIGHTS MOVEMENT

Although the Democratic platform of 1960 contained the most far-reaching civil rights pledges that had yet been made by a major political party in the United States, the Kennedy administration demonstrated great reluctance in sponsoring a broad civil rights program in Congress. The reason was not hard to find: Kennedy feared that administration pressure for such legislation would jeopardize the enactment of other important New Frontier measures, espe-

John Fitzgerald Kennedy and Robert Francis Kennedy (*courtesy John F. Kennedy Library/Imagefinders, Inc.*)

cially among powerful southern Democrats. The administration did exert its influence to help secure a two-year extension of the Civil Rights Commission in 1961, and during the following year it endorsed two voting rights proposals. One of these measures, a constitutional amendment outlawing the poll tax as a prerequisite for voting in federal elections, was approved by Congress.[3]

In sharp contrast to its relative inactivity in the legislative field, the Kennedy administration proved to be vigorous in its use of executive action to promote greater equality in such areas as voting rights, employment, transportation, and education. The Kennedy government expanded the appointment opportunities for blacks; Carl Rowan became ambassador to Finland, Andrew Hatcher served as White House associate press secretary, and five black Americans were appointed to federal judgeships. The president gave firm support to the civil rights division in the Department of Justice, which emerged under Robert F. Kennedy's leadership as the strategic center of the administration's early efforts to advance the cause of Negro rights. The younger Kennedy was perhaps more deeply committed to the civil rights movement than any other top administration leader, and he brought into his department a remarkable group of talented and dedicated young people to work on the civil rights frontier.

One of the administration's most spectacular achievements through the use of its executive prerogatives was its effective desegregation of interstate transportation, including terminal facilities. Following the freedom rides in the spring of 1961, the Justice Department obtained from the Interstate Commerce Commission a self-enforcing order integrating interstate buses and railroads and the terminals they used. The department also moved against discrimination in airport facilities, securing voluntary desegregation in most cases and in a few instances resorting to litigation to effect changes. The president conferred at the White House with delegations of southern businessmen, theater owners, and newspaper editors in the interest of voluntary desegregation, and administration members like Secretary of Commerce Hodges of North Carolina worked to persuade southern leaders to cooperate with the administration.

The government also moved against racial discrimination in employment and housing. Soon after assuming office, Kennedy established the President's Committee on Equal Employment Opportunity to combat racial discrimination in the employment policies of government agencies and private firms holding government contracts. Under the chairmanship of Vice President Johnson, the committee won agreements from several large government contractors. Although Kennedy had criticized Eisenhower during the campaign of 1960 for failing to eliminate racial discrimination in housing, he waited almost two years before issuing an executive order on the matter. The order he finally signed on November 20, 1962, banned discrimination in federally owned and federally financed housing. But unfortunately certain types of housing were exempted from the antidiscrimination requirement, and in practice the order covered only about one-fifth of the new houses constructed in the United States.

Administration officials did their best through private conversations and behind-the-scenes work to smooth the way for school desegregation in southern cities such as Memphis and New Orleans. In Virginia the Justice Department cast itself as the plaintiff in requesting the federal courts to compel the reopening of schools in Prince Edward County, which had been closed to forestall desegregation. Abraham A. Ribicoff, secretary of health, education, and welfare, announced in the spring of 1962 that only integrated schools would qualify for federal aid in "impacted" school districts,[4] and that the government was making plans to establish on-base schools where there were no desegregated public institutions in the vicinity of military bases.

The administration's greatest stress and its chief success in the civil rights struggle was voting reform. The right to vote was basic, Robert Kennedy declared, "and from it all other rights flow." Whereas the Eisenhower administration had filed only six voting suits, the Justice Department under Kennedy brought thirty-two in less than two years. The Democratic administration emphasized the ballot in part because it seemed to offer a safer alternative to the more volatile direct action campaigns being waged by such organizations as CORE and SNCC. Although the Justice Department sent several hundred federal marshals to protect the beleaguered freedom riders in Montgomery in May 1961, such intervention troubled the president and his aides, who redoubled their efforts to produce change through administrative measures. Attorney General Kennedy, asking for a "cooling-off period," encouraged civil rights groups to undertake large registration drives in the southern states.

As the pressure for changes in racial practices mounted, the White House was eventually drawn into a dramatic confrontation with intransigent white supremacists in the Deep South. The spirit of defiance in Mississippi, the citadel of white supremacy, came to a climax in the early fall of 1962, with the threatened desegregation of the state university. The federal courts had ordered the admission of James H. Meredith, a black Mississippian who had served eight years in the Air Force. Governor Ross Barnett, who had been elected with strong support from the Citizens' Council and other resistance elements, aroused the state with demagogic rhetoric and talk of nullification. The governor defied the court orders and denied Meredith's enrollment in the University of Mississippi. The Kennedy administration tried persuasion at this point, but Barnett proved to be a devious adversary, and he secretly encouraged the gathering mob to attack Meredith and his escort of federal marshals when they appeared on the Ole Miss campus.

With a crisis at hand, the president addressed the nation over television, urging the students and people of Mississippi to comply with the court ruling. "The eyes of the nation and all the world are upon you and upon all of us," Kennedy said, "and the honor of your university and state are in the balance." Such pleas were to no avail. Meredith's appearance was greeted by an outbreak of violence, and only after a night of terror and a pitched battle involving thousands of students and segregationist sympathizers, on the one hand, and 400 federal marshals and a contingent of army troops, on the other, was the lone Afro-American enrolled. Kennedy moved to quell the riot by sending in regular troops and federalizing the state's National Guard. Two people were killed and 375 were injured in the

melee. Meredith was registered under federal bayonets, and some of
the troops remained on the campus until the university's first black
student was finally graduated.

The force of events in the South, the rising tide of discontent in
the black community, and mounting sympathy for the equal rights
crusade among white Americans combined to bring about a decided
alteration in President Kennedy's position. Among the developments that influenced the administration was a series of demonstrations beginning in early April 1963 against the segregated institutions and business places of Birmingham, Alabama. The
demonstrations were led by Dr. King and the Reverend Fred Shut-
tlesworth. When the Birmingham police, under the leadership of
the outspoken segregationist "Bull" Connor, met the peaceful demonstrators with clubs, fire hoses, guns, and police dogs, vivid pictures of the brutal repression were seen in the news media and on
television screens all over the country. The president eventually
sent federal troops to restore order in the city. In June 1963, when
Governor George C. Wallace threatened to "bar the entrance" of
two black students whom the federal courts had ordered admitted
to the University of Alabama, Kennedy federalized part of the
state's National Guard in order to guarantee the enrollment of the
students.

In an eloquent television address immediately after the Alabama
episode, on June 11, Kennedy declared that America was confronted
"primarily with a moral issue." Continuing, he warned that "the
fires of frustration and discord are burning in every city, North and
South, where legal remedies are not at hand."

> One hundred years of delay have passed since President Lincoln freed the
> slaves, yet their heirs, their grandsons, are not fully free. They are not yet
> freed from social and economic oppression. And this nation, for all its
> hope and all its boasts, will not be fully free until all its citizens are free.

On the night of the same day the president spoke, Medgar Evers,
the field secretary of the NAACP in Mississippi, was killed from
ambush as he entered his home in Jackson.

On June 19 Kennedy sent Congress a comprehensive civil rights
bill. Since a focal point of recent equal rights demonstrations had
been the exclusion of blacks from lunch counters, restaurants, theaters, and the like, a public-accommodations provision was said to
be the "symbolic heart" of the administration's bill. Kennedy proposed a limited ban on discrimination in public places, requested
power to enable the Justice Department to sue for school desegregation when an aggrieved citizen asked its help, and urged a broad
provision authorizing the government to withhold funds for federal

assistance programs in cases of discrimination. Administration leaders moved energetically to develop grass-roots support for the proposed legislation and to rally backing for it in Congress.

The struggle for black equality now seemed to be moving inexorably toward enactment of a broad civil rights law. The Birmingham demonstrations in the spring had sparked one black protest after another, and by the end of the year demonstrations, involving growing numbers of whites, had taken place in more than 800 cities and towns. The culmination came when 200,000 blacks and whites staged the great March on Washington on August 28, which the president praised for its "deep fervor and quiet dignity." When Martin Luther King, Jr., delivered his powerful address on that occasion, he warned of the "whirlwind of revolt" that would sweep over the country if the rights of blacks were delayed any longer. But it was soon apparent that Congress would be in no hurry to pass the civil rights bill. The Senate Judiciary Committee, under the chairmanship of Mississippi's James O. Eastland, held hearings on the proposed legislation but took no further action during the session. The most significant activity took place in the House, where the critical groundwork was laid for ultimate success as a result of intensive negotiations between administration spokesmen and congressional leaders of both parties.

The Kennedy administration became a full-fledged supporter of the equal rights movement only hesitantly and under considerable pressure. Nevertheless, no previous president had made more vigorous efforts to enforce the Constitution with regard to blacks. Kennedy's administration contributed substantially to the advancement of the nonviolent phase of the equal rights revolution. Despite the likelihood of losing several southern states in 1964 and signs of the "white backlash" in northern suburbs, Kennedy continued until his death to fight for civil rights legislation.

THE DEATH OF A PRESIDENT

In the fall of 1963 the president and his advisers were devoting more attention than usual to politics. In September Kennedy made a tour of eleven western states, and he later made a number of appearances throughout the East. Democratic prospects in the South were a particular cause of concern to administration leaders, and Texas was especially critical because of a widening cleavage between a Democratic faction identified with Senator Ralph W. Yarborough and a more conservative element associated with Governor John B. Connally. Following a visit to Florida in mid-November, Kennedy flew to Texas for appearances in several cities, an inspection of space installations, and an effort to patch up differences between the feuding factions in the state's Democratic party.

Having been met by cheering crowds in San Antonio, Houston, and Fort Worth, President Kennedy and his wife, accompanied by Vice President Johnson, arrived in Dallas on November 22. Kennedy and the other dignitaries then set out that sunny Friday morning in a motorcade from Love Field for the Dallas Trade Mart, where the president was to make a luncheon address. The people of Dallas, a dynamic city of modern commerce but also the center of a virulent form of right-wing fanaticism, greeted JFK warmly, despite some recent rhetorical outbursts by local critics of the administration and several displays of violence by the radical right during the past few weeks. As the president's open car moved through the cheering crowds in downtown Dallas, three shots were fired from an upper window of the Texas School Book Depository. Kennedy was hit in the neck and the head, and Governor Connally, sitting in front of the president, was also wounded, though not fatally. Kennedy's car sped to nearby Parkland Memorial Hospital, but efforts to save the chief executive proved futile, and he died half an hour later, at 1 P.M. Shortly afterward, Lyndon B. Johnson took the oath of office as president; the oath was administered on board *Air Force One*, as the jet plane prepared to take the body of the fallen leader back to Washington.

Within an hour of Kennedy's death, an employee of the Texas School Book Depository named Lee Harvey Oswald was arrested, after having allegedly shot a Dallas policeman, and was charged with the assassination. Oswald, a twenty-four-year-old former Marine, was a self-styled Marxist who had lived for a while in the Soviet Union and married a Russian woman. Unstable and frustrated, probably psychotic, the young Texan was at one time a member of the Fair Play for Cuba Committee. He maintained his innocence through several hours of questioning, and then in a bizarre sequel two days after the president's assassination, Oswald was himself shot and killed while being moved to another jail. His assailant was a Dallas nightclub operator named Jack Ruby.[5]

News of John Kennedy's sudden and tragic death stunned and saddened the American people as had no other public happening since Roosevelt's death in 1945. When the word reached Washington, crowds gathered in front of the White House, gazing silently and sadly through the iron fence at the deserted mansion. A grief-stricken nation paused to watch the solemn funeral rites, which culminated with the mass conducted by Richard Cardinal Cushing in St. Matthew's Cathedral and interment in the Arlington National

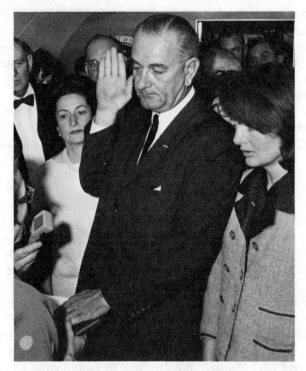

A new president assumes office aboard *Air Force One*, Dallas, Texas, November 22, 1963 (*courtesy Lyndon B. Johnson Library*)

Cemetery. Television made the whole event indescribably poignant. As William L. O'Neill has vividly written:

> To sit before the screen day after day exposed Americans to such images as no people had ever been. Films of the President's life punctuated the chronicle of somber events. The terrible moments were shown again and again, so were the great ones, and the most touching of all, the merely happy. Shots of his lovely wife Jacqueline, radiant at some public event, alternated with the ghastly pictures of her stricken face and bloodstained clothes. John F. Kennedy was alive and vigorous on some film clip in one instant, and lying in state the next. The drums rolled, the bells tolled, the heads of state marched in grim procession, and all the while his familiar voice filled the air.[6]

One of President Johnson's first official acts was to appoint a special seven-member commission under Chief Justice Earl Warren to investigate the assassination. The commission presented a report and a twenty-six-volume supplement on September 27, 1964. The report concluded that Lee Harvey Oswald, "acting alone and without advice or assistance," had shot President Kennedy. Unfortunately, the Warren Commission's findings, which were meant to reassure the public and put to rest the many rumors and suspicions surrounding the president's murder, left a good deal to be desired. Despite its bulk, the report was not a thorough and careful piece of research. Critics of the Warren Commission soon challenged its lone-assassin and "one-bullet" theories. A variety of hypotheses about the assassination were given currency in scores of articles and books, including one that pictured Oswald as only a decoy set up by the real assassin and another that attributed the murder to some U.S. agency like the CIA.

Having been struck down in his prime and at a time when his presidency seemed on the verge of realizing its promise, Kennedy was transformed almost overnight into a mythical figure surrounded by an aura of romance. "What was killed in Dallas," journalist James Reston wrote, "was not only the President but the promise. The death of youth and the hope of youth, of the beauty and grace and the touch of magic." Americans found it difficult to comprehend such tragedy; only the province of mythology seemed capable of lending meaning to an act so shocking and irrational. Out of this need was born the legend of Camelot, whose gallant young prince gave the nation a moment of glory before dying for its sins, but who also opened the way for change and reformation.

The slain president's admirers spoke of the glowing prospects his leadership had kindled and of the great progress that would have come in 1964 and later years had he lived. In *A Thousand Days* Arthur M. Schlesinger, Jr., wrote movingly of how Kennedy had "reestablished the republic as the first generation of our leaders saw it—young, brave, civilized, rational, gay, tough, questing, exultant in the excitement and potentiality in history." Kennedy's youth, vitality, and modernity made him, in Adlai Stevenson's phrase, the "contemporary man." He understood better than most Americans the challenge of change, and he had a feeling for the way the world was going. Yet, in spite of its outward brilliance, the Kennedy administration did not bring extensive changes. The journalist I. F. Stone wrote, for example, "Kennedy, when the tinsel was stripped away, was a conventional leader, no more than an enlightened conservative, cautious as an old man for all his youth, with a basic distrust of the people." Even so, the impact of John F. Kennedy's example and of his "style" was quite remarkable. No public figure since Franklin D. Roosevelt did as much as Kennedy to stimulate the idealism and self-sacrifice of young Americans. At the time of his death, he seemed to be in the process of capturing the imagination of the American people as had few of his predecessors. And his dreams, while largely unfulfilled, were prophetic.

A New President and a Democratic Landslide

"Let us continue" was the advice the new president gave to Congress in his first address on November 27, 1963. Lyndon Johnson took over the Oval Office of the White House confidently and with a firm hand. He conducted himself well, moving through the difficult days of his predecessor's funeral and memorialization with dignity and tact. Taking advantage of a more sober and supportive mood in Congress and throughout the country, Johnson adroitly maneuvered to break the long congressional deadlock. During the first hundred days of his administration the legislative logjam began to break up; the foreign aid bill was approved, the Higher Education Facilities Act was passed, the tax reduction bill was enacted, and the Kennedy civil rights legislation was passed by the House of Representatives. In 1964 during the second session of the Eighty-eighth Congress, Johnson's legislative accomplishments were still more impressive. Johnson also succeeded, in the spring of 1964, in arranging a labor-management agreement for the nation's railroads, thereby preventing a serious national strike and the possible resort to compulsory arbitration.[7]

While Johnson was consolidating his national leadership, the two major political parties were making preparations for the presidential election of 1964. The Republicans, racked by internal conflict and frustrated by the resurgence of Democratic strength in the late fifties and early sixties, turned abruptly from the moderate course followed by their presidential nominees since 1940 and launched a militantly conservative campaign for control of Washington. A variety of right-wing organizations had sprung up, among them the John Birch Society, the Christian Anti-Communist Crusade, the Citizens' Council, and the Minutemen. A kind of intellectual "new conservatism" found expression in the *National Review*, edited by William F. Buckley, Jr., and news commentators such as Fulton Lewis, Jr., Clarence Manion, and Dan Smoot added their voices to the "radical right" refrain. In general these zealous anti-liberals stressed economic freedom; opposition to governmental intervention, social democracy, and heavier taxes; and unrelenting hostility toward international communism, which they interpreted as a pervasive and subversive threat within the United States.

The radical right found a political figure to rally around in Senator Barry M. Goldwater of Arizona. Goldwater, a millionaire department-store owner who was first elected to the Senate in 1952, had been a staunch supporter of Senator Joseph R. McCarthy. By 1960, when he made a strong impression on conservatives at the Republican national convention, the senator had become an aggressive spokesman for right-wing elements. Goldwater summed up the tenets of his conservative Republicanism in *The Conscience of a Conservative*, a book he published in 1960. He urged a sharp cutback in federal power and spending; a reassertion of state rights, including those involving school desegregation decisions; an end to farm subsidies and the restoration of agriculture to free-market conditions; and a restriction of big labor power. He believed that America's objective in foreign policy should be "total victory" over "the all-embracing determination of Communism to capture the world and destroy the United States." The political columnist Richard Rovere suggested that there were two Goldwaters: "the agreeable man with the easy, breezy Aw Shucks Western manner who speaks in rightist platitudes but has only a loose grip on ideology," on the one hand, and "the dour authoritarian polemicist whose name is signed to *The Conscience of a Conservative*," on the other.

While the conservative revival during the early 1960s was an important factor in the emergence of Barry Goldwater as a national figure, it was a group of little-known Republicans that converted the movement into an effective political organization. Beginning in 1961, such GOP organization men as Clifton F. White of New York (head of the Young Republicans), Peter O'Donnell of Texas, and John Grenier of Alabama began the task of capturing the party machinery for the senator from Arizona. The leaders of the Goldwater movement aimed both at securing the Republican nomination for the senator in 1964 and at remaking the GOP as a vehicle of militant conservatism. Bitterly resentful of the long domination of Republican presidential nominations by the moderate, eastern wing of the party, they were convinced that the "me too" leadership of men like Thomas E. Dewey had led to disaster and that a vast silent vote would respond to a nominee who presented "a choice, not an echo." Goldwater himself was tireless in his campaigning.

Meanwhile, the moderate wing of the Republican party was in disarray. Eisenhower was reluctant to take an active part in the drive for a moderate candidate; Nixon had retired after losing his bid for the governorship of California in 1962; and Rockefeller, while a proven vote-getter in New York, had been badly hurt by his recent divorce and remarriage to a divorcée whose former husband had gained custody of her children. The New York governor continued to seek the GOP nomination, however, and while he defeated Goldwater and Henry Cabot Lodge, Jr., in the Oregon presidential primary, he lost the crucial California primary to the Arizona senator on June 2. Governor William W. Scranton of Pennsylvania made an energetic campaign in the few remaining weeks before the Republican National Convention. But it was too late. Goldwater had won too many delegates in the selection process that reached from the local precincts to the state conventions.

At the Republican convention in San Francisco, July 13–16, the conservatives completed their long-awaited conquest of the Grand Old Party. Tightly controlled by Goldwater partisans, the convention rejected moderate, international Republicanism and revenged itself with verbal abuse of Governor Rockefeller and others who advanced anti-extremist positions. Goldwater was easily nominated on the first ballot, and William E. Miller, a conservative congressman from upstate New York and chairman of the GOP National Committee, was selected as the vice-presidential nominee. The platform was forthright in its conservatism. In his acceptance speech Goldwater asserted that "extremism in the defense of liberty is no vice!" and that "moderation in the pursuit of justice is no virtue!"

The situation in the Democratic party was far simpler than that of the Republican. While Republican factionalism was threatening to destroy the GOP, President Johnson was preparing the way for the greatest Democratic victory since the days of Franklin Roosevelt. Johnson, as William S. White has observed, was a "compulsive competitor," and he set out to win the presidency in his own right—and to win big. His remarkable success with Congress and his impressive performance as executor of Kennedy's political legacy made him all the more formidable. Public opinion polls in the preconvention period showed him far in front of any Republican candidate. There were few surprises and not much drama in the Democratic National Convention, which met in Atlantic City, New Jersey, August 24–27. Johnson was nominated by acclamation. His running mate, whose identity the president revealed only at the last minute, was Senator Hubert H. Humphrey of Minnesota. The convention's placidity had earlier been disturbed briefly by a fight over the seating of the all-white Mississippi delegation and the subsequent walkout of most of the Mississippi and Alabama delegates.[8] But otherwise the convention seemed to be united behind the president and his program.

In spite of the ideological contrast between the candidates and platforms, the presidential campaign of 1964 was a dull contest, filled with strenuous campaigning and a plethora of platitudes. A leading theme of Goldwater's campaign was that "something basic and dangerous is eating away at the morality, dignity and respect of our citizens." The Republican standard-bearer continued to urge the need for a more militant foreign policy and to assert that the United States was pursuing "no win" policies abroad. In one campaign speech he declared: "I charge that this Administration is soft on Communism . . . I charge that this Administration has a foreign policy of drift, deception, and defeat."

Goldwater's campaign gave Johnson the great advantage of running as a social reform candidate and still seeming less "radical" than his opponent. At the same time, Senator Humphrey's selection for the vice-presidential nomination reassured many people as to Johnson's commitment to liberalism. When Goldwater tried to associate violence in the streets with civil rights demonstrations, the Democrats accused him of bidding for a white backlash, anti-Negro vote. When the GOP nominee said he wanted to strengthen social security, the Democrats recalled his earlier statements about making the system "voluntary." Over and over Goldwater demanded, "What kind of country do we want to have?" To which Johnson replied, "The kind we've made it," and then proceeded to talk about prosperity, progress in education, and the goals of his Great Society. Charging that Goldwater was "trigger-happy" and would endanger world peace if elected, the Democrats reminded the voters that he had earlier recommended that NATO commanders be given control of tactical nuclear weapons and that he had once said, "I'd drop a low-yield atomic bomb on the Chinese supply lines in North Vietnam or maybe shell 'em with the Seventh Fleet." Johnson, by contrast, played down the war in Vietnam and urged a more prudent course in foreign affairs.

The election returns on November 3 confirmed the opinion polls' forecast of a Democratic landslide. The Johnson-Humphrey ticket received a total of 43.1 million popular votes (61.4 percent) to 27.1 million for Goldwater and Miller. The Democrats carried forty-four states and the District of Columbia, with 486 electoral votes, while the Republicans won only five Deep South states and Goldwater's home state of Arizona, with 52 electoral votes. Only an unusual amount of ticket splitting saved the Republicans from total destruction in the congressional races, in which the Democrats added to their existing majorities by gaining thirty-eight seats in the House and two in the Senate. Republican candidates in state legislative races experienced numerous defeats, with the GOP losing over 500 seats it had previously held. Since almost all state legislatures were faced with the compulsory reapportionment of their own bodies and with congressional redistricting as a result of *Baker* v. *Carr* (1962) and *Wesberry* v. *Sanders* (1964), the Democrats were in a good position to draw the new lines to their own long-range advantage.[9]

The sweeping Democratic victory at the polls in 1964 was based in considerable part on Johnson's record of accomplishment as president and on his emergence as a genuine national leader. But it also mirrored the split in the Republican party and the alarm many moderates and conservatives felt over Goldwater's call for radical changes at home and abroad. The times favored the Democratic administration. The economy was booming, and the tensions of the cold war had steadily eased since 1963. The president used the power of his incumbency with telling effect, and he attracted support from every segment of the population (receiving over 90 percent of the black vote). Lyndon Johnson intended to discredit thoroughly Goldwater's brand of conservatism and also to help elect a congressional majority large enough to build his Great Society. He appeared to have achieved both objectives.

NOTES

1. Estes was an amazingly successful Texas promoter who made a fortune in a complicated series of business deals such as obtaining loans on fictitious liquid-fertilizer tanks, bribing farmers to acquire false cotton-acreage allotments, and receiving government storage fees for surplus grain that was often nonexistent. Estes was eventually prosecuted and sent to prison. The case provided a spectacular example of the possibilities of fraud and mismanagement in the nation's costly and bureaucratic farm subsidy system.

2. A congressional report in 1963 revealed that less than 1 percent of the nation's elderly citizens were receiving benefits under the Kerr-Mills Act, and most of them were concentrated in five states. Those who received medical care through this federal program, moreover, were required to sign what some critics described as virtually a "pauper's oath."

3. Anti-poll-tax bills had been passed by the House of Representatives no less than five times during the 1940s, only to die in the Senate. The Twenty-fourth Amendment was ratified by the required majority of the states in 1964. Its only real effect was in the five states that still retained a poll tax: Alabama, Arkansas, Mississippi, Texas, and Virginia.

4. Impacted school districts were those with large numbers of pupils resulting from the location of federal installations in the area. Congress had long provided federal aid for such districts.

5. Despite his plea of insanity, Ruby was convicted in March 1964 of "murder with malice" and sentenced to life imprisonment. He died of cancer before the courts had completed a consideration of his appeal.

6. William L. O'Neill, *Coming Apart: An Informal History of America in the 1960's* (1971), pp. 90–91.

7. The railroad dispute had been developing for many years and came to a head in August 1963 when management demanded the elimination of some 30,000 firemen on diesel locomotives and 19,000 train crewmen on the grounds that they were no longer needed and their jobs amounted to featherbedding. The railroad unions argued that maintenance of the jobs was necessary for railway safety. With a strike imminent in the summer of

1963, Congress passed the first peacetime compulsory arbitration act to deal with the problem, but the life of the arbitration act was only six months, and thus a new crisis developed the following spring. The president, with the help of Secretary of Labor W. Willard Wirtz, brought the two sides together at the White House for intensive negotiations, which resulted in an agreement signed in April 1964.

8. The regular Mississippi delegation had been challenged by the insurgent, largely black Mississippi Freedom Democratic party. The convention sought to allay this potentially explosive conflict by adopting a compromise permitting the regular delegates to take their seats if they would sign a party loyalty pledge. The compromise resolution also gave two convention seats to the challenging group and established an antidiscrimination requirement in the selection of delegates to future party conventions.

9. The federal courts, in a series of landmark decisions beginning with *Baker* v. *Carr*, stipulated that the criterion in congressional and state legislative districting and apportionment should be, "as nearly as practicable," that "one man's vote . . . is to be worth as much as another's."

SUGGESTIONS FOR FURTHER READING

Reform and domestic politics during the Kennedy years are examined in three general works cited in chapter 10: Heath, *Decade of Disillusionment;* Matusow, *The Unraveling of America;* and Parmet, *JFK: The Presidency of John F. Kennedy.* The books by Donald, Fairlie, O'Neill, Schlesinger, and Sorensen, also referred to earlier, are useful in providing an introduction to the Kennedy administration and the politics of the early 1960s. In this connection see as well James T. Crown, *The Kennedy Literature: A Bibliographical Essay on John F. Kennedy* (1968); Richard E. Neustadt, *Presidential Power: The Politics of Leadership* (rev. ed., 1968); Bruce Miroff, *Pragmatic Illusions: The Presidential Politics of John F. Kennedy* (1976); and Harris Wofford, *Of Kennedys and Kings: Making Sense of the Sixties* (1980). Tom Wicker's *JFK and LBJ: The Influence of Personality upon Politics* (1968) is a revealing comparison of the two Democratic presidents. Lawrence H. Fuchs, *John F. Kennedy and American Catholicism* (1967), is a useful specialized study.

Economic trends and economic reforms during the early 1960s are treated in Jim F. Heath, *John F. Kennedy and the Business Community* (1969), and several previously cited works: Collins, *The Business Response to Keynes;* Rowen, *The Free Enterprisers;* Stein, *The Fiscal Revolution in America;* and Stein, *Presidential Economics.* The steel crisis of 1962 is described by Grant McConnell in *Steel and the Presidency—1962* (1963). James L. Sundquist's *Politics and Policy: The Eisenhower, Kennedy, and Johnson Years* (1968) is indispensable for an understanding of the economic and social reforms of the Kennedy administration. Richard Harris, *The Real Voice* (1964), is a critical evaluation of the Kennedy administration's role in the passage of the drug legislation of 1962. On another controversial issue, see Max J. Skidmore, *Medicare and the American Rhetoric of Reconciliation* (1970). Walter A. McDougall, *The Heavens and the Earth: A Political History of the Space Age* (1985), concentrates on the politics of the space program.

The best study of the Kennedy administration and civil rights is Carl M. Brauer, *John F. Kennedy and the Second Reconstruction* (1977). Pat Watters and Reese Cleghorn, *Climbing Jacob's Ladder: The Arrival of Negroes in Southern Politics* (1967), is an unusually good contemporary account. Robert Kennedy's contributions are described by Schlesinger, *Robert Kennedy and His Times*, mentioned in chapter 10, and Victor S. Navasky, *Kennedy Justice* (1971). For the "movement" itself, see the trenchant account by Harvard Sitkoff, *The Struggle for Black Equality, 1954–1980* (1981), and the interviews with participants in Howell Raines, *My Soul Is Rested: Movement Days in the Deep South Remembered* (1977). The books by Lewis, Lomax, and Muse, cited in chapter eight, are also useful for the Kennedy administration and the equal rights movement in the early 1960s. Alexander M. Bickel's *Politics and the Warren Court* (1965) is helpful in understanding national policy in this period. James W. Silver, *Mississippi: The Closed Society* (1964), is a compelling account of the federal intervention at Ole Miss in 1962 and its background.

An absorbing though controversial description of John F. Kennedy's assassination is contained in William R. Manchester's *The Death of a President, November 20–November 25, 1963* (1967). Edward Jay Epstein advances a different interpretation of events in *Inquest: The Warren Commission and the Establishment of Truth* (1966). Jim Bishop, *The Day Kennedy Was Shot* (1968), is another popular treatment. Michael Amrine has written a journalistic account of the presidential succession in 1963 entitled *This Awesome Challenge: The Hundred Days of Lyndon Johnson* (1964).

A good beginning place for study of the presidential election of 1964 is Theodore H. White, *The Making of the President, 1964* (1965). For a more scholarly work, see Milton C. Cummings (ed.), *The National Election of 1964* (1966). Barry Goldwater and the Republican campaign are dealt with by Bernard Cosman and Robert J. Huckshorn, *Republican Politics: The 1964 Campaign and Its Aftermath for the Party* (1968); Bernard Cosman, *Five States for Goldwater: Continuity and Change in Southern Presidential Voting Patterns* (1966); and Robert D. Novak, *The Agony of the G.O.P., 1964* (1965). The revival of the extreme right is discussed in Arnold Forster and Benjamin R. Epstein, *Danger on the Right* (1964); Seymour Martin Lipset and Earl Raab, *The Politics of Unreason: Right-Wing Extremism in America, 1790–1970* (1970); and David W. Reinhard, *The Republican Right Since 1945* (1983).

CHAPTER TWELVE

Toward the Great Society

LYNDON B. JOHNSON moved easily into the role of domestic reformer, working with skill, energy, and resourcefulness to advance first the Kennedy program and then his own more ambitious legislation. Johnson wanted desperately to be "president of all the people," and during his first years in the White House he seemed to have succeeded in creating a national consensus. The new president hoped to improve the quality of American life and thus achieve a "Great Society," which "asks not only how much, but how good; not only how to create wealth, but how to use it." Johnson repeatedly assured the American people that "we have the power to shape the civilization that we want."

There was irony—indeed, tragedy—in the presidency of Lyndon Johnson. For in spite of his impressive record of domestic reforms and the overwhelming mandate of 1964, Johnson soon began to lose the support of the public and to have a serious "credibility" problem. The Great Society lost its momentum, and, as we shall see in the next chapter, the administration virtually collapsed before LBJ left office.

THE THIRTY-SIXTH PRESIDENT

Lyndon Baines Johnson's ascent to the pinnacle of national politics was quite as remarkable, in its own way, as that of Harry Truman or Dwight Eisenhower. Born near Stonewall, Texas, on August 27, 1908, Johnson grew up in the bleak Texas hill country surrounding Johnson City, which his grandfather had founded. The Johnsons, sturdy and self-reliant, were influential in the local community, and both Lyndon Johnson's father and grandfather had served in the state legislature. But the rural economy was depressed and times were hard as Lyndon grew up, and in order to complete Southwest Texas State Teachers' College at nearby San Marcos, he was forced to work at a variety of jobs. After teaching school for a year or two following his graduation, he went to Washington in late 1931 as secretary to the congressman from his district. In 1935 the young Texan was appointed director of the National Youth Administration in his home state. Meanwhile, he had married Claudia (Lady Bird) Taylor. In 1937 he won a special election to fill a congressional vacancy and was regularly reelected thereafter. He was an ardent New Dealer. After losing a bid for the U.S. Senate in 1941, he ran again in 1948 and managed to win (by 87 votes) in an extraordinarily close election.

Johnson rose like a meteor in the Senate. His qualities of leadership so impressed powerful Democrats like Richard B. Russell that he was chosen as Senate minority leader in 1953. After the Democrats won the congressional elections of 1954, Johnson became majority leader in the upper house. Although the Texas senator suffered a severe heart attack in 1955, he made a good recovery; by the late fifties he had become perhaps the most dominant Democrat in Washington. Johnson became a master of parliamentary maneuver, made effective use of "unanimous consent" agreements to limit debate, and was adept at applying and relaxing pressure on senators who were undecided or opposed on a particular question. He had an unlimited capacity for courtesies, flattering attentions, and small favors in his personal relations with his colleagues, and he also frequently used what some observers called "the treatment." Journalists Rowland Evans and Robert D. Novak have described the majority leader in action: "He moved in close, his face a scant millimeter from his target, his eyes widening and narrowing, his eyebrows rising and falling. From his pockets poured clippings, memos, statistics. Mimicry, humor, and the genius of analogy made the Treatment an almost hypnotic experience and rendered the target stunned and helpless."

The Texan's record in the Senate was neither liberal nor conservative, although he had shown some pronounced conservative leanings in supporting Taft-Hartley, opposing Truman's civil rights program, and manifesting special concern for the oil and gas interests of the Southwest. At the same time, he was not basically ideological. He was, first and foremost, a professional politician. Still, his fundamental outlook had been enduringly shaped by his background and formative experiences. For one thing, he was a southerner—a white southerner who had grown up in a depressed regional economy and society; his own experiences and observations as well as the attitudes and stereotypes he encountered among non-southerners in Washington made him sensitive to his regional and cultural disadvantages. Whether or not he was influenced by southern populism, he was imbued with real concern for the poor and the deprived, and he accepted the Populist prescription of positive governmental action as a means of restoring opportunity. The New Deal reinforced these convictions, and Johnson later would recall that FDR "was like a daddy to me." Though strongly influenced by his regional heritage, the Texan moved steadily toward a wider perspective. In 1960 he sought to portray himself as a westerner as well as a southerner, and his role as a conciliator and harmonizer in the Senate served to lessen his provincialism and to broaden his views.

A tall, powerfully built man, Johnson provided a marked contrast to John F. Kennedy; his rural, southwestern background, small-college education, drawling speech, and backslapping demeanor seemed the antithesis of Kennedy's northeastern, metropolitan youth, Harvard training, eloquence, and urbanity. Johnson lacked his predecessor's graceful style on the speaker's platform, and his unadorned language and effusive rhetoric caused some sophisticated liberals to wince. But Johnson had a flair for the dramatic, and he was a man of enormous energy, drive, and determination. He was also a vain man, eager for approval and sensitive to criticism. One discerning observer described him as "a man of contradictions":

> a Southerner, yet one who intuitively understood the black revolution long before many northern politicians did; a Southerner, and at the very same time a Westerner; a man who understood poverty because he had known it, but who belonged also to a little rural oligarchy, a man with politics in his blood, and now also a man of self-made wealth. He was proud, domineering, insecure, persuasive, egotistical, subtle, coarse, sentimental, vindictive, intelligent (though not at all intellectual), insistent upon loyalty (yet capable of the most brutal ingratitude to those who had been loyal to him), needing love (yet not always able to repress upwelling bitterness and anger).[1]

Johnson entered the White House with a great deal of congressional support and goodwill. "If the President decides that it would be nice to have a coast-to-coast tunnel," remarked political journalist Richard Rovere at the outset of the Eighty-ninth Congress (1965–66), "he need only call in some engineers and lawyers to put the scheme in order, advise Congress of his wishes, and begin letting contracts." Relishing the whirligig of congressional action and his own role in the process from 1600 Pennsylvania Avenue, Johnson seemed to know every detail of the administration's program and every pressure that affected its disposition. He made a point, especially during his first year in office, of stressing his commitment to the realization of Kennedy's New Frontier. Congress and the public responded positively to the administration's articulation of these reform goals, as they did to the president's announcement of his own Great Society. Following his electoral triumph in 1964, Johnson amplified the Great Society and explained it in greater detail. Presenting his State of the Union message to Congress early in 1965, he outlined a far-reaching and unprecedented program of domestic reform.

Having achieved a series of spectacular successes during his first year in office, Johnson proceeded to guide through Congress the most impressive array of domestic reforms since the 1930s. The first session of the Eighty-ninth Congress (1965) was particularly productive. The coalition of Republicans and conservative Democrats, where it did appear in the House of Representatives roll call votes, was victorious only 25 percent of the time in 1965, as compared with 67 percent in 1963 and 1964 and 74 percent in 1961.[2] Gallup and Harris polls showed that two-thirds of the American people liked LBJ's performance in the White House. Then the Great Society began to slow down, and within a year polls revealed a mounting loss of confidence in the president extending almost uniformly across the range of his responsibilities.

THE QUEST FOR EQUALITY

In his first address to Congress, in late November 1963, President Johnson urged the lawmakers to complete action on the Kennedy administration's tax-cut proposal. He also called for "the earliest possible passage" of Kennedy's civil rights bill, which had recently been reported favorably by the House Judiciary Committee. The new chief executive soon made it clear that he was totally committed to the enactment of this broad equal rights measure and that he was prepared to push on boldly to advance the cause with additional legislation and with executive action. "We have talked long enough in this country about equal rights," Johnson declared on November 27, 1963. "We have talked for one hundred years or more. It is time now to write the next chapter, and to write it in the books of law." Civil rights represented a test of Johnson's credentials as a reformer and national leader. "If I didn't get out in front on this issue," he recalled, the liberals would "throw up my background against me, they'd use it to prove I was incapable of bringing unity. . . . I had to produce a civil rights bill that was even stronger than the one they'd have gotten if Kennedy had lived."

When the second session of the Eighty-eighth Congress began its work in January 1964, the Johnson administration mobilized all of its powers behind the effort to enact an omnibus civil rights statute. The threat of a discharge petition that would force action persuaded the House Rules Committee to clear H.R. 7152 for floor action by late January, and the bill was passed with strong bipartisan support on February 10, by a vote of 290 to 130. In steering the measure through the lower house, Emanuel Celler, the floor manager, was greatly assisted not only by liberal party members identified with the Democratic Study Committee but also by such Republican leaders as William H. McCulloch, the ranking minority member of the House Judiciary Committee. Thousands of people poured into Washington in early 1964 to press for congressional approval, and scores of national organizations participated in the movement through the Leadership Conference on Civil Rights.

Prospects for the passage of such far-reaching civil rights legislation in the Senate were much less encouraging, given the strategic positions of southern leaders in that body and the difficulty of overcoming filibusters. Southern senators hoped to bury the House-approved bill in James Eastland's Judiciary Committee, but administration leaders skillfully avoided that trap and persuaded the Senate on February 26 to place the measure directly on the upper chamber's calendar. Hubert H. Humphrey, who managed the drive for Senate passage, and other supporters of the proposed law succeeded in creating a sturdy coalition and in preventing its disruption as a result of partisan politics, an ever-present danger. Senate leaders of both parties and administration spokesmen carried on intensive negotiations in an effort to work out an agreement that would make it possible to halt debate and enact the bill. The pivotal figure in these negotiations was minority leader Everett M. Dirksen of Illinois. The administration undertook painstaking conferences with the minority leader, and so intensive were the discussions that, in the words of one White House aide, Johnson "never let him alone for thirty minutes." The Illinoisan slowly moved toward a compromise, and in mid-May, during the seventh week of floor debate, a package of compromise amendments was agreed to in these negotiations and incorporated into a "clean bill" to be offered as a substitute for H.R. 7152.

On June 10 the Senate adopted a cloture resolution by a vote of 71 to 29, and for the first time in history the upper house had voted to close debate on a civil rights bill. Senator Richard B. Russell and his southern colleagues had made a strategic error in demanding unconditional surrender. Had they sought an agreement with Republican moderates earlier in the debate, they might well have obtained significant concessions and seriously weakened the final enactment. Yet as Dirksen said, quoting words attributed to Victor

Hugo, "Stronger than all the armies is an idea whose time has come." After cloture the Senate approved a few minor amendments, voted down a large number designed to weaken the measure, and passed the bill on June 19 by a roll call vote of 73 to 27. The House accepted the Senate version, and President Johnson signed it on July 2.

The Civil Rights Act of 1964 was the most sweeping affirmation of equal rights and the most comprehensive commitment to their implementation ever made by a U.S. Congress. The law contained new provisions to help guarantee black voting rights; assured access to public accommodations such as motels, restaurants, and places of amusement; authorized the federal government to bring suits to desegregate public facilities and schools; extended the life of the Civil Rights Commission for four years and gave it new powers; provided that federal funds could be cut off where programs were administered discriminatorily; required most companies and labor unions to grant equal employment opportunity; and authorized the Justice Department to enter into pending civil rights cases. Compliance was not universal, but the act was generally obeyed throughout the South, in part because of careful preparations by federal and local officials. A startling change in the daily behavior if not the thinking of millions of southerners took place with incredible swiftness.

Johnson soon decided to take advantage of the reform impulse in civil rights by seeking additional legislation in the field of voting rights, an area where the 1964 law was considered weak. Such ancient obstructions as literacy tests, discriminatory treatment by local officials, economic pressure, and intimidation were still prevalent in much of the South, particularly in the lower part of the region. The ballot, it was widely assumed, would provide the most practical means of changing the status of southern blacks. Thus hundreds of students—black and white—came to Mississippi in 1964 to participate in the Freedom Summer project, an undertaking that involved the registration of blacks. White resistance was bitter. Negro churches were burned, many civil rights workers were beaten, and several of the students were killed.

Early in 1965 Martin Luther King, Jr., launched a series of demonstrations that were centered in Selma, Alabama, to dramatize the absence of black voting rights in the Deep South. Dallas County, in which Selma is located, had a black majority, but only 325 Negroes were registered to vote as compared with 9,800 whites. In some other black-belt counties not a single black man or woman was enfranchised. King announced plans for "a march on the ballot boxes throughout Alabama," moving from Selma to Montgomery, the state capital, fifty-four miles away. Governor George C. Wallace refused to permit such a march, and when the demonstrators tried to proceed without his approval, they were met with clubs and tear gas. The president finally stepped in, federalizing the Alabama National Guard, and the march was completed between March 21 and 25. The violent clashes that took place in the Selma area provoked national outrage and set the stage for congressional action on voting rights legislation.

Having become committed to the passage of a strong voting rights statute, the Johnson administration submitted a carefully developed proposal on March 17, 1965. From March until August, the voting rights coalition never lost its momentum. It was a bipartisan effort, with solid administration support and powerful assistance from the Leadership Conference on Civil Rights and other groups. After a compromise anti-poll-tax provision was approved, the Senate adopted a cloture motion on May 25—the second one in two years. The bill was passed on the following day. The House passed a similar measure on July 9, and after a conference committee worked out an agreement reconciling the differences between the two houses, the revised measure was approved in early August. The president signed it on August 6. "They came in darkness and they came in chains," he said of the first American blacks. "Today we strike away the last major shackle of those fierce and ancient bonds."

The Voting Rights Act of 1965 authorized direct federal action to enable blacks to register and vote. It empowered the attorney general to appoint federal examiners to supervise voter registration in states or voting districts where a literacy test or similar qualifying devices existed and where fewer than 50 percent of the voting-age residents were registered or cast ballots in the 1964 presidential election.[3] Stiff penalties were provided for interference with voter rights. The Department of Justice moved quickly to implement the new statute. The act of 1965, the invalidation of the poll tax, and the "one man, one vote" principle handed down by the Supreme Court went a long way to democratize southern—and American—politics. The number of black voters in the southern states steadily increased as a result of these reforms and the work of such campaigns as the Southern Regional Council's Voter Education Project.

The Johnson administration brought many more blacks into important government jobs, and Johnson was the first chief executive to appoint a black to his Cabinet and to the Supreme Court. Robert C. Weaver was named to head the new Department of Housing and Urban Development, while the famous NAACP attorney Thurgood

Marshall was elevated from the federal circuit court to the nation's highest court. Johnson also pressed on, along with many civil rights leaders and organizations, to secure still more congressional action. In his State of the Union message of January 1966, the president urged the passage of legislation to prevent discrimination in jury selection, to guarantee the physical security of all citizens, and to outlaw discrimination in the housing field. The House of Representatives proceeded to pass this legislation, though the margin of victory on the housing title was very narrow; but the proposals failed in the Senate when efforts to adopt a cloture resolution were twice unsuccessful.

Black impatience and white resistance mounted even as the structure of legal segregation was being dismantled. Equality, many black leaders had come to realize, would be only a mirage unless tangible opportunities for self-improvement could be created. This awareness was reflected in the growth of black militancy, in declining white participation and leadership in the movement for equal rights, and in a mood of heightened black bitterness over conditions in the urban ghettos. Frustration and rage found expression in "black power," an angry reaction against nonviolence as a tactic and integration as a goal. Racial tension increased throughout the country, white and black attitudes were rapidly polarized, and the civil rights coalition began to splinter. By the summer of 1966 a "white backlash" was being manifested in many northern and midwestern areas, open-housing demonstrations were causing violent racial conflicts, and "law and order" was emerging as a key political issue.

Some of the basic problems facing American blacks were touched upon in a controversial memorandum on the black family written in 1965 by Daniel Patrick Moynihan, an official in the Johnson administration. The Moynihan report, while pointing out that perhaps half of the nation's blacks could be classified as middle class in socio-economic status, emphasized the disintegration of the black family in the great urban centers. The report angered blacks and depressed many whites. A more comprehensive treatment of racial problems was contained in *The Report of the National Advisory Commission on Civil Disorders* (1968). The work of a special commission appointed by President Johnson and headed by Otto Kerner, a former governor of Illinois, the report stated that "white racism is essentially responsible for the explosive mixture which has been accumulating in our cities since the end of World War II." The commission cited the growing concentration of blacks in cities; the chronic discrimination and segregation in employment, education, and housing; the oppressive effects of ghetto life upon the young and the increase in crime, drug addiction, and welfare dependency; and the fact that 2 million "hard-core disadvantaged" urban blacks were making no significant economic gains.

By early 1967 the civil rights movement appeared to have collapsed. While the urban riots raged out of control during the summer of 1967, the House of Representatives voted down rent subsidy and rat control legislation. The assassination of Martin Luther King, Jr., on April 4, 1968, touched off the most widespread rioting that had yet occurred in Afro-American areas throughout the country and contributed further to black disillusionment and alienation. King's assassination did help bring the enactment of one additional civil rights measure during the Johnson years. The Civil Rights Law of 1968, which had been pending for more than two years, outlawed racial discrimination in the sale and rental of 80 percent of all U.S. houses and apartments. It also imposed stringent criminal penalties on persons found guilty of interfering with anyone's civil rights. With the passage of the Open Housing Act of 1968, the right of American blacks to equal treatment in most aspects of the national life was established in law.

Lyndon Johnson was, as the black novelist Ralph Ellison has said, "the greatest American President for the poor and for the Negroes." Johnson, even more than Kennedy, contributed to the quickening pace of the civil rights movement during the 1960s and to the great progress made since World War II toward the goal of equal rights for all. Even so, the task of converting equal rights into truly equal opportunity was far from finished. Most white Americans were still opposed to open housing, the urban ghettos remained volatile, millions of blacks were working in menial jobs or were unemployed, and in the 1970s and 1980s the nation seemed to have lost a sense of urgency about the terrible condition of its minorities.

THE WAR ON POVERTY

Like all modern American presidents, Lyndon Johnson was continually concerned with the effort to promote the nation's economic security and growth. He quickly embraced the Kennedy administration's tax reduction plan, which had passed the House of Representatives in September 1963, and pushed it through the Senate in February 1964, though without many of the tax reforms Kennedy had originally recommended. Johnson's sympathetic attitude toward business, as well as his early budgetary restraint, appealed to businessmen, and for a time, at least, he succeeded in bringing the business class into his broad-gauged coalition. The tax cut of 1964 seemed to work brilliantly, and even though the legislation favored established interests, a new principle of economic policy had been enacted. The continued expansion of the economy during 1964 and 1965, the steady decline of unemployment, and the marked increase of sales and profits lent support to the claims of the administration for its fiscal policy and justified the slash in excise taxes enacted by Congress in June 1965.

The Johnson administration also moved to help less fortunate Americans in more direct ways. In 1966 the administration got Congress to raise the minimum wage from $1.25 to $1.60 an hour, effective in 1968. The Manpower Development and Training Act of 1964 was designed to train the unskilled or technologically displaced worker in new skills. Congress established a permanent food stamp program in 1964. Taking Kennedy's embryonic war-on-poverty plans, Johnson developed his own legislative program and gave it the impetus of his administration's all-out support. Poverty, LBJ asserted in his first State of the Union message, was a national problem against which his administration "here and now declares unconditional war." At the University of Michigan a few months later, the president declared that "the Great Society rests on abundance and liberty for all. It demands an end to poverty and racial injustice, to which we are totally committed in our time."

Most Americans were slow to recognize the extent of poverty in the United States during the post-1945 period. Until 1964 the term "poverty" did not appear as a heading in the index of either the *Congressional Record* or the *Public Papers of the Presidents*. Yet in 1960 more than one-fifth of all American families—perhaps as many as 40 million people—were living on less than $4,000 a year, that is, below the official poverty line. Twice as many blacks as whites, relative to population, were the victims of poverty, but in chronically depressed areas like Appalachia as well as rural pockets and city slums all over the country there were millions of impoverished white people, as well as Indians, Mexican-Americans, and Puerto Ricans. Local welfare officials in San Antonio, Texas, for example, reported in 1967 that between 100,000 and 150,000 of that city's residents were suffering from hunger or malnutrition. Public awareness of the nation's extensive poverty grew in the early 1960s, stimulated by the vivid portrayal in Michael Harrington's *The Other America*, by the analyses of Robert J. Lampman and other scholars, and by the Kennedy administration's commitment to an antipoverty program.

President Johnson submitted his specific recommendations to Congress on March 16, 1964. If Johnson's most spectacular victories came in the field of civil rights, his most ambitious and original program was the war on poverty. He requested an initial outlay of

$962.5 million to support a variety of programs. The antipoverty bill encountered a good deal of opposition in Congress, especially from Republicans, who called it a partisan scheme to win votes in an election year. But once Johnson had made the proposal the "centerpiece" of his 1964 program, it was impossible to prevent its passage. Congress gave the administration virtually all that it asked, appropriating almost a billion dollars for the first year of the antipoverty war.

The Economic Opportunity Act of 1964 established ten separate programs to be administered by an Office of Economic Opportunity (OEO), which was given broad discretionary powers. The president appointed R. Sargent Shriver, director of the Peace Corps, to head the OEO. The act provided funds for job training, community projects, small farm and business loans, and much more. Many of the new programs were designed to help the young and to do so primarily by giving them opportunities for further education and training. Thus Head Start was a program for preschoolers, while Upward Bound was for college students. VISTA (Volunteers in Service to America) was intended to function as a domestic peace corps in behalf of the poor and disadvantaged. The most innovative and controversial part of the legislation was Title II, which authorized community action programs to develop employment opportunities and to improve performance and motivation by providing for "maximum feasible participation" of the poor themselves in directing and developing the projects.

In 1965, with the administration vigorously pursuing the realization of the Great Society, the war on poverty was stepped up still further. Congress passed amendments to the 1964 legislation that more than doubled the first year's authorization. By 1966 the Office of Economic Opportunity was devoting about two-fifths of its budget to an assortment of community action programs, another two-fifths to its youth programs, and most of its remaining funds to work experience projects. One of Johnson's major congressional accomplishments in 1965 was the passage of the Appalachian Regional Development Act, which had passed the Senate but failed to win House approval in 1964. Emphasizing economic development rather than welfare support, the act provided $1.1 billion in subsidies for highway construction, health centers, and resource development in a depressed region stretching from Pennsylvania to Alabama. Another 1965 statute, the Public Works and Economic Development Act, extended the same concept to other depressed areas.

The war on poverty began to slow down in 1966, as the administration became more engrossed in the struggle over Vietnam and as growing inflationary pressure resulted from the sharp increase in defense expenditures. Congressional Republicans found new Democratic allies in their efforts to curb the Great Society's spending and social reform programs. A measure to overhaul the unemployment compensation system, for instance, was left languishing in conference as the session ended in 1966.

For all its call to arms and good intentions, the war on poverty during the 1960s was never given more than a fraction of the funds it needed. Its entire cost during the years of its most active support—1964–1967—was only $6.2 billion. Much of this money went to landlords and construction companies; to big corporations like International Telephone and Telegraph and Litton Industries that received contracts for antipoverty projects; and to construction of highways, airports, and other facilities that benefited the middle classes and the affluent much more than the needy. In the end, the Great Society did little for the central cities and their inhabitants, and the depressed rural areas received even less help from Washington. Many of the antipoverty projects were hastily initiated, there was the usual bureaucratic inertia and inefficiency, and the control exercised by local officials frequently prevented progress. There was also waste in the OEO undertakings, as well as a substantial amount of pork-barrel funds in such programs as those begun in Appalachia. The rent supplement provisions of the housing legislation of the mid-sixties were never really implemented.

Rather than seeking to organize the poor to combat alienation, the war on poverty might have been more effective in the long run with legislation providing for public employment and an incomes program guaranteeing a minimum standard of living. Still, there were some gains, not all of which resulted from action by the national government. By the end of the 1960s, only 11 percent of the nation's families received an annual income of less than $4,000, as compared with 22 percent at the beginning of the decade (this does not take into account the losses resulting from inflation). The antipoverty programs, as well as Medicare and increased social security benefits, did help many poor people, young Americans, and elderly folk. The effort to involve the poor in community action programs, while alarming to many local leaders and the subject of much criticism, did represent a new approach by government to the problem of poverty. Finally, the war on poverty did constitute a beginning, even if an extremely limited one, toward the solution of a great social ill in the United States.

BREAKTHROUGHS IN EDUCATION AND HEALTH

One of the goals of the Great Society, proclaimed President Johnson in early 1965, was to improve the quality of American life. "We begin with learning," he said. "Every child must have the best education our nation can provide." Johnson was fond of saying that all young Americans should have open to them as much education as they could absorb. Several factors had served to obstruct direct federal intervention in this area: the historic church-state issue, the conservative suspicion of increased governmental involvement in such matters, southern congressional fear that a federal program would become an instrument of school desegregation, and the insistence of Representative Adam Clayton Powell and others that federal aid must be accompanied by the banning of racial discrimination in education. The Kennedy administration had mounted a new attack on the problem, but without much immediate success. Johnson's efforts in 1964 to secure the passage of direct federal-aid-to-education legislation were also unsuccessful.

When the first session of the Eighty-ninth Congress convened in January 1965, Johnson was ready to submit a series of educational proposals. Some of these recommendations had originated in a presidential task force on education headed by John W. Gardner, president of the Carnegie Corporation.[4] Assistant Secretary Wilbur J. Cohen and other HEW staff members had been working on the problem of the church-state issue as an obstacle to a general education statute, and both sides of the religious controversy seemed to have become more amenable to compromise. Johnson's consensus-building technique and his legislative skill were much in evidence on the educational front. The administration won the support of both the National Education Association and the National Catholic Welfare Conference for a new approach to federal aid based on the needs of individual students rather than assistance to schools per se.[5] Democratic leaders were able to push the general education bill through Congress by April 1965, despite the opposition of conservatives who objected to the expenditure of federal funds and to the growing role of the national government in the field of education.

The Elementary and Secondary Education Act of 1965 was the first general federal aid to education law in U.S. history. The act authorized the expenditure of over a billion dollars in federal funds for textbooks, library materials, special educational programs for adults and the handicapped, and the strengthening of state educational agencies. Large sums were to be devoted to improving the teaching of students in the urban slums and in impoverished rural areas. Private schools, whether religious or not, could benefit from this federal support in several ways, including educational television and the use of library materials.

Another feature of the Great Society was a wide-ranging program of aid to higher education. The Higher Education Act of 1965 expanded federal assistance to colleges and universities, providing scholarships and low-interest loans for students, aid to struggling colleges and community service programs, and grants for college libraries. The law made scholarships available to more than 140,000 capable but needy students and authorized a National Teacher Corps to work in poverty-stricken areas.

By mid-1965 resistance to federal aid to education had been shattered, and Congress was pouring more than $4 billion a year into all levels of the national education system. In 1966 Congress provided further massive infusions of federal aid, including $3.9 billion over a three-year period for colleges and universities and $6.1 billion for public schools in a two-year extension of the Elementary and Secondary Education Act. Although the lawmakers refused to appropriate funds in 1966 for the new Teacher Corps, they did approve several additional educational measures during the Ninetieth Congress. Meanwhile, the U.S. Office of Education issued broad new guidelines for the desegregation of schools, hospitals, and other medical facilities under Title VI of the Civil Rights Act of 1964. Lyndon Johnson liked to be called "the education president," and he deserved the designation.

Johnson also achieved a dramatic breakthrough with the approval of Medicare in 1965. The final legislation was the product of fifteen years of refinement and liberalization since the first comprehensive medical care proposal had been made by the Truman administration. But like the educational enactments of the mid-sixties, it reflected the special circumstances and pressures associated with the Johnsonian Great Society. By the early 1960s, polls indicated that over two-thirds of the American people favored the idea. Organized labor, the elderly, and other groups increased the pressure for congressional approval. Johnson took up the cause in 1964, but while numerous expiring laws, including Hill-Burton hospital legislation, were extended and broadened that year, Medicare was defeated once again.

The Democratic landslide of 1964 went a long way toward settling the question. Practically the entire Democratic "class of '64" in the House—numbering sixty-five—was committed to Medicare. Johnson made the issue his top priority measure in 1965, and the administration's bill, introduced by Representative Cecil R. King and Senator Clinton P. Anderson, was appropriately numbered H.R. 1 and S. 1. The American Medical Association, sensing the swelling tide of support for congressional action, now presented its own legislative plan, calling for a program to be financed through private insurance companies. Congressional Republicans also introduced comprehensive medical care legislation, but they adhered to the voluntary concept and financing through insurance companies. Congress effectively resisted the lobbying of the AMA and other opponents of Medicare, in part by incorporating some features of the other proposals into the King-Anderson bill, which was considerably broadened in scope during the process. Both houses passed the bill by large majorities.

Two major health care programs for persons sixty-five and older were established by the $6.5 billion Medical Care Act of 1965. The basic plan, usually referred to as Medicare, would cover most hospital and some nursing home costs, diagnostic studies, and home health care visits. It was to be compulsory, financed mainly by a payroll tax and administered by the social security system. The second health care program, called the supplementary plan, would be voluntary and was to be financed by monthly premiums from participants and by general revenue. It was designed to cover about 80 percent of the costs of a variety of health services, including doc-

Spending on Health, 1965–1984

Total public and private spending on health care for each year in billions of dollars and as percentage of the gross national product.

Source: Department of Health and Human Services

tors' bills. A little-noticed feature of the Medical Care Act was the provision authorizing Medicaid, a program making federal funds available to the states to help cover medical expenses of the needy, regardless of age. The act of 1965 had its flaws. The program it established helped only the elderly, and then in a cumbersome and limited way. It gave control over fees to physicians, some of whom abused the system. Nevertheless, the aged did receive immediate relief from the unbearable costs of health care.

LBJ AND THE URBAN NATION

The increasing problems of American cities provided a major focus for Lyndon Johnson's Great Society. The crisis of the city grew steadily worse with the continuing middle-class flight to the suburbs, with the shrinking tax base in the inner city, and with "the revolution of rising expectations" among the urban poor. The condition of the great cities had become extraordinarily precarious, as a *Newsweek* article in March 1969 suggests:

> Choking in air so polluted that it filters out a quarter of the sun's light; stifled by traffic jams; plagued by strikes that cripple essential services; victimized by muggers who fill the streets with fear, America's cities daily appear to confirm Thomas Jefferson's sour conviction that they would be "penitential to the morals, the health and the liberties of man."

LBJ signs the Medicare Bill (*courtesy Lyndon B. Johnson Library*)

During the sixties the Kennedy and Johnson administrations pushed hard for such programs as urban renewal, public housing, mass rapid transit, and water pollution control, and following the election of 1964, Congress enacted an unprecedented number of urban-oriented measures.

Although the assault on the slums drew the most attention, Washington's response to the urban crisis was broad and varied. One approach was the community-centered character of the antipoverty programs. This approach sought to meet the sharp criticism of the traditional urban renewal process—charges, for example, that it involved haphazard and undemocratic destruction of communities, the forced relocation of families, and the replacement of older houses and buildings with high-rise apartment complexes. The Johnson administration also attempted to reduce the political fragmentation of metropolitan districts. The Housing and Urban Development Act of 1965,[6] for example, authorized support for areawide planning, and during the following year Congress gave the newly created Department of Housing and Urban Affairs power to require that a locally appointed and financed regional council or planning board review all applications for federal funds from governmental units within a given metropolitan area. The elaborate housing law of 1965 not only extended the existing urban renewal programs but also provided federal funds for community health and recreation centers and for urban beautification, grants to low-income home-owners for home repairs and improvements, and a controversial rent supplement program.

The most prominent feature of the administration's urban program was the Demonstration Cities and Metropolitan Area Redevelopment Act of 1966. This so-called Model Cities Act was designed to improve the quality and efficiency of urban life by authorizing $1.2 billion to be spent in slum areas for the improvement of housing, health, education, job training, recreational facilities, welfare, and transportation. Calling for an intensive attack on urban blight, the act sought to encourage slum clearance and rehabilitation in some sixty or seventy cities by covering up to 80 percent of the costs of planning and construction, to encourage metropolitan area planning, and to underwrite the building of new model communities by providing land development mortgage insurance. The model cities program attempted to improve the "total environment" of the slum resident by going beyond the traditional physical treatment of urban renewal and including antipoverty and educational projects.

Part of the trouble in urban America was the result of inadequate, inefficient, and expensive transportation. Although public transit was cheaper, safer, and more efficient for the user, it was costly to provide and much less central to the economy than the automobile system, in which there was a huge existing investment. In 1964 Congress enacted a $375 million mass transit bill to aid in planning and developing areawide urban transit systems. The federal grants aimed at relieving the heavy traffic congestion in most major metropolitan areas were supplemented by appropriations in the Urban Mass Transportation Act of 1966. Congress also responded to another administration request in 1966 by creating a Cabinet-level Department of Transportation, with full responsibility for the development of a coordinated transportation system for the United States.

A growing consumer movement in the second half of the sixties spurred the Johnson administration to sponsor other measures somewhat related to its urban programs. The Highway Safety Act and the Traffic Safety Act of 1966 allocated federal funds for state and local traffic safety programs and applied safety standards to automobile manufacturers. Ralph Nader's muckraking book, *Unsafe at Any Speed* (1965), and his research and lobbying played an important part in the enactment of these laws. The young lawyer soon became a full-time advocate of the public interest, investigating and criticizing numerous products, industries, and government agencies. Congress also took action in 1966 to broaden federal controls over the labeling and packaging of foods, drugs, cosmetics, and household supplies. The Consumer Credit Protection Act of 1968 established a Commission on Consumer Finance to oversee the operations of the consumer finance business and consumer credit transactions in general. The Truth in Lending Act, as it was popularly called, did not limit the charge for credit, but it did require lenders and creditors to give their customers full, honest, and comparative information on the interest rates they were paying—and on a uniform, annual basis.

"A prime national goal," the president told Congress in 1965, "must be an environment that is pleasing to the senses and healthy to live in." During the early postwar years little was said in Washington to suggest that the purity of air and water, the pressure of population upon outdoor open space, and the beauty of countryside and city were *national* concerns. There was a growing awareness, however, of the environmental implications of the postindustrial pattern of metropolitan growth; writers like Rachel Carson and Barry Commoner warned of increasing ecological dangers; and such groups as the Sierra Club began to attract some political support in their battles for conservation and an end to the wholesale destruction of the environment. President Kennedy endorsed the idea of more federal spending for conservation and environmental controls. By the time Johnson sent Congress the first presidential message ever devoted to natural beauty, in February 1965, the national government had adopted or was in the process of adopting a long series of measures designed to protect the environment.

According to President Johnson and Secretary of the Interior Stewart L. Udall, the Eighty-eighth Congress was a "conservation Congress." Among the conservation measures it passed was the National Wilderness Preservation Act of 1964, which incorporated federally held wilderness areas into a National Wilderness System. Congress also set up a Land Conservation Fund in 1964 to provide for future state and federal recreation area needs. Each year thereafter brought new legislation and increased appropriations for conservation and environmental protection, an enlargement of federal responsibilities in that field, and an intensified attack on the problem through the formation of regional control agencies and planning commissions. In 1965 Senator Edmund S. Muskie of Maine and other congressional advocates of conservation cooperated with the administration to secure the passage of the important Water Quality Act. The Solid Waste Disposal Act of 1965, the Clean Water Restoration Act of 1966, and a variety of other enactments provided federal support for air and water purification; for the construction of sewage and waste treatment plants; and for research, planning, and the establishment of mandatory standards and enforcement procedures.

Among the "working groups" Johnson created to develop Great Society programs was one on "natural beauty." Appointed in July 1964, this task force reported to the president during the following November. Its recommendations, which were used as the basis for LBJ's congressional message on natural beauty early in 1965, included a highway beautification proposal. Known as "Lady Bird's bill," because of the first lady's identification with the natural beauty campaign, the bill became the Highway Beautification Act of 1965. It attacked the human-made blight that lined the country's highways.

Despite the variety and scope of the Kennedy and Johnson attacks on the urban crisis, their programs did little to halt the deterioration of America's cities. The city-suburban conflict persisted, and the critical questions of race and metropolitan fragmentation remained largely unresolved. For all their good intentions, most of the urban renewal and redevelopment programs dislocated thousands of poor families, reduced the supply of low-rent housing, increased rents, and enabled private business interests to make enormous profits from slum clearance and construction loans and subsidies. Many of the urban programs died before their impact could be felt, some were badly conceived, and others were destroyed by the conflicting and overlapping intra-urban governments. Lack of money was also an acute problem.

Lyndon Johnson sponsored the most advanced program of social reform in the history of the republic. Congress responded to his leadership by enacting an extraordinary burst of social legislation: civil rights, the war on poverty, Medicare, aid to education, housing and urban development, increased social security benefits, conservation measures, a new immigration law, and even the subsidization of American "culture." The Great Society sought to correct old racial wrongs, to provide badly needed educational and medical services, to advance social justice by mounting a broad-based attack on poverty and urban blight, and to demonstrate man's capacity to master his environment. There were genuine successes in moving toward greater racial equality, in offering expanded educational opportunities and better health care, and in launching important federal programs in such areas as the war on poverty and environmental control. If the Great Society was a failure in many respects, it was nevertheless an audacious failure. A leader of uncommon ability and impressive accomplishments, Johnson set his sights on becoming a great president. The tragedy was that he lacked the capacity to inspire the confidence and trust of the people.

NOTES

1. Godfrey Hodgson, *America in Our Time* (1976), pp. 167–68.
2. Liberal Democratic strength in the House in the Eighty-ninth Congress also resulted in a revision of the rules in a way that gave the speaker authority to bring legislation to the floor if blocked by the Rules Committee.
3. This brought the federal registration machinery to bear on seven states—Alabama, Alaska, Georgia, Louisiana, Mississippi, South Carolina, and Virginia—plus thirty-four counties in North Carolina and one county each in Arizona, Idaho, and Maine.
4. Realizing the importance of presenting Congress with a carefully developed blueprint for the implementation of his Great Society, Johnson decided in 1964 to create fifteen task forces, made up of both government and nongovernment members, to formulate the legislative proposals he would send to Capitol Hill in 1965.
5. The new formula centered on the child benefit instead of the school benefit concept, a distinction the federal courts had made during recent years. As early as 1947, in *Everson* v. *Ewing Township*, the Supreme Court had upheld a New Jersey law providing bus transportation for parochial school children because the benefit went to the individual rather than the school. Under the federal statute of 1965, aid would be given to all children, but public agencies would control expenditures.
6. The act provided aid for the construction of 240,000 units of housing and $2.9 billion for urban renewal.

SUGGESTIONS FOR FURTHER READING

Although the literature on Lyndon Johnson and his administration is extensive, the thirty-sixth president still awaits his biographer. Paul K.
Conkin's *Big Daddy from the Pedernales: Lyndon Baines Johnson* (1986), a brief but
perspicacious and revealing treatment, provides a good introduction to the
man and his politics. Alfred Steinberg, *Sam Johnson's Boy: A Close-up of
the President from Texas* (1968), should be used with caution. More reward-
ing are two critical examinations of Johnson's early career: Ronnie Dugger,
The Politician: The Life and Times of Lyndon Johnson (1982), and Robert
A. Caro, *The Years of Lyndon Johnson: The Path to Power* (1982). Leonard
Baker, *The Johnson Eclipse: A President's Vice Presidency* (1966), recounts
a neglected story. Merle Miller, *Lyndon: An Oral Biography* (1980), is interesting but thin. Johnson's own views are presented in his *The Vantage
Point: Perspectives of the Presidency, 1963–1969* (1971) and in *Public Papers of the Presidents of the United States: Lyndon B. Johnson* (12 vols.,
1965–1970). See also Claudia Alta (Taylor) Johnson, *A White House Diary*
(1970).

Allen J. Matusow, *The Unraveling of America: A History of Liberalism
in the 1960s* (1984), offers a fresh and critical evaluation of Johnson's presidency. Heath, *Decade of Disillusionment*, Sundquist, *Politics and Policy*,
and O'Neill, *Coming Apart*, all referred to in the previous chapter, are also
valuable for LBJ's domestic policies. Vaughn Davis Bornet's *The Presidency
of Lyndon B. Johnson* (1983) is informative but rather difficult to use. Robert A. Divine (ed.), *Exploring the Johnson Years* (1981), contains a number
of valuable essays on the Johnson administration. *Lyndon B. Johnson: The
Exercise of Power, a Political Biography* (1966), by Rowland Evans, Jr., and
Robert D. Novak, is a shrewd journalistic account. For interesting and revealing works by two scholars who worked for Johnson, see Eric F. Goldman, *The Tragedy of Lyndon Johnson* (1969), and Doris Kearns, *Lyndon
Johnson and the American Dream* (1976). Wicker, *JFK and LBJ*, cited in
chapter eleven, is perceptive. Hamby, *Liberalism and Its Challengers*, also
cited before, contains a thoughtful essay on Johnson, who is characterized
as "a man of excess and overcompensation." For other books on Johnson's
presidency, see Jack Bell, *The Johnson Treatment: How Lyndon B. Johnson
Took Over the Presidency and Made It His Own* (1965); Frank Cormier,
LBJ: The Way He Was (1977); Richard Harwood and Haynes Johnson, *Lyndon* (1973); and Louis Heren, *No Hail, No Farewell* (1970). Harry Mc-
Pherson, *A Political Education* (1972), is an unusually perceptive memoir
by one of LBJ's aides.

Several books mentioned in chapters eight and eleven, including those
by Muse and Sitkoff, are useful for civil rights and the black revolution
during the Johnson period. *Black Protest in the Sixties* (1970), edited by
August Meier and Elliott Rudwick, is a good anthology of *New York Times*
articles. *The Report of the National Commission on Civil Disorders* (1968)
is an indispensable document for the urban riots of the 1960s. Robert E.
Conot's *Rivers of Blood, Years of Darkness* (1967) deals with the Watts riot
of 1965. For the Selma-to-Montgomery march and the voting rights legislation, see Charles E. Fager, *Selma, 1965* (1974), and David J. Garrow, *Protest at Selma: Martin Luther King, Jr., and the Voting Rights Act of 1965*
(1978). The consequences of federal intervention in the South are explored
in Gary Orfield, *The Reconstruction of Southern Education: The Schools*

and the 1964 Civil Rights Act (1969), and Steven F. Lawson, *Black Ballots: Voting Rights in the South, 1944–1969* (1976).

The goals and achievements of the Great Society are examined by Marvin Gettleman and David Mermelstein (eds.), *The Failure of American Liberalism: After the Great Society* (1971), and Sar A. Levitan and Robert Taggart, *The Promise of Greatness* (1976). For various aspects of the war on poverty and welfare reform, see James T. Patterson, *America's Struggle Against Poverty, 1900–1980* (1981); Kenneth Davis, *The Paradox of Poverty in America* (1969); John C. Donovan, *The Politics of Poverty* (1973); Stephen Goodell and Bennet Schiff, *The Office of Economic Opportunity During the Administration of President Lyndon B. Johnson, 1963–1969* (1973); Frances Fox Piven and Richard A. Cloward, *Regulating the Poor: The Functions of Public Welfare* (1971); J. David Greenstone and Paul E. Peterson, *Race and Authority in Urban Politics: Community Participation and the War on Poverty* (1973); Marc and Phyllis Pilisuk (eds.), *How We Lost the War on Poverty* (1973); Karen Davis and Cathy Schoen, *Health and the War on Poverty: A Ten Year Appraisal* (1978); Daniel Patrick Moynihan, *Maximum Feasible Misunderstanding: Community Action in the War on Poverty* (1969); Ernest H. Woldenberg, *The Geography of Poverty in the United States* (1971); and William Graebner, *A History of Retirement: The Meaning and Function of an American Institution, 1885–1978* (1980). Charles Murray advances a biting critique of national welfare policy since mid-century in *Losing Ground: American Social Policy, 1950–1980* (1984).

Johnson's educational reforms are considered by Ravitch, *The Troubled Crusade*, cited in chapter nine. Urban social policy is discussed by Mark I. Gelfand, *A Nation of Cities: The Federal Government and Urban America, 1933–1965* (1975); Scott A. Greer, *Urban Renewal and American Cities: The Dilemma of Democratic Intervention* (1966); and Zane L. Miller, *The Urbanization of Modern America: A Brief History* (1973). Jon C. Teaford, *City and Suburb: The Political Fragmentation of Metropolitan America, 1850–1970* (1979), is useful for the rising political difficulties of metropolitan areas.

Congress and the Nation, 1965–1968 (1969), by the Congressional Quarterly, Inc., is a valuable reference work on the Johnson years.

CHAPTER THIRTEEN

Johnsonian Foreign Policy and the War in Vietnam

LIKE THOSE OF ALL PRESIDENTS of the post–World War II period, Lyndon B. Johnson's administration was beset by a series of difficult international problems. "World affairs will continue to call upon our energy and courage," Johnson declared in his State of the Union message in January 1965. "But today we can turn increased attention to the character of American life." Unfortunately, however, there was to be little time after 1965 in which the administration could concentrate upon the task of advancing the Great Society at home. Although U.S. relations with the Soviet Union were improving when Johnson assumed the presidency, he also inherited a set of thorny foreign problems from John F. Kennedy. The Atlantic alliance was undergoing severe strain, the pressure for large-scale economic and social change in Latin America was steadily mounting, the Middle East remained in an unsettled and volatile condition, and the nature of America's role in Southeast Asia, which was then but a small cloud on the horizon, would soon have to be resolved.

THE PATTERN OF AMERICAN POLICY IN THE MID–1960S

An internationalist schooled in the struggles of World War II and the cold war, Johnson accepted implicitly the threat of international communism, the wisdom of containment, the need to live up to commitments to one's allies, and the special obligation to maintain an American presence in the Far East. LBJ was not well prepared either by temperament or experience to meet the challenges of international leadership. His instinct was to seek consensus in waging the cold war abroad just as he did in creating the Great Society at home. Following Johnson's overwhelming victory at the polls in 1964, his consciousness of the immense power at his disposal and his faith in his capacity to use it nourished his globalist pretensions and his determination to master intractable problems in the international arena.

Although the U.S. conflict with the Soviet Union and with international communism was no longer quite such an obsession by the mid-sixties, that dual conflict was still the single most important international factor in the shaping of American policy. There was some concern in Washington when Khrushchev was suddenly deposed in October 1964, but his successors, Leonid Brezhnev and Alexei N. Kosygin, soon revealed their desire for a continuation of peaceful coexistence. In 1964 the Americans and the Russians worked out arrangements for cultural exchanges involving teachers, researchers, and artists. They reached a joint understanding not to place nuclear warheads into orbit. They inaugurated direct air service between New York and Moscow and signed a new consular treaty establishing additional consulates in both countries. The invasion and occupation of Czechoslovakia by Russian troops in August 1968 in order to crush the liberalization program of Czech party leader Alexander Dubček provoked strong criticism in the United States; but even this turn of events failed to disrupt the improved relations between the two great powers.

The Johnson administration also took up the cause of a nonproliferation treaty with the Soviet Union in 1965. Years of effort to reach an agreement to prevent the spread of nuclear weapons culminated in July 1968, with the signing of a nonproliferation treaty by the United States, the Soviet Union, Great Britain, and fifty-eight nonnuclear nations. The treaty forbade the transfer of nuclear weapons to any nation not possessing such devices; the nonnuclear nations agreed not to manufacture or to receive nuclear weapons.[1] Before Johnson left office, the United States and Russia had agreed to hold talks on the more fundamental problem of limiting the arms race.

This relaxation of tension did not mean that the two superpowers had abandoned their rivalry for the support of the unaligned nations and the Third World. The explosive situation in the Middle East made that clear. Following Israel's spectacular military victory in the Six Day War of 1967, in which the American role was essentially that of a passive spectator, the Arab nations aligned themselves more closely with the USSR. The Russians denounced Israel's "aggression," provided new military aid to their Arab friends, and dispatched naval forces into the eastern Mediterranean to

Kosygin and Johnson confer at Glassboro State College, June 1967 (*courtesy Lyndon B. Johnson Library*)

counter the U.S. Sixth Fleet. The UN was unable to bring the Arab-Israeli dispute much closer to a permanent settlement, and in later years the problem was further complicated by the guerrilla attacks carried out by bands of Palestinian refugees against the Israelis. President Johnson and Premier Kosygin made no real progress in dealing with the Middle East crisis when they held a series of friendly conversations at Glassboro State College, New Jersey, June 23–25, 1967.

In Western and Central Europe, Johnson hoped to carry forward the Kennedy administration's plans for the strengthening of defense and trade relations within the Atlantic community. He made little progress, however, and the NATO alliance continued to lose cohesiveness as its members grew more independent of Washington. Franco-American relations were exacerbated in 1964 when France extended diplomatic recognition to Communist China, and U.S. annoyance with Charles de Gaulle grew as a result of the French leader's overtures to Eastern Europe and criticism of U.S. policies. In early 1966 de Gaulle announced that France would formally withdraw from the NATO military organization within three years, and the alliance's commands and installations were thus forced to leave French soil.[2] A bitter quarrel between Greece and Turkey over the relative political status of their respective nationals on the island of Cyprus also strained the Atlantic alliance.

The United States encountered similar difficulties in its efforts to promote further economic integration of the Atlantic community. France blocked British membership in the Common Market, and the tariff negotiations made possible by the Trade Expansion Act of 1962 failed to produce the hoped-for trading area stretching from West Germany to Japan in which goods and services could move with relative freedom. In the bargaining preliminary to the so-called Kennedy Round negotiations within the General Agreement on Trade and Tariffs, the United States and the Common Market nations engaged in sharp debate over some issues. Nevertheless, the completion of the Kennedy Round in 1967 resulted in reductions averaging 35 percent between the United States and the Common Market.

Meanwhile, American involvement in Africa grew larger. The United States replaced Belgium as the most powerful foreign element in the Congo, and after a left-wing nationalist attempt to overthrow the central government was repulsed by General Joseph D. Mobutu in 1964, U.S. influence with the Congolese increased still further. Another rebellion in 1967 and rising protest in the United States against additional aid to Mobutu, coupled with the growing American preoccupation with Vietnam, limited Washington's initiatives in the Congo. The same was also true in other newly emerging countries.

During the campaign of 1964 Lyndon Johnson pictured himself as a peaceful and prudent president, in contrast to a warmongering and trigger-happy Barry Goldwater. The president talked about strengthening the United Nations, reducing cold-war tensions, expanding economic aid to underdeveloped countries, increasing world trade, and employing patience and moderation in dealing with international crises. Yet Johnson also urged a powerful military system for the United States. By 1965, in fact, Secretary McNamara's energetic efforts to enlarge the country's military capability were producing impressive results. Substantial increases had been made in the nuclear missile force, military aircraft, combat-ready divisions, special forces, and such specialized apparatus as tactical airlift and helicopter inventories.

U.S. IDEALS AND SELF-INTEREST IN LATIN AMERICA

While the United States in the twentieth century had emerged as one of the major world power centers, the vast region to its south remained a power vacuum. Lacking unity and political stability, Latin America was backward, agrarian, and undiversified in its economic life. It was a land of mass illiteracy, grinding poverty, and inadequate social services. Long dominated by foreign capitalists, local elites, and right-wing military dictatorships, most of the Latin American countries faced an enormous task of modernization. Millions of Latin Americans resented the record of U.S. intervention in their affairs during earlier decades; they were also both envious of their powerful neighbor to the north and unhappy over its relative neglect of them in the post-1945 period. It was the challenge of the "revolution of rising expectations" in Latin America that eventually resulted in Kennedy's Alliance for Progress.

Johnson was determined to prevent a recurrence of Castroism in the Western Hemisphere, not only because of his commitment to the containment of communism, but also because of his keen awareness of the political use the Republican party had made of the Cuban situation during the early 1960s. LBJ's ambassador to Chile later recalled the president's "romantic, Tex-Mex view of Latin America." One indication of the administration's approach to Latin America came with the appointment of Thomas C. Mann as assistant secretary of state for Inter-American Affairs. Mann, a Texas lawyer and former ambassador to Mexico, wanted above all else to stabilize Latin American politics, to protect the private interests of the United States in the area, and to wage a vigorous struggle against communism. Johnson and Mann took a hard line toward Castro's regime. They resisted Cuban pressure on the U.S. naval base at Guantanamo and maintained the economic boycott of the island.

President Johnson was confronted with his first foreign affairs crisis early in 1964 when long-festering anti-Americanism in Panama erupted into violence. In January 1964 controversy over the displaying of the American and Panamanian flags resulted in rioting, property destruction, and the loss of several lives. American troops finally were used to restore order. Meanwhile, President Roberto Chiari of Panama severed diplomatic relations with the United States and demanded a revision of the treaty of 1903 under which the Americans had built and operated the canal. Chiari also brought charges against the United States before the United Nations and the Organization of American States (OAS). The Johnson administration adopted a moderate position in dealing with the crisis, and with the encouragement of the OAS, secret talks were held between representatives of the two countries, leading to some easing of tensions and a decision to discuss the Panamanian grievances in a more formal way. In subsequent negotiations the United States made a major concession that helped pave the way for the historic treaty of 1978 between the two countries. Earlier the Johnson administration had pursued a constructive approach by cooperating with Eduardo Frei's moderate reform government in Chile.

The major crisis in Johnson's Latin American diplomacy resulted from his precipitous decision in the spring of 1965 to send a contingent of U.S. Marines into the Dominican Republic, ostensibly to protect American lives and property. The government of Juan Bosch, a non-Communist intellectual and nationalist reformer, had been overthrown by a military coup in September 1963. In April 1965 an odd coalition of democrats, radicals, and junior military officers launched a countercoup with the object of restoring constitutional government under Bosch. A bloody struggle ultimately broke out in the streets of Santo Domingo. The U.S. embassy in Santo Domingo and the State Department in Washington, which from the beginning had sided with the conservative military elements against the Bosch rebels, hastily urged the use of U.S. troops to stop the fighting.

On April 28, four days after the revolt began, Johnson sent in the Marines. They were followed during the next few weeks by more than 20,000 Army troops. The president defended the intervention by charging that the rebels had carried out mass executions, which proved not to have been the case. He also asserted that "people trained outside the Dominican Republic are seeking to gain control." Suspecting that the revolt was part of a larger conspiracy, probably masterminded by Castro, Johnson had acted decisively. "We don't expect to sit here on our rocking chairs with our hands folded and let the Communists set up any government in the Western Hemisphere," he explained. Once the American troops had restored some order, Washington sought to broaden the basis of its intervention by securing OAS support. The two sides finally accepted a cease-fire, and an interim government was agreed upon. More than a year after the revolt, on June 1, 1966, Joaquín Balaguer, a moderate, was chosen president in a peaceful election.

Johnson's police action and diplomatic moves had apparently accomplished their purpose. A strife-torn Caribbean republic had been stabilized, and the possible establishment of another Castro-like government in the Western Hemisphere had been prevented. Johnson could also claim to have supported the cause of free elections. Furthermore, the Dominican Republic venture appeared to confirm the promise of the Kennedy-McNamara strategy of flexible response. Johnson's apparent success in the Caribbean almost certainly encouraged him to push forward with his military intervention in Vietnam. On the other hand, the intervention raised serious doubts about American intentions throughout Latin America and about Johnson's capacity for the wise and restrained exercise of power. It led to new charges of U.S. imperialism and U.S. support of right-wing dictatorships. It reinforced many long-standing Latin American fears and placed new strains on the relations between the United States and the nations to its south. It also created Johnson's first credibility crisis at home.

The Johnson administration's gunboat diplomacy in the Dominican Republic threatened to undo the good it had accomplished through the Alliance for Progress. American support of the *Alianza* began to decline in the mid-sixties, and with Johnson's encouragement, its initial ten-year timetable was lengthened to eighteen years. As American fears of Castro declined, U.S. appropriations for Latin American aid dropped. Furthermore, Alliance aid was not predicated, as originally intended, on local reforms. After 1945 non-revolutionary democratic change seemed less urgent to American leaders, as was demonstrated by U.S. acceptance and in some cases support of military coups in Brazil, Bolivia, and Argentina. Little land reform was undertaken, and income distribution throughout Latin America remained almost unchanged. Although the United States had spent $9.2 billion on the Alliance program by 1969, so great was the population increase resulting from the high birthrate that the per capita increase in real productivity per year amounted to only about 1.5 percent.

The United States continued to use the rhetoric of its democratic creed, even as it showed a willingness to cooperate with right-wing military leaders in many Latin American countries. President Johnson, for example, met with leaders from twenty Latin American nations at Punta del Este, Uruguay, in April 1967. But he was unable to overcome the ill effects of his Caribbean intervention two years before. Even the military regimes in some South American countries began to behave in strange and unpredictable ways. A military coup toppled the Peruvian government in the fall of 1968. The new government proceeded to nationalize the local subsidiary of Standard Oil, to capture U.S. fishing boats within 200 miles of its coast, and to establish diplomatic and commercial ties with the Soviet Union. Soon afterward, a new military government in Bolivia began to act in a somewhat similar manner. The United States responded cautiously to these provocations, partly because there was no ready solution for such difficulties and partly because American attention was focused on a more serious and distant international challenge in Southeast Asia.

VIETNAM: THE MAKING OF A QUAGMIRE

When Lyndon Johnson entered the White House in late November 1963, he hoped to continue John Kennedy's policies in Southeast Asia, as in other parts of the world. It was assumed that this would require only a limited American involvement, largely in the form of military advisers to instruct the South Vietnamese, and that the Communist threat in the region could be blunted with economic and military aid. Having made South Vietnam a client state, the United States had reorganized, equipped, and trained that country's army. It had also provided the South Vietnamese with a great deal of economic assistance. When South Vietnam's National Liberation Front made overtures to General Duong Van Minh, head of the new Saigon government, for the possible negotiation of a cease-fire and a coalition government, Johnson asserted that "neutralization of South Vietnam would only be another name for a Communist take-over." He promised Minh "American personnel and material as needed to assist you in achieving victory." Later in the year LBJ declared, "I am not going to be the President who saw South Vietnam go the way China went."

The situation in South Vietnam became more uncertain in 1964, as the Vietcong enlarged its operations and the political instability in Saigon continued. In June 1964, when the Pathet Lao fired upon American planes making reconnaissance flights over Laos, the president ordered retaliatory air strikes against the rebel positions. American advisers continued to assist the Army of the Republic of Viet Nam (ARVN) in carrying out raids and acts of sabotage in the north. Furthermore, the U.S. Navy had begun to send destroyers on reconnaissance missions off the coast of North Vietnam.

In early August the U.S.S. *Maddox* was attacked while on such a mission in the Gulf of Tonkin by North Vietnamese PT boats, and two days later the *Maddox* and a second destroyer were allegedly fired upon during a night so dark and rainy that the two U.S. ships could not even see each other. Johnson seized upon this encounter to broaden his discretionary authority in the Vietnam conflict. He ordered retaliatory air attacks against three North Vietnamese torpedo-boat bases and an oil storage depot. More importantly, he asked Congress for a blanket authorization to use military force to defend the American position in Southeast Asia.

Congress speedily complied with the president's request. By August 25 the two houses had passed the Gulf of Tonkin Resolution with only two opposing votes being cast against the measure. The resolution authorized the chief executive "to take all necessary measures to repel any armed attack against the forces of the United

States and to prevent further aggression." It also stated that the United States was prepared, "as the President determines," to take "all necessary steps, including the use of armed force," to assist any nation covered by SEATO that requested assistance "in defense of its freedom."

Despite the Gulf of Tonkin, Johnson, in his public statements, continued to urge restraint. He resisted pressures for the United States to begin bombing the north in the fall of 1964, even after a Vietcong mortar attack on an American base near Saigon in early November. Yet when Hanoi put out peace feelers soon after the November election, neither Johnson nor his advisers were interested in the kind of compromise solution that would likely have resulted from such peace negotiations. Nothing came of UN Secretary General U Thant's efforts during the following winter to bring the United States and North Vietnam to the conference table. The Americans had lost their illusions of easy success in Vietnam, and by the end of 1964 the Johnson administration had decided to expand its military role in the struggle.

Having rejected negotiations, Johnson's problem was how to win the war in Vietnam. The position of South Vietnam—and of the United States—had steadily deteriorated. The Vietcong, receiving supplies and some military reinforcements from North Vietnam by way of the Ho Chi Minh Trail through Laos, controlled great sections of the southern countryside. In Saigon seven different governments came to power in 1964 as one coup followed another. While the generals feuded in Saigon, there were student demonstrations, Buddhist protests, and other evidence of disunity among the South Vietnamese. Virtually all of the president's advisers on foreign affairs recommended an expansion of American military force in Vietnam. They believed that Hanoi was directing and controlling the Vietcong insurgency, and they were convinced that the demonstration of U.S. military power north of the 17th parallel would persuade the North Vietnamese to withdraw. They also assumed that a Communist victory in South Vietnam would result in the collapse of all Southeast Asia and dominance of the area by the People's Republic of China. Once again, as so often in the past, American policy makers talked about the Munich appeasement analogy, the test-of-will hypothesis, and the need to maintain "our credibility vis-à-vis the Communists." Furthermore, North Vietnam was, in LBJ's pungent phrase, only a "raggedy-ass little fourth-rate country."

A fateful decision was made in the wake of an attack on February 6, 1965, by Vietcong guerrillas on an American military advisers' compound in Pleiku in the Central Highlands and on a nearby U.S. helicopter base. Johnson ordered an immediate reprisal on a North Vietnam barracks forty miles north of the Demilitarized Zone

(DMZ). New incidents provoked similar reprisals later in the month, and on March 2 a systematic bombing campaign of the north began. Within a week Operation Rolling Thunder, as this campaign was called, was spreading destruction by dropping incendiary bombs containing napalm on North Vietnam's villages and countryside. "We seek no wider war," the president declared in a nationwide television address following the attack on Pleiku. "We want nothing for ourselves, only that the people of South Vietnam be allowed to guide their own country in their own way."

When Operation Rolling Thunder had no perceptible effect on the position of North Vietnam or the National Liberation Front, the Johnson administration made another crucial decision. It committed U.S. ground troops to the war in Vietnam. On March 8, 3,500 Marines came ashore near Danang, and in late April Johnson authorized the dispatch of 40,000 additional combat troops. These ground forces were expected to help implement the "enclave strategy" devised by General Maxwell D. Taylor. By the summer of 1965, the "advisory" role of the American military units had been abandoned; the mission of U.S. ground forces in Vietnam was changed from defense to offense. They also increased steadily in number. In July Johnson raised the troop level in Vietnam to 125,000 men, and by the end of 1965 more than 184,000 troops were stationed there. Johnson's decisions in the summer of 1965 represented an open-ended commitment to employ U.S. military forces as the situation might demand.

While the United States was doing its best to force North Vietnam to end its support of the NLF and to recognize the independence of South Vietnam under an anti-Communist government, its leaders talked of peace. Thus in an important address at Johns Hopkins University on April 7, 1965, Johnson urged an end to the war on the basis of self-determination by the South and a massive U.S. investment of a billion dollars for the development of the rich Mekong Valley, a development in which North Vietnam would share. Reiterating the American commitment to the independence of South Vietnam, the chief executive made it clear that the United States would not withdraw, "either openly or under the cloak of a meaningless agreement." From time to time in the years that followed, beginning with a bombing pause at Christmas in 1965 that eventually lasted thirty-seven days, Washington launched other peace offensives. But Johnson increasingly relied on military pressure in dealing with the problem in Vietnam.

In the meantime, the tempo of the war continually increased. By the spring of 1966, B-52 bombers were regularly conducting large-scale raids on North Vietnam, and in June of that year their strikes were extended to include oil installations and other targets near the major cities of Hanoi and Haiphong. The total number of American troops in Vietnam had grown to 385,000 by the end of 1966 and to more than 485,000 a year later. But escalation was a two-way street. North Vietnam responded to the American buildup by sending additional forces to the South, leading General William C. Westmoreland, the U.S. commander in South Vietnam, to plead for more and more troops. By October 1967, 40 percent of America's combat-ready divisions, half of its tactical air power, and a third of its naval strength were involved in the Vietnam War.

The war developed into a costly stalemate. As American men and equipment poured into South Vietnam, it became clear that North Vietnam lacked the military power to drive the United States out of

The Vietnam Conflict, 1966

Southeast Asia. On the other hand, it eventually became equally apparent that the United States, in spite of its enormous military predominance, could neither prevent Communist infiltration into the South nor force the enemy to enter into what U.S. leaders considered genuine negotiations. The United States carefully avoided an invasion of North Vietnam, fearing large-scale Chinese intervention as a consequence; but the American air assault above the 17th parallel was unprecedented in its severity. Yet this air war failed either to break the enemy's morale or to stop the flow of supplies to the Vietcong from the north.

General Westmoreland's ground strategy was no more successful than the U.S. air bombardment. Periodically he sent "search-and-

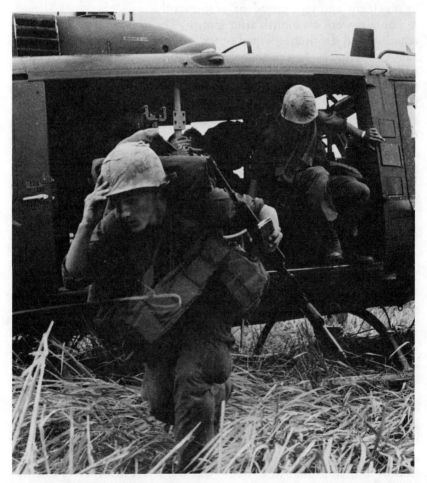

American Marines on a search and destroy mission, South Vietnam, October 1967 (*Defense Department photograph [Marine Corps] by SSgt. W. F. Schrider*)

destroy" missions through the countryside in an effort to demolish the Vietcong. The Americans also carried on a "pacification campaign" that was intended to win the loyalty of the South Vietnamese peasants. Yet neither the military operations nor the pacification programs accomplished their purpose. The NLF guerrillas would habitually fade away in the face of search-and-destroy sweeps, only to reappear and resume control as American and ARVN forces withdrew. Washington found some satisfaction in the greater stability of the Saigon government that resulted from Air Marshal Nguyen Cao Ky's accession to power as premier in 1965. In 1967 a new constitution for South Vietnam was approved, and in an effort to display its democracy, the Saigon government held national elections in which Nguyen Van Thieu and Ky were selected as president and vice president, respectively.

The war went on month after month. The employment of bombs, napalm, and defoliants wiped out whole villages and created thousands of refugees. In the absence of established battle lines, American officials measured progress not in the amount of territory won but by the number of enemy killed. By 1968 the "body count" in this numbers game had exceeded 400,000 of the enemy—surely an exaggerated figure. For U.S. policy makers, American involvement had a certain incremental character. Each step along the way seemed no more than a modification of past practice, and thus to obviate the need for a full-scale reassessment of basic policies.

Americans had never experienced anything quite like the Vietnam War. As one historian has written:

> It was a bizarre struggle, in which correspondents could drive or helicopter into the countryside, film or watch an engagement, come home, change clothes, open a cold beer, and report it all—uncensored—to the people at home. Americans, gathered around their television sets, saw unforgettable scenes from this "living room war"—bound and frail-looking Vietcong captives, equipment-burdened Americans setting fire with PX cigarette lighters to hootches, screaming wounded being lifted into choppers, piles of anonymous dead that were the stuff of body counts, sweating men pinned down in tall grass by fire from invisible machine guns, black-and-red billowing explosions of a tactical air strike on the enemy.[3]

Then, on January 31, 1968, came a surprise offensive in which the enemy launched powerful, simultaneous attacks against dozens of key cities and towns in South Vietnam. Days and even weeks of bitter fighting ensued before the military adversary was finally dislodged. The "Tet offensive"—which took place during the celebration of Tet, the lunar new year—was the most destructive enemy attack of the war. The offensive inflicted heavy losses on U.S. and

U.S. soldiers in the streets of Hue, February 1968 (*Defense Department photograph [Marine Corps]*)

ARVN forces, though at a heavy cost to the Vietcong and North Vietnamese. Although Westmoreland described the all-out offensive as the "last gasp" of the enemy, he also requested that an additional 206,000 American troops be sent to Vietnam. The Tet offensive was, as Townsend Hoopes remarks, "the eloquent counterpoint to the effusive optimism" that had long held sway in the White House and the Pentagon. After years of heavy fighting in Vietnam, victory for the Americans and their allies seemed as remote as ever.

ANTIWAR PROTEST

The war in Vietnam shattered the political consensus that Lyndon Johnson prized so highly and ultimately created profound suspicion and disillusionment among the American people. Indeed, the war became the most divisive issue in the modern history of the United States. It provoked a far-reaching protest movement, tested the basic assumptions underlying U.S. foreign policy, and encouraged a critical reappraisal of the nation's political institutions, culture, and values. The mounting violence in Vietnam was closely paralleled by the heightened turmoil and social disorder at home—by urban riots, black militancy, and campus unrest. The very legitimacy of the national government came into question, and there was, as Senator Eugene McCarthy said, a "growing sense of alienation from politics." The war, observes the journalist Godfrey Hodgson, "became the organizing principle around which all the doubts and disillusionments . . . all the deeper discontents hidden under the glossy surface of the confident years coalesced into one great rebellion."

Defenders of Johnson's policies generally believed that the United States must contain Communist expansion in every part of the world. Accepting the logic of the domino theory, they endorsed the administration's promise to contain Communist aggression everywhere by fighting in Southeast Asia. They stressed Johnson's often-expressed willingness to negotiate a general withdrawal of "foreign" forces from the south, which the Communists continued to reject. Some "hawks," as supporters of the war were dubbed, disapproved of the president's approach as too limited and urged that a quick and total American victory should be sought.

Liberal critics of the American war in Vietnam, who were called "doves," pictured Johnson as too quick to resort to force. They tended to view the Vietnam conflict as fundamentally a civil war, and they questioned the administration's assumption that the North Vietnamese, in view of their traditional distrust of the Chinese, were pawns of Peking. They scoffed at the domino theory; charged the administration with exaggerating the Communist threat in Vietnam; called attention to the repressive, reactionary character of the Saigon government; objected to the massive aerial bombing of Vietnam; deplored the heavy loss of American life and the enormous cost of the war; and denied that the United States was advancing the cause of democracy or of a stable peace. Questioning the official explanation of the war, Johnson's critics expressed doubts about the sincerity of his peace efforts and accused him of rejecting opportunities for negotiation and of stiffening his demands upon the enemy.

University students and professors were among the earliest critics of the American escalation, and antiwar protests called "teach-ins" were held on various campuses in the spring of 1965. Beginning at the University of Michigan in late March, the teach-ins quickly spread. During a two-day demonstration at Berkeley, California, 12,000 students heard such speakers as Dr. Benjamin Spock, the noted authority on baby care, Socialist leader Norman Thomas, and Dick Gregory, the well-known black comedian, condemn the government's policy in Vietnam. In mid-May a national teach-in was held in Washington, D.C., and during the following August representatives of several peace, civil rights, and church groups organized a National Coordinating Committee to End the War. This committee sponsored a series of mass demonstrations during the fall of 1965. The teach-ins and other campus demonstrations, while initially supported by only a small minority of students, were important because they helped make dissent respectable.

Antiwar sentiment also began to appear in some newspapers and journals of opinion, in radio and television commentaries, and in Congress. The first congressional doves were an intrepid little group of critics led by Wayne Morse, Ernest Gruening, and Gaylord Nelson, who risked their political futures by opposing the administration's policy. But congressional opponents soon began to multiply in both houses following the great escalation of 1965. The most important defector from the president's cause was Senator J. William Fulbright. In January 1966 Fulbright's Foreign Relations Committee commenced televised hearings on the Vietnam situation, and this inquiry was followed by another set of hearings that probed the war's impact on Chinese affairs.

Many civil rights leaders, including Martin Luther King, Jr., eventually joined the peace ranks. King argued that blacks were being called upon to make disproportionately large sacrifices in Vietnam and that the conflict there was undermining badly needed reforms at home. In April 1967 King led a march of over 100,000 people from New York's Central Park to United Nations headquarters in an antiwar demonstration. A few days earlier he had characterized the United States as "the greatest purveyor of violence in the world today." King's death in the early spring of 1968 completed the disillusionment that many blacks had begun to feel over the American war in Vietnam.

Much of the antiwar protest in the United States was based on moral considerations, including traditional pacifism and revulsion against the war's brutality. The corrupt and repressive regimes of Ky and Thieu seemed to make a mockery of American intervention in support of democracy and self-determination in Vietnam. Photography and television brought daily illustrations of the war's inhumanity into American homes: the death and maiming of U.S. soldiers, the killing of civilians by U.S. military operations, the wholesale destruction of Vietnamese villages, the use of napalm and defoliants to ruin forests and crops, and the savage spoliation of an ancient culture by modern warfare. In March 1968, for example, an American platoon led by Lieutenant William Calley, Jr., indiscriminately machine-gunned and bayoneted more than 100 old men, women, and children in the South Vietnamese hamlet of My Lai.[4] One soldier later described the behavior of a friend on the scene that day:

> He was covered with smoke, his face streaked with it, and it looked like there was blood on him, too. You couldn't tell, but there was blood everywhere. Anyway, he was kneeling there holding this grenade launcher, and he was launching grenades at the hootches. A couple of times he launched grenades at groups of people. The grenades would explode, you know, KAPLOW, and then you'd see pieces of bodies flying around.[5]

While all of the major American religious groups were represented in the antiwar movement, young Catholic priests and nuns were notably outspoken in their dissent. One of the most active of the Catholic peace advocates was Father Philip Berrigan, a Josephite priest and a veteran of World War II. In late October 1967, Berrigan and three other men broke into a Baltimore draft office, drenched the board records with blood, and waited to be arrested. They were tried and sent to prison. During the following spring, while out on bail, Berrigan was joined by his brother Daniel, a Jesuit priest, and seven other Catholic priests and lay people in the destruction of draft records at Catonsville, Maryland. The "Catonsville Nine," as they came to be called, were tried, convicted, and sentenced to prison. These shocking acts provided one measure of the tumultuous changes taking place in American society as a consequence of the far-off war in Southeast Asia.

One of the effective forms of antiwar protest was the draft-resistance movement. The government's increasing reliance on the Selective Service System imposed an enormous burden of uncertainty, coercion, and risk upon young American men, especially those from the lower and lower-middle classes who were unable to attend college and obtain educational deferments. Draft card "turn-ins" began to occur, and the public burning of such cards became a dramatic means of refusing to fight in Vietnam. Thousands of young men exiled themselves to Canada or Europe in order to avoid military duty. Mass protests were held outside induction centers. In October 1967 some sixty thousand demonstrators conducted a spectacular march on the Pentagon, hated symbol of the U.S. war machine. Resistance eventually began to appear within the military. The desertion rate from the armed forces mounted, and sizable communities of American deserters developed in Canada, Sweden, and other Western European countries. By the time the war finally ended for the United States in March 1973, it had produced 570,000 draft offenders and 563,000 less-than-honorable discharges from the service.

The continuing escalation of the war tended not only to polarize public opinion on the issue but also to radicalize a significant proportion of the antiwar protestors. According to such New Left groups as the Students for a Democratic Society (SDS), the war in Vietnam was an expression of fundamental ills in American society, including political hypocrisy, the oppression of nonwhite people, imperialism, and the capitalist drive for raw materials, markets, and investment opportunities. Vietnam, as one young rebel remarked, was for a goodly number of students "a symbol of the deeper ills of American society." The Free Speech Movement at the University of California, Berkeley, in 1964–65, an early manifestation of campus protest, played a key role in radicalizing college and university students, and it served as a bridge between the civil rights and the antiwar movements. SDS and other New Left groups grew rapidly during the next few years. The counterculture also contributed to the polarization of U.S. society and to the increasing disillusionment over the war. Many of the same people passed from cultural rebellion to political activism and back again.

THE LOST CRUSADE

Plagued by ghetto riots, campus unrest, rising inflation, and sharp divisions over the Vietnam War, Lyndon Johnson lost popularity rapidly after 1965. While 63 percent of the people approved of Johnson's handling of the presidency at the beginning of 1966, only 44 percent did so in October of that year. The president's problems were complicated by what many Americans began to perceive as his duplicity—his "credibility gap." Johnson, hoping and believing that every new increase in the American military effort in Vietnam would bring victory into sight, persisted in his course for a long time. He lashed out at his critics, contemptuously referring to "some Nervous Nellies and some who will become frustrated and bothered and break ranks under the strain."

In the fall of 1967 the White House launched an energetic campaign to win renewed support for the war, and the Pentagon reiterated its confidence in an early military victory for the United States. But the administration's problems were steadily exacerbated.

President Johnson visits Seoul, South Korea, October 1966 (*courtesy Lyndon B. Johnson Library*)

The president's neglect of the ambitious reform programs of the mid-sixties dissipated much of his support within the United States. The economy was in trouble by 1967, with the cost of the war going up drastically and the resulting inflation becoming more and more acute. Some of the administration's ablest Great Society architects, including Secretary John W. Gardner of HEW, resigned because of the president's absorption in Vietnam. Secretary of Defense McNamara, who had been instrumental in formulating the strategic and technological rationale for the American escalation, left office in November 1967, having become increasingly unhappy over U.S. policy in Vietnam and dubious as to its effectiveness.

Early in 1968 the administration was dealt a series of heavy blows. First came the seizure by North Korea of the U.S.S. *Pueblo*, an intelligence ship cruising off the North Korean coast. This incident created a new American crisis in the Far East and led to drawn-out negotiations that finally secured the release of the crew (but not the ship) almost a year later. The Tet offensive followed hard on the heels of the *Pueblo* affair, and for many Americans that psychological setback was the last straw. Then, on March 12, Senator Eugene J. McCarthy, an announced candidate for the Democratic presidential nomination in 1968, made a surprisingly strong showing in the New Hampshire primary, winning 42.4 percent of the votes to President Johnson's 49.5 percent. Private polls indicated that McCarthy would defeat Johnson in the forthcoming Wisconsin primary. Four days after the New Hampshire primary, Robert F. Kennedy entered the Democratic presidential race as an active candidate. It was obvious that the president's renomination would be bitterly challenged and that the party was confronted with a bruising intraparty fight in the coming months. The mood of the country had become intensely bitter, public opinion was polarized, much of the nation's youth had been politicized, Johnson's popularity had sunk to a new low, and the president himself had become a divisive force in a badly fragmented nation.

Nevertheless, the administration's problem was not that a majority of the people opposed the war in 1968. The problem was that many of the most influential groups had withdrawn their support. As Clark Clifford explained, "Major elements of the national constituency—the business community, the press, the churches, professional groups, college presidents, students, and most of the intellectual community have turned against this war." Johnson had tried to carry out a responsible policy in waging the war and to follow a moderate course without abandoning what he considered vital American interests. But he was also influenced by another consideration. He feared that the "loss" of Vietnam would set off "a mean and destructive debate," one that would "shatter my Presidency, kill my administration, and damage our democracy." Johnson's greatest failure was his inability to be honest with the American people—and with himself—about the war in Vietnam. Perhaps he could not have behaved differently. "The natural gifts which made him the most successful Senate majority leader in history rendered him unfit to lead the nation in times of crisis," the British journalist Louis Heren concludes. "National leadership could not be exercised from a back room, with cajolery, fixing, and the rest of his tricks, and Johnson knew no other way."

Johnson finally heeded those who contended that the United States must abandon the search for a decisive victory in Vietnam. A high-level review of U.S. policy, brilliantly conducted by Clark Clifford, the new secretary of defense, convinced Johnson that further escalation would not guarantee greater success. By 1968 the conflict in Vietnam had become the longest war in American history. It was also one of the bloodiest, having involved more casualties than the Korean War. It had cost almost $100 billion, had brought incalculable losses to the Vietnamese people, and had become the least popular war in the nation's experience. In a major address to a national television audience on March 31, the president announced that he was restricting the bombing of North Vietnam and inviting Hanoi to discuss a settlement of the war. At the end of his speech, Johnson made an even more startling announcement. "I have concluded," he declared, "that I should not permit the Presidency to become involved in the partisan divisions that are developing in this political year. . . . Accordingly, I shall not seek, and I will not accept, the nomination of my party for another term as your President."

ELECTION OF 1968: THE CENTER HOLDS

Ho Chi Minh responded with unexpected promptness to Johnson's peace overture of March 31, and after weeks of painfully slow progress, the two sides managed to begin formal negotiations in Paris on May 10. Although the war thereafter lost some of its terrible intensity, the military operations dragged on month after month, while the peace talks soon bogged down in the quicksand of basic differences separating the negotiators. Meantime, the bitter social division and conflict within the United States showed no signs of diminishing. With the nation on the verge of social disintegration, its citizens turned to politics and the national elections that would be held in November.

The focus of interest during the first half of the year was the struggle going on in the Democratic party. Three contestants for the party's presidential nomination dominated the center of the stage in the hectic spring of 1968: Eugene McCarthy, Robert Kennedy, and Hubert Humphrey. McCarthy, a handsome, soft-spoken congressional liberal with a sharp wit and an intellectual bent, brought thousands of students actively into his campaign. As the "peace candidate," he appealed to many elements of the New Left, as well as to various other groups calling for a "new politics" emphasizing a more moral and intellectual approach to national problems.

In announcing his candidacy on March 16, Senator Kennedy told a press conference in the Senate caucus room where his older brother had declared his candidacy eight years earlier: "I run to seek new policies, policies to end the bloodshed in Viet Nam and in our cities, policies to close the gap that now exists between black and white, between rich and poor, between young and old in this country and around the rest of the world." Kennedy plunged into a characteristically energetic campaign. Charismatic, ambitious, and hard-driving, "Bobby" aroused either passionate approval or intense dislike; he appealed strongly not only to those who venerated the memory of his martyred brother but also to blacks, the lower-middle classes, and urban ethnic groups, many of whom looked on him as a zealous champion.

Vice President Humphrey announced his candidacy on April 27.

Having the tacit support of President Johnson, Humphrey could count on the backing of party leaders throughout the country. While the two Democratic senators fought it out in the primaries, the vice president proceeded to gather a large number of convention delegates in the nonprimary states. A reluctant defender of the administration's foreign policies, Humphrey was also closely identified with the civil rights acts of the mid–1960s and with other reforms of the Great Society. His strength was centered in the old Democratic coalition.

Meanwhile, Kennedy's vigorous and well-financed campaign was picking up steam. In May the New York senator defeated his Minnesota colleague in Indiana and Nebraska, but then received a setback at the end of the month when McCarthy won the Oregon primary. The two candidates turned to California for a final showdown in the June 4 primary where 174 convention votes were at stake. The Kennedy forces were elated when they won a narrow victory in California with a 46 to 42 percent edge in primary votes. Then came another of those incredible and bizarre acts of violence, which seemed almost more than the American people could bear. Robert Kennedy was fatally shot early on June 5 as he was leaving a victory celebration being held in Los Angeles's Ambassador Hotel. The police seized a young Jordanian immigrant named Sirhan Bishara Sirhan, a confused Arab zealot who probably resented the New York senator's support of Israel. Once again the nation paused, stunned and saddened, as funeral rites were held for a second Kennedy.

The Democratic party never really recovered in 1968 from the shock of Robert Kennedy's assassination. McCarthy attracted much, though by no means all, of Kennedy's more than 300 delegates, and he consistently led the vice president in the public opinion polls. Yet McCarthy's quest for delegates was attended by many handicaps, including his own introspective and enigmatic personality, the image of his campaign as a "children's crusade," the fact that most professional politicians distrusted him, and the success Humphrey achieved among party regulars in lining up delegates.

The convention itself, which was held in Chicago's Amphitheater in late August, was a bitter affair. After an angry debate, a "peace" plank calling for "an unconditional end to all bombing in North Vietnam" was voted down in favor of an endorsement of the president's efforts to achieve "an honorable and lasting settlement." Humphrey was easily nominated on the first ballot. He decided upon Edmund S. Muskie, a respected senator from Maine, as his running mate. The Democrats adopted a platform in keeping with their traditional liberalism, and in spite of the steamroller tactics sometimes employed by the Humphrey managers, the delegates abrogated the long-established unit rule, refused to seat the segregationist Mississippi delegation, and initiated an unprecedented democratization of delegate selection to take effect in 1972.

In the meantime, a drama of street violence unfolded in downtown Chicago. Some 10,000 antiwar youths had descended upon the city, including such elements of the New Left as the Youth International Party (Yippies), to demonstrate against Johnson's Vietnam policy. In the tense atmosphere that resulted, a series of acrimonious and bloody clashes took place between the youthful demonstrators and the city police, who operated under the tight control of Mayor Richard J. Daley, a powerful old-time political boss and strong Humphrey partisan. Given orders to restrict the organized activities of the protestors and whipped into a frenzy by taunts, obscenities, and showers of stones, the police went berserk and turned brutally on their tormentors with clubs, tear gas, and mace. A nationwide television audience watched in fascinated horror as scenes of party warfare and of mayhem in the streets followed each other.

Republicans were spared such fierce intraparty struggles and bitter differences as they prepared for the campaign of 1968. The party's leading candidate at the outset was Governor George W. Romney of Michigan, a dynamic businessman who had built the failing American Motors Company into a going concern before entering politics. Although a series of forthright but undiplomatic statements on Vietnam and other issues had hurt Romney's prestige, he formally announced his candidacy in November 1967. New York's Governor Nelson A. Rockefeller, who had foresworn future presidential ambitions in 1965, once more became interested in heading the national ticket following his election to a third gubernatorial term in 1966. Still a third aspirant from the ranks of the Republican governors was Ronald Reagan of California, who had defeated Governor Edmund G. "Pat" Brown in 1966 by more than a million votes.

The fourth major candidate was Richard M. Nixon, who had undergone a remarkable rehabilitation following his humiliating defeat at the hands of Pat Brown in 1962. Nixon left California following his failure to win the governorship and joined a prominent New York law firm. But he remained active in Republican affairs, speaking frequently and attending party meetings all over the country. He won the gratitude of hundreds of Republican candidates and party leaders by his extensive efforts in the campaign of 1966.[6] Nixon did not formally announce his candidacy until February 1, 1968, but he had determined long before to undertake a strenuous campaign in most of the party primaries in order to demonstrate his popular support and to erase his loser's image. The New Hampshire primary brought forth the "new Nixon"—relaxed and confident, gracious and unhurried, seemingly without bitterness or rancor.

Nixon quickly established his dominance in the Republican contest for the presidential nomination. Romney abandoned his campaign two weeks before the New Hampshire election, while Rockefeller entered the race too late to mount an effective challenge to Nixon. Meanwhile, the former vice president won a number of significant preferential primaries and steadily added to his delegate strength in nonprimary states. Nixon was concerned over the threat that Reagan posed in the South and in other conservative quarters, but he dealt with that potential barrier by holding private talks with a number of important southern Republicans in Atlanta on May 31 and June 1. He assured such Republican leaders as Senator J. Strom Thurmond of South Carolina of his sympathy for their position on questions like school busing and law and order.

When the Republican National Convention was held in Miami Beach, Florida, in early August, Nixon was nominated on the first ballot. To the surprise of most observers, he chose Governor Spiro T. Agnew of Maryland for second place on the ticket. Agnew was acceptable to conservatives like Thurmond, and the selection of the governor, rather than a representative of the liberal wing of the party, was another indication of what became known as Nixon's "southern strategy." The GOP platform emphasized an "all-out" campaign against crime, reform of the welfare laws, an end to inflation, and a stronger national defense. On Vietnam, the platform promised to "de-Americanize" the war, to engage in "clear and purposeful negotiations," and not to accept "a camouflaged surrender."

The national campaign was well under way by early September. The Republicans, confident that they would be able to smash the divided Democrats, unleashed the most elaborate and expensive presidential campaign in United States history. Nixon campaigned at a deliberate, dignified pace, seeking to dramatize the nation's decline at home and abroad under two Democratic administrations. The Democratic campaign, by contrast, started very badly. The disastrous Chicago convention still hung like a pall over the party. Humphrey and Muskie also faced a serious challenge from the third-party candidacy of Governor George C. Wallace of Alabama.

Increasingly unhappy with the Democratic party's national policies, Wallace finally organized what he labeled the American Independent party; he selected General Curtis E. LeMay, former chief of the Strategic Air Command, to run with him on a national ticket.

Well-financed by wealthy conservatives and many grass-roots dona-
tions, the new party was able to get itself listed on the ballots of all
fifty states. Wallace developed surprising strength, not only among
white southerners but also among blue-collar groups and the lower-
middle class in other regions, where there was often rising tension
between white and black America. A short, pugnacious man with a
quick wit and a folksy speaking style, Wallace liked to assert that
there was not "a dime's worth of difference" between the two major
parties. He promised a policy of victory in Vietnam and tough measures at home against dope users, hippies, and Communists. The
feisty governor titillated his audiences by declaring, "If any dem-
onstrator ever lays down in front of my car, it'll be the last car he'll
ever lay down in front of." He condemned federal "meddling," the
"coddling" of criminals, and forced desegregation of the schools.

     Nixon, in a subtle way, appealed to many of the same fears and
prejudices that Wallace aroused. But the Republican nominee's basic strategy was to seize the middle by stressing peace and healing,
in contrast to the demagogic Wallace and the divided Democrats,
whose failings Nixon promised to repair. Offering himself as a harmonizer, Nixon promised to bring Americans together and to
achieve "peace with honor" in Vietnam. Agnew, on the other hand,
was given the task of capturing as much of the right as possible
from Wallace. Exploiting the "social issue," the Maryland governor
fulfilled this assignment with a series of blunt speeches, attacks on
left-wing dissident groups, and racial slurs.

     For the Republican party, Humphrey appeared to be an ideal op-
ponent: he could not dissociate himself from his party's record in
Washington without provoking a counterrevolution within the
Democratic organization itself. Nevertheless, from the rock-bottom
position his campaign had reached in September, Humphrey began
to move upward. During October the vice president's aggressive,
underdog campaigning began to have an effect. Senator Muskie's
low-keyed personality and calm and forceful style made him a distinct asset to the Democratic cause. Humphrey was searching for a
way in which to take an independent line without actually repu-
diating President Johnson. He made what seemed to be a significant
move in that direction in a televised speech in Salt Lake City on
September 30. "As President," he declared, "I would stop the bombing of the North as an acceptable risk for peace." On November 1,
just before the election, Johnson made a dramatic effort to get the
stalled peace talks moving and to help his party win. He proclaimed
a complete halt in the bombing of North Vietnam on that day.[7]

     By early November the Humphrey surge had brought the Demo-
crats almost abreast of the Republican ticket in the public opinion

polls. But Nixon won a narrow victory, receiving 31.7 million votes to 31.2 million for Humphrey and 9.9 million for Wallace. Nixon carried thirty-two states and 301 electoral votes, while Humphrey was successful in thirteen states with 191 electoral votes. Wallace carried five southern states and received 46 electoral votes. Both houses of Congress remained in Democratic hands.

The Republicans obviously took advantage of the disarray and division in the Democratic party. Vietnam was clearly both an immediate cause of Democratic enervation and a symbol of more widespread dissatisfaction with the party's programs and policies. Many youthful idealists sat out the campaign, a good many liberals failed to vote at all, support from various of the traditional Democratic components declined somewhat, and even the usually reliable black vote dropped 11 percent from 1964. The Democrats suffered defections on the part of the South, blue-collar workers, and the left. The Republicans conducted a well-organized and well-financed campaign. Nixon solidified the "law and order" tendencies of the GOP center, and his southern strategy enabled him to divide the South with Wallace, without subtracting much from his support in the Midwest and West. The public, it seemed, sought out the "decisive middle ground" in the politics of 1968, and as David

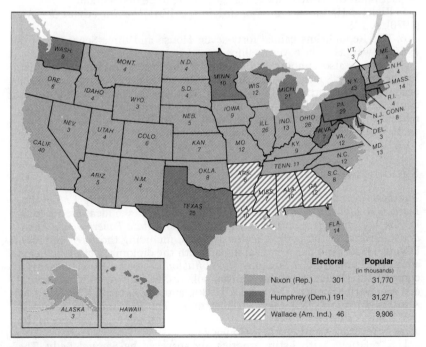

	Electoral	Popular (in thousands)
Nixon (Rep.)	301	31,770
Humphrey (Dem.)	191	31,271
Wallace (Am. Ind.)	46	9,906

The Election of 1968

S. Broder has remarked, the central paradox of the election is that, in a year of almost unprecedented violence, turmoil, and political oscillations, the electorate gave "a terribly conventional result."

The result was hardly conventional from the point of view of the Democratic party and President Johnson. In four years a Democratic presidential plurality of 16 million votes had evaporated. From 1965 on, the Johnsonian consensus had declined in a steady curve, its fragile structure shattered by war, inflation, racial strife, and widespread disillusionment with the leadership and personality of the president. Thus the election of 1968 was the final scene in the tragedy of Lyndon Johnson.

NOTES

1. France and the People's Republic of China refused to enter into the agreement.

2. NATO command headquarters were subsequently shifted to Brussels.

3. Bernard A. Weisberger, *Cold War, Cold Peace: The United States and Russia since 1945* (1984), p. 240.

4. The American public did not learn of this massacre until two years later, when Calley was court-martialed and convicted. By that time, similar incidents had come to light, and the full meaning of the Vietnam War's impact upon the United States was beginning to be understood.

5. Richard Hammer, *One Morning in the War: The Tragedy at Son My* (1970), p. 128.

6. The Republicans gained forty-seven House and three Senate seats in 1966, as well as eight governorships.

7. Johnson also announced that the United States and North Vietnam had agreed that South Vietnam and the NLF could begin taking part in the peace talks. Unfortunately, the South Vietnam government, hoping no doubt for greater backing from a Republican administration in Washington, refused to join in the discussions, thereby neutralizing the Democratic advantage resulting from Johnson's action on November 1.

SUGGESTIONS FOR FURTHER READING

The best introduction to Johnson's foreign policies is Philip L. Geyelin, *Lyndon B. Johnson and the World* (1966). Johnson's own ideas are set forth in *The Vantage Point* and relevant volumes of *Public Papers of the Presidents*. Several of the books previously cited, including those by Ambrose, Divine, Heath, and LaFeber, deal in part with the diplomacy of the Johnson administration. Walt W. Rostow, *The Diffusion of Power* (1972), presents a comprehensive defense of the Johnson policies. For the views of two advisers, see Warren Cohen, *Dean Rusk* (1980), and George Ball, *The Past Has Another Pattern* (1982). David Halberstam's *The Best and the Brightest* (1972) offers a critical assessment of several key presidential advisers in the areas of military strategy and diplomacy.

U.S. relations with Latin America are surveyed by Samuel Baily, *The United States and the Development of South America, 1945–1975* (1976).

More specialized works include Jerome Slater, *The OAS and United States Foreign Policy* (1967), on the operation of the inter-American organization; Jerome Levinson and Juan de Onis, *The Alliance That Lost Its Way* (1970), on the Alliance for Progress; and Cole Blasier, *The Hovering Giant* (1976), on North American reactions to South American revolutions. Piero Gleijeses, *The Dominican Crisis: The 1965 Constitutionalist Revolt and American Intervention*, trans. Lawrence Lipso (1978), is good on Dominican politics and the situation leading to U.S. intervention. Also see Theodore Draper, *The Dominican Revolt: A Case Study in American Policy* (1968); Jerome Slater, *Intervention and Negotiation* (1970); and Abraham Lowenthal, *The Dominican Intervention* (1972).

The literature on Vietnam is vast and still growing. The best overview of U.S. involvement is provided by George C. Herring, *America's Longest War: The United States and Vietnam, 1950–1975* (2nd ed., 1986). Frances Fitzgerald, *Fire in the Lake: The Vietnamese and the Americans in Vietnam* (1972), is particularly valuable because of the author's understanding of Vietnamese politics and culture. For other general studies, see George M. Kahin and John W. Lewis, *The United States in Vietnam* (rev. ed., 1969); Robert Shaplen, *Road from War: Vietnam, 1965–1970* (1970); Dennis Bloodworth, *An Eye for the Dragon: Southeast Asia Observed, 1954–1970* (1970); Guenter Lewy, *America in Vietnam* (1978); Leslie Gelb and Richard Betts, *The Irony of Vietnam: The System Worked* (1979); Paul Kattenburg, *The Vietnam Trauma in American Foreign Policy, 1945–1975* (1980); James Pinckeney Harrison, *The Endless War: Fifty Years of Struggle in Vietnam* (1982); and Stanley Karnow, *Vietnam: A History* (1983). Neil Sheehan and others, *The Pentagon Papers as Published by the New York Times* (1971), is a convenient edition of an important source. Robert L. Gallucci, *Neither Peace Nor Honor: The Politics of American Military Policy in Vietnam* (1975), is a critical analysis.

Among several books on the Gulf of Tonkin incident are John Galloway, *The Gulf of Tonkin Resolution* (1970), and Eugene C. Windchy, *Tonkin Gulf* (1971). Larry Berman's *Planning a Tragedy* (1982) deals with Johnson's decision to escalate the war. His peace efforts are described in David Kraslow and Stuart H. Loory, *The Secret Search for Peace in Vietnam* (1968), and Allan E. Goodman, *The Lost Peace* (1978). For three important studies of American policy in Vietnam, consult Robert W. Tucker, *Nation or Empire: The Debate over American Foreign Policy* (1968); Townsend Hoopes, *The Limits of Intervention: An Inside Account of How the Johnson Policy of Escalation in Vietnam Was Reversed* (rev. ed., 1973); and Chester L. Cooper, *The Lost Crusade: America in Vietnam* (1970).

A good beginning place for the military side of the war is Dave Richard Palmer's *Summons of the Trumpet* (1978), a concise and readable history. For two accounts by U.S. generals, see William C. Westmoreland, *A Soldier Reports* (1976), and Bruce Palmer, Jr., *The 25-Year War: America's Military Role in Vietnam* (1984). Bernard Fall's *The Two Viet-Nams: A Political and Military Analysis* (2nd rev. ed., 1967) is the work of a veteran French reporter. Various aspects of the war are examined in Frank Harvey, *Air War—Vietnam* (1967); Tony Fuller, *Charlie Company: What Vietnam Did to Us* (1983), on the ordinary soldier; Francis J. West, *The Village* (1972), on the impact of pacification; Philip Caputo, *A Rumor of War* (1977), a memoir by a Marine lieutenant that evokes the mood of the war; and Jonathan Schell, *The Village of Ben Suc* (1967), on the devastation of search-and-destroy operations. The brutality and horror of the war are revealed in Jonathan Schell, *The Military Half: An Account of Destruction in Quang Ngai and Quang Tin* (1968); Seymour M. Hersh, *My Lai 4: A Report on the Massacre and Its Aftermath* (1970); Richard Hammer, *One Morning in the War: The Tragedy at Son My* (1970); Don Oberdorfer, *Tet* (1971); Joseph Goldstein and others, *The My Lai Massacre and Its Cover-up: Beyond the Reach of Law?* (1976); Michael Herr, *Dispatches* (1977); and Robert Pisor, *The End of the Line: The Siege of Khe Sanh* (1982). For the media's coverage of the war, see Edward Jay Epstein, *News from Nowhere* (1974), and Peter Braestrup, *Big Story: How the American Press Reported and Interpreted the Crisis of Tet 1968 in Vietnam and Washington* (1983).

The domestic consequences of the Vietnam conflict are illuminated by Heath, *Decade of Disillusionment*, Hodgson, *America in Our Time*, and Matusow, *The Unraveling of America*, all cited earlier. Todd Gitlin's *The Whole World Is Watching* (1980) provides an overview of the antiwar movement. J. William Fulbright, *The Arrogance of Power* (1966), is an important critique by a leading Senate critic of American policy in Vietnam. Among critical works by revisionists on the left are Noam Chomsky, *American Power and the New Mandarins* (1969), and Richard J. Barnet, *Roots of War* (1972). Norman Mailer, *Armies of the Night: History as a Novel, the Novel as History* (1968), is concerned with the march on the Pentagon in October 1967. The best contemporary account of the new radicals is Christopher Lasch's *The Agony of the American Left* (1969). Other useful studies of the New Left include Kirkpatrick Sale, *SDS* (1973); Edward J. Bacciocco, *The New Left in America* (1974); and Irwin Unger, *The Movement: A History of the American New Left, 1959–1972* (1974). For the role of the draft, see Michael Useem, *Conscription, Protest, and Social Conflict: The Life and Death of a Draft Resistance Movement* (1973), and Lawrence M. Baskir and William A. Strauss, *Chance and Circumstance: The Draft, the War, and the Vietnam Generation* (1978).

Indispensable background for the election of 1968 is provided by Herbert Y. Schandler, *The Unmaking of a President: Lyndon Johnson and Vietnam* (1977). Kathleen J. Turner, *Lyndon Johnson's Dual War: Vietnam and the Press* (1985), is also useful. The campaign and election are described in two readable and informative books: Theodore H. White, *The Making of the President, 1968* (1969), and Lewis Chester, Godfrey Hodgson, and Bruce Page, *American Melodrama: The Presidential Campaign of 1968* (1969). More restricted accounts include Joe McGinniss, *The Selling of the President, 1968* (1969); Jules Witcover, *The Resurgence of Richard Nixon* (1970); Witcover, *85 Days: The Last Campaign of Robert Kennedy* (1969); Carl Solberg, *Hubert Humphrey: A Biography* (1984); Marshall Frady, *Wallace* (enlarged and updated, 1976); and Jody Carlson, *George C. Wallace and the Politics of Powerlessness, 1964–1976* (1981). Kevin Phillips, *The Emerging Republican Majority* (1969), offers an interesting analysis of the broader implications of Nixon's election in 1968. Richard M. Scammon and Ben J. Wattenberg, *The Real Majority* (1970), considers the "social issue" in contemporary American politics.

CHAPTER FOURTEEN

The Nixon
Years Begin

RICHARD M. NIXON'S VICTORY in the election of 1968 and his inauguration as the nation's thirty-seventh president on January 20, 1969, seemed to mark the beginning of a new era in American politics. Yet the meaning of the transfer of power in Washington was far from clear, and the prospects for the new Republican era were uncertain. Nixon had not won a clear-cut mandate; he was a minority president facing a Congress controlled by the opposition party. The center he represented was apparently holding, but there was widespread discontent over taxes, big government, bureaucracy, special privilege, and the war in Southeast Asia. Foreign affairs reflected a similar ambiguity involving such developments as the emergence of the People's Republic of China as a third great power center, the growing U.S. concern with Asia and the Third World, increasing opposition to foreign aid programs, and an upsurge of isolationist sentiment. Could the new chief executive "bring the American people together," as he had promised?

THE RETURN OF RICHARD NIXON

Richard Milhous Nixon, the second of five sons in a hard-working Quaker family, was born on January 9, 1913, in Yorba Linda, California, a farming community in the southern part of the state. He grew up in nearby Whittier, was graduated from Whittier College, and attended the Duke University Law School in North Carolina, where he worked hard and compiled a good academic record. After receiving his law degree, he returned to Whittier to practice and in 1940 married a local schoolteacher named Thelma "Pat" Ryan. During World War II the young lawyer served as a naval supply officer in the South Pacific. After the war Nixon was presented with an opportunity to enter politics, and he made the most of his chance, unseating Congressman Jerry Voorhis with a hard-hitting and somewhat demagogic campaign in 1946. In Washington Nixon soon made a name for himself as a member of the House Committee on Un-American Activities. He moved up to the Senate in 1950 by defeating Helen Gahagan Douglas in another campaign in which he charged his opponent with radicalism and used guilt-by-association tactics. Two years later Senator Nixon was selected by General Eisenhower as his running mate on the Republican national ticket.

Nixon continued to be a controversial figure during his eight years as vice president. His loss of the presidency by an eyelash in 1960 and his devastating defeat in the California gubernatorial election of 1962 set the stage for an incredible recovery and political vindication in 1968. Totally absorbed in political affairs, this intensely ambitious and rigorously disciplined man was determined to succeed. There was a streak of ruthlessness in his character, a tendency toward arrogance and self-righteousness, and the self-made man's emphasis upon the moral value of success. Basically a somewhat shy and introverted person, Nixon was also secretive, sensitive, and rather lonely—easily hurt, prone to lash back at his critics, always careful not to reveal too much of himself. "Absolutely central to his sense of identity," the historian Alonzo L. Hamby suggests, "was a self-image as a crusading underdog fighting against a host of privileged, unscrupulous enemies." The Californian was neither charismatic nor eloquent, but in the troubled sixties he appealed to more and more Americans because he gave expression to, indeed he embodied, traditional American virtues and aspirations which millions of people continued to cherish and desperately wanted to maintain.

During the interim between his election and his inauguration, Nixon and Johnson cooperated in effecting a smooth transition in the presidency. The president-elect announced the makeup of his Cabinet in December. William P. Rogers, an urbane New York lawyer who had served as attorney general under Eisenhower, was appointed secretary of state. David M. Kennedy, a Chicago banker, was named secretary of the treasury, while Representative Melvin R. Laird, a hawkish member of the House Armed Services Committee from Wisconsin, took over as secretary of defense. Nixon's New York law partner and campaign manager, John N. Mitchell, became attorney general. The other Cabinet members did not alter the conventional character of the collective portrait. Two Harvard University professors were brought into the new administration as presidential advisers: Henry A. Kissinger in the area of national security

Inauguration of the thirty-seventh president, January 20, 1969 (*U.S. Army photograph*)

and foreign affairs and Daniel Patrick Moynihan in the field of urban affairs and domestic policies.

President Nixon sought to foster a spirit of moderation, and he pledged himself to put an end to inflated rhetoric and exaggerated promises emanating from the White House. Stressing organization with clearly defined lines of authority and areas of responsibility, the new president established the most elaborate array of assistants and councils in the history of the executive branch. Nixon was far more interested in international questions than in domestic problems, in part no doubt because his party's dominant constituency and orientation gave him somewhat greater latitude in that sphere. He carefully set about defusing the explosive tensions surrounding U.S. involvement in Vietnam. At the same time, there were signs that the Nixon administration would not drastically change Johnson's policies in Southeast Asia. The selection of Henry Cabot Lodge as chief negotiator in Paris and the retention of Ellsworth Bunker as ambassador to Saigon were straws in the wind. Nixon's increasing reliance on the tough-minded Henry Kissinger, who emphasized stability as the goal of policy and military power as the most trusted instrument, provided another clue to the president's basic ideas on foreign policy.

Astronaut Edwin E. Aldrin, Jr., walks on the moon (*NASA photograph by Neil A. Armstrong*)

Nixon's restrained and prudent course elicited general approval in the United States. Tensions subsided and the public mood changed, not to one of optimism as much as to one of relief over the passing of the bitter divisions associated with the Johnson administration. People seemed prepared to give the new administration a chance to end the war, unify the country, and formulate policies for the solution of troublesome social problems. In July 1969, while this mood persisted, *Apollo 11* landed on the moon after a long and dramatic flight. Americans everywhere felt a thrill of exultation as Commander Neil Armstrong and Colonel Edwin E. Aldrin made a perfect landing on the Sea of Tranquility and became the first earth men to walk on the moon.

THE PERSISTENCE OF VIETNAM

The Nixon administration's most pressing task was to end the Vietnam War. Not only had he committed himself to the solution of the Vietnamese problem, but failure to end it, or at the very least to remove most American combat forces before 1972, might well drive him from the presidency. The U.S. position was that all outside forces should be withdrawn from South Vietnam and that the voters of that country should decide their future in internationally supervised elections. The North Vietnamese and the National Liberation Front insisted upon a complete withdrawal of American forces and the installation in Saigon of a coalition government that would include the NLF. The Thieu regime was fiercely resolved to continue as the dominant element in any postwar government, and the United States, while trying from time to time to persuade South Vietnam to moderate its position, was unwilling to sacrifice the existing government, which Washington associated with the right of self-determination for the South Vietnamese. Its survival thus became, to the United States, an essential requirement for a peace settlement.

A variety of proposals and counterproposals were presented as the peace talks dragged on. The talks frequently stalled and sometimes broke down completely, only to be resumed after a few weeks. The United States sought to convince the other side of its error in two ways. One was the process of "Vietnamization"—building up the ARVN forces and preparing them to take over an increasingly large part of the fighting. The other was the massive use of U.S. air power, tactical and strategic, in direct support of ground operations and in attacks upon North Vietnamese supply routes, bases, and production centers. In March 1969 American planes began "Operation Menu," a long series of secret raids on Communist bases in Cambodia. In spite of their talk of "peace with honor," Nixon and Kissinger were determined to secure an independent, non-Communist South Vietnam.

The administration hoped to disarm its critics and to ease the antiwar pressures at home by a systematic reduction of U.S. combat troops in South Vietnam. The president announced in June 1969 that 25,000 men were being sent home without replacements, and

American troops move up a canal near Dong Tam, August 1969 (*U.S. Army photograph by SP4 James Boak*)

in December 1969 he ordered the withdrawal of an additional 50,000 soldiers. The process continued until the number of American troops had declined from a high of 543,000 in the spring of 1969 to approximately 255,000 by May 1971. Meanwhile, monthly draft quotas were reduced, and the administration eventually reorganized the Selective Service System and replaced its unpopular director.[1] Nixon also outlined what became known as the Nixon Doctrine. The United States, he declared, would remain a Pacific power safeguarding Asia's peace, but the principal responsibility for Asian security and development must rest with the Asians themselves. America would provide its Asian allies with economic assistance, nuclear reassurance, and moral support.

Despite the general disposition in the United States to give the administration time in which to work out a settlement in Vietnam and the widespread approval of troop reductions and such pronouncements as the Nixon Doctrine, antiwar feeling remained strong. In the autumn of 1969 a number of antiwar demonstrations erupted throughout the country. Hundreds of rallies and mass observances were held on October 15, and a second "moratorium" staged a month later drew still larger crowds. Some 250,000 persons

U.S. Military Forces in South
Vietnam, 1965–1973

Year	Number
1965	184,300
1966	385,300
1967	485,600
1968	536,100
1969	475,200
1970	334,600
1971	157,800
1973*	23,500

*As of January 27, 1973, when the
cease-fire agreement was signed.
Sources: U.S. Department of Defense,
Office of the Secretary, *Selected Manpower Statistics*, annual and unpub-
lished data; *New York Times*, Feb. 28,
1973.

participated in a three-day demonstration in the national capital,
with a "March against Death" proceeding from Arlington National
Cemetery to Capitol Hill.

President Nixon denounced the demonstrators in a television address on November 3, 1969, stated that he planned to remove all
American ground forces from Vietnam (though he failed to be specific about such plans), and pleaded for support from "the great silent majority of my fellow Americans." Vice President Agnew also
spoke out caustically against the peace demonstrators, condemning
them on one occasion as "an effete corps of impudent snobs who
characterize themselves as intellectuals." The public response to
the administration's actions was encouraging, and the president's
popularity rose sharply. American troops were coming home, the
draft was less threatening, and the financial costs of the war were
beginning to go down.

Then came the shock of Cambodia. In late April 1970, in a step
long urged by U.S. military leaders, the president announced an
American-South Vietnam invasion of Communist staging areas in
Cambodia. This Cambodian "incursion" was also justified as necessary to prevent the Communists from taking over all of Cambodia. Addressing the American people on the evening of April 30,
Nixon called the military move "indispensable" for the continuing
success of his withdrawal program. "If when the chips are down,"
he declared, "the United States acts like a pitiful helpless giant, the
forces of totalitarianism and anarchy will threaten free nations and
free institutions throughout the world." The advancing troops, sup-

ported by powerful U.S. air forays, failed to uncover the elusive command headquarters of the enemy, but they located extensive Vietcong supply centers and huge stores of materials.

The Cambodian invasion triggered an outbreak of violence and turmoil in the United States. Just when Nixon was supposedly winding down the war, he had extended it to another country in Southeast Asia. The contradictions between Nixon's earlier claims for Vietnamization and his alarmist statements about powerful enemy forces threatening South Vietnam were especially disturbing to many Americans. Reaction to the president's announcement was notably violent on college and university campuses. In one of the demonstrations, at Kent State University in Ohio, a confrontation between students and national guardsmen ended on May 4 with four students fatally shot and eleven others wounded.[2] Student protests soon forced more than 400 colleges and universities to close, and many of these institutions did not reopen until summer or fall.

The severe criticism of the Cambodian invasion and the upheaval it produced on college campuses shook the president. He agreed to talk to six Kent State students who had traveled to Washington, conferred with the presidents of eight universities, and asked Chancellor Alexander Heard of Vanderbilt University to serve as a special liaison between the universities and the White House. Still, Nixon's interest in placating his critics did not last long, partly perhaps because a good many Americans seemed to approve of his Cambodian policy and to oppose the antiwar protests. On May 8, 1970, for example, a group of protesting students in New York City was brutally attacked by helmeted construction workers who bludgeoned them with wrenches and clubs. Shouting "all the way, U.S.A.," the hard hats then marched on City Hall and raised the American flag. Similar incidents as well as rallies in support of the administration occurred during the next few weeks. And Peter Brennan, head of the construction workers' union, visited the White House, presented the president with a hard hat, and pinned an American flag on his lapel.

Nixon had not consulted or even informed Congress prior to announcing his move into Cambodia, and the congressional response to the invasion was sharp and critical. A bipartisan amendment to a military bill, sponsored by Senators Frank Church of Idaho and John Sherman Cooper of Kentucky, sought to require the president to withdraw all American troops from Cambodia by June 30, 1970, and to forbid any new strikes into that country. Although the measure was adopted by the Senate, it was defeated in the House of Representatives. Meanwhile, many of the lawmakers were incensed when they learned for the first time of the administration's secret air attacks on Cambodia. Late in 1970 Congress repealed the Tonkin Gulf resolution and voted to deny funds for any further U.S. ground operations in Cambodia. Meanwhile, Senators Mark Hatfield of Oregon and George S. McGovern of South Dakota presented an unsuccessful amendment that would have required the withdrawal of all U.S. troops from Vietnam by the end of 1971.

The progress of Vietnamization was tested in February 1971, when South Vietnamese troops invaded Laos, which had long been subjected to heavy air bombardment by U.S. bombers. Assuming that a major offensive by the South Vietnamese army was now feasible, American leaders approved a large-scale ARVN offensive, with strong U.S. air support, in an attempt to cut the Ho Chi Minh Trail in eastern Laos, the vital supply route for men and materials flowing south from North Vietnam. The offensive went badly for the invaders. Communist forces outflanked the South Vietnam units, destroying some of them and forcing others into headlong retreat. In the meantime, the Vietcong challenged the pacification efforts in South Vietnam, shelling cities and raiding villages that were assumed to be invulnerable to attack.

The invasion of Laos provoked new antiwar protests, and in April 1971 demonstrators were back in Washington. The reaction against the Laotian venture was heightened when Americans began to learn that approximately 25,000 South Vietnamese civilians had been killed and 100,000 wounded during the past two years of fighting. Public awareness of the massacres of Vietnam civilians by U.S. servicemen was intensified by the military trial of Lieutenant William Calley, which began at Fort Benning, Georgia, in November 1970. On March 29, 1971, a court composed of six Army officers found Calley guilty, personally, of the premeditated murder of at least twenty-two unarmed civilians. He was sentenced to life imprisonment.[3]

Nixon countered the antiwar protests and criticisms of his policies in Vietnam with a combination of rebuffs to the peace advocates and a continuation of the troop withdrawals. Yet as the war ground on, there was a growing loss of credibility in administration policies and pronouncements concerning Vietnam. These doubts were increased by the publication, in June 1971, of excerpts from the so-called Pentagon Papers. Daniel Ellsberg, a military analyst who had worked for the Defense Department, had photocopied a massive study of U.S. involvement in Vietnam that had been commissioned by the Pentagon. Ellsberg made these documents available to the press. The Pentagon Papers not only suggested that the Kennedy and Johnson administrations had made a fairly steady effort to widen the American role in the Vietnam War, but they also revealed the government's lack of candor in explaining certain details of this policy to the public. Americans had grown weary of the war, and even the military forces still in Vietnam showed the strain. After 1969 combat units sometimes refused to fight, drugs became a serious problem, and numerous "fragging" incidents occurred as a result of attempts by enlisted men to kill or injure their own officers, usually with fragmentation grenades.

At the end of March 1972, the Communists launched their heaviest offensive since the Tet campaign four years earlier. With most of the American ground forces gone and the burden of defense on the South Vietnamese troops, the enemy soon overran Quangtri Province in the north, made substantial advances in the central and southern sections, and inflicted heavy losses on the ARVN units before the situation was stabilized and some of the lost ground was recovered. With his Vietnamization program in jeopardy, Nixon again resorted to drastic action. Contending that the Communist offensive violated the implicit understanding under which President Johnson had halted the bombing of North Vietnam in 1968, Nixon ordered renewed attacks north of the DMZ, first with sporadic retaliatory raids and then with sustained air bombardments. In a television address on May 8, the president announced an even bolder move—the mining of Haiphong and other North Vietnamese ports, along with a naval blockade of North Vietnam.

Although Richard Nixon had promised to end the war, it was still going on. Fifteen thousand Americans had lost their lives in Vietnam during the first three years of the Nixon administration. In 1971 the United States dropped 800,000 tons of bombs—an amount equal to that of 1967—in Indochina. The war had assumed a surrealistic quality. As one staff officer remarked, "Often it reminded me of the caucus race in 'Alice in Wonderland.' Everyone runs in circles, no one really gets anywhere, and when the race is over, everybody gets a medal."[4]

DOMESTIC PROBLEMS

In domestic affairs the thirty-seventh president was also confronted with pressing problems. While Nixon failed to launch any bold new programs during the first part of his presidency, he made a special effort to identify his administration with the "silent majority" and "middle America," as against militants, radicals, and youthful dissenters. After a brief period of amicability, Nixon's relations with Congress worsened as partisan tensions increased and recurrent deadlocks occurred. The chief executive frequently succeeded in dominating the Democratic-controlled Congress by masterful timing, skillful maneuvering, and effective presentation of his case through television and other media. One of Nixon's first triumphs was the approval of the antiballistic missile program originally sponsored by the Johnson administration. Despite strong opposition, Congress authorized an ABM system by a narrow margin in the summer of 1969.

One area in which Nixon hoped to effect substantial change was the composition of the Supreme Court. He was eager to add "strict constructionists" to the tribunal and to overcome the liberal majority that had dominated the Warren Court. The president thought the Court had swung too far in the liberal direction under Chief Justice Warren, and thus he threw his weight on the side of the wide-ranging criticism of Supreme Court decisions in such fields as civil rights, school prayers, and obscenity cases. The Court's broadened interpretation of the defendant's rights in criminal cases, as spelled out in *Gideon* v. *Wainwright* (1963), *Escobedo* v. *Illinois* (1964), and *Miranda* v. *Arizona* (1966), was especially upsetting to many people intent upon maintaining "law and order." In the *Miranda* case the Court held, in a 5 to 4 decision, that, before the police question a person suspected of crime, they must inform him of his constitutional right to remain silent and to have counsel, as well as warn him that any statement he makes may be used against him.

President Nixon's first appointment to the Supreme Court was Warren E. Burger, who was named chief justice when Earl Warren retired in June 1969. Burger, a respected conservative who had served as a court of appeals judge, was readily confirmed by the Senate. This was not the case with Clement F. Haynsworth, Jr., whom Nixon appointed to replace Abe Fortas in 1969.[5] Haynsworth, a federal circuit court judge from South Carolina, was strongly opposed by several civil rights groups and labor organizations because of his conservative opinions. It was also charged that he had owned stock in a company involved in litigation before his court. A furious debate broke out over the nomination, and in November 1969 the Senate voted 55 to 45 against his confirmation. Much annoyed by this rebuff, Nixon then submitted the name of G. Harrold Carswell, a Floridian who had recently been appointed to the Fifth Circuit Court of Appeals. Carswell was not only open to the charge of having been a racist earlier in his career, but his record on the bench was decidedly mediocre and he had been frequently overruled on appeal. The Senate rejected Carswell by a vote of 51 to 45. Nixon was furious, but in his next effort he was finally successful. The Senate, in May 1970, unanimously approved the nomination of Harry A. Blackmun, a federal judge from Minnesota known for his judicial scholarship.

The conservatism of the Burger Court was further strengthened in the fall of 1971 when Justice Hugo L. Black died and Justice John Marshall Harlan resigned. Nixon replaced them with two staunch conservatives: Lewis F. Powell, a well-known Virginia lawyer, and Assistant Attorney General William H. Rehnquist of Arizona. Thus within three years Nixon had been able to transform the high court, and before the end of his first term the new conservative majority had begun to chip away at some of the Warren Court's rulings, particularly in criminal law decisions. Nevertheless, the Court did not entirely reverse the humane precedents laid down under Chief Justice Warren. In *Furman v. Georgia* (1972), the Court advanced to a new liberal position by holding capital punishment unconstitutional as "cruel and unusual," except when the law made it mandatory.

Nixon also tried in other ways to identify himself as a champion of law and order. His administration made greater use of wiretapping and other electronic surveillance of organized crime, obtained increased support for the Law Enforcement Assistance Administration, and in a bid for symbolic leadership sponsored a special District of Columbia Criminal Justice bill, which Congress finally passed in 1970. Other new statutes, including the organized crime law of 1970, limited immunities under the Fifth Amendment, permitted a judge to lengthen the sentence of a dangerous criminal, and provided the death penalty for bombings involving loss of life.

In promising to "get tough on crime" and in condemning drugs and pornography, the Nixon administration sought to take advantage of the backlash against rising crime rates, antiwar protests, campus disorders, black militancy, and moral permissiveness. Middle Americans, the president and his advisers believed, were moving to defend the flag, traditional authority, and older values. Among the administration's concerns were the so-called white ethnics, whose new self-consciousness and distrust of the social ferment of the 1960s made them sensitive to the "social" issue. A broader group of "middle" Americans—some 55 percent of the population—included families with annual earnings between $5,000 and $15,000. Many of these people, feeling neglected, resented the civil rights and welfare programs sponsored by liberals and reformers; they often felt victimized for the advantage of others who had not struggled as they had to make good and to abide by the rules. There was also a pervasive sense of crisis in cultural values that manifested itself in apprehension over such traditions as the sanctity of marriage and the morality of work. The popular television comedy *All in the Family*, first produced in 1970, gave expression to many of the cultural stereotypes associated with the "middle" American.

The Nixon administration's approach to civil rights and the condition of blacks was clearly meant to implement his southern strategy. The Department of Justice, in sharp contrast to its position under Kennedy and Johnson, opposed the extension of the Voting Rights Act of 1965, proposing unsuccessfully to replace it with a uniform national law. The administration lobbied in Congress to defeat the fair-housing enforcement program. It also attempted to slow the pace of school desegregation in the South. In 1969 HEW relaxed its policy against five school districts in South Carolina and flip-flopped in handling litigation involving thirty-three Mississippi school districts (after having earlier approved desegregation plans for the fall term).[6]

President Nixon defended his administration's civil rights policies in a comprehensive statement issued in March 1970. He announced that he would ask Congress for $1.5 billion to improve education in racially impacted areas and to help school districts meet problems caused by court-directed desegregation. But Nixon emphasized the distinction between *de jure* segregation based on discriminatory laws and *de facto* segregation based on residential patterns, and he promised that "transportation beyond normal geographical school zones for the purpose of achieving a racial balance will not be required." In January of the following year the president announced his firm opposition to federal efforts to "force integration of the suburbs," calling such measures "counterproductive, and not in the interest of race relations."

One of the administration's boldest domestic proposals was its plan for the revision of the nation's welfare programs. Strongly influenced by Daniel Patrick Moynihan, the president sent Congress a message in August 1969 recommending "the transformation of welfare into 'workfare,' a new work-rewarding system." Instead of the existing federal welfare grants, the government under the Nixon-Moynihan Family Assistance Plan (FAP) would make a cash payment to guarantee a prescribed minimum income level—$1,600 a year for a family of four in which there was no wage earner. Such a family could also receive food stamps valued at $820 a year. Nixon's welfare reform proposal created quite a stir, and during the controversy that followed the measure's introduction, it was attacked by both the right and the left. The House passed a bill containing the basic features of the Nixon program in 1970, but the Senate Finance Committee failed to report it. A new and somewhat more ambitious version of the measure was approved by the House in June 1971, but the Senate remained divided over the issue. Thus the FAP was not enacted during Nixon's first term, and the president himself, sensing the deep middle-class resentment against welfare recipients, eventually abandoned the scheme.

Nixon looked to the midterm elections of 1970 for popular endorsement and legislative support of his program. The president believed that a major party realignment was in progress, and he accepted journalist Kevin P. Phillips's thesis that a new conservative majority of "middle" Americans might be emerging—a majority that came from the suburbs, the U.S. heartland, and "the Sunbelt" stretching from Florida through the Southwest to southern California. Nixon's southern strategy was designed to win support from many Wallace sympathizers, while his attempts to exploit the more conservative aspects of cultural politics were aimed at middle-class Americans throughout the country. Nixon and Agnew joined other Republican leaders in conducting a strenuous campaign in 1970. Agnew had emerged as an outspoken and controversial champion of the administration, and in numerous speaking engagements he lashed out at dissident college students, critics of American involvement in Vietnam, radicals, hippies, and network television commentators, whom he described as "a tiny and closed fraternity of privileged men" biased toward the eastern establishment. Nixon took a more elevated road, but he too assumed the familiar role of partisan campaigner. The outcome was extremely disappointing to the administration: while the Democrats lost two seats in the Senate, they gained nine in the House.

When the new Congress convened in January 1971, Nixon urged its members to prepare the way for "a New American Revolution." The president's extravagant rhetoric on this occasion was somewhat reminiscent of the "new federalism" he had first enunciated to Congress in the summer of 1969. The most substantial result of the new federalism was "revenue sharing," which Nixon repeatedly advocated and formally presented in his State of the Union message in January 1971. In order to halt the steady enlargement of the central government and return more responsibilities to the local communities, the plan would eliminate a number of specific federal programs and substitute general-purpose grants to the states and cities to administer as they thought best. Revenue sharing soon became mired in controversy, but it was eventually approved, in October 1972, as the State and Local Fiscal Assistance Act. The act provided for the sharing of $30.2 billion in federal revenue over a five-year period, with $5.2 billion to be allocated in 1972 on the basis of two-thirds to local governments and one-third to the states.

Local officials soon began to complain that the new system, which coincided with drastic reductions or freezes in various federal programs, was likely to worsen rather than relieve their revenue plight.

The administration's timid approach to conservation and environmental issues reflected its probusiness orientation and the fact that the principal polluters were large corporations in such industries as automobiles, aviation, and petroleum. Most environmentalists opposed Nixon's efforts to win continued support for the development of a supersonic transport (SST), and in this case the president suffered a setback when the Senate, under the leadership of William Proxmire of Wisconsin, voted against further appropriations for the SST in December 1970. Nixon had appointed Walter J. Hickel of Alaska as secretary of the interior, and surprisingly Hickel became something of an environmentalist. He halted drillings in the Santa Barbara Channel after a severe oil spill, persuaded the Justice Department to prosecute the Chevron Oil Company for polluting the Gulf of Mexico, took firm action to protect the Florida Everglades from a proposed jet airport, and held up construction of the trans-Alaskan oil pipeline that threatened the native tundra, before being fired in November 1970. Pushing ahead, the Democratic Congress was largely responsible for the Occupational Safety and Health Act of 1970, the Clean Air Act of 1970, and new statutes to control water pollution in 1970 and 1972.

Perhaps the most pressing domestic problem facing Nixon was the mounting inflation, which had intensified during the last years of the Johnson administration. The cost of living rose more than 7 percent in 1969, and it continued to go up at a high rate. Nixon realized the importance of halting inflation, but he was limited in dealing with the problem by his conservative economic policy. The administration's anti-inflation program at first revolved around tighter credit and a cut in government spending. The Federal Reserve Board raised interest rates so sharply during the first six months of 1969, however, that many businessmen became alarmed, and the tight money policy was relaxed in the fall. Nixon's attempt to reduce federal expenditures proved equally unsuccessful; the budget was increased every year, and there were large annual deficits ($23 billion in fiscal 1971, for example). The president's program for the ABM, space exploration, and continued involvement in Vietnam wiped out any economies he managed to make in health, education, and housing.

In May 1970 the Dow-Jones index of stock prices dropped from almost 1,000 to below 700. During the following month the Penn Central Railroad went bankrupt. Corporate profits, industrial production, automobile sales, and new construction slipped. Someone coined the word "Nixonomics" to describe the curious combination of lagging output and soaring prices. With the economy still sluggish and the price index continuing to rise, Nixon finally adopted a new economic policy. In a television address on August 15, 1971, he announced that, under authority previously given him by Congress (which he had vowed never to use!), he was freezing all wages, prices, and rents for ninety days. In an effort to improve the position of the dollar abroad, he cut its tie with gold and permitted it to "float" freely in foreign exchange. He imposed a 10 percent surtax on a wide list of imported goods and requested Congress to change the tax laws as a stimulus to industry. He established a Cost of Living Council headed by Secretary of the Treasury John B. Connally to administer the new program. In December 1971, at an international monetary conference held in Washington, the United States agreed to reduce the exchange value of the dollar by about 12 percent and to drop the 10 percent import surtax in return for increases in the exchange rate of foreign currencies and other trade concessions. Phase Two of the president's plan was initiated in November 1971, with the introduction of a system of mandatory guidelines for subsequent wage and price increases under the supervision of a federal agency.

Nixon's new economic policy was only partially successful. The rate of inflation declined to 3.2 percent during the first year of the policy's operation, wages were generally held within the 5.5 percent increase, and production rose substantially. But food prices went up at a 4.2 percent rate, unemployment did not drop below 5.5 percent, and American trade deficits continued to be large. At the same time, the Nixon administration could point to several achievements on the domestic front. It could claim some credit for increases in social security benefits, for large federal outlays in support of medical training, for the continuation of federally subsidized housing programs, for the Tax Reform Act of 1969, for large educational appropriations in 1972, and for a law to regulate campaign spending in federal elections.

OLD APPROACHES AND NEW INITIATIVES ABROAD

Although Nixon seemed to appreciate the need to change the nation's overextended and overbearing international posture, his basic instincts were those of the cold warrior. As the *New York Times* observed after two years of the Nixon administration, "President Nixon has labored to protect and to perfect the foreign-affairs concepts of the last two decades against the widespread disenchantment with Vietnam and against the allure of insular doctrines."

Nixon was consistently able to dominate Congress in dealing with international affairs.[7] He also moved quickly to centralize the most critical aspects of foreign policy formulation and implementation within the White House. With the passage of time, it became evident that Nixon had brought to the Oval Office a new and more realistic outlook on world affairs. Despite his cold war instincts, he seemed to realize that the cold war had undergone great change, that the old polarity had broken down, and that power had become multidimensional. Somewhat surprisingly, he was more flexible than his predecessors in his perception of global interests and less concerned with ideology as the chief criterion by which to identify threats. There were indications that he recognized the limits of American power and that he was willing to accept "sufficiency" rather than the traditional U.S. insistence on nuclear "superiority." Nixon and Kissinger wanted to maintain an overall balance of power and to achieve a "structure of peace" in the world. As Nixon declared in an interview early in 1972, "I think it will be a safer world and a better world if we have a stronger, healthy United States, Europe, Soviet Union, China, Japan, each balancing the other, not playing one against the other, an even balance."

The tentative steps Kennedy and Johnson had taken toward a détente with the Soviet Union were endangered during the late 1960s by the Vietnam War and the tense situation in the Middle East. Nixon hoped to ease tensions between the two superpowers through a mutual agreement to limit strategic nuclear weapons. He expressed great satisfaction over the Senate's approval of the Nuclear Nonproliferation Treaty in March 1969, and during the following November he unilaterally renounced American use of biological warfare and chemical weapons except for defense. The Strategic Arms Limitation Talks (SALT) were resumed in Helsinki, Finland, in November 1969. The two cold war antagonists agreed in 1971 to modernize and strengthen their hot-line communications link. More important was the breakthrough that came in August 1971, when the Russians offered new guarantees to keep the access routes open into West Berlin from West Germany, in exchange for an Allied promise to reduce the city's political significance for the West and allow a Russian consulate in West Berlin. While moving to ease the conflict over Berlin, Brezhnev suggested the possibility of a general settlement in Central Europe under which NATO and the Warsaw Pact allies would reduce their forces. Nixon responded positively to this overture.

In the Middle East the Russians had begun to supply the Arabs with new military resources soon after the swift Israeli triumph in the war of 1967. Though committed to the defense of Israel, the

Nixon administration delayed sending additional arms to the Israelis, while negotiating with the Soviet Union and Egypt on a plan
calling for Israeli withdrawal from the occupied territories in return
for recognition of Israel's right to exist and to use the Suez Canal
and other waterways. The United States did help to obtain an
Israeli-Egyptian cease-fire along the Suez, but Secretary Rogers's efforts to secure a more permanent settlement were unsuccessful.
Soviet intrigue in Egyptian affairs eventually caused President Anwar Sadat, in a surprise move in July 1972, to expel all Russian
technicians and military advisers from Egypt, a step that somewhat
reduced American anxieties about the Middle East. The United
States had earlier used its influence to prevent a Middle East explosion when Palestinian commandos attacked the forces of Jordan's
moderate King Hussein. Despite the intervention of Syria on the
side of the rebels, Hussein's air force soon subdued the attackers.

Farther to the east, the United States suffered a diplomatic setback when it became involved in a new crisis between India and
Pakistan. When the Pakistan government attempted to suppress a
nationalistic rebellion in East Bengal, India intervened in behalf of
the Bengali rebels. Washington supported Pakistan, hoping that India would be deterred from going to war against Pakistan, while the
Soviet Union made clear its sympathy for India and the rebels.
When the Bengali nationalists won their independence and became
the new state of Bangladesh, the Russians emerged with enhanced
prestige in South Asia.

In general the United States under Nixon demonstrated little tolerance toward political change in the developing nations. The limits
of its tolerance were determined by the expected consequences of
such change. The administration's Latin America policy illustrates
Nixon's approach to the Third World. Governor Nelson Rockefeller,
who made a special investigation for the president in 1969, emphasized serious problems and deficiencies in the Latin American
economies and called for greater U.S. assistance in strengthening
them. President Nixon, like his predecessors, counted on extensive
private U.S. investments in developing regions, but Washington
could not control the investment policies of the large multinational
corporations, which became relatively less interested in such uncertain areas. Terrorism and guerrilla activities increased in Venezuela,
Colombia, Guatemala, and Bolivia, and in 1970 Salvador Allende,
the head of the Socialist party in Chile, won the presidency of that
country as a coalition candidate of the left-wing parties. The United
States used its influence against his election. Allende was the first
avowed Marxist to come to power in the Western Hemisphere
through free elections. He soon began to nationalize the large U.S.

investments in Chile (most notably the copper industry), opened diplomatic relations with Cuba, and signed a trade agreement with the Soviet Union. Allende's government was overthrown in 1973, a result the United States had covertly encouraged for the past two years.

In 1971 Nixon achieved a startling new departure in the established policy toward the People's Republic of China. The turnabout in Chinese-American relations came as the People's Republic was emerging from a prolonged period of political and social upheaval. In April 1971 the Chinese leaders unexpectedly invited the American champion table tennis team, then playing in Japan, to visit mainland China. Significantly, this friendly gesture was made just at the time that the USSR was convening a Communist party congress to line up opposition against the People's Republic. In any case, the United States accepted the invitation, and the table tennis players went to China in May, thus becoming the first group of Americans to visit the mainland since 1949.

Nixon and Kissinger had concluded as early as 1969 that Communist China should be brought out of its isolation and that U.S. relations with the Asian nation should be improved. When the Chinese overtures came in the spring of 1971, Washington quickly responded, not only by accepting Peking's invitation, but also by relaxing U.S. trade and travel restrictions against the People's Republic. Then, in mid-July 1971, the president informed the American people that Kissinger had just returned from a secret trip to Peking and that he himself had accepted an invitation to visit China sometime before May 1972. The State Department, during the following month, let it be known that the United States would no longer oppose the admission of the People's Republic to the United Nations.[8]

President and Mrs. Nixon, accompanied by a large number of advisers and journalists, began their spectacular visit to the Far East by landing at the Peking airport on February 21, 1972. They remained in China for a crowded week of ceremonial functions, high-level talks, and visits to other parts of the country. The concrete results of Nixon's series of conferences with Premier Chou En-lai were not very impressive, but as a symbolic event in the search for more normal relations, the meetings were extremely significant. Nixon seemed to agree that Taiwan was really part of China and that American forces would eventually leave the island, as tensions "in the area" subsided. In a joint statement following their discussions, Nixon and Chou discussed other areas of agreement and wider contacts in such fields as science, sports, and culture. A delegation of Chinese doctors soon visited the United States, the Chinese bought ten Boeing 707 transport planes and $50 million worth of American grain, and early in 1973 the two countries agreed to exchange diplomatic missions.

The Chinese adventure had another consequence as well: it contributed to a new détente with the Soviet Union. Nixon's visit to Peking made Soviet leaders suspicious of American and Chinese motives in arranging such an unprecedented meeting. As for the Nixon administration, it had sought since 1969 to promote greater harmony with the USSR in the SALT meetings, in Berlin, and in the Middle East. Rapprochement with the Soviet Union might also contribute to a settlement in Southeast Asia, while strengthening the president's position at home and in the election campaign of 1972. In May Nixon made his second sensational trip abroad in 1972—a visit to the Soviet Union.

After several days of talks with Leonid Brezhnev and other Russian leaders, President Nixon came home with a number of signed agreements. The Moscow summit meeting focused on an arms limitation treaty and a series of agreements concerning trade, scientific and space cooperation, and environmental problems. Nixon was unable to negotiate a comprehensive trade agreement, but the two nations did establish a joint commission to discuss that question in detail. Later in the year a harvest shortage led the Russians to make a large purchase of American wheat. The arms limitation agreements Nixon signed in Moscow represented the consummation of the first phase of the SALT efforts. One of these agreements was a treaty on defensive weapons limiting the building of antiballistic missile systems to two sites in each country. On the more difficult question of offensive weapons, an interim agreement was signed placing a five-year freeze on the number of strategic offensive weapons in both arsenals, including ICBMs, modern ballistic missile submarines, and submarine-launched missiles. Senator Henry M. Jackson charged that the nuclear arms agreements conceded too much to the Russians, and he succeeded in securing a proviso that in any future accords the United States would not accept any inferiority to the USSR.[9] Otherwise, the Nixon arms limitation agreements won overwhelming congressional approval. Public reaction was equally favorable.

By the late summer of 1972, the Nixon administration had reason to be pleased with its foreign policy initiatives of the past year. "It is difficult to think of anything the Nixon administration could have done," John L. Gaddis has recently written, "that would have produced a more dramatic shift in world power relationships of greater benefit to the United States at less cost." American leaders could even be hopeful about the final ending of the long U.S. involvement in the Vietnam War. In August 1972 the last American ground combat unit in Vietnam was deactivated, leaving fewer than 40,000 U.S. military men in the country. Although the Paris peace talks remained deadlocked, secret meetings between Henry Kissinger and the principal North Vietnam diplomats, Xuan Thuy and Le Duc Tho, had been held with growing frequency in 1972. On October 8, Tho made a significant concession in those talks. No longer insisting on a new government in Saigon, he offered to accept an internationally supervised cease-fire and promised to release American prisoners of war in return for the withdrawal of U.S. forces from Vietnam. Kissinger quickly accepted these terms. The Hanoi government soon announced that a nine-point agreement would shortly be signed.

Nixon's Triumph: The Election of 1972

Despite the president's initiatives on the economic front and in the international sphere, his political prospects were not altogether favorable as the election year 1972 opened. Nixon and other Republican leaders could not forget their party's congressional setback in 1970. Senator Edmund Muskie, the favored Democratic presidential candidate, had pulled even with Nixon in public opinion polls. The Vietnam War dragged on, inflation had not been brought under control, and although public discourse had become less strident, controversy and division continued to disrupt American life.

The favorite presidential possibility among most Democrats during the early part of Nixon's presidency was Senator Edward M. Kennedy of Massachusetts, the surviving Kennedy brother and the recently chosen party whip in the upper house. Not only did Kennedy have the advantage of his famous family name, but he had also proved, to the surprise of many observers, to be an able senator, a strong campaigner, and a popular figure with both party regulars and Democratic liberals. While driving back from a party on Chappaquiddick Island, off Martha's Vineyard, on the night of July 18, 1969, Kennedy was involved in a tragic accident that suddenly altered his prospects for 1972. The car he was driving careened off a bridge, and a young woman with him was drowned in the submerged vehicle, despite his efforts to rescue her. These circumstances and Kennedy's inexplicable failure to report the accident until the following morning raised many questions in the public mind,[10] damaged the senator's reputation, and removed the Democrats' best hope for 1972.

After Kennedy became unavailable, Senator Muskie emerged as the Democratic front-runner. But the senator from Maine was forced to share the Democratic center with Hubert Humphrey, who had reentered the Senate in January 1971. A third aspirant from the Senate was George S. McGovern of South Dakota, a liberal and an early opponent of the war in Vietnam. One other Democrat cast a long shadow over the contest for the party's presidential nomination in 1972—Governor George C. Wallace. There were several minor candidates: Senator Henry Jackson of Washington, the peppery black congresswoman Shirley Chisholm of New York, and Mayor John V. Lindsay of New York (who had recently left the Republican party to affiliate with the Democrats).

Senator Muskie continued to lead the field of Democratic hopefuls until early 1972, when his drive lost momentum and the middle ground he had cultivated so well suddenly became untenable. Although Muskie won the New Hampshire primary, his performance there was unimpressive, and during the next few weeks his campaign failed to arouse genuine enthusiasm. With Muskie's decline, Humphrey's prospects brightened somewhat even though he suffered in many quarters as a result of his identification with the Johnson administration and the ill-fated Chicago convention of 1968. The most noteworthy primary campaigns were those of McGovern and Wallace, the candidates of the left and right, respectively. Starting from far back in the pack, the South Dakota senator won a series of primary victories in states like Wisconsin, Massachusetts, and New York. Wallace likewise demonstrated impressive strength, sweeping several southern primaries as well as such northern states as Michigan and Maryland. Then, as he rattled "the eyeteeth of the Democratic party," fate intervened: the governor was critically wounded by a gunman while campaigning in Maryland on May 15.[11] Left paralyzed from the waist down, he was unable to continue his campaign for the Democratic nomination. Thereafter, McGovern advanced rapidly to a dominant position, defeating Humphrey in the important California primary and winning that state's 271 delegate votes.

The composition and conduct of the Democratic National Convention, which convened in Miami Beach, Florida, on July 10, also favored McGovern. The South Dakota senator himself, as chairman of a Democratic reform committee, had taken a leading part in liberalizing the rules under which convention delegates were selected. It was now stipulated that the makeup of each delegation must "reasonably" reflect that state's relative proportion of women, minorities, and young people—all groups with which McGovern was strong. The reform faction was able to establish control of the convention, and McGovern was easily nominated on the first ballot. Senator Thomas F. Eagleton of Missouri, a liberal, a Catholic, and a friend of organized labor, was selected by McGovern as his running mate. In his acceptance speech McGovern pleaded with Americans to "come home"—to abandon their imperialistic ambitions, turn their energies to pressing domestic problems, subordinate their differences, and renew the idealism and faith of the American dream.

Republicans were spared the internecine conflict that took place within the Democratic party during the first half of 1972. President Nixon was in an unassailable political position by the spring of the election year, and the GOP convention, opening on August 21 at Miami Beach, brought few surprises. Although Nixon had been challenged in the primaries by Representative Paul N. "Pete" McCloskey, Jr., of California, a liberal who opposed the Vietnam War, and Representative John Ashbrook of Ohio, a conservative who was unhappy with the administration's economic policies and with its rapprochement with the Communist powers, he was overwhelmingly renominated on the first ballot. Vice President Agnew was also nominated for a second term. The president, in the midst of much pageantry, rhetorical acclaim, and a galaxy of movie stars and other celebrities, called for "a new America bound together by our common ideals." For Nixon the convention was like a coronation.

Although Nixon was strongly favored to win in November, McGovern's preconvention appeal seemed to reveal a widespread desire among Americans for new approaches and new solutions to national problems. Unfortunately for Democratic hopes, McGovern's campaign failed to capture the public imagination or to carry forward the momentum of the Miami Beach convention. The South Dakotan ran into bad luck soon after his nomination when it was revealed that his attractive young running mate, Senator Eagleton, had been hospitalized on three occasions during the 1960s for "nervous exhaustion and fatigue" and had undergone brief psychiatric treatment for "depression." McGovern, who had not known about Eagleton's hospitalization, at first supported the Missouri senator, but as the pressure for his removal from the ticket mounted, the Democratic leader capitulated and asked his colleague to withdraw. McGovern then selected Sargent Shriver, a former director of the Peace Corps and brother-in-law of Senator Kennedy, to replace Eagleton.

Having identified himself as an uncompromising and forthright progressive in the battle for the Democratic nomination, Senator McGovern discovered that he could not easily change direction and move into the vitally important center. Many long-time party stalwarts were unhappy because of the new Democratic rules, which they associated with McGovernism. The Democratic nominee's demand for immediate U.S. withdrawal from Vietnam disturbed some Democrats, while his promise to cut $30 billion from the Pentagon budget alarmed thousands of defense workers. Labor leaders were unhappy with McGovern's labor record, and many of the union spokesmen disliked the senator's dovish position on Vietnam. His desire to grant amnesty to those who had fled the country or otherwise evaded military service upset others. His earlier statements led critics to charge that he favored liberalizing abortion laws and legalizing marijuana.

The strife-torn Democrats and McGovern's image as a candidate of the left gave President Nixon a decided advantage, and his campaign succeeded in attracting the votes of millions of dissatisfied Democrats and independents. The country was relatively tranquil, and, in contrast to the widespread pessimism of early 1971, the public assessment of the state of the nation was rather favorable. Although Nixon remained in seclusion for the most part, the Republicans were able to wage an impressive campaign on the basis of a huge election fund. Kissinger enhanced Republican prospects by announcing shortly before the election that "peace is at hand" in Vietnam.

McGovern and Shriver campaigned hard, but they made little headway. Acting as if he were conducting a religious crusade, the Democratic standard-bearer urged the need for changes in the tax laws to ease the burden on disadvantaged groups, pledged himself to cut the huge defense budget, and advocated better programs in education, health, and welfare. The senator also hit hard at the alleged corruption associated with the Nixon administration. Some McGovernites suspected that a large contribution to the Nixon campaign by the International Telephone and Telegraph Company was linked to the favorable settlement of an antitrust suit against ITT in 1971, and that a sizable sum contributed by the dairy interests was related to an increase in the price support of milk. McGovern and his associates cited the break-in, on June 17, at the Washington headquarters of the Democratic national committee. Five men had been apprehended in the party headquarters located in the office and apartment building known as the Watergate, including two former White House aides and a member of the Committee to Reelect the President. They were charged with breaking and entering, planting wiretaps and electronic bugging devices, and stealing and photographing documents. Administration spokesmen dismissed the Watergate break-in as a "third-rate burglary attempt" of little importance.

The election results confirmed the polls, which had shown President Nixon ahead all the way. In fact, the president won by a landslide, receiving 47.1 million popular votes to McGovern's 29.1 million and carrying every state except Massachusetts and the District of Columbia. With 60.7 percent of the popular vote (a percentage surpassed only by Lyndon Johnson in 1964) and 520 electoral votes, Nixon made the best showing of any Republican presidential nominee in history. He captured 65 percent of the votes of middle-income Americans, who comprised over half of the electorate. The Democrats, in the face of Nixon's one-sided margin, retained control of both houses of Congress.[12] Nixon thus became the first president in U.S. history to begin two terms with an opposing Congress. Nevertheless, in Richard Nixon's eyes, the voters had given him a strong mandate in 1972 to govern as he wished. The polls revealed, as the new year began, that almost 70 percent of the people approved of his performance, and in February *Time* chose Nixon and Kissinger as its "men of the year."

NOTES

1. The complicated deferment system was replaced with a lottery, which enabled most young men to learn at the age of nineteen what the probability was of their having to enter the armed forces, either then or after completing college. In 1973 Nixon did away with the draft altogether by creating an all-volunteer army.

2. A report made subsequently by the President's Commission on Campus Unrest, while critical of actions by the student protestors at Kent State, condemned the casual issuance of live ammunition to guardsmen and denounced their "indiscriminate firing" as "unnecessary, unwarranted and inexcusable."

3. Calley's conviction was reversed by a federal court in 1974 because of serious flaws in his prosecution under military law.

4. Quoted in William L. O'Neill, *Coming Apart: An Informal History of America in the 1960's* (1971), pp. 405–406.

5. Fortas resigned in May 1969 after it was learned that he had received an annual stipend from a family foundation established by promoter Louis Wolfson, who was subsequently sent to prison for illegal stock manipulation. Ironically, President Johnson had nominated Fortas as chief justice in June 1968, when Warren indicated his desire to retire. The nomination was severely criticized in the Senate on the ground that Justice Fortas was a "crony" of the president and had violated judicial ethics by continuing to act as a White House adviser. Fortas finally asked Johnson to withdraw his nomination.

6. The Supreme Court eventually overruled the delaying action in the Mississippi case, and in *Alexander* v. *Holmes County Board of Education* (1969) Chief Justice Burger, speaking for a unanimous Court, declared that "the obligation of every school district is to terminate dual school systems at once and to operate now and hereafter only unitary schools." Two years later the Court ruled unanimously, in *Swann* v. *Charlotte-Mecklenburg Board of Education* (1971), that cities must bus students out of their neighborhoods if this was necessary to achieve school integration.

7. Nixon's reliance upon Henry Kissinger in the formulation and conduct of his personal diplomacy worried some members of Congress. Several senators publicly warned that Kissinger exerted far more influence in the shaping of American diplomacy than did Secretary William P. Rogers. Unlike the secretary of state, Kissinger could not be summoned before congressional committees to explain and defend his policies. As the president's personal adviser, he was able to invoke executive immunity. According to *Time* magazine, Kissinger's role had become that of a "combination of professor-in-residence, secret agent, ultimate advance man and philosopher-prince."

8. When the General Assembly convened in October, the American proposal of a "two-China" policy was rejected, and the Assembly voted, 76 to 34, to admit the Peking government and to oust Taiwan. The People's Republic thus replaced Nationalist China on the UN Security Council as well as in the General Assembly.

9. The agreement on offensive weapons provided for a five-year freeze at the current missile levels—1,054 land-based and 635 sea-based missiles for the United States, 1,550 land-based and 740 sea-based missiles for the Soviet Union. The apparent Russian superiority was misleading, since the American multiple independently-targeted reentry vehicles (MIRVs) gave the United States a substantial advantage.

10. Kennedy explained his nine-hour delay in reporting the accident as a result of the shock and confusion he had experienced. The senator then made a televised statement to the people of Massachusetts in which he asked them to let him know whether or not they wished him to remain in the Senate. Not surprisingly, this emotional appeal elicited a heavy majority in favor of Kennedy's continuing in office and running for reelection in 1970.

11. Wallace's would-be assassin was an unstable young "loner" from Milwaukee named Arthur Bremer. Immediately apprehended and later indicted and tried, Bremer was sentenced to life imprisonment.

12. The Democrats lost 12 House seats but gained 2 Senate seats. The new party alignment gave the Democrats an advantage of 57 to 43 in the Senate and 242 to 192 in the House. The Democrats also won 2 new governorships and led in that category 31 to 19.

SUGGESTIONS FOR FURTHER READING

The literature on Richard M. Nixon and his presidency is uneven. Nixon's own views are presented in *RN: The Memoirs of Richard Nixon* (1978) and the various volumes of *Public Papers of the Presidents*. The best introductions to Nixon, in the absence of a good biography, are a stimulating essay in Alonzo Hamby's *Liberalism and Its Challengers*, cited earlier, and Garry Wills's *Nixon Agonistes: The Crisis of a Self-Made Man* (1970), a perceptive and wide-ranging study. Earl Mazo and Stephen Hess offer a sympathetic account of the pre-presidential period in *Nixon: A Political Portrait* (1968). For Nixon's comeback and first months in the presidency, see Jules Witcover, *The Resurrection of Richard Nixon* (1970); Paul Hoffman, *The New Nixon* (1970); and Richard J. Whalen, *Catch the Falling Flag* (1972). Helpful for Nixon's first administration are Rowland Evans, Jr., and Robert D. Novak, *Nixon in the White House: The Frustration of Power* (1971); James David Barber, *The Presidential Character: Predicting Performance in the*

White House (1972); and Jonathan Schell, *The Time of Illusion* (1976). William Safire, *Before the Fall* (1975), is a good account by an insider, while Raymond Price, *With Nixon* (1977), is a useful memoir.

James Keough, *President Nixon and the Press* (1972), is an illuminating appraisal. James Reichley's *Conservatives in an Age of Change: The Nixon and Ford Administrations* (1981) is a perceptive treatment of the influence of neoconservatism in the 1970s. The men around Nixon are described by Dan Rather and Gary Paul Gates, *The Palace Guard* (1974). John Osborne, a columnist for the *New Republic*, published five volumes of his observations on the theme of *The Nixon Watch* (1970–1974). Two psychobiographies, Bruce Mazlish's *In Search of Nixon: A Psychohistorical Inquiry* (1972) and Fawn M. Brodie's *Richard Nixon: The Shaping of His Character* (1981), are interesting but speculative and tendentious.

Important features of the Nixon administration's domestic policies are discussed in Daniel P. Moynihan, *The Politics of a Guaranteed Income: The Nixon Administration and the Family Assistance Plan* (1973); Vincent Burke and Vee Burke, *Nixon's Good Deed: Welfare Reform* (1974); R. P. Nathan (ed.), *Monitoring Revenue Sharing* (1975); and Leon E. Panetta and Peter Gall, *Bring Us Together—The Nixon Team and the Civil Rights Retreat* (1971). Nixon's influence on the Supreme Court is analyzed by Richard Harris, *Decision* (1971), and Leonard W. Levy, *Against the Law: The Nixon Court and Criminal Justice* (1974). The administration's sudden shift in economic policy is described by Roger L. Miller, *The New Economics of Richard Nixon: Freezes, Floats, and Fiscal Policy* (1972), and Leonard Silk, *Nixonomics: How the Dismal Science of Free Enterprise Became the Black Art of Controls* (1972).

Ethnic and class conflict and the world of the "middle" American are explored in Louise Kapp Howe (ed.), *The White Majority: Between Poverty and Affluence* (1970); Samuel Lubell, *The Hidden Crisis in American Politics* (1970); Michael Novak, *The Rise of the Unmeltable Ethnics* (1972); Peter Schrag, *The Decline of the Wasp* (1971); Irving Howe (ed.), *The World of the Blue Collar Worker* (1972); Michael Wenk (ed.), *Pieces of a Dream: The Ethnic Worker's Crisis with America* (1972); and Orlando Patterson, *Ethnic Chauvinism: The Reactionary Impulse* (1977).

John L. Gaddis's *Strategies of Containment*, cited in chapter two, contains an excellent chapter on Nixon's new diplomacy. Two other general works mentioned in the same chapter, Ambrose's *Rise to Globalism* and LaFeber's *America, Russia, and the Cold War*, are useful for foreign policy during the Nixon years. Henry Brandon, *The Retreat of American Power* (1973), is a good contemporary account of the Nixon policies. Tad Szulc, *The Illusion of Peace: Foreign Policy in the Nixon Years* (1978), is a more critical assessment. Stanley Hoffman, *Primacy or World Order: American Foreign Policy Since the Cold War* (1978), is an academic overview. Lloyd C. Gardner (ed.), *The Great Nixon Turnaround: America's New Foreign Policy in the Post-Liberal Era* (1973), is also helpful. For Vietnam and Southeast Asia, see Herring, *America's Longest War*; Goodman, *The Lost Peace*; and Gelb and Betts, *The Irony of Vietnam*, all cited in chapter 13; Gareth Porter, *A Peace Denied: The United States, Vietnam and the Paris Agreement* (1975); Larry Berman, *Planning a Tragedy: The Americanization of the War in Vietnam* (1982); and William Shawcross, *Sideshow: Kissinger, Nixon, and the Destruction of Cambodia* (1979). For the impact of the Kent State tragedy, see I. F. Stone, *The Killings at Kent State: How Murder Went Unpunished* (1971), and Scott L. Bills (ed.), *Kent State/May*

4: Echoes Through a Decade (1982). The disarmament negotiations are dealt with by Harland B. Moulton, *From Superiority to Parity: The United States and the Strategic Arms Race, 1961–1971* (1973), and John Newhouse, *Cold Dawn: The Story of SALT* (1973).

Henry Kissinger's influential role is examined by David Landau, *Kissinger: The Uses of Power* (1972); Marvin and Bernard Kalb, *Kissinger* (1974); John G. Stoessinger, *Henry Kissinger: The Anguish of Power* (1976); Coral Bell, *The Diplomacy of Détente: The Kissinger Era* (1977); and Seymour M. Hersh, *The Price of Power: Kissinger in the Nixon White House* (1983). See also Kissinger's own *The White House Years* (1979) and *Years of Upheaval* (1982).

Several works cited in the previous chapter are useful for an understanding of the background of the election of 1972. Other significant studies are Herbert S. Parmet, *The Democrats: The Years After FDR* (1976); Theodore H. White, *The Making of the President, 1972* (1973); Byron E. Shafer, *Quiet Revolution: The Struggle for the Democratic Party and the Shaping of Post-Reform Politics* (1983); Robert Sam Anson, *McGovern: A Biography* (1972); Jules Witcover, *White Knight: The Rise of Spiro Agnew* (1972); and David S. Broder, *The Party's Over: The Failure of Politics in America* (1972).

CHAPTER FIFTEEN

Crisis of Confidence: America in the 1970s

BOLSTERED BY HIS great electoral triumph of 1972, Richard Nixon began his second term in the White House with a new sense of power and assurance. On the international front he completed the settlement of the Vietnam War and strengthened his administration's cooperative relationship with mainland China and the Soviet Union. In domestic affairs Nixon moved forthrightly toward a conservative position, and he quickly concentrated more power over the domestic arena within the White House, where he had earlier concentrated power over foreign affairs. But the new administration had scarcely begun before it encountered a series of challenges and setbacks that ultimately shattered the president's confidence, destroyed his capacity to govern effectively, and forced his resignation in August 1974. Meanwhile, as the seventies unfolded, Americans still clung to their historic ideals but were less confident than at any time since the Great Depression of their ability to solve the nation's major problems or to cope with mounting social ills.

LAUNCHING THE SECOND NIXON ADMINISTRATION

At the outset of his second term, Nixon reorganized his Cabinet and made new appointments to many other upper-level positions in the executive branch. Henry Kissinger continued to play a leading role in the administration's foreign policy, and when William P. Rogers resigned in the fall of 1973, Kissinger assumed his position as secretary of state. Relying heavily on such aides as H. R. "Bob" Haldeman and John D. Ehrlichman, Nixon seemed to increase his isolation in the White House, much to the displeasure of some Republican leaders. He held few press conferences, preferring to deliver prepared addresses to national television audiences.

The second Nixon administration got off to a good start in foreign affairs. A formal settlement of the Vietnam War was finally negotiated. In mid-December 1972, with the agreement so confidently predicted in late October still unrealized, the president ordered the resumption of massive bombing and mining attacks on North Vietnam, apparently as a tactical move to put pressure on the enemy to assume a more conciliatory position. These assaults resulted in heavy U.S. losses of aircraft and airmen, and they were soon suspended north of the 20th parallel. But in January 1973 Kissinger and Le Duc Tho resumed intensive negotiations in Paris, and a formal accord was signed on January 27. The peace agreement provided for the complete withdrawal of all U.S. troops and military advisers from Vietnam within sixty days; for the dismantling of all U.S. military bases; for the return within sixty days of all prisoners of war held by both sides; and for the maintenance of a demilitarized zone at the 17th parallel to serve as a provisional dividing line between North and South Vietnam, with the reunification question to be settled by peaceful means. While the agreement left the Thieu government intact, it also allowed North Vietnamese troops to remain in the south and accorded status to the People's Revolutionary Government (the formal name assumed by the NLF in 1969).[1] President Thieu, under great pressure from the United States, reluctantly accepted the treaty, after Nixon assured him of continued U.S. support and promised to "respond with full force" if North Vietnam violated the agreement.

In general, foreign policy promised to be more subdued during the 1970s. "The time has passed," Nixon declared in his second inaugural address, "when America will make every other nation's conflict our own, or make every other nation's future our responsibility, or presume to tell the people of other nations how to manage their own affairs." America's longest and most unpopular war was over, all U.S. combat forces had left Vietnam by the end of March 1973, and the Americans who had been prisoners of war came home to rejoin their families. In the meantime, the administration ended the draft, thus removing the prospect of compulsory military service for the first time in a quarter-century. Nixon and Kissinger talked not only of strengthening their rapprochement with the great Communist powers, but also of reassuring their NATO allies and of making 1973 the "year of Europe." Nevertheless, U.S. prestige and influence in Europe and in many other parts of the world were not restored. The outbreak of the October War in 1973 threatened to engulf the Middle East and to undermine the American-Soviet détente. Fighting in Vietnam continued, and U.S. bombers, operating out of Thailand, kept up their raids on Cambodia until Congress adopted an amendment prohibiting the use of any funds for bombing or other military action in either Cambodia or Laos. Nixon and Kissinger assisted South Vietnam in every way they could, but by the end of 1973 the president was preoccupied with Watergate and had lost much of his autonomy in foreign affairs. In November, for instance, Congress passed, over Nixon's veto, the so-called War Powers Act, which required the chief executive to inform Congress within forty-eight hours of the deployment of U.S. military forces abroad and obligated him to withdraw them within sixty days in the absence of explicit congressional endorsement.

The administration's domestic policies reflected the president's sweeping electoral conquest of 1972. Although Nixon refrained from directly attacking the reform programs instituted by Johnson and Kennedy, he made clear his intention of eliminating numerous Great Society programs, including the Office of Economic Opportunity, and of restricting federal spending. He gave up altogether on his own programs for welfare reform and health insurance. He dismissed the liberal and forthright Theodore M. Hesburgh as chairman of the Civil Rights Commission. He used his veto power more freely, disapproving congressional measures providing for environmental control, hospital construction, the establishment of child day-care centers, and the like. The administration's budget proposals, while providing generously for defense and aerospace development, slashed funds for welfare, medical services, housing, and training programs.

Nixon now assumed a tough stance in dealing with Congress. One of his tactics was to impound billions of dollars appropriated by Congress for social services; that is, the president simply refused to spend congressional appropriations larger than he wanted, contending that it was his prerogative to exercise this kind of executive discretion. He refused to spend almost $9 billion appropriated by Congress in 1972. Several federal courts eventually ruled that the chief executive had exceeded his authority in impounding certain federal funds and eliminating some federal programs. Another source of presidential-congressional contention was the administration's assertion of the doctrine of executive privilege—the privilege to refuse to make its documents accessible to Congress and to refuse to testify before congressional committees.

The erratic performance of the economy confronted the administration with a continuing problem in 1973 and 1974. On January 11,

1973, Nixon suddenly terminated most wage and price controls and substituted reliance on "voluntary cooperation." Phase Three, as the new economic program was labeled, worked badly. Food prices skyrocketed, and such items as rents, fuel, and manufactured goods rose rapidly in cost. In June the president acknowledged the failure of Phase Three by imposing a sixty-day ban on all price increases except for food products at the farm level. The American dollar also suffered further humiliation in the foreign money markets in 1973, and on February 12 Nixon announced a second devaluation of the dollar—this time by about 10 percent.

In August 1973 the administration introduced a system of moderate controls allowing price adjustments. Since food prices were unfrozen before Phase Four was instituted, the cost of living continued to climb. Nixon's countermeasures were limited. The Federal Reserve System followed a tight money policy. The president also signed a new price support measure designed to increase domestic farm production, thus reversing the restrictive programs introduced in the 1930s. The economic situation worsened during the winter of 1973–74 when the country suddenly found itself in the midst of a fuel crisis. Inflation during the first half of 1974 increased at an annual rate of over 11 percent, unemployment mounted once more, and the gross national product for the first quarter actually declined at a rate of 5.8 percent. Year after year, meanwhile, the federal deficit was very large.

WATERGATE: THE MAKING OF A SCANDAL

To the surprise of most Americans, the burglary of the Democratic national committee headquarters in mid-June 1972 did not fade out of public consciousness, despite the limited impact it had on the campaign of 1972. The trial of the seven defendants in January 1973 set off a startling chain of developments and revelations that eventually showed that Watergate was part of a larger effort involving covert and illegal activities to influence the outcome of the election in 1972. It also developed that a systematic effort had been made to cover up the administration's involvement in the Watergate affair. By the spring of 1973, the outlines of an unprecedented political scandal were emerging.

The Watergate trials began in Washington on January 9, 1973. Five of the men arrested for the crime pleaded guilty as charged. The other two—G. Gordon Liddy, counsel for the Committee to Reelect the President (CRP), and James W. McCord, security officer for CRP—were tried and convicted. The presiding judge, John J. Sirica, pressed the defendants to tell all they knew about the incident, and during the trial he made it clear that he thought they were withholding information. In late March, shortly before Sirica pronounced the sentences in the case, he revealed that McCord had informed him that perjury had been committed at the trial, that the defendants had been under pressure to plead guilty and divulge nothing, and that people in the White House or higher up in the reelection committee had been involved in the Watergate break-in and bugging. A Washington grand jury began to investigate these charges.

McCord's revelations exposed the cover-up operation and set off a succession of further disclosures in the Watergate affair. Much of the story was brought to light through the probing inquiries of persistent journalists, particularly those employed by the *Washington Post* and the *New York Times*. It quickly became evident that some of the president's aides and former advisers were willing to divulge information in the hope that they could gain immunity or partial immunity from prosecution. Thus Jeb Stuart Magruder, a former special assistant to Nixon and later deputy director of CRP, was reported to have implicated John N. Mitchell and John W. Dean III, counsel to the president, in the Watergate intrusion and subsequent efforts to buy the silence of the convicted conspirators. Dean himself informed the press that the Nixon administration had decided to make him the "scapegoat" in the affair, and he charged that Haldeman and Ehrlichman had supervised the whole Watergate cover-up. On May 10, 1973, a New York grand jury indicted Mitchell and former Secretary of Commerce Maurice H. Stans for conspiracy to defraud the United States and to obstruct justice.[2] Meanwhile, a Senate committee considering the nomination of L. Patrick Gray to be director of the Federal Bureau of Investigation[3] also uncovered evidence linking presidential aides with Watergate. Gray, who eventually asked that his name be withdrawn from consideration, admitted that he had destroyed certain documents relating to the Watergate incident.

On April 27, Judge W. Matthew Byrne, who was presiding at the trial of Daniel Ellsberg for stealing and making public the Pentagon Papers, reported that two of the men convicted in the Watergate case had burglarized the office of Ellsberg's psychiatrist in an attempt to obtain the physician's files on Ellsberg. On May 11 Judge Byrne dismissed all charges against Ellsberg and his codefendant, Anthony Russo, on grounds of improper government conduct.[4] John Ehrlichman later reported that Nixon had ordered him to reinforce the FBI investigation of the leaks that led to the publication of the

Pentagon Papers. Ehrlichman then assembled the "plumbers" to stop such leaks, and some of them were subsequently involved in the Ellsberg case and in the Watergate burglary. The plumbers also bugged the telephones of several journalists and government officials suspected of giving sensitive information to the press.

When the Watergate disclosures began early in 1973, the administration first tried to ignore the rising furor; but it soon became defensive and gradually acknowledged the involvement of certain White House aides. Nixon eventually conceded that "major developments" had led him to make a new inquiry into the case. On April 30 the president made a nationwide television address on Watergate. Flanked by a bust of Lincoln and a photograph of his family, Nixon accepted official "responsibility" for the Watergate events and asserted that "there can be no whitewash at the White House." Yet he denied any foreknowledge of these events or any part in their cover-up, declaring that there had been an effort "to conceal the facts both from the public—from you—and from me." He announced the resignations of Attorney General Richard G. Kleindienst, John Dean, and his close aides Ehrlichman and Haldeman, whom he described as "two of the finest public servants it has been my privilege to know." Nixon implied that Dean had, for reasons of his own, masterminded the entire Watergate cover-up and kept the chief executive in the dark about the whole affair.

Nixon soon made another move to strengthen his position in the eyes of the nation. He issued a long written statement to the press on May 22, declaring, first, that he had no intention of resigning, as some reports had suggested he might. He acknowledged, for the first time, that there had been extensive White House involvement in the plumbers' activities and in the subsequent cover-up. The president admitted that some "highly motivated individuals" might have been engaged in "specific activities that I would have disapproved had they been brought to my attention," and he conceded that there were apparently "wide-ranging efforts" to limit the investigation or to conceal the possible complicity of members of the administration and of the campaign committee. But he denied any personal involvement or knowledge in all areas except certain limited "national security" matters, which he tried clearly to distinguish from Watergate.

Under pressure to authorize the selection of an independent special prosecutor, Nixon agreed to such a course, and Attorney General Elliot L. Richardson chose Professor Archibald Cox of the Harvard Law School for this task. While Cox set about his work, another inquiry into Watergate was getting under way on Capitol

Hill. The Senate had voted on February 7 to establish a seven-member select committee to investigate the Watergate break-in and other campaign election violations. The committee, headed by Senator Sam J. Ervin, Jr., of North Carolina, began its public hearings on May 17. During the weeks and months that followed, the committee heard a parade of witnesses, including Mitchell, Stans, Dean, Haldeman, Ehrlichman, McCord, and Magruder. J. Fred Buzhardt, special counsel to the president, presented a memorandum in which he claimed that John Dean was "the principal actor in the cover-up." The Ervin committee hearings, televised by the national networks, assumed the character of a great dramatic spectacle in the summer of 1973.

The committee—and the American people—learned that various individuals connected with the Nixon administration and the presidential campaign committee had been involved in burglary, bugging, spying on the sex lives of political opponents, and other "dirty tricks," destruction of evidence, blackmail, perjury, and pledges of executive clemency to buy silence. It was also disclosed that an attempt had been made after the initial Watergate arrests to put the FBI off the trail by implying that secret CIA activities might be uncovered if the search were continued. Senator Howard H. Baker of Tennessee posed the essential question: "What did the President know and when did he know it?" Dean told the committee that the president had known of the attempted cover-up almost from the beginning. He had warned Nixon on March 27 that "there was a cancer growing on the presidency" as he described the nature of the cover-up under way since the burglary in June 1972. It was also learned, from Dean's testimony, that the White House had maintained a "Political Enemies Project," and that the "enemies" on this list were to be subjected to income tax audits and other kinds of harassment.

Another sensational discovery was that the Secret Service, on Nixon's orders, had made regular tape recordings of everything said in the presidential offices and on the presidential telephones. The Ervin committee sought access to these presidential tapes for several specified days, as did special prosecutor Cox. The White House denied those requests, however, on the grounds of executive privilege and the principle of separation of powers. The Senate committee and the special prosecutor then asked the courts to issue a subpoena for the tapes, and in the hearings that ensued before Judge Sirica, the president's lawyers argued that the subpoenas should not be granted.

After the Ervin committee recessed, President Nixon on August

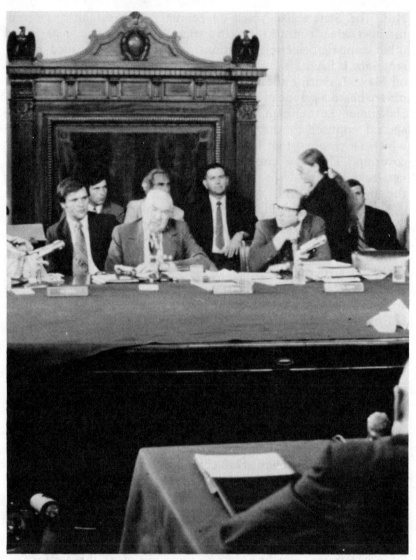

The Watergate hearings (*courtesy Congressional Quarterly, Inc.*)

15 made another television speech on Watergate. He also issued a supplementary statement to the press. He denied once again that he had any knowledge of or complicity in the Watergate burglary or cover-up. Nixon defended his decision not to release the disputed tapes. The chief executive said he had ordered an investigation soon after the Watergate break-in, and he repeated his earlier assertion that he had not known of a cover-up until March 1973. He appealed

to the nation to leave Watergate to the courts and to turn to such pressing concerns as foreign affairs and inflation.

A variety of other revelations in 1973 cast the president in an unfavorable light. Some of these disclosures and allegations involved money. The dairy industry, for example, contributed heavily to the Nixon campaign fund in 1972, presumably in return for the imposition of selective import quotas and an increase in milk price supports. Nixon had paid federal income taxes of only $792.81 in 1970 and $878.03 in 1971, about what a person with an income of $8,500 a year would have paid.[5] Rumors of huge federal expenditures for repairs and construction at the president's private homes in San Clemente, California, and Key Biscayne, Florida, were finally confirmed, after first being denied by the General Services Administration. The administration suffered still further setbacks. After Judge Sirica ordered that the disputed White House tapes be turned over to him for review, a presidential assistant told the judge that two of the tapes (possibly the most important ones) had never existed.

In the early fall of 1973, another crisis in Washington momentarily diverted the public's attention from the Watergate scandal, but this new development represented a further blow to the reeling Nixon administration. The Watergate disclosures had not involved Vice President Agnew in any way, but in August 1973 he was informed that a federal grand jury in Baltimore was probing his connection while governor of Maryland with certain alleged kickbacks to state and Baltimore County officials. The vice president vigorously denied these allegations, and as rumors of his probable indictment spread, he spoke out sharply in maintaining his innocence. But in a dramatic move on October 10, Agnew resigned the vice-presidency and pleaded *nolo contendere* to a charge of income tax evasion. His lawyers had earlier engaged in plea bargaining with the prosecutors. The judge fined Agnew $10,000 and gave him a suspended prison sentence, thus bringing down the most outspoken "law and order" champion in the administration. President Nixon, following the provisions of the Twenty-fifth Amendment, soon nominated Gerald R. Ford, Republican leader in the House of Representatives, to succeed Agnew, and both houses readily confirmed his nomination.

Shortly after Agnew's resignation, another major development occurred in the Watergate case. It grew out of the efforts by the Ervin committee and Archibald Cox to subpoena nine presidential tapes. When the president refused to comply with the subpoenas, Ervin and Cox sought an order from Judge Sirica to force their release, and after hearing arguments from both sides, Sirica in late August ordered Nixon to turn over the tapes and related documents to him for review, after which he would decide whether the tapes were protected by the doctrine of executive privilege or whether they should be turned over to the special prosecutor. The White House appealed Sirica's decision to the Circuit Court, which upheld the district judge on October 12. Seeking to avoid an appeal to the Supreme Court, Nixon and his advisers then sought a "compromise" with the Ervin committee and the special prosecutor. They offered to provide a summary of the nine tapes, which Senator John C. Stennis of Mississippi could "authenticate" after listening to the tapes in question. Senator Ervin apparently agreed to this proposal at first, but Cox rejected it on the ground that no trial court would accept summaries of evidence when the full evidence existed. On October 19 Nixon directed Cox "to make no further attempts by judicial process to obtain the tapes, notes, or memoranda of Presidential conversations." Cox refused to accept this order, at which point the president directed Attorney General Richardson to fire the special prosecutor. Richardson resigned rather than carry out this order, as did Deputy Attorney General William D. Ruckelshaus. But the next man down the line, the solicitor general, fired the special prosecutor.

The "Saturday night massacre," coming only hours before the deadline for filing an appeal with the Supreme Court, shocked the country and immediately stimulated talk of impeachment in Congress.[6] One White House spokesman described the reaction to the president's defiant action as a "firestorm." This was doubtless one reason Nixon soon abandoned his adamant position on the White House tapes and directed his attorneys to inform Sirica that the White House would comply with the judge's order. Some observers suspected, however, that Nixon had contrived a way to get rid of Cox, possibly because his careful investigation was likely to implicate the president. There was also criticism in some quarters of Nixon's decision, on the night of October 24, to order a worldwide alert of American military units as a result of a new outbreak of war in the Middle East. The chief executive's credibility had sunk so low that some people interpreted the alert as a desperate ploy to divert attention from Nixon's domestic difficulties. The president finally held a televised press conference in an effort to improve his standing in the eyes of the public. He named Leon Jaworski, a respected Houston lawyer, to succeed Cox as special prosecutor in the Watergate case and Senator William B. Saxbe of Ohio to replace Richardson as attorney general.

As the year ended, Watergate was still very much in the news. Although the Ervin committee had completed most of its investigation, its final report had not yet been made. Jaworski and his staff were continuing their quiet but methodical probe, including an effort to obtain access to additional White House tapes. Perhaps of even greater significance was the full-fledged impeachment inquiry being undertaken by the House Judiciary Committee. George Gallup's polls indicated that Nixon's popularity had dropped from a high of 68 percent early in 1973 to a mere 27 percent a year later.

THE ENERGY CRISIS AND THE ENVIRONMENT

Most Americans were worried and exasperated during the winter of 1973–74 by a more immediate problem than Watergate. The United States was suddenly hit by an acute fuel shortage, particularly of gasoline. The possibility of inadequate fuel supplies first became meaningful to Americans soon after Egypt and Syria attacked Israel on *Yom Kippur*, October 6, 1973. Within two weeks of the resumption of war in the Middle East, the Arab nations announced an outright ban on oil exports to the United States, the major supplier of arms to Israel; the embargo would apparently remain in effect until the Israeli forces withdrew from the territories occupied in 1967 and 1973. This would deprive the United States of a million barrels of oil a day.

Neither President Nixon nor Congress had done much to anticipate the energy shortage, but in November 1973 Congress passed the Emergency Petroleum Allocation Act. It provided for a mandatory allocation program of available fuel supplies within thirty days, with additional time permitted for the allocation of gasoline and products already being allotted under the administration's plan of distribution. Early in December William E. Simon took over as director of the administration's new omnibus energy agency. While warning of higher fuel prices, Simon stated that gasoline rationing would be employed only as a last resort.

Congress adopted other energy legislation in late 1973, including the Trans-Alaska Oil Pipeline bill. The act cleared the way for the construction of a 789-mile pipeline, to be built by a consortium of seven oil companies at an estimated cost of $4.5 billion. The pipeline was designed to carry oil from the North Slope to the southern Alaskan port of Valdez, whence it would be transported by tanker to West Coast ports. By 1980, the sponsors of the bill predicted, the pipeline would be supplying the United States with 2 million barrels of oil a day. In December Congress completed action on a measure instituting daylight saving time on a year-round basis, an innovation expected to save as much as 1½ percent of the nation's fuel consumption during the winter months.

Both the legislative and executive branches of the national government were preoccupied with the energy crisis during the winter of 1973–74. An avalanche of proposed laws descended upon Congress, and in his State of the Union message on January 30, 1974, President Nixon declared that "the number one legislative concern must be the energy crisis." Nixon urged the development of "reliable new energy sources," but he also cautioned Americans to adjust "to the fact that the age of unlimited supplies of cheap energy is ended." The administration proposed a five-year research program costing $10 billion, which Senator Henry Jackson, the Senate's chief authority in the energy field, criticized as altogether inadequate. In late February Congress passed the Emergency Energy bill, only to have the president veto the measure on March 6. The legislation would have resulted in a substantial rollback in domestic crude oil prices. Opponents of this provision argued that it would discourage petroleum companies from exploring and drilling for new wells. While the debate continued, fuel prices rose spectacularly.

Meanwhile, Americans tried to conserve energy. The country shifted to daylight saving time early in January, the president and other leaders urged people to turn their thermostats down to 68 degrees, and Congress established a national speed limit of 55 miles an hour. Citizens everywhere suffered from a gasoline shortage unknown in the United States since the grim days of World War II. "The scene is the same in one area after another," the *U.S. News & World Report* noted late in the winter: "scores, even hundreds of cars, stretching as far as the eye can see, winding around corners, creating traffic jams. Inside the cars are drivers trying—not always with success—to control their tempers as they spend an hour or more waiting their turn at the gasoline pumps." Many people expressed their exasperation and resentment to their representatives in Congress. "As an average American housewife," one Floridian wrote Senator Lawton Chiles, "I am fighting mad. I've had it with the high prices for food, the chicanery of Watergate and now the so-called gasoline shortage." Shortages were accompanied by sharply rising prices. The cost of gasoline to the average American driver rose from 36 cents to over 60 cents a gallon within a few weeks.

The Federal Energy Office under William Simon moved clumsily to allocate gasoline and other scarce fuels among the states and regions of the country. Several states resorted to various types of rationing their gas supplies, but the Nixon administration, continuing to blame the Arab oil embargo for the crisis, steadfastly opposed federal rationing. Gradually, by the early spring of 1974, the fuel shortage began to ease. One of the contributing factors was the success of voluntary efforts to conserve heating fuel, which eventually made it possible to begin refining more gasoline. The winter in most parts of the country providentially turned out to be exceedingly mild. The Arab oil-producing countries ended the embargo on March 18.

There was widespread suspicion in the United States that the giant petroleum concerns were reaping inordinate profits from the energy crisis and that they might even have conspired to cause it. The great oil companies operated with the advantage of concentrated economic resources and technological expertise. They maintained powerful political lobbies in Washington and the state capitals. The National Petroleum Council, made up entirely of industry representatives, served as the Department of Interior's official advisory body on all aspects of oil policy. For the past fourteen years U.S. oil producers had demanded and obtained restrictive import quotas on petroleum products. The industry enjoyed a 22 percent depletion allowance on domestic and foreign operations. In addition, for more than two decades American petroleum companies had been permitted by the federal government to use the royalties they paid to foreign producing countries to offset, dollar for dollar, their U.S. taxes. "A small group of businessmen," the economist James Patterson wrote early in 1974, "could, and did, decide to let gasoline demand catch up with refining capacity in the United States while expanding refining capacity at a breakneck rate over the rest of the world." The profits of American petroleum companies were up 61 percent in the last quarter of 1973, as compared with a similar period a year before.

The fuel crisis led to much discussion of "alternative energy." There was even talk of solar power and fusion power, although the development of such projects on a large scale did not appear to be realistic possibilities in the near future. On the other hand, a boom in coal and domestic fuel production seemed certain during the next few years. Whatever course the search for energy took, it was likely to be surrounded with difficulties. National policy apparently assumed that increased energy use was desirable, and by sponsoring long-term investment to meet expected needs, government action probably would reinforce existing patterns of energy demand.

The energy crisis of the 1970s also evoked the image of an economic "catastrophe." Some Americans expressed fear that economic growth would soon have to be curtailed, that it would be necessary to place a ceiling on the nation's historic trend of industrial and business expansion. Even more disturbing was the growing awareness of the fact that U.S. economic growth was accompanied by unwanted side effects, including a steady decline in the quality of the air and water, a series of human-made disasters of ecological imbalance, and widening alarm over the imminent destruction of the natural environment. In its first report, the Council on Environmental Quality observed that the Santa Barbara oil spill early in 1969 showed the nation how one accident could temporarily devastate a large area. "Since then," the report continued, "each environmental issue—the jetport project near Everglades National Park, the proposed pipeline across the Alaskan wilderness, the worsening blight of Lake Erie, the polluted beaches off New York and other cities, smog in mile-high Denver, lead in gasoline, phosphates in detergents, and DDT—flashed the sign to Americans that the problems are everywhere and affect everyone." *U.S. News & World Report* estimated in 1970 that it would cost $71 billion within the next five years to clean up the American environment.

By that time the environment and its degradation had emerged as a compelling public issue. Television brought pictures of ecological disaster into every American home, politicians began to discuss the problems of environmental collapse, a new vocabulary of words like *ecology* and *population explosion* entered everyday speech, and such scientists as Barry Commoner began to argue that "the proper use of science is not to conquer nature, but to live in it." Environmentalism, supported by middle-class and professional recruits, had become a major movement in the United States. The cause was promoted by groups such as the Sierra Club, Friends of the Earth, Ecology Action, and the National Wildlife Federation. Deeply concerned about the quality of the physical environment, the environmentalists also tended to be suspicious of the American obsession with economic growth and to have a skeptical attitude toward the claims of the consumer culture. In April 1970, millions of schoolchildren and other Americans took part in the first Earth Day, a remarkable symbol of the new enthusiasm for environmental matters. "Ecology," remarked a California politician, "has become the political substitute for the word 'mother.'"

Although the movement had deep roots in the American past, it began to take shape and to gather momentum in the 1960s. Rachel Carson helped to spotlight the perils of ecological imbalance in her book *Silent Spring* (1962), in which she showed the disastrous side effects of massive use of chemical pesticides. Ralph Nader, the most prominent of the new public-service lawyers, encouraged the environmental movement with his work for consumer protection and corporate responsibility. Beginning with his exposé of automobile safety hazards, he broadened his investigations to include topics ranging from air and water pollution to the depredations of agribusiness. Controversy was intensified in the late 1960s and early 1970s over the environmental impact of strip mining, the burning of coal, and automobile engine emissions, as well as the question of radioactivity and reactor safety in nuclear production. The energy crisis of 1973–74 heightened public awareness of the fact that natural resources were not inexhaustible. There also seemed to be a growing consciousness of hidden costs in a system of mass production and high technology based on the profligate use of energy and other resources. Even so, not all Americans joined the environmental crusade. Many industrialists and business people criticized new regulations for cutting into their profit margins, while labor leaders and minority representatives often opposed protective measures that might jeopardize or limit jobs.

Environmentalism had gained national attention, but it proved difficult to secure the adoption of a comprehensive national policy for safeguarding the environment. Significant beginnings were made in the 1960s with the passage of federal legislation designed to guarantee clean air and water and to facilitate the disposal of solid wastes. President Nixon signed the National Environmental Policy Act on January 1, 1970. Calling for a new national responsibility for the environment, this act established the Council on Environmental Quality to review governmental activities pertaining to the environment. The Clean Air Amendments of 1970 introduced stringent air pollution controls. In 1971 Congress authorized the creation of the Environmental Protection Agency (EPA), which was charged with the operation of the pollution control programs and the evaluation of impact statements. While the Nixon administration accepted these reforms, its leadership in this area was limited; the problems of the economy, the energy crisis, and Watergate complicated the task of developing effective policies for the protection of the environment. The search for such policies would continue through the 1970s and into the 1980s.

THE DOWNFALL OF A PRESIDENT

The dramatic succession of revelations and confrontations in the Watergate controversy dominated public affairs in the United States in 1973 and 1974. By the beginning of the latter year, the issue of overwhelming importance in the Watergate affair had become President Nixon's possible involvement in the scandal. The focus of the Watergate inquiry had become a movement to impeach the president. What had seemed unthinkable during the early stages of the various investigations into the matter had become a realistic possibility, especially in the aftermath of the notorious Saturday night massacre in October 1973. The House Judiciary Committee, under the chairmanship of Peter W. Rodino, Jr., of New Jersey, was formally considering impeachment charges against the chief executive.[7]

Public reaction to the firing of special prosecutor Cox in the fall of 1973 was so hostile that the president had agreed to turn over the disputed tapes to Judge Sirica. But a week later the White House informed the court that two of the nine subpoenaed tapes were missing and that another of the specified conversations had never been recorded. Three weeks later it was further revealed that one of the other tapes contained an eighteen-minute gap in a conversation between Nixon and Haldeman on June 20, 1972—three days after the Watergate break-in. Embarrassed White House spokesmen tried to explain the gap as resulting from an accidental erasure by the president's secretary, Rose Mary Woods, but a panel of electronics experts reported to Sirica, after studying the tape, that "someone" had deliberately erased it in at least five efforts.

With only 27 percent of the American people approving his performance as chief executive, Nixon launched "operation candor" in November 1973. This bid for public support through speeches and travel to various parts of the country served only momentarily to improve the president's image. Even the traditional bases of his support—the business community, middle-of-the-road and conservative Republicans, and the South—seemed to be eroding. Congress had learned to say "no" to the White House. The *Congressional Quarterly* reported that the executive branch had got its way on only 50.6 percent of the legislative votes on which it had expressed its wishes in 1973, as compared with 66 percent in 1972 and 77 percent in 1970.

Both Leon Jaworski and the House Judiciary Committee requested further evidence from the White House, including a large number of recorded conversations between the president and his subordinates. Nixon adamantly refused to provide this information, arguing that to do so would infringe upon executive privilege and interfere with the stability and authority of the presidency. Nixon's strategy was to delay, to assert that the president was unimpeachable in the absence of explicit proof of serious criminality, and to refuse to surrender evidence that could either provide such proof or demonstrate his innocence. On April 11 the Judiciary Committee voted 33 to 3 to issue a subpoena ordering the chief executive to deliver the tapes of forty-two presidential conversations within two weeks. A week later the special prosecutor subpoenaed sixty-four White House tapes for his own use.

Nixon decided, in a carefully staged move, to make public edited transcripts of thirty-one of the forty-two tapes demanded by the House committee.[8] Having provided the committee with what he described as voluminous materials, the president made it clear that there would be no further White House disclosures concerning Watergate. Before the transcripts were released, James D. St. Clair, the president's top lawyer, gave the press an account of the transcripts; the White House also approached key Republican leaders and lined up television programs in an effort to blitz the media. Nixon took his "case" for the Watergate transcripts directly to the people in a televised speech on April 29, 1974. He projected a forceful and controlled image, and as a TV "presentation" his address seemed to be a success. The bulky transcripts—1,308 pages in length—were made public on May 1. Although cleansed of profanity ("expletive deleted") and filled with sections marked "unintelligible," the transcripts were published in several editions and read by millions of people. They did not have the effect the president had evidently intended, for at crucial points such as the conversation involving Nixon, Haldeman, and Dean on March 21, 1973, they contained talk of extortion, blackmail, cover-ups, hush money, and other desperate measures.

President Nixon's Watergate transcripts, Eric Sevareid of the Columbia Broadcasting System remarked, "constitute a moral indictment without known precedent in the story of American government." The *Wall Street Journal* thought the transcripts revealed "a flawed mentality." Leaders of the Republican party and long-time Nixon supporters in the press voiced dismay at the quality of Nixon's thinking and leadership. The president's authority, as the *New York Times* noted, was "visibly disintegrating."

Still, Nixon held on. His recalcitrance finally led Jaworski, in a cogent letter to the Senate Judiciary Committee on May 20, to point out that he had been personally assured by General Alexander M. Haig, Jr., Nixon's chief aide, that the White House recognized his right as special prosecutor to seek any evidence he considered necessary, including that in the president's personal possession. Ten days later the Supreme Court agreed to Jaworski's request that it rule directly on Nixon's refusal to turn over the sixty-four subpoenaed tapes for use in the approaching trials of leading Watergate defendants. It was revealed in early June that the grand jury that indicted those persons involved in the Watergate cover-up had also named the president as an "unindicted co-conspirator." This prompted the White House to ask the Supreme Court to hear arguments about whether the grand jury had overstepped its authority in this instance. The Court agreed to hear such arguments. At about the same time, the House Judiciary Committee voted 37 to 1 to issue still another subpoena for tapes, calling on the president to produce, by June 10, forty-five Watergate-related conversations held between November 15, 1972, and June 4, 1973. Nixon refused to comply.

The beleaguered president was apparently determined to ride out the worsening Watergate storm. His tactics were those of "fighting," "counterattacking," "toughing it out," and resorting insistently to his international role in an effort to vindicate himself at home. In mid-June, hard on the heels of Secretary of State Kissinger's successful negotiations in arranging a military disengagement between Syria and Israel, Nixon made a well-publicized five-day visit to the Middle East in search of a more lasting peace. The Nixon entourage was delighted with the reception given the president, and it almost seemed that the exhilarating pre-Watergate days had returned. In late June and early July Nixon made another spectacular visit to the Soviet Union, where he signed a limited underground nuclear test-ban treaty.

In early July the president's chances of escaping impeachment appeared to be improving. But there was a recurrent phenomenon in the Watergate affair: every time the outlook for Nixon brightened, a series of new developments renewed the storm. The second week of July brought a spate of new disclosures and setbacks for the White House. John Ehrlichman was convicted by a federal court of having authorized the 1971 break-in of Ellsberg's former psychiatrist.[9] The House Judiciary Committee released a mass of presidential transcripts and other evidence indicating that the transcripts approved and released by Nixon with such fanfare in the spring had been edited to make the president's involvement appear less extensive than it was. A 2,500-word segment of a March 22, 1973, conversation had been left out entirely. In that conversation Nixon had told his aides, "I want you all to stonewall it, let them plead the Fifth Amendment, cover up or anything else, if it'll save it—save the plan."

The Senate Watergate committee published its final report at about this time. While refraining from making charges that would interfere with the impeachment procedure or the Watergate trials, the Ervin committee expressed alarm over indications that people in high office were indifferent to public morality and operated "on the belief that the end justifies the means, that the laws could be flouted to maintain the present Administration in office." The committee recommended broad legislative reforms "to safeguard the electoral process and to provide the requisite checks against the abuse of executive power." A few days later, on July 24, the Supreme Court ruled 8 to 0 that the president must turn over the sixty-four subpoenaed tapes to Judge Sirica so that whatever relevant material they contained could be used by the special prosecutor.

The final scenes of the Watergate drama were now enacted. The House Judiciary Committee held six days of nationally televised debate in late July, and the committee members adopted three articles of impeachment. The committee recommended that the president be impeached by the House of Representatives for obstruction of justice in the Watergate cover-up, for general abuse of his powers, and for refusing to comply with its subpoenas for White House tapes. Several Republican members voted for impeachment, and virtually all informed observers agreed that Nixon would be impeached by the House. In a surprise move on August 5, the president made public the transcripts of three of the tapes recently surrendered to Sirica. The three conversations took place between Nixon and Haldeman on June 23, 1972—six days after the Watergate break-in—and they showed that the president had sought to use the CIA to slow the FBI investigation of the crime. Thus Nixon was involved in the cover-up almost from the beginning. He acknowledged that he had monitored the "damaging" tapes in May 1974 and had kept the information from the Judiciary Committee as well as his lawyers. Many influential Republicans now joined the call for Nixon's resignation or impeachment. It was clear that he would have to stand trial in the Senate for "high crimes and misdemeanors."

While the nation waited, Richard Nixon made his decision. Addressing a nationwide television audience on the evening of August 8, Nixon announced that he would resign the presidency on the following day. He made no mention of Watergate, admitting nothing beyond misjudgment and the erosion of his "political base." But behind "the dazzling succession of events of this most extraordinary week in American political history," as the *New York Times* put it, "lies one fact of surpassing importance: the long and unmistakable drift toward concentration of power in the hands of one elected official, the President of the United States, has been stopped." At noon on August 9, Vice President Gerald Ford was sworn in as the nation's thirty-eighth president.[10] "Our long nightmare is over," he declared. "Our Constitution works. Our great republic is a government of laws and not of men." Americans could take some satisfaction in the constructive role of the press, Congress, the courts, and an aroused public opinion in responding to the challenge of Watergate.

Watergate was unquestionably the most serious political scandal in American history. But the Watergate crimes were more than that: they constituted an attempt to use government power to subvert the political process in the broadest sense of the term. This audacious venture involved a cover-up by conspirators in such high

The new president (*David Hume Kennerly, the White House*)

places that they were in position to manipulate the investigation that should have ferreted them out. Senator Jacob Javits of New York referred to Watergate as "a symptom of political decadence," and few thoughtful Americans could doubt that the scandal was in some measure a reflection of the nation's social environment and cultural themes. Some commentators suggested that Watergate was a consequence of the "imperial presidency"—the tradition of presidential supremacy that had developed during recent decades. Watergate was also rooted in a cold-war mentality that justified the most dubious activities to overcome a single totalitarian enemy. Thus the affair was only the other side of the clandestine operations of the cold war, the falsified records, and the Cambodian bombings. But there were other factors as well in this story of hubris and tragedy. The excesses of Nixon's abuse of power and his refusal to speak candidly to the American people were the acts of a man haunted by insecurity, fear of failure, and the delusion that powerful enemies were determined to obstruct his presidency. Finally, Watergate reflected the problem of moral leadership in Nixon's politics. As one historian has written, "Nixon, Agnew, and Mitchell had passed down to the third and fourth echelons an attitude that the opposition was illegitimate and that the political contest with them might reasonably have a dimension of secret warfare not unlike that waged by the CIA against its Soviet counterparts."[11]

Watergate sparked a reconsideration of political ethics, mounting distrust of intelligence activities, a searching reappraisal of federal power, and widespread criticism of the vast authority lodged in the executive branch in Washington. The shadow of the president's abuses stimulated discussion of how to restore the balance between the legislative and executive branches and how to prevent future abuses of power by the White House. There were indications that Congress might be moving to reassert its authority, despite the characteristic lack of unity and basic purpose in the Democratic majority.[12] One corrective step was the passage over Nixon's veto of the War Powers Act, limiting presidential ability to commit troops abroad by executive action. Congress also passed the Federal Election Campaign Act of 1974, which set campaign contribution and spending limits for candidates in federal elections and provided for public financing of presidential campaigns. In addition, the lawmakers strengthened the Freedom of Information Act to prevent the government from denying access to official documents "arbitrarily or capriciously." There were also other signs of reform vigor, among them the activities of public-interest groups like Common Cause and the network of Nader organizations. An Associated Press survey in the late spring of 1974 showed that twenty-one states had adopted political reforms in 1974 establishing ethics commissions, regulating campaign spending and lobbying, and requiring the disclosure of campaign contributions.

REFORM IN A NEW MODE

By the early 1970s a deep crisis of the spirit had settled over America, accompanied by a pervasive pessimism unknown in the United States since the depths of the Great Depression. A series of enervating events contributed to this sense of foreboding. As community organizer Saul Alinsky remarked in 1969, "Every time you turn around, there's a crisis of some sort. You have the black crisis, the urban crisis—it's just one goddam crisis after another. It's just too

much for the average middle-class Joe to take." The widespread repudiation, especially by the young, of long-established norms and
values heightened the mood of anxiety and despair. External threats
constituting a "civilizational malaise" further undermined American confidence. Robert L. Heilbroner wrote, in *The Human Prospect* (1974), that "we are entering a period in which rapid population
growth, the presence of obliterative weapons, and dwindling resources will bring international tensions to dangerous levels for an
extended period."

The American experience in Vietnam, more than any other aspect of the nation's contemporary history, demonstrated the limits
of U.S. power, destroyed a large part of the public's confidence in
the country's capacity to deal with foreign and domestic problems,
and bruised the national spirit as had no other development in the
twentieth century. Then came Watergate, which made Americans
acutely aware of the fragility of their political institutions, deepening the doubts that had already entered the public consciousness.
The events of the late sixties and early seventies showed how difficult it was to apply political solutions to social problems. The
frightful outbreak of prison violence at Attica, New York, in September 1971 was only one example of the seemingly endless social
problems that Americans had made little headway in solving.[13] The
Attica revolt set off a national debate, not only about the problem
of rising crime rates but about the whole system of American justice as well.

American loss of assurance stemmed in considerable part from
some hard realities, one of which was the crisis of the national
economy. The cost of living rose almost 7 percent in 1973, and during the following year its galloping gait reached 11 percent. The
gross national product actually declined in 1974. Unemployment
continued to be a problem, reaching 6.5 percent by late 1974 and 9
percent by the spring of 1975. The mounting cost of living confronted more and more people with a drastic loss of purchasing
power. The U.S. economy was far less self-contained than it had
been before World War II, and many Americans began to fear that
their capitalist system would not function if most of Europe and
Asia should abolish free enterprise, as appeared likely. Faith in the
"new economics" had also been shaken, including the assumption
that capitalism would manifest a steady trend to economic growth
and that its undesirable results—poverty, unemployment, social neglect—could be adequately dealt with by governmental intervention. Most Americans still adhered to the idea that growth was indispensable, but a strong movement was clearly under way to

modify the measurements of growth to take into account such factors as social costs.

Although racial tensions seemed to subside somewhat during the early 1970s, the reality of inequality was everywhere apparent in the United States. The black community was one of the principal victims of the reaction that had set in against radicalism, and of the reaction's instrumentality, the Nixon administration. Black Americans were hard hit by the severe inflation, the high unemployment rates in their ranks, and the contraction of the welfare system. Crime, drug addiction, and bad housing made life in slum areas almost intolerable for millions of blacks and Puerto Ricans. Genuine school integration in northern cities was delayed by the resistance of white parents to busing and the Supreme Court's increasing tolerance of racial imbalances in school systems.[14] The end of the "Second Reconstruction" was punctuated, in the early seventies, by a debate among scholars over the alleged genetic inferiority of blacks.

If the civil rights movement had lost its momentum, one group complaining about its discriminatory treatment showed signs of new vitality. Stimulated by the civil rights movement, student protests, and antiwar demonstrations, as well as the new "sexual revolution," a movement for women's liberation came into being. It was manifested in a variety of feminist organizations, protests, and campaigns. Female activists demanded equal employment opportunities in professional associations, spoke out against the oppression of a "sexual politics," sat in at the editorial offices of Newsweek and Ladies' Home Journal, picketed the Miss America contest, and even forced their way into male bars and restaurants. Feminism suddenly became a national concern and a topic of absorbing interest in the media. On August 26, 1970—the fiftieth anniversary of the ratification of the Woman Suffrage Amendment—feminists conducted a "Strike for Equality," with a big parade in New York City and smaller demonstrations in numerous other cities. The demonstrators emphasized such objectives as equal opportunity for women in jobs and education, free twenty-four-hour child-care centers, and free abortions on demand.

The objective conditions and attitudes of American women had undergone considerable change between 1940 and 1960. Millions of women had entered the work force during the war, and the number of women at work had increased rapidly in the 1950s. But most of these workers were concentrated in traditional "female" jobs, they were paid less than men, and there was no real challenge to the dominant attitudes on sex roles and the place of women. This would soon change. "Just as World War II had served as a catalyst to behavioral change among women," William H. Chafe writes, "the ferment of the sixties served as a catalyst to ideological change." The new ideological perspective was articulated in Betty Friedan's brilliant polemic, The Feminine Mystique (1963), which identified an invisible culture that pervaded women's lives and continually reaffirmed their traditional roles. Reacting against the "sterility" of the consumer culture, Friedan described the plight of the middle-class woman trapped in a daily routine of housework and child care. In the 1960s many American women were attracted to the civil rights movement, since they were increasingly sensitive to the theme of social inequality, and they soon adopted much of the tactics, message, and moral commitment that would soon characterize their own movement. It also gave some of them valuable experience, including, ironically, being subjected to sexual discrimination in groups like SNCC and SDS.

Among the goals of the women's liberation movement were equal opportunity and equal pay in employment; ending discrimination against women in education, the professions, and tax laws; changes in anti-abortion laws; and the sharing by husbands and wives in child-raising responsibilities. The reformers demanded equality of opportunity for advancement and promotion in private as well as government enterprises. While feminists agreed that men were the dominant sex and that women as a group were oppressed, they differed in their analysis of causes and solutions. Some extremists went beyond a call for equal partnership with men to demand an all-out assault on male supremacy and even to advocate the abolition of marriage and the family. Rape, Susan Brownmiller charged in Against Our Will: Men, Women, and Rape (1975), was "nothing more or less than a continuous process of intimidation by which all men keep all women in a state of fear." The mainstream of the movement, represented by the National Organization for Women (NOW), founded by Friedan and others in 1966, devoted itself initially to a campaign for equal rights, equal opportunity, and an end to discrimination. The National Women's Political Caucus, organized in 1971, concerned itself with politics and government, lobbying for women's rights within both major parties.

Many of the feminist activists turned their attention to legislation. Some gains had been made during the Kennedy administration, including the enactment of a measure to outlaw discrimination in the civil service. Title VII of the Civil Rights Act of 1964, which prohibited job discrimination based on sex, became the cornerstone in the drive for economic equality. It resulted in a flood of complaints of sexual discrimination. President Johnson had issued an executive order in 1968 forbidding federal contractors from discriminating against women, and two years later the Office of Federal Contract Compliance, under heavy pressure from women's groups, promulgated guidelines to strengthen the anti-discrimination ban. In 1972 Congress passed the Equal Pay Act, prohibited sexual discrimination in federally supported educational programs, and enlarged the jurisdiction of the Equal Employment Opportunity Commission to include local government agencies and educational institutions. Under Title IX of the Educational Amendments Act of 1972, colleges and universities were required to establish programs of "affirmative action" to ensure equal opportunity for women. Meanwhile, NOW, the Women's Equity Action League (WEAL), and other organizations had also been working at the state and local levels. By 1972 all fifty states had enacted legislation to prevent sex discrimination in employment. Congress approved the Equal Rights Amendment (ERA) in 1972, and American feminists spent the next decade in an intensive campaign to secure its ratification by two-thirds of the state legislatures.

By the mid–1970s, affirmative action programs were helping women even more than members of racial minorities. Universities, business institutions, and the professions began to employ more women, in part because of pressure exerted by Washington. Women assumed high-level positions in government, business, labor, the judiciary, and the military. They moved into new roles such as television commentators, airline pilots, and police officers, to mention only a few, and they began to make their way into the skilled trades and other formerly restricted areas of employment. The number of women workers increased dramatically, and by 1980 about half of all adult females were working outside the home. Women also began to play a more conspicuous part in politics. They made other gains as well. Several states, including New York, liberalized their abortion laws, and in 1973 the Supreme Court, in *Roe* v. *Wade*, upheld a woman's right to have an abortion during the first three months of pregnancy. Great changes were occurring in the way U.S. women conducted their lives. Many of them had begun to enjoy unaccustomed economic and professional advantages. Being more financially independent, freer from traditional sexual constraints, and with ready access to birth control pills and other effective contraceptives, middle-class women in particular were marrying later, having fewer children, and getting more education. In the early 1980s, for example, the percentage of women in college had come to equal that of men.

Although the movement for women's liberation accomplished many of its objectives and brought notable changes to American society, it encountered strong opposition and received several set-backs. There was much evidence of tokenism in the acceptance of women, just as there was in the case of blacks and other minorities. Despite the tangible gains made in the economic sphere, about 80 percent of all working women in the early 1980s were still concentrated in gender-segregated, low-paying occupations. They earned only about two-thirds as much as men. Women continued to carry the brunt of household tasks, and by 1980 over one-fourth of them headed households, as compared with 15 percent in 1950. Since two out of every three poor persons in the United States were females, social analysts began to refer to the "feminization of poverty." Women faced growing opposition on other fronts in the 1970s and early 1980s. The very success of the drive to liberalize abortion statutes encouraged a powerful "right to life" movement, especially among Catholics and fundamentalist Protestants. In the battle over ERA, women tended to divide along lines of social class, with middle-class and professional women providing most of the support for the amendment. Conservatives like Phyllis Schlafly attracted broad support with fervent appeals to older values and traditional ideas about women's place in society. When the ERA failed, by a narrow margin, the women's movement had been dealt a great symbolic defeat.

Still, feminism is far from dead in America. Women's liberation

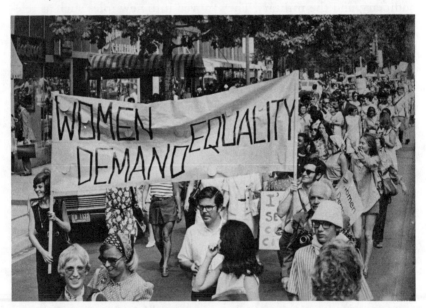

Women's Equality Day march, in Washington, D.C., August 26, 1970 (*Washington* Star *staff photo/Imagefinders, Inc.*)

has profoundly affected behavior and attitudes involving the place of women and sexual roles in U.S. society. Millions of women—and men—have become conscious of the biological, economic, and political rights of females in a democratic society, and a new feminist ideology has begun to spell out the meaning of sexual equality in the social order. One example of institutional change, often unnoticed, is the way sex roles and child-rearing practices have been evolving to accommodate families in which both husband and wife have full-time jobs outside the home.

THE PRESIDENCY OF GERALD FORD

The man suddenly elevated to the presidency on August 9, 1974, was a successful but undistinguished politician from Michigan. Gerald Ford was born in Omaha, Nebraska, on July 14, 1913. He grew up in Grand Rapids, Michigan, was graduated from the University of Michigan, where he was a varsity football player, and worked his way through the Yale Law School. He served in the Navy during the Second World War and was elected as a Republican to Congress in 1948. A conservative on domestic issues, Ford was something of an internationalist, though of an aggressive, interventionist type. He prided himself on following the approach of Michigan's Senator Arthur H. Vandenberg. As the representative gained seniority, he moved slowly up through GOP ranks, and in 1965 defeated Charles Halleck to become minority leader. His greatest ambition was to become speaker of the House of Representatives. During the Nixon years, he was a staunch administration supporter, which was an important factor in his selection as vice president in 1973. Most people liked Ford. Amiable and gregarious, he was a warm, open, and unpretentious man. He did not have his predecessor's sense of insecurity and distrust of people.

Ford's first weeks in the White House were reassuring. The press and the public responded enthusiastically to the new president's low-key approach and to his promise of an "open, candid" administration. He acted with marked restraint. He made no changes in the Cabinet and delayed bringing in his own personal aides. Ford's honeymoon lasted only a short time, however. One reason it ended was the president's announcement on September 8 that he had granted Nixon a full pardon, apparently because of the virtual certainty that the former president would be indicted and tried for obstruction of justice. The press then turned on Ford, many people questioned his judgment and motives, and his popularity dropped precipitously, declining to an approval rating of only 50 percent by the end of September. Ford's agreement to give Nixon custody of the disputed presidential tapes and papers, which was subsequently invalidated by an act of Congress, also damaged the new chief executive's standing, as did the controversy that arose over his choice of Nelson Rockefeller as vice president. November brought another setback with substantial Democratic gains in the midterm congressional elections.

Basically, Ford continued the conservative policies of the Nixon administration. Like Nixon, Ford wanted to reduce federal expenditures and to cut back on welfare programs and the structure of bureaucracy. He opposed vigorous action by federal regulatory agencies that might prevent "maximum freedom for private enterprise." Nor was he a champion of civil rights measures. He was against almost every bill Congress passed that would have assisted the black poor. He was extremely hostile to the use of busing as a means of achieving school desegregation. Indeed, he was criticized by the U.S. Civil Rights Commission for accelerating the trend toward resegregation by his resistance to open housing and school desegregation.

One of the problems Ford inherited was the precarious state of the economy, which had entered a severe recession and was plagued by rising unemployment, soaring inflation, and a shortage of energy. A drastic increase in energy prices in 1973 and 1974 contributed to inflation and slowed economic activity. The president adopted a conservative approach to these problems, calling for a cut in federal spending, a tight money policy, and voluntary action to hold down the cost of living. In September 1974 he held a series of meetings with experts from various sectors of the economy, followed by a big conference in Washington on approaches to the nation's economic difficulties. Little came of these efforts, although Ford tried for a time to promote a rather droll voluntary program he called Whip Inflation Now (WIN). In late 1974 the chief executive called for a tax increase to combat inflation. But when the first session of the Ninety-fourth Congress convened in January 1975, Democrats pressed for a massive tax cut, emergency jobs for the unemployed, housing construction subsidies for an industry hard hit by the economic downturn, and a number of tax reforms. The Republican president and the Democratic-controlled Congress were frequently at loggerheads during the months that followed. Ford, who was anxious to restrain federal spending and hold down inflation, vetoed no fewer than 17 bills in 1975. Congress overrode only 4 of these vetoes. Democratic leaders denounced Ford as "the most veto-prone Republican President in the twentieth century."

The economic crisis deepened in early 1975, and President Ford was eventually forced to accept both an increase in federal spending and a tax cut. Ford managed to head off some liberal measures, but Congress passed a number of significant bills in 1975, including an extension of the Voting Rights Act of 1965, a compromise energy bill, and a $4 billion public works act. During the previous year, the lawmakers had increased social security benefits, raised the minimum wage, and appropriated sizable amounts of money for highways, mass transit, and public service jobs. In 1976 Congress passed a tax revision bill that included several provisions promoted by "tax reformers." The measure extended the personal and corporate tax cuts of 1975. In general Congress rejected Ford's proposals for cutbacks in domestic programs and concentrated new federal spending on several jobs programs. The president's major setback on the domestic front was his failure to formulate and establish a comprehensive energy policy. Congress, in effect, wrote its own legislation, the Energy Policy and Conservation Act of 1975, which continued price controls and the mandatory allocation of domestic oil.[15]

In its foreign policy the Ford administration had to adjust to the relative decline of American power in the 1970s. This decline reflected economic problems at home, a weakening dollar abroad, the ending of U.S. superiority in nuclear arms and the rapid development of new Russian strategic weapons systems, strains in the U.S. alliance system, and the crisis in the American presidency. Ford, as might have been expected, leaned heavily on Secretary of State Kissinger. On the whole, the foreign affairs initiatives of Ford and Kissinger were not very successful. Relations with the Soviet Union, however, remained reasonably good. In November 1974 President Ford met with Leonid Brezhnev in Vladivostok, where they negotiated a modest arms-control agreement. Under this rudimentary SALT II, each side would be limited to 2,400 delivery vehicles and could not place multiple warheads on more than 1,320 of its missiles. Ford and Brezhnev, along with the heads of all major European states, met again in August 1975 at a summit conference in Helsinki. The conferees signed a declaration on European security that recognized existing frontiers. The United States thereby accepted the postwar Soviet annexations in Eastern Europe. Although the question of nuclear arms was also discussed at Helsinki, further agreement could not be reached on the terms of SALT II.

In the spring of 1975, Kissinger's Indochina peace suddenly fell apart. In April the Khmer Rouge captured the Cambodian capital of Phnom Penh and brought the collapse of the government, despite American efforts to save the Lon Nol regime. About the same time, a North Vietnamese offensive swept into Saigon and took control of South Vietnam. The United States evacuated more than 40,000 Americans and South Vietnamese before the last helicopter left the U.S. embassy roof on April 20. The defeat, while long expected, was humiliating to Americans. In all, 56,000 Americans had died in Vietnam, 270,000 others had been wounded in battle, and the war

President Ford and Leonid Brezhnev toast the success of their arms talks, November 1974 (*David Hume Kennerly, the White House/Imagefinders, Inc.*)

had cost a staggering $150 billion. Two weeks after the fall of Saigon, a final Indochina incident captured U.S. headlines. When the new Cambodian government seized an American merchant ship, the *Mayagüez*, off the mainland, Ford authorized the use of force to reclaim the vessel and its crew. Though a number of Americans lost their lives in the rescue operation, the mission was successful. It precipitated an outburst of martial pride in the United States.

Kissinger, with Ford's approval, continued his search for a formula that would establish peace between Israel and the Arab states. After arranging a disengagement of Israeli forces from those of Egypt and Syria, the secretary of state was able to work out an interim agreement between Egypt and Israel in September 1975. The United States basically guaranteed this settlement, in part by providing Israel with a large amount of military equipment, including sophisticated weapons. This was only a beginning, however, no more than a step along the tortuous path to peace in the Middle East. In Africa another American venture turned out badly. The United States provided covert assistance in the mid–1970s to an anti-Marxist faction in a three-way struggle for control of newly independent Angola. The U.S.-backed faction lost out in the struggle.

Meanwhile, Congress demonstrated a new assertiveness in deal-

The Collapse of South Vietnam, 1975

ing with international issues. In 1975 the legislators refused, in a series of votes, to approve $722 million the Ford administration sought in extra aid for South Vietnam. They insisted on a thorough examination of Kissinger's request for authority to station American civilians in the Sinai as part of the agreement between Egypt and Israel. They imposed a ban on arms shipments to Turkey. They forced the administration to modify a sale of missiles to Jordan, to delay construction of a proposed U.S. refueling facility on the Indian Ocean island of Diego Garcia, and to proceed slowly in negotiations for a new Panama Canal treaty. Congress also stepped up its oversight of federal intelligence agencies.

Despite the administration's limited success at home and abroad, Gerald Ford brought a measure of calm and a more optimistic outlook to public affairs in the United States. As Americans approached the bicentennial of their independence in 1976, they could face the future with greater confidence following the upheaval of the sixties and the agony and disillusionment of Vietnam and Watergate. President Ford no doubt shared this renewed sense of possibilities. He also looked ahead to the national election of 1976 and a chance to win the presidency in his own right.

NOTES

1. The peace settlement also called for the withdrawal of all foreign troops from Cambodia and Laos and for the creation of an international control commission to supervise the cease-fire and enforce other provisions.

2. They were charged with accepting $200,000 in cash for the Nixon campaign of 1972 from a financier named Robert L. Vesco, who at the time was being sued by the Securities and Exchange Commission in a $224 million securities fraud case. Mitchell was alleged to have interceded with the SEC in Vesco's behalf. Mitchell had directed the activities of the Committee to Reelect the President until his resignation soon after the Watergate break-in, while Stans had been chairman of the CRP finance committee. A jury ultimately acquitted both men of these charges.

3. FBI Director J. Edgar Hoover died in May 1972.

4. The judge did not refer to another defense complaint: two conversations Byrne had with Ehrlichman during the trial about the possibility of Byrne's becoming the next FBI director. The judge refused to consider the matter while the trial was in progress.

5. Nixon had made large deductions as a result of giving his vice-presidential papers to the National Archives. It was later revealed that the deed transferring the papers was not signed until several months after the expiration of the law permitting such deductions. The president eventually agreed to pay $467,000 in back taxes.

6. Forty-four Watergate-related bills and resolutions were introduced in the House of Representatives on October 23 and 24—twenty-two calling for impeachment of the president or for an investigation of impeachment procedures. The House Judiciary Committee began an impeachment inquiry on October 30.

7. In early February 1974, the House of Representatives voted overwhelmingly to empower the Judiciary Committee to subpoena anything and anyone, including the president.

8. Nixon's attorneys stated that the other eleven tapes were missing or had never been recorded.

9. Nixon had testified, in a written statement, on Ehrlichman's behalf. By August 1974, fourteen of Nixon's former administrative or campaign aides and twenty-one other men had pleaded guilty or had been convicted for crimes related to Watergate.

10. Soon afterward, Ford nominated Governor Nelson Rockefeller for the vice-presidency, and after extended consideration, Congress voted in December to confirm the nomination.

11. Alonzo L. Hamby, *Liberalism and Its Challengers: FDR to Reagan* (1985), p. 333.

12. Watergate as well as the worsening economic situation probably contributed to Democratic successes in the midterm elections of 1974. The Democrats picked up 43 House seats and 3 senatorships, increasing their totals to 291 in the House and 61 in the Senate.

13. A thousand inmates of the state prison in Attica—mostly minority-group members—revolted on September 9, 1971, seizing thirty-three guards as hostages and demanding a long list of concessions. When negotiations failed to end the uprising, state troopers and deputy sheriffs stormed the prison and subdued the prisoners on September 13. Nine hostages and twenty-nine inmates were killed. Many prison officials around the country criticized the way the revolt was handled by New York authorities.

14. In July 1974 the Supreme Court prohibited, by a 5 to 4 decision, busing into the suburban Detroit school districts. This ruling appeared to be a reversal of the long trend that began with the *Brown* decision of 1954.

15. The act of 1975 made a number of important structural changes. It abolished the Atomic Energy Commission and established three new agencies: the Energy Research and Development Administration, the Nuclear Regulatory Commission, and the Energy Resources Council.

SUGGESTIONS FOR FURTHER READING

Although there is not yet a first-rate history of the Watergate scandal, a good place to begin is with Jonathan Schell's *The Time of Illusion* (1976). Other general accounts include Lewis Chester and others, *Watergate: The Full Inside Story* (1973); Theodore H. White, *Breach of Faith: The Fall of Richard Nixon* (1975); and J. Anthony Lukas, *Nightmare: The Underside of the Nixon Years* (1976). The Congressional Quarterly's two-volume *Watergate: Chronology of a Crisis* (1973–1974) is very useful. *All the President's Men* (1974), by Bob Woodward and Carl Bernstein, is a fascinating account of the Watergate cover-up and the press's role in the early Watergate disclosures. Other aspects of the episode are explored in Delmer D. Dunn, *Financing Presidential Campaigns* (1972); the *New York Times* edition of *The White House Transcripts* (1974); Peter Schrag, *Test of Loyalty: Daniel Ellsberg and the Rituals of Secret Government* (1974); and Bob Woodward and Carl Bernstein, *The Final Days* (1976). Arthur M. Schlesinger, Jr., *The Imperial Presidency* (1973), places Nixon's abuses in an illuminating historical context. Robert Gilmour and Robert Lamb, *Political Alienation in Contemporary America* (1975), examines the mounting distrust of the political process among Americans.

Personal accounts and memoirs of participants make up a sizable collection of Watergate materials. One of the most informative of these is John Dean's *Blind Ambition: The White House Years* (1976). Among others are Jeb Stuart Magruder, *An American Life: One Man's Road to Watergate* (1974); James W. McCord, Jr., *A Piece of Tape: The Watergate Story, Fact and Fiction* (1974); Charles Colson, *Born Again* (1976); H. R. Haldeman, *The Ends of Power* (1978); Gordon Liddy, *Will* (1980); and John Ehrlichman, *Witness to Power* (1982). Light is thrown on the various judicial and congressional inquests by Fred D. Thompson, *At That Point in Time: The Inside Story of the Senate Watergate Committee* (1975); Samuel Dash, *Chief Counsel: Inside the Ervin Committee—The Untold Story of Water-*

gate (1976); Leon Jaworski, *The Right and the Power: The Prosecution of Watergate* (1976); and John J. Sirica, *To Set the Record Straight: The Breakin, the Tapes, the Conspirators, the Pardon* (1979). See also James Doyle, *Not Above the Law: The Battles of Watergate Prosecutors Cox and Jaworski, a Behind-the-Scenes Account* (1977).

The relationship between energy and the environment is discussed in an excellent general history by Martin V. Melosi, *Coping with Abundance: Energy and Environment in Industrial America* (1985). S. David Freeman, *Energy: The New Era* (1974), deals with the origins of the fuel crisis and offers a blueprint for future action. Other aspects of the energy crisis are treated in Lawrence Rocks and Richard P. Runyon, *The Energy Crisis* (1972); John C. Fisher, *Energy Crises in Perspective* (1974); Frank R. Wyant, *The United States, OPEC, and Multinational Oil* (1977); Loring Allen, *OPEC Oil* (1979); Ian Seymour, *OPEC: Instrument of Change* (1980); Roger M. Anders, *The Federal Energy Administration* (1980); and Jack M. Holl, *The United States Department of Energy* (1982). Among the helpful books on the environmental movement are Frank Graham, Jr., *Since Silent Spring* (1970); John C. Esposito, *Vanishing Air: The Ralph Nader Study Group Report on Air Pollution* (1970); Paul R. Ehrlich and Anne Ehrlich, *Population, Resources, Environment: Issues in Human Ecology* (2nd ed., 1972); Barry Commoner, *The Closing Circle: Nature, Man, and Technology* (1971); Emma Rothschild, *Paradise Lost: The Decline of the Auto-Industrial Age* (1973); Charles McCarry, *Citizen Nader* (1972); William Ophuls, *Ecology and the Politics of Scarcity: Prologue to a Political Theory of the Steady State* (1977); Allan Schnaiberg, *The Environment: From Surplus to Scarcity* (1980); Thomas R. Dunlap, *DDT: Scientists, Citizens, and Public Policy* (1981); S. David Aviel, *The Politics of Nuclear Energy* (1982); Craig R. Humphrey and Frederick R. Buttel, *Environment, Energy, and Society* (1982); and Jerome Price, *The Antinuclear Movement* (1982).

For the historical background of the modern feminist movement, readers should consult William H. Chafe's *The American Woman: Her Changing Social, Economic, and Political Roles, 1920–1970* (1972) and Carl N. Degler's *At Odds: Women and the Family in America from the Revolution to the Present* (1980). Linda K. Kerber and Jane De Hart Mathews (eds.), *Women's America: Refocusing the Past* (1982), is a valuable anthology. Joseph P. Lash's biography of Eleanor Roosevelt, *Eleanor: The Years Alone* (1972), is helpful for the 1940s and 1950s. The organization and politics of the women's movement are considered by Judith Hole and Ellen Levine, *Rebirth of Feminism* (1971); Jo Freeman, *The Politics of Women's Liberation: A Case Study of an Emerging Social Movement and Its Relation to the Social Policy Process* (1975); Sara Evans, *Personal Politics: The Roots of Women's Liberation in the Civil Rights Movement and the New Left* (1979); and Donald G. Mathews and Jane De Hart Mathews, *The Equal Rights Amendment and the Politics of Cultural Conflict* (1986). Ideological dimensions are analyzed in Peter Gabriel Filene, *Him/Her/Self: Sex Roles in Modern America* (1975); Susan Brownmiller, *Against Our Will: Men, Women, and Rape* (1975); William H. Chafe, *Women and Equality: Changing Patterns in American Culture* (1977); and Albie Sachs and Joan Hoff-Wilson, *Sexism and the Law: A Study of Male Beliefs and Legal Bias in Britain and the United States* (1978). Economic and occupational patterns are discussed in Helena Z. Lopata, *Occupation: Housewife* (1971); Mary Roth Walsh, *Doctors Wanted, No Women Need Apply: Sexual Barriers in the Medical*

Profession, 1835–1975 (1977); Susan Estabrook Kennedy, *If All We Did Was to Weep at Home: A History of White Working Class Women in America* (1979); Rae Andre, *Homemakers: The Forgotten Workers* (1981); and Alice Kessler-Harris, *Out to Work: A History of Wage-Earning Women in the United States* (1982).

Literature on the Ford administration is limited. Ford's own views are set forth in his *A Time to Heal: The Autobiography of Gerald R. Ford* (1979) and in the relevant volumes of *Public Papers of the Presidents*. Ford and his administration are treated by James Reichley, *Conservatives in an Age of Change*, cited earlier; Jerald F. terHorst, *Gerald Ford and the Future of the Presidency* (1974); Richard Reeves, *A Ford, Not a Lincoln* (1975); and Clark Mollenhoff, *The Man Who Pardoned Nixon* (1976). Other perspectives are provided by John Osborne, *White House Watch: The Ford Years* (1977); John J. Casserly, *The Ford White House: The Diary of a Speechwriter* (1977); Ron Nessen, *It Sure Looks Different from the Inside* (1978); and Robert T. Hartmann, *Palace Politics: An Inside Account of the Ford Years* (1980).

Several of the books cited in chapter 14, particularly John Gaddis's *Strategies of Containment*, are important for an understanding of foreign affairs during the years 1973–1977. In addition see Roy Rowan, *The Four Days of the Mayaguez* (1975), Earl C. Ravanal, *Never Again: Learning from America's Foreign Policy Failures* (1978), Frank Snepp, *Decent Interval: An Insider's Account on Saigon's Indecent End Told by the CIA's Chief Strategy Analyst in Vietnam* (1977), and James F. Veninga and Harry A. Wilmer (eds.), *Vietnam in Remission* (1985), on Southeast Asia; Edward R. F. Sheehan, *The Arabs, Israelis, and Kissinger* (1976), and William B. Quandt, *Decade of Decision: American Policy toward the Arab-Israeli Conflict, 1967–1976* (1977), on the Middle East; and Jerah Johnson, *Africa and the West* (1974), Anthony Lake, *The "Tar Baby" Option: American Policy toward Southern Rhodesia* (1976), and John Stockwell, *In Search of Enemies: A CIA Story* (1978), on Africa.

Chapter Sixteen

Post-Watergate Politics and the Carter Administration

IN THE AFTERMATH of Watergate, Democratic leaders, heartened by their gains in the midterm elections of 1974, looked expectantly to the presidential campaign of 1976 and the opportunity to recapture control of the executive branch of government. The intense competition for the Democratic presidential nomination produced a new party leader, a one-term governor of Georgia named James Earl Carter, Jr. Campaigning in a new mode, Carter seemed to speak to the sense of betrayal following Watergate, to understand the new realities that confronted the United States in the 1970s, and to represent traditional values that would restore the faith of Americans in their political process. Launching his administration early in 1977, after he had narrowly defeated Gerald Ford, Carter set about the difficult task of finding solutions to the nation's troublesome economic and social problems. Despite his hard work and good intentions, the new president was not very successful, particularly on the domestic front. He did not hit it off well with Congress, failed to develop a coherent design of action, and was unable to unify and inspire the American people. New crises near the end of Carter's term heightened the mood of futility and impotence that surrounded his presidency and contributed to his defeat in 1980. Thus, like his four immediate predecessors, the president from Georgia was brought down. While his own limitations were partly responsible for the frustration of his administration, more fundamental factors were also involved such as the intractability of many contemporary problems, the depletion of American liberalism, and the shifting nature of U.S. political parties.

THE ELECTION OF JIMMY CARTER

After Senator Edward M. Kennedy, the early favorite, withdrew for personal reasons in September 1974, a large number of candidates entered the contest for the Democratic presidential nomination in 1976. Among these Democratic aspirants were Senator Henry Jackson of Washington, Representative Morris K. Udall of Arizona, Governor George Wallace of Alabama, and former governor Jimmy Carter of Georgia. To the surprise of most observers, Carter led the nine candidates in the party's New Hampshire primary in January 1976. The Georgian had traveled all over the country for the Democratic national campaign committee in 1974, and by early 1976 he had been campaigning for more than a year. Carter had a disarming smile, adopted an earnest and folksy approach, and employed a style of campaigning that emphasized personal contact with ordinary people. Running as an outsider, he promised to bring a fresh perspective to Washington. Having established himself as a serious candidate, Carter began to win other primaries, including a key victory in March over Governor Wallace in Florida. He went on to win additional primaries and to establish an insurmountable lead in committed delegates, despite late challenges from Senator Frank Church of Idaho and Governor Jerry Brown of California. Carter was nominated on the first ballot when the Democratic National Convention assembled in New York City in July. His choice of Senator Walter F. Mondale of Minnesota as his running mate gave the ticket ideological balance and helped unify the party.

Meanwhile, President Ford and former governor Ronald Reagan of California were locked in a hard-fought struggle for the Republican nomination. Capitalizing on his incumbency and picturing himself as a conciliator and moderate, Ford defeated Reagan in the first three Republican primaries. But in March Reagan won an upset victory in North Carolina. Reagan's outspoken conservatism attracted many southern sympathizers of George Wallace, and the Californian moved on to defeat the president in several Sunbelt primaries, as well as the one in Indiana. But Ford clung to a narrow lead and was nominated on the first ballot at the GOP convention in Kansas City in August. Senator Robert Dole of Kansas was named the party's vice-presidential nominee.

When the formal campaign began in the late summer, Carter was far ahead of Ford in the polls. Recognizing how Watergate had changed the public mood, the Democratic leader talked about restoring morality and integrity to the national government. "I will never tell a lie to the American people," he declared. Carter did not emphasize his party's New Deal and Great Society traditions, but

Jimmy Carter campaigning in 1976 (*The Library of Congress*)

instead pledged himself to balance the budget by 1980, to stream-line existing programs, and to dismantle bureaucratic regulations in areas like banking and transportation. Ford sought to take advantage of his position in the White House and to identify his presidency with moderation and constructive leadership. Although the two nominees met in a series of nationally televised "debates," which added some interest to the campaign, it was not a very exciting contest. Starting from far behind, Ford's campaign began to gain momentum, and by election day he and his challenger were almost even in the polls.

Carter managed to win, but not by much. By contrast, the Democratic party retained a comfortable lead in congressional seats and governorships. The Georgian received 40.8 million popular votes

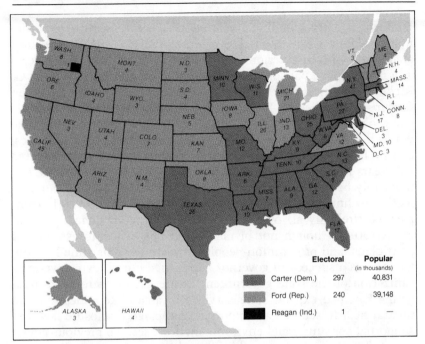

	Electoral	Popular
		(in thousands)
Carter (Dem.)	297	40,831
Ford (Rep.)	240	39,148
Reagan (Ind.)	1	—

The Election of 1976

(50.1 percent) to 39.1 million (48 percent) for Ford, who actually carried two more states than his opponent. The electoral vote was 297 to 240. Carter swept the South, except for Virginia, and ran well in the Northeast, while Ford carried most of the western states. The pollster Louis Harris concluded that the Democratic nominee had won, not because of his personal qualities, but because of "the revival of the old coalition that first sent Franklin D. Roosevelt to the White House in 1932." There was a good deal of truth in Harris's analysis, for Carter had brought together a diverse collection of supporters that included blacks, southerners, labor members, and ethnic groups. Strong black support was a major factor in his election. Mondale also made an important contribution to the success of the Democratic ticket, since his urban liberalism attracted many blue-collar workers and low-income city voters. Nor should Watergate be overlooked. As the *New York Times* observed, Carter was "the candidate of the Watergate backlash."

Hearing Carter's name for the first time before the campaign of 1976, many Americans had asked, "Jimmy Who?" It was a fair question, given the Georgia politician's obscurity at the time. Carter was born on October 1, 1924, in Plains, a small town in southwest Georgia. His ancestors had lived in Georgia since the late eighteenth century, and his father was a successful businessman and landowner. After spending a year at the Georgia Institute of Technology, young Carter was able to enter the U.S. Naval Academy, graduating with distinction in 1946. He spent the next seven years as a naval officer, part of the time working with Admiral Hyman G. Rickover in developing the Navy's first nuclear submarines. When Carter's father died in 1953, the young officer returned to Georgia and took charge of the family farm supply and peanut business. He did well in business, involved himself in numerous civic activities, and in 1962 was elected to the state senate. After being reelected two years later, he ran unsuccessfully for governor in 1966. He immediately began to perfect an organization and to develop more effective techniques for another gubernatorial bid in 1970. He campaigned tirelessly all over the state, projecting an image of social conservatism (though not of racism), of opposition to established politicians, and of common-people sympathies. This time he won. Carter was a successful governor. He carried out an extensive reorganization of the state government, made use of "zero-based budgeting," helped expand state services in areas like education and mental health, secured an important campaign disclosure law, and supported consumer and environmental causes. No previous governor of Georgia went as far as he did in championing human equality. He was one of a new breed of southern governors elected in the 1970s.

A leader of great energy and driving ambition, Jimmy Carter, as he was invariably called, had an analytical mind, a capacity for hard and disciplined work, and an unshakable faith in his own abilities. Carter described himself as a "born-again" Christian, and it would seem that his Southern Baptist religion reinforced his drive and self-confidence. His engineering training in college and in the Navy probably strengthened his concern for organization and efficiency. The new president could not be called a sparkling speaker, and he lacked magnetism as a leader. On the other hand, he was effective in working with small groups and could inspire loyalty and devotion among his subordinates.

In his inaugural address Carter proclaimed "a new beginning, a new dedication within our government, a new spirit within us all." The Carter administration did seem to represent "a new beginning" in some respects. For one thing, Carter was the first president from the Deep South in well over a century, and his election appeared to provide dramatic proof that the southern region had finally been fully integrated into national politics. In staffing the White House, the new chief executive appointed many Georgians who had served in his adminstration as governor, including Hamilton Jordan as chief aide, Jody Powell as press secretary, Stuart Eizenstadt as domestic policy adviser, and Bert Lance as director of the Office of

Management and Budget. Carter also appointed many blacks and women to high-ranking positions in the government. Six women were selected as ambassadors; two women, one of whom was black, were named to the Cabinet; and the black congressman Andrew Young of Georgia was appointed ambassador to the United Nations. The Cabinet, as a whole, was more conventional; several of its members had served in the Kennedy and Johnson administrations. Cyrus R. Vance, a New York lawyer, became secretary of state. Among the other Cabinet members were W. Michael Blumenthal as secretary of the treasury, Harold Brown as secretary of defense, and Joseph A. Califano as secretary of health, education, and welfare. Zbigniew Brzezinski, a Columbia University specialist in international affairs, was selected as the president's national security adviser. Carter also relied upon his wife, Rosalynn, for advice.

Although many able people were brought into the new administration, they were not always able to work together as a team. For example, the White House staff—referred to by some journalists as the "Georgia mafia"—tended to be overly protective of the president. Its members were soon involved in serious quarrels with department heads, and some of the White House functionaries antagonized congressional leaders. Debilitating conflict also developed within the administration over the formulation and conduct of foreign policy, centering in differences between Secretary Vance and the State Department, on one hand, and Brzezinski and the National Security Council, on the other. Carter made Vance the sole spokesman for the United States on international questions, but he allowed Brzezinski to control the flow of advice and recommendations to the Oval Office on all matters of national security. The more aggressive and hawkish Brzezinski gradually overcame Vance, a strong advocate of détente and arms limitation. Meanwhile, President Carter was unwilling or unable to mend these rifts in the ranks of his advisers.

RESPONDING TO PROBLEMS AT HOME

Gerald Ford left his successor a large number of unresolved and perplexing problems, including an economy characterized by sluggish growth, high unemployment, an adverse trade balance, and increasing dependence on foreign sources of energy. Carter hoped to respond effectively to these and other national problems. In his first year he unveiled an estimated eighty legislative proposals to Congress. He began his term by working hard to develop popular support for his administration. Seeking to restore confidence in the federal government and to mobilize the public behind his programs,

The president and his lady walk down Pennsylvania Avenue on January 20, 1977 (*courtesy the White House*)

the new chief executive portrayed himself as a "people's president" deeply concerned with morality, compassion, openness, frugality, and simplicity. In seeking congressional action, he was quick to resort to television as a medium of appeal. According to one source, Carter "gave Americans a series of populist symbols—town meetings, fireside chats and blue jeans—to get his message across, rather than delivering a clearly defined program to Capitol Hill."[1]

In an effort to stimulate the economy and to reduce unemployment, the Carter administration pushed for increased federal spending and a sizable tax cut. Carter's first economic stimulus proposal featured a two-year, $31.6 billion combination of tax cuts and job-creation programs. The Democratic-controlled Congress was generally receptive to the president's recommendations, although the legislation it passed was substantially reshaped from its original form. The lawmakers appropriated $6 billion in federal grants for local public works, provided $7.9 billion for public-service jobs, and voted to increase farm price supports. They reduced taxes by $34 billion over a three-year period, with incentives for employers who hired additional workers. They also approved a phased increase in the minimum wage from $2.30 to $3.35 an hour by 1981. Unemployment declined, whether as a result of these initiatives or other factors, and the rate had fallen from 7.9 percent in December 1976 to 6.4 percent a year later, and to less than 6 percent by mid-1978. As time passed, Carter showed less enthusiasm for tax reductions and more concern over federal deficits and the problem of inflation. His recovery plans struck some of his supporters as too cautious.

The administration was less successful in its efforts to formulate and secure the enactment of social welfare reforms. One program that demanded attention was the social security system, whose several funds for old-age, disability, and medical benefits were under mounting pressure from rising costs and population changes. In December 1977 Congress acted on the administration's recommendation by increasing payroll taxes in gradual increments and by raising the salary limit for such taxes. Secretary Califano's proposals for more fundamental reforms in the social security system, such as raising the minimum retirement age from sixty-two to sixty-five, failed to survive strong opposition within the administration. Califano also urged the consolidation of all welfare payments into one cash payment to recipients. His plan would provide a family of four with an income of $4,200 a year, while creating 1.4 million public-service jobs. Fearful of the large costs involved, Carter was reluctant to give welfare reform high priority, and a more modest proposal in 1978 made little headway in Congress. Though committed to the idea of a national health plan, the president was slow in agreeing to sponsor such a program. In 1978 he finally approved Califano's comprehensive scheme, which would make use of both private and public insurance, in contrast to Senator Edward Kennedy's ambitious plan based on public insurance. By this time it was too late, since Congress was badly divided and other issues had moved to the fore.

Energy was a major focus of the administration's efforts from the outset. Since the Ford administration had been unable to come to grips with the energy crisis or to work out a long-range policy for its solution, Carter devoted much of his time to developing an energy policy. He presented a wide-ranging energy proposal in mid-April 1977 and soon after sent it to Congress. The energy problem, the president asserted in a phrase taken from the philosopher William James, represented "the moral equivalent of war." Referring to the way in which energy costs had multiplied since 1973 and to the fact that the United States was currently importing almost half of the petroleum it used, Carter urged the adoption of an energy policy that would end the crisis and meet the nation's future needs. The administration plan emphasized a conservation program designed to reduce the rate of increase in overall energy use, to lower gasoline consumption by 10 percent, and to cut oil imports to one-eighth of total energy consumption. In all, the plan included dozens of features ranging from taxes and incentives for conservation to alternative energy sources and new transportation studies. In general the administration wanted to reduce dependence on imported oil, retain domestic price controls with a new pricing system, and bring supply and demand into balance. Carter also recommended the construction of more nuclear power plants and a two-thirds increase in coal production. Finally, he called for deregulation of natural gas, which would result in higher prices and encourage domestic exploration, and a "windfall profits" tax on the petroleum companies, whose profits would increase following deregulation.

Congress debated Carter's energy bill for eighteen months. After being passed by the House in August 1977 with relatively few important changes, the measure was torn apart in the Senate, which eventually voted for a bill so different from the House version that it took the conference committee almost a year to work out a compromise. The deregulation of natural gas precipitated a bitter struggle. Liberal members of Congress opposed it because it would mean higher prices for consumers, while conservatives were generally against the windfall profits tax. Special-interest lobbies exerted great weight, party discipline among the Democrats collapsed, and the president found it impossible to mobilize public opinion in support of his plan, since most people were not convinced that the energy problem was really as serious as it was pictured by the administration. The National Energy Act, which was finally passed in October 1978, contained many of Carter's original recommendations, but some of its central provisions were quite different and much weaker than those first proposed. The president lost his proposal for a crude oil tax to bring domestic oil prices up to world levels, and a recommended tax on industrial users of oil and gas failed to win approval. As a result, the act had no provisions for oil pricing. Carter put the best face possible on the new energy statute, but he could hardly claim it as a major achievement.

By the time the energy legislation was finally approved in the late autumn of 1978, the administration was caught up in a hopeless struggle to solve another economic problem, the rapidly rising rate of inflation. Stimulated by the spending and tax-cut policies of 1977, as well as more deep-seated factors, the inflation rate had risen from about 5.5 percent when Carter took office to 9.6 percent in 1978. The president, initially preoccupied with the development of unemployment, economic growth, and energy programs, had trouble in devising a consistent and effective solution to the inflation problem. Like Ford, he was opposed to mandatory controls. Meanwhile, as the cost of living continued to rise, Carter began to show more budgetary restraint and to resist appropriation bills he considered inflationary. Casting about for a workable approach, he finally decided, in April 1978, to propose a freeze on the salaries of top-level federal officials and a limit of 5.5 percent a year on raises for the government's white-collar employees. In May he asked Congress to reduce the size of the previously adopted tax cut and to push back its effective date. He also vetoed several appropriation measures. Then in October, following a sharp decline in stock market prices and the weakening of the dollar in foreign money markets, the president proclaimed a new anti-inflation program containing voluntary guidelines designed to limit annual wage increases to 7 percent and to keep price hikes from exceeding 6.5 percent. The new guidelines had little practical effect. In the meantime, the Federal Reserve Board raised the rediscount rate to a record 9.5 percent and tightened credit in other ways as well. And the United States managed to head off a financial panic by acting to sustain the price of the dollar against speculative sales in currency markets abroad.

Worsening inflation and a contrary economy clearly had an adverse effect on President Carter's popularity, which had declined steeply by the middle of his term. But the administration experienced a variety of other difficulties as well. Businessmen, labor leaders, and even black spokesmen found fault with the president's domestic policies. A long and enervating coal strike in the winter of 1977–78 forced Carter to resort to an injunction under the Taft-Hartley Act. His close friend and adviser Bert Lance resigned as budget director in September 1978, following a series of embarrassing allegations of illegal campaign contributions and questionable practices in his earlier banking career. Carter was also dealt several setbacks by Congress. It rejected his proposals for tax reform, a new labor law, and major changes in election procedures. After a long delay, the lawmakers voted against the administration's recommendation that increases in hospital costs be limited to 9 percent a year. Carter's plan for dealing with the swelling number of illegal aliens in the United States, presented in August 1977, was caught in a congressional cross fire and not enacted. The Georgian had committed himself to federal gun-control legislation as a means of preventing crime, but after eighteen months in office, he dropped the issue without making a real effort to secure its adoption. But the deteriorating economy overshadowed these defeats, as the cost of living skyrocketed and unemployment once again began to increase.

Carter's own limitations were partly to blame for his unimpressive record in the domestic arena. Although he eventually attempted to develop better relations with Congress, he and his lieutenants were too often arrogant and insensitive in trying to work with congressional leaders. In the spring of 1977, for example, the new president abruptly and without consulting Congress proposed the elimination of eighteen ongoing federal water projects, creating unnecessary hard feelings as a result. Some observers thought Carter's problems on Capitol Hill were largely the result of poor communications with members of the House and Senate. Congress itself was resistant to executive pressure and eager to defend its prerogatives in the wake of Vietnam and Watergate. There was, moreover, a rising tide of conservatism in the two houses, despite the Democratic majorities,[2] and liberal members could not always be relied on by the administration, since many of them had doubts about the specifics of Carter's programs and had begun to question the desirability of a strong presidency. Another difficulty was that in trying to balance the budget, cut down on the size of government, and control inflation, Carter frequently found that he had to deny favors and to say "no" rather than "yes" to individual members of Congress. In retrospect it is apparent that the thirty-ninth president tried to move on too many fronts at the beginning of his term; he needed a more coherent, focused set of proposals. More fundamentally, however, Jimmy Carter served in a time of deep divisions in Congress and the electorate, multiplying special interests, and the absence of a consensus to facilitate concerted action. As Meg Greenfield wrote in *Newsweek* in April 1978, "I can't remember a time in Washington when interest-group issues and politics so dominated events."

Nevertheless, the Carter administration could point to some significant achievements—to its recognition of blacks and women, to the creation of Cabinet-level departments of Education and Energy, and to its success in reducing unemployment. Carter established a federal task force to deal with draft evaders during the Vietnam War, and amnesty was eventually extended to thousands of American youths who had fled the country to avoid fighting in the war. The administration was successful in sponsoring several important conservation measures: controls over strip mining, a "superfund" of $1.6 billion to clean up chemical waste sites, and the Alaska Lands Protection Act of 1980 establishing a forest reserve of over 100 million acres. Congress also approved other Carter proposals, including the extension of the ratification period for the ERA, legislation reinstating presidential authority to reorganize the executive branch of government, civil service reform, and deregulation of the nation's transportation system and banking industry.

SEARCHING FOR SOLUTIONS ABROAD

In the realm of foreign policy, President Carter seemed to challenge his predecessors' preoccupation with the containment of international communism. The time had come, he declared in his first major address on foreign affairs, to move beyond the belief "that Soviet expansion was almost inevitable but that it must be contained," beyond "that inordinate fear of communism which once led us to embrace any dictator who joined us in that fear," and beyond the tendency "to adopt the flawed and erroneous principles and tactics of our adversaries, sometimes abandoning our own values for theirs." Carter called for a new American foreign policy "based on constant decency in its values and on optimism in our historical vision." Yet, ironically, this idealistic president eventually fell back on a forceful reassertion of the containment doctrine, urging the development of new strategic weapons, a return to the military draft, and fewer constraints on intelligence collection capabilities.

Perhaps Carter's most striking departure from the foreign policies of his predecessors was his emphasis on human rights. "We can never be indifferent to the fate of freedom elsewhere," he asserted in his inaugural address. "Our commitment to human rights must be absolute." He later described human rights as "the soul of our foreign policy." The administration soon issued statements criticizing the Soviet Union and Czechoslovakia for intimidating citizens who tried to exercise their right to protest. The president expressed his sympathy for prominent Russian dissidents. Carter's criticisms of the Russians for human rights violations came, unfortunately, just at the time the United States was trying to negotiate an arms-limitation agreement with the USSR. He also signed the Inter-American Convention on Human Rights, urged Congress to approve the UN Human Rights Covenants of 1966, and expanded American refugee and asylum programs. Critics, of whom there were many, charged that the administration's insistence on human rights abroad was naive and impractical. For one thing, they contended, such a policy would bring the United States into conflict with its own allies—with nations such as South Korea, Iran, and the Philippines, notorious for having repressive regimes. When the United States accompanied its annual offer of $50 million in military aid to Brazil with a critical report on the status of human rights in that country, the Brazilian government rejected the offer. Several other Latin American countries followed Brazil's lead. In general the human rights policy brought few if any positive results.

The Carter administration's sponsorship of the so-called Panama Canal treaties was, by contrast, one of its most signal triumphs. Building on years of earlier negotiations between the United States and the Republic of Panama, the administration agreed to two treaties pertaining to the canal in September 1977. The heart of the agreements was the promise to give Panama full control of the canal by the year 2000. The treaties also provided for the immediate abolition of the canal zone and for the transformation of the canal into an international waterway, with U.S. and Panamanian ships having priority of use in times of emergency and war. A long and acrimonious debate followed the president's submission of the treaties to the Senate for ratification. Led by Carter himself, the administration worked hard to rally support for the agreements, which attracted bipartisan backing in the Senate and the endorsement of Gerald Ford, Henry Kissinger, and other influential leaders. President Carter argued that the treaties would strengthen U.S. security and trade opportunities as well as improve the American image abroad. Many Americans opposed the agreement, however. One Gallup poll showed 46 percent of the people opposed and only 39 percent in favor. Conservatives were especially critical, asserting that the treaties would jeopardize American security. The issue seemed less one of control of the Panama Canal than the alleged decline of America as a global power. In the end administration forces prevailed, though not until an amendment had been adopted giving the United States the right to use military force to defend the canal after it was turned over to Panama. Then, in March and April 1978, the two treaties were narrowly ratified by identical votes of 68 to 32.

Carter's most celebrated diplomatic achievement came in the Middle East, where efforts to secure a comprehensive peace had been deadlocked for three years following the truce in the Yom Kippur War. The United States was eager to restore peace and stability to this strategic region, to strengthen the position of such allies as

Israel and Iran, and to protect its future access to vital sources of petroleum. But the problems were formidable and intractable. They included the refusal of the Arab states to recognize the legitimacy of Israel; the disposition of Israeli-occupied territories resulting from the wars of 1967 and 1973, particularly the west bank of the Jordan River; and the insistence by the Palestine Liberation Organization and other militant groups on the return of all Arab territory and the creation of a permanent homeland for the Palestinian Arabs. Despite American efforts to follow the course set by Henry Kissinger's Middle East diplomacy, the impasse continued until the fall of 1977, when a ray of hope suddenly altered the gloomy outlook. President Anwar Sadat of Egypt, burdened with economic problems and anxious to strengthen his country's position, announced his willingness to visit Israel and enter into direct negotiations with Prime Minister Menachem Begin. After the two leaders held friendly discussions in Tel Aviv, they continued their negotiations in 1978, but without significant results. The talks eventually broke down, but President Carter, assuming the role of mediator, was able to persuade Begin and Sadat to resume their negotiations in the United States.

Meeting at Camp David for almost two weeks in September 1978, the two leaders responded to Carter's patient and persistent efforts

Menachem Begin, Jimmy Carter, and Anwar Sadat at Camp David (*courtesy the National Archives, Office of Presidential Libraries/Imagefinders, Inc.*)

by working out a tentative agreement. It seemed to be a momentous breakthrough. Begin and Sadat agreed to negotiate a separate treaty between their two countries and to initiate a "peace process" in which it was hoped other states might later join. Even so, the Camp David accords did not guarantee a definitive agreement, and it was not until Carter's dramatic journey to the Middle East early in 1979 that a treaty was finally accepted by the two sides. Begin and Sadat then returned to Washington, where they signed the formal treaty on March 26, 1979. The treaty provided for Egyptian recognition of Israel, for peace between the two nations, and for a phased Israeli withdrawal from the Sinai Peninsula. The agreement was less clear in dealing with the West Bank, calling for gradual self-government for West Bank Palestinians over a five-year period. That part of the treaty soon began to come unraveled. Although the treaty failed to touch on such crucial questions as the fate of the displaced Palestinians, it represented an important advance. It was Carter's most notable achievement.

In the Far East the Carter administration completed the establishment of diplomatic relations with the People's Republic of China, a process begun by Richard Nixon. The administration hoped that this step would encourage the Soviet Union to be more cooperative. An agreement between China and the United States was announced in December 1978, following months of secret negotiations. Relations between the two countries would be placed on a normal basis as of January 1, 1979. The United States promised to end diplomatic relations with Taiwan, to remove its troops from the island, and to abrogate its mutual defense treaty with the Taipei government within a year. While the Americans could continue to provide Taiwan with defensive weapons and could maintain cultural and trade relations, they accepted Peking's claim that Taiwan was a part of mainland China. Conservative critics, led by Senator Barry Goldwater, subjected the agreement to bitter attack, condemning Carter for the "betrayal" of an American ally. The president was able, nonetheless, to implement the treaty.

The outcome of Carter's relations with the Soviet Union was much less satisfactory. During its first year in office, the Carter administration followed a moderate approach in its dealings with the USSR. Seemingly eager to halt the arms race, the president ordered the immediate withdrawal of American nuclear weapons from South Korea and delayed approval of the B-1, a new manned bomber sought by the Air Force. He later announced a delay in the production of the neutron bomb, a weapon designed to make nuclear war more conceivable. Early in his tenure, Carter decided upon a "deep-cut" proposal in the arms-limitation talks, only to have the Russians summarily reject it. Negotiations were continued, however, and Secretary Vance and Foreign Minister Andrei Gromyko were finally able to work out a new strategic arms limitation treaty. It was signed by Carter and Brezhnev in Vienna in June 1979. SALT II set a limit of 2,400 long-range missiles and bombers on each side, to be reduced to 2,250 by 1981. Each country was limited to 1,320 MIRVed warheads and airborne cruise missiles.

SALT II encountered a barrage of criticism in the United States. Many liberals found it overly modest and predicted that it would do nothing to prevent the development of new destabilizing weapons systems. Conservatives argued that it would give the Russians a great advantage and that compliance would be impossible to verify. Carter, who had earlier ordered the construction of the intermediate-range cruise and Pershing II missiles, soon authorized a new missile system—the MX—to be housed in a vast complex of underground tunnels. Under the influence of Brzezinski, Carter was increasingly disturbed by the Soviet Union's military buildup, by its export of arms and technicians to Third World countries, and by the threat it posed in the Middle East and Africa. In Africa Ambassador Andrew Young and other American spokesmen had attempted to pursue a policy based on more than opposition to the USSR and to encourage the survival of independent black regimes. Yet the Soviet-Cuban presence was both expansive and mischievous, including activities in strategic areas like the Horn of Africa. The U.S. State Department announced in the spring of 1978, for instance, that Fidel Castro was maintaining 37,000 military personnel in twenty African countries.

President Carter gradually adopted a tougher and more aggressive posture toward the Russians. Speaking at the Naval Academy in June 1978, he bluntly declared, "The Soviet Union can choose either confrontation or cooperation. The United States is adequately prepared to meet either choice." One consequence of the president's growing suspicion of and hostility toward the Soviets was the loss of support for SALT II, whose ratification appeared increasingly problematic. Meanwhile, Carter called for a significant increase in the military budget for fiscal 1979, the strengthening of NATO forces, and development of the neutron bomb. Notwithstanding the administration's human rights rhetoric, Panama Canal treaties, Camp David accords, and normalization of relations with the People's Republic of China, it had apparently come around to a reaffirmation of the cold war strategy of containment.

YEARS OF TROUBLE: 1979–80

Things went from bad to worse for Jimmy Carter, who was almost overwhelmed by a plethora of new and perplexing problems in 1979

President Carter's Approval Rating in the Gallup Poll

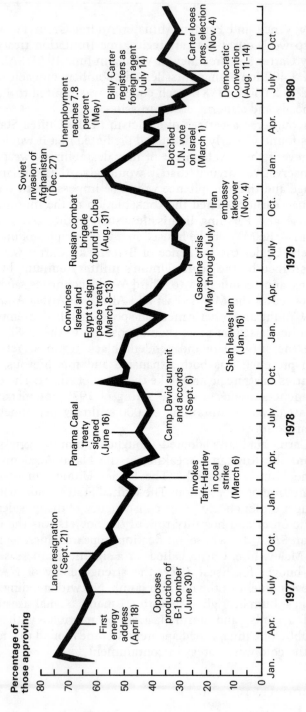

Percentage of those approving

First energy address (April 18)

Lance resignation (Sept. 21)

Opposes production of B-1 bomber (June 30)

Panama Canal treaty signed (June 16)

Invokes Taft-Hartley in coal strike (March 6)

Camp David summit and accords (Sept. 6)

Convinces Israel and Egypt to sign peace treaty (March 8-13)

Shah leaves Iran (Jan. 16)

Russian combat brigade found in Cuba (Aug. 31)

Gasoline crisis (May through July)

Soviet invasion of Afghanistan (Dec. 27)

Iran embassy takeover (Nov. 4)

Botched U.N. vote on Israel (March 1)

Unemployment reaches 7.8 percent (May)

Billy Carter registers as foreign agent (July 14)

Democratic Convention (Aug. 11-14)

Carter loses pres. election (Nov. 4)

1977   1978   1979   1980

The president's popularity is measured in the Gallup Poll by asking the question: "Do you approve or disapprove of the way Carter is handling his job as president?" Shown above are the percentages of those who approve.

Source: Congressional Quarterly, Inc., *President Carter, 1980* (Washington, DC, 1981), p. 3.

and 1980. Tension mounted between the United States and the Soviet Union. At home the economy was in serious trouble. In the spring of 1979 the index of leading economic indicators dropped more than 3 percent, automobile sales and new housing starts declined, and evidence accumulated that the country was moving into a new recession. The situation was exacerbated by rising inflation, which reached 10 percent in 1979 and kept climbing. Interest rates were at record heights. Nor was that the end of it. Another energy crisis threatened to paralyze the United States in the spring and summer of 1979. President Carter tried to respond effectively to these vicissitudes, but his leadership seemed less and less adequate, while his approval rating plunged to 25 percent, lower even than that of Richard Nixon during the controversy over Watergate.

The new energy crisis highlighted the woes of the Carter administration. The crisis was precipitated by a worldwide shortfall in oil production, resulting in part from a revolution in Iran, and the heavy American dependence on foreign sources. Despite the president's earnest efforts to lessen this dependence, the United States was importing about 9 million barrels of oil a day by 1979. Declining production led the Organization of Petroleum Exporting Countries (OPEC) to raise prices, and the effect was quickly felt by Americans. Gasoline prices rose sharply, approaching a dollar a gallon within a few weeks, and shortages in some parts of the country resulted in long lines of motorists at service stations. Some localities witnessed displays of anger, frustration, and near-panic. In April 1979 Carter recommended several long-term measures as a means of hastening American self-sufficiency in energy, but Congress took no immediate action. One of the proposed remedies for the energy problem was greater use of nuclear power. But many Americans had begun to have second thoughts about that alternative following a frightening accident in March at the nuclear power plant at Three Mile Island, near Harrisburg, Pennsylvania.[3] A catastrophe was averted, but the consequences of a possible meltdown of the reactor core and the emission of large amounts of radioactive gas were almost too horrible to contemplate.

As the energy crisis deepened, Carter searched for a way to resolve it. He decided to deliver a nationwide television address on energy in early July. Then he canceled that address and spent several days at his Camp David retreat talking with a cross section of American leaders about the nation's problems. On the evening of July 15, the chief executive attempted to explain his position and to inspire support among the mass of American people. An estimated 100 million people heard his speech. Acknowledging his own mistakes, Carter made a moving appeal for cooperation and assistance. He quoted a southern governor who had said to him, "Mr. President, you're not leading this nation, you're just managing the Government." America's problems, Carter declared, were all rooted in an underlying "crisis of confidence," which was threatening to destroy the nation's social and political fabric. "For the first time in the history of our country," Carter said, "a majority of our people believe that the next five years will be worse than the past five years. Two-thirds of our people do not even vote. The productivity of American workers is actually dropping and the willingness of Americans to save for the future has fallen below that of all other people in the Western world."

The more substantive part of Carter's address laid out the details of a new energy plan. The president announced a freeze on imports of petroleum at a maximum level of 8.5 million barrels a day, and he expressed the hope that oil imports could be cut in half by 1990. He stressed the need for increased domestic production through the construction of new and safer nuclear plants, a giant "solar energy bank" to promote the use of solar energy in commercial buildings and private homes, and the rapid development of synthetic fuels. Carter renewed his call for the deregulation of domestic oil and natural gas and for a windfall profits tax. A few days later he reorganized his Cabinet by replacing Blumenthal, Califano, and Secretary of Energy James Schlesinger. While the initial reaction to the president's address was favorable, Congress showed little disposition to approve his energy recommendations.[4] Carter's popularity soon dropped once more. Clearly he had failed to restore the confidence of the American people in his leadership.

An even more frustrating problem suddenly confronted the Carter administration in the fall of 1979. It began with the abrupt, drastic change in the role of Iran as policeman of the Persian Gulf, brought about by the collapse of the shah's regime in January 1979 and an Islamic revolution led by a revered holy man, Ayatollah Ruhollah Khomeini. The United States had relied on the shah as a source of stability, an opponent of communism, and a voice of moderation in OPEC. But the shah was identified with the American CIA, which had saved his throne in 1953 and had trained SAVAK, his secret police. The Ayatollah Khomeini was virulently hostile to America, which he described as the "great Satan" behind the wicked shah. When the former Iranian ruler, suffering from incurable cancer, was allowed to enter the United States for surgery in October 1979, it produced mobs on the streets of Teheran shouting anti-American slogans. On November 4, a crowd of about 400 "students" rushed the U.S. embassy in the Iranian capital and took over the building and 66 American diplomatic personnel and visitors. They demanded that the shah be returned for trial or the hostages would be held indefinitely, or even tried as American spies.[5]

Since the United States was neither willing nor able to force the return of the shah, it found itself in a cruel dilemma. Its options were few. The president appealed to the United Nations, protesting the violation of diplomatic immunity and international law in the holding of the American hostages. He suspended arms sales to Iran, froze Iranian assets in U.S. banks, announced an embargo on Iranian oil, and sought without much success to persuade American allies to join him in a trade embargo. He threatened to deport the 50,000 Iranian students in the United States. The chief executive also ordered a contingency plan for military action to rescue the hostages. But nothing worked, in part because of the unstable situation in Iran and the difficulty of finding a responsible party with whom to negotiate. American leaders wanted at all costs to avoid sacrificing the lives of the captives.

In December 1979, soon after the beginning of the hostage crisis, the Soviet Union sent an army into the ostensibly neutral state of Afghanistan. This mountainous buffer country between Pakistan and the USSR had been controlled by a pro-Communist government, which was threatened by a Muslim-based, anti-Communist opposition. Carter, unable to express his wrath publicly over the hostage situation, strongly condemned this Soviet use of military power, which he called "the greatest threat to peace since the Second World War." Carter offered military and economic aid to Pakistan, suspended the shipment of grain to Russia, outlawed the export of high-technology equipment to countries behind the Iron Curtain, and called for a boycott of the summer Olympics in Moscow. He ordered the Sixth Fleet to the eastern Mediterranean, alerted U.S. units in Turkey, and recommended a crash program to create a Rapid Deployment Force for action in the Persian Gulf. He also decided to withdraw SALT II from further Senate ratification consideration. Fearing that the Soviet Union would exploit the unstable situation in Iran to cut off the flow of Persian Gulf oil to the West, the president soon enunciated the Carter Doctrine: "An attempt by any outside force to gain control of the Persian Gulf region will be regarded as an assault on the vital interests of the United States of America, and such an assault will be repelled by any means necessary, including military force."

The crisis over the American hostages in Iran dominated the foreign affairs agenda of the Carter administration for the last fourteen months of its tenure. Carter himself was almost consumed by the crisis. He met repeatedly with the families of the hostages and refused to participate in the Democratic preconvention campaign on the ground that he needed to devote full time to the problem. Meanwhile, the American people, daily assaulted by media coverage of the hostage question, were baffled and outraged. It was difficult for the State Department to negotiate with the Iranian government, whose demands seemed to include the return of the shah for trial, the repatriation of his wealth to the Iranian people, admission of guilt and an apology by the United States for its past actions in Iran, and an American promise not to interfere in Iranian affairs in the future. For a moment in the early spring of 1980, the administration thought it had worked out an agreement with President Abol-Hassan Bani-Sadr, but it proved ephemeral. Carter finally approved a military operation to rescue the hostages in late April. Poorly planned and botched in its execution, the rescue mission failed.[6] The crisis continued week after week. Not even the shah's death, in July 1980, brought an end to the ordeal. Meanwhile, Carter was placed at a great disadvantage in his campaign for reelection.

THE REPUDIATION OF A PRESIDENT: 1980

Senator Edward Kennedy challenged President Carter's renomination in 1980, and for a time the Massachusetts senator led the president in the polls. Kennedy portrayed Carter as a weak and ineffectual leader who had abandoned the Democratic party's tradition of domestic reformism and was unable to forge a successful foreign policy. Carter defended his policies but refused to engage in an active preconvention campaign, electing to foster the impression of a chief executive fully preoccupied with urgent national problems. In the end this tactic seemed to work, for Carter won a series of preferential primaries and thus turned back the Kennedy challenge. The Democratic National Convention then renominated the Carter-Mondale ticket.

The Republicans, sensing victory, began their search for a presidential nominee with a more open field. Gerald Ford disclaimed interest in the nomination, but several other Republican leaders entered the race. Among these aspirants were two senators, Howard Baker of Tennessee and Robert Dole of Kansas; George Bush of Texas, a former director of the CIA and one-time ambassador to the United Nations; and Ronald Reagan, an ex-governor of California who had come close to winning the GOP nomination in 1976. This time the Californian was successful, and he chose Bush as his running mate. The conservative Reagan provided a sharp contrast to Carter. He urged a reduction of federal spending and promised to "take government off the backs of the people." He blamed the Carter administration for the nation's economic doldrums and accused it of weakening the national defense and allowing the Soviet Union to achieve an advantage in strategic striking power.

When the campaign between Carter and Reagan got under way after Labor Day, the president, as one historian has remarked, was widely perceived as "having gone from blunder to blunder." He remained on the defensive throughout the campaign, buffeted by a faltering economy, deteriorating relations with the Soviet Union, and the humiliating hostage crisis, which seemed to symbolize the bankruptcy of the president's leadership. The worsening economy seriously weakened Carter's reelection chances. By the first part of 1980, inflation had skyrocketed to a quarterly rate of 20 percent, interest rates were climbing in the wake of the Federal Reserve System's tight-money policy, and unemployment was rising, approaching 8 percent before the election.

The Reagan campaign was quick to place the blame for these trends on the Carter administration. Reagan kept referring to the "misery index"—the combined inflation and unemployment rates. Republican speakers also stressed Reagan's record as governor of California and his success in attracting "good people" to work in his administration. Carter's campaign was complicated by the independent candidacy of Representative John B. Anderson of Illinois, an unsuccessful candidate for the Republican nomination earlier in the year. Anderson's campaign threatened to deprive the president of millions of votes.

Reeling under the barbs of his GOP opponents, Carter struck back. Reagan's election, he warned, would result in the undoing of hard-won domestic reforms and would favor the rich at the expense of the poor and elderly. The Democratic leader accused the Republican nominee of offering simplistic solutions to complex problems, and he suggested that Reagan was a warmonger. Republican attacks on the administration's defense policies no doubt influenced Carter's decision to request supplementary appropriations for the Pentagon, to announce an agreement with NATO to deploy nearly 600 medium-range cruise and Pershing missiles in Europe in the early 1980s, and to issue Presidential Directive 59, introducing greater flexibility in the nation's nuclear-deterrence doctrine. The president had earlier secured congressional approval of a new military draft registration. Near the end of the campaign, the two major contestants met in a well-publicized television debate. A rather somber and defiant Carter lashed out at his challenger, while a smiling and confident Reagan easily parried the president's attack. Turning to the millions of Americans watching the confrontation, the Republican rhetorically asked, "Are you better off now than you were four years ago?"

The televised debate gave added momentum to the Reagan campaign, and the election results in early November swept Carter from office. In an election that brought the lowest U.S. turnout in the twentieth century, Reagan received 43.9 million popular votes (51 percent) to 35.5 million (41 percent) for Carter. The vote in the electoral college was an overwhelming 489 to 49, with Carter winning only six states. Anderson had 5.7 million votes, about 7 percent of the total. The Republicans did especially well in the South and West. To their delight, they won control of the Senate for the first time in a quarter-century and made sizable gains in the House of Representative contests.[7] Among the defeated Democrats were such prominent liberals as George McGovern, Frank Church, Birch Bayh, and John Brademas.

Reagan proved to be a skillful campaigner. The incumbent president's image as a weak and luckless leader played into Reagan's hands, and the persistence of the hostage crisis seriously damaged Carter's chances of reelection.[8] But the state of the economy, particularly the rising cost of living, was the chief obstacle to the Democratic president's bid for a second term. The Republicans conducted a unified and well-organized campaign, in contrast to the Democrats' loosely organized and poorly integrated campaign. The re-

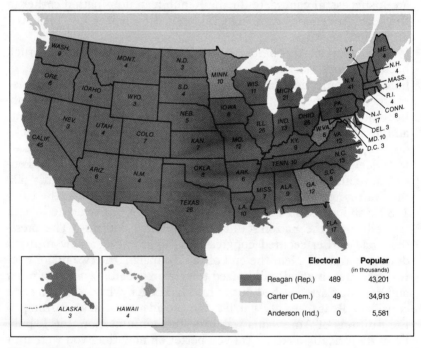

	Electoral	Popular (in thousands)
Reagan (Rep.)	489	43,201
Carter (Dem.)	49	34,913
Anderson (Ind.)	0	5,581

The Election of 1980

turns represented an unmistakable repudiation of the thirty-ninth president's leadership. Some observers thought the election signified a shift in party realignment, the end of the New Deal coalition, and the beginning of a new era of Republican control. Others questioned this interpretation. A *New York Times*–CBS poll, for example, suggested that the electorate had hardly made "a clear move to the right," noting that there was still "strong public support for a substantial government role in economic matters and for a variety of government programs in health care and education." Much of Carter's difficulty on election day, the historian William E. Leuchtenburg concludes, "came not from being too liberal but from being so little in the image of FDR that millions in the Roosevelt coalition did not go to the polls and many others were so uninspired that they did nothing in the campaign save cast a dutiful vote."

Few American presidents have worked harder or sought more exalted objectives than the man from Georgia. His administration was not without accomplishment, particularly in the realm of foreign affairs, most notably in the Panama Canal treaties and the Camp David accords. Carter was confronted by a number of unusually perplexing problems in a period in which political consensus was noticeably lacking. Ironically, while Carter was a product of Watergate, that controversy and other developments were undermining the concept of the presidency described by one writer as "activist, innovative, and the single source for creative national social reforms." Thus Carter found himself limited by a resurgent Congress, a more critical press, and a more suspicious public. The Georgian himself was at fault. He made too many promises, tried to do too much at once, waited too long to develop a clear set of priorities, and was too self-righteous and insensitive in dealing with Congress. His ability to inspire the people—to enlighten and to lead—was limited. Yet he was a leader who possessed admirable qualities as well. Like Herbert Hoover, a president he resembled in many ways, Jimmy Carter was in a sense overtaken by events. One of those events was the rising tide of conservatism in America.

NOTES

1. Congressional Quarterly, Inc., *President Carter, 1980* (1981), p. 2.
2. In the Ninety-fifth Congress (1977–78), the party division in the House favored the Democrats 292 to 143, while the Democratic margin in the Senate was 62 to 38. The Republicans made only modest gains in the midterm elections of 1978: 12 seats in the House and 3 in the Senate.
3. A combination of faulty equipment and inadequate safety provisions caused the radioactive core of the plant to overheat, coming dangerously close to a meltdown.

4. In March 1980 Carter proposed, as part of an anti-inflation program, an import fee of $4.62 per barrel on foreign oil. This would have resulted in higher gasoline prices for motorists. But Congress killed the scheme, handing the president a major defeat.

5. Thirteen of the captives—blacks and women—were released later in November. Another was released in July 1980 because of an undiagnosed illness.

6. The mission, undertaken by a commando team, was aborted in the Iranian desert because of equipment failures. Eight Americans were killed in an accident that occurred as the rescue team was about to leave the area.

7. The party lineup in the Ninety-seventh Congress (1981–82) would be 53 Republicans, 46 Democrats, and 1 Independent in the Senate. In the House the Democrats had a majority, 243 to 192.

8. A breakthrough in the U.S.-Iranian impasse over the hostages did not come until shortly before Reagan's inauguration. An agreement was finally worked out in the last days of the Carter administration providing that the United States would return the $8 billion of frozen Iranian assets in exchange for the release of the 52 hostages. The United States paid no ransom and made no apologies for past misconduct. The agreement, which came too late to help Carter politically, did offer him a measure of vindication.

SUGGESTIONS FOR FURTHER READING

Jimmy Carter and his presidency still await convincing treatment. Many of the works on Carter are flawed by an uncritical approach or excessive animosity toward him. The following books are helpful but should be used with caution: Betty Glad, *Jimmy Carter: In Search of the Great White House* (1980); James T. Wooten, *Dasher: The Roots and the Rising of Jimmy Carter* (1978); William Lee Miller, *Yankee from Georgia: The Emergence of Jimmy Carter* (1978); Victor Lasky, *Jimmy Carter: The Man and the Myth* (1979); and Haynes Johnson, *In the Absence of Power: Governing America* (1980). Numan V. Bartley, "Jimmy Carter and the Politics of the New South," *Forum Series* (1979), is a perceptive essay on the Georgian's political roots and emergence. Gary M. Fink, *Prelude to the Presidency: The Political Character and Legislative Leadership Style of Governor Jimmy Carter* (1980), is a scholarly monograph on Carter's governorship. For Carter's own ideas and statements see, in addition to the appropriate volumes of *Public Papers of the Presidents*, the Georgian's *Why Not the Best?* (1977) and *Keeping Faith: The Memoirs of a President* (1982).

Several books deal with the electoral politics of 1976 and 1980. See in particular Jules Witcover, *Marathon: The Pursuit of the Presidency, 1972–1976* (1977); Gerald Pomper (ed.), *The Election of 1980* (1981); and Theodore H. White, *America in Search of Itself: The Making of the President, 1956–1980* (1982). Other perspectives are provided by Martin Schram, *Running for President, 1976: The Carter Campaign* (1977); Kandy Stroud, *How Jimmy Won: The Victory Campaign from Plains to the White House* (1977); Austin Ranney, *The American Elections of 1980* (1981); Rowland Evans and Robert Novak, *The Reagan Revolution* (1981); Congressional Quarterly, Inc., *President Carter, 1980* (1981); and Elizabeth Drew, *American Journal: The Events of 1976* (1977), and *Portrait of an Election: The 1980 Presidential Campaign* (1981).

Various aspects of the Carter administration are discussed by Robert Shogan, *Promises to Keep: Carter's First Hundred Days* (1977); Joseph Califano, *On Governing America* (1981); Griffin Bell, *Taking Care of the Law* (1982); and Laurence Lynn and David Whiteman, *The President as Policymaker* (1981). The last of these is concerned with welfare reform.

The best study of Carter's foreign policy is Gaddis Smith's *Morality, Reason, and Power: American Diplomacy in the Carter Years* (1986). Briefer evaluations are contained in four previously cited books: Ambrose, *Rise to Globalism*; Gaddis, *Strategies of Containment*; LaFeber, *America, Russia, and the Cold War*; and Weisberger, *Cold War, Cold Peace*. Two useful personal accounts are Zbigniew Brzezinski, *Power and Principle: Memories of the National Security Adviser, 1977–1981* (1983), and Cyrus Vance, *Hard Choices* (1983). For the Middle East, see Steven L. Spiegel, *The Other Arab-Israeli Conflict: Making America's Middle East Policy From Truman to Reagan* (1985). The Panama Canal treaties are discussed by Walter LaFeber, *The Panama Canal* (1978), and George D. Moffett III, *The Limits of Victory: The Ratification of the Panama Canal Treaties* (1985). Strobe Talbott, *Endgame: The Inside Story of SALT II* (1979), is an absorbing account. Barry Rubin's *Paved with Good Intentions: The American Experience in Iran* (1980) is good on the background of the Iranian crisis. Other books on Iran and the hostage problem include John Stempel, *Inside the Iranian Revolution* (1981); Hamilton Jordan, *Crisis: The Last Year of the Carter Presidency* (1982); and Warren Christopher and others, *American Hostages in Iran: The Conduct of a Crisis* (1985).

CHAPTER SEVENTEEN

Ronald Reagan and the Revival of American Conservatism

WITH THE ELECTION of Ronald Reagan as the fortieth American president, the political landscape began to undergo a radical change. This was true not merely because of Reagan's Republicanism, but also because of his dedication to conservative principles. The new president came to office with a definite agenda, and he presented Congress and the public with a set of clear alternatives to established policies. Indeed, he proposed nothing less than a revolution in national policy—a drastic transformation in the role of the government at home and a sweeping change in its posture abroad. Reagan was successful in getting most of his domestic proposals through Congress, and despite the onset of a severe recession in 1981, a strong economic recovery was under way by late 1983. The administration's international initiatives, less certain and more controversial than its domestic proposals, resulted in few noteworthy achievements during Reagan's first term, aside from a substantial increase in the nation's defense forces. Yet the Californian became the best-liked chief executive since Dwight Eisenhower, and he was overwhelmingly reelected in 1984. It was obvious that he had become the dominant figure in American politics. But how extensive and how durable his politics and policies would be remained problematic in the mid-1980s.

SPOKESMAN FOR NEOCONSERVATISM

Ronald Reagan was born in 1911 and reared in a succession of small northern Illinois towns. He attended Eureka College, a denominational school near Peoria. Growing up in this environment, he was strongly influenced by traditional ideas about freedom, hard work, and morality. But his development was shaped even more power- fully by the modern consumer culture, and especially by what one of his biographers describes as "the new ethos of entertainment and pleasure." Following his graduation from college, he began work as a radio announcer, spending five years as a sports announcer for station WHO in Des Moines, Iowa. In 1937 he went to Hollywood, where initiative and luck gave him an opportunity as an actor. Rea- gan made a series of grade B movies during following years, the best of which was probably *King's Row* in 1941. One of his fifty-three films was *The Knute Rockne Story*, in which he played the part of George Gipp and gained a certain notoriety as "the Gipper." While preferring action pictures and the role of a successful "good guy," however, he seldom seems to have got the girl!

By the late 1940s, Reagan's acting career appeared to be at a stand- still, his first marriage had ended in divorce, and he was becoming increasingly interested in public affairs and politics. He had become active in the Screen Actors Guild and would soon serve as its pres- ident and take the lead in a campaign to prevent Communists from gaining control of the organization. He had not been a conservative in the 1930s and 1940s. In fact, he came from a Democratic family, was a supporter of the New Deal, and admired Franklin D. Roose- velt, for whom he had voted. In 1947 he helped organize the Cali- fornia branch of the Americans for Democratic Action and in 1950 backed Helen Gahagan Douglas in her campaign against Richard Nixon for the United States Senate. Reagan later explained his de- fection from the Democratic party by saying, "I didn't desert my party. It deserted me."

The Californian's political orientation changed in the 1950s. His ideological shift was encouraged by his experience in working for the General Electric Corporation during the years 1954–1962. In addition to serving as the host of a television series sponsored by GE, he traveled widely over the country, promoting the company's interests, meeting with its employees, and making hundreds of speeches. In these talks he increasingly attacked collectivism and centralization in Washington. By the early 1960s, Reagan had be- come identified as a conservative Republican. In 1964 he was an ardent supporter of Barry Goldwater's nomination and election, speaking for him in the party's national convention and delivering a national television address in his behalf near the end of the cam- paign. Reagan soon began to emerge as a new hero of the Republi- can right. "Although he was as fully committed to the ideas and assumptions that animated Goldwater," Robert Dallek writes, "he was a more flexible, accommodating, and ingratiating personality

with whom great numbers of middle-class citizens could identify."
Two years later Reagan was elected governor of California, winning
reelection in 1970. While maintaining his commitment to conservative principles, he demonstrated a capacity to compromise and to
adjust to political realities. He made a tentative bid for the GOP
presidential nomination as early as 1968, when he showed impressive strength in the South, and in 1976 he almost succeeded in taking the nomination from President Ford.

Just as Jimmy Carter was, in large part, the product of the Watergate crisis, so was Ronald Reagan the beneficiary of a resurgent conservatism in the 1970s and 1980s. This conservative renewal had
begun to manifest itself in the Nixon administration. As Alonzo L.
Hamby has written:

> The Nixon policies had considerable strength and appeal independent of
> the man who had adopted them. Their survival and ultimate resurgence
> were all but assured by the major themes of the post-Nixon seventies:
> the decline of the party system, the retreat of economic growth, the fail-
> ure of liberalism to address the nation's problems convincingly, and a
> vacuum of political leadership unparalleled in contemporary American
> history.

Many people had become critical of the "failure" of an expanded
welfare system, of affirmative action programs, and of a rise in
crime they tended to associate with an indulgent liberalism. The
writer Robert Heilbroner called attention in 1974, for instance, to
"a recrudescence of an intellectual conservatism that looks askance
at the possibilities for large-scale social engineering, stressing
the innumerable cases . . . in which the consequences of well-
intentioned acts have only given rise to other, sometimes more formidable problems than those they had set out to cure."

Demographic forces contributed to this rising tide of conservatism, particularly the large increase in the older population in the
1970s and the growth of the Sunbelt states of the South and West.
These developments enhanced the political and economic power of
regions that were already hostile to "big government." The revival
of evangelical religion in the seventies also strengthened the conservative movement in the United States. One survey in 1977 revealed that more than 70 million Americans considered themselves
"born-again" Christians who had "a direct personal relationship
with Jesus." The more powerful evangelical groups owned their own
radio and television stations and operated their own schools and
universities. The Reverend Jerry Falwell's Moral Majority spoke for
most of the "religious right" in its fervent support of free enterprise
and opposition to big government and international communism

and in its demand for prayer in the public schools, anti-abortion laws, and harsher treatment of criminals. A majority of these evangelical Christians became enthusiastic backers of Reagan.

The conservative revival, in turn, owed a good deal to Ronald Reagan. He brought its loose strands together into the semblance of a whole, gave it greater respectability, and provided it with a sounding board in the White House. Reagan's emergence as a successful politician was not solely the result of a revitalized conservatism. His own personal qualities were important. Although the oldest man, at sixty-nine, ever to be elected president, he was physically fit, was extraordinarily personable, and had a ready smile and a quick wit. He was, in the words of one historian, "at ease with the members of the working press and with all the paraphernalia of mass communications. The camera, the microphone, the sincere appearance, the well-delivered lines were the tools of his trade."[1] The Californian had a magnetic stage presence, and he was remarkably effective in projecting himself over radio and television. He came to Washington after eight years of experience as governor of the nation's most populous state, and in that position he had been adept at focusing on moral or symbolic issues without being perceived as a right-wing ideologue.

DOMESTIC POLICIES: GETTING BACK TO BASICS

At the outset, the Reagan administration concentrated on the economy. The cost of living had increased by more than 12 percent in 1980, unemployment had risen to 7.4 percent, the prime lending rate was an astonishing 20 percent, and the government was facing a projected budget deficit of $56 billion. "In this present crisis," Reagan said in his inaugural address, "government is not the solution to our problem; government is the problem." It was time, the new president declared, "to reawaken this industrial giant, to get government back within its means and to lighten our punitive tax burden." Reagan's solution to the nation's economic problems was one he had long urged—the reduction of the power and control of the federal government and the expansion of the freedom of individuals and private enterprise.

Reagan proposed a comprehensive four-point program consisting of reductions in taxes and in the growth of government spending, elimination of unnecessary regulations, and a policy of monetary restraint to slow down the rate of inflation. He asked Congress to cut direct federal spending by $41.4 billion in fiscal 1982. Social security and Medicare payments would not be reduced, and the administration insisted that an adequate "social safety net" would be assured for the poverty-stricken, the disabled, and the elderly. The heart of the president's program was a 30 percent reduction in both personal and corporate income taxes over the next three years. This proposal was based on supply-side economics, a set of ideas identified with Professor Arthur Laffer of the University of Southern California. Supply-siders argued that very large tax cuts constituted a painless way to eliminate budget deficits and achieve prosperity. Reagan and his advisers reasoned that the tax cuts—by increasing the incentives of individuals and businesses to work, save, and invest—would greatly stimulate economic growth so that, even with much lower tax rates, tax revenues would actually rise, deficits would narrow, and a balanced budget could be reached during Reagan's first term.

Most economists were dubious about "Reaganomics," and Senator Howard Baker, the Senate majority leader, who helped get the measure through the upper house, called it a "riverboat gamble." But public reaction was extremely favorable, and Congress was in no mood to sidetrack the administration's economic proposals. The lawmakers began by considering the Reagan budget, which included large increases for military spending and substantial reductions in social services and welfare benefits. Reagan and his tough-minded budget director, David A. Stockman, pushed hard for these reductions, which were strongly criticized by many liberals. Thus Benjamin Hooks of the NAACP predicted that they would bring new "hardship, havoc, despair, pain, and suffering on blacks and other minorities." But the administration prevailed, with the aid of a large number of conservative southern Democrats in the House of Representatives who were dubbed "boll weevils." Reagan won an even more impressive victory when Congress passed a $280 billion tax-cut bill. The administration had made only a slight concession by lowering the first year's reduction to 5 percent, to be followed by a 10 percent decrease in each of the next two years. By the summer of 1981, the president's entire package of economic proposals had been enacted without major modification.

Congress was less responsive in 1981 to several administration recommendations to strengthen the social security system, whose trust fund reserves were declining at an alarming rate. When Congress refused to go along with the administration's solution, Reagan appointed a bipartisan commission to study the problem. The Social Security Commission, headed by the economist Alan Greenspan, submitted its report late in 1982. The commission recommended a series of reforms in the system. Congress approved most of these recommendations in March 1983. Designed to guarantee

President Reagan holds a press conference (*Michael Evans, the White House*)

the solvency of the social security trust funds, the legislation provided for the future raising of the basic retirement age from sixty-five to sixty-seven, for a six-month delay in the next cost-of-living increase, and for the taxing of benefits paid to the well to do.

In its efforts to deregulate the private sector and to restrict the federal bureaucracy, the Reagan administration relied on administrative appointments and procedures. Reagan immediately ended all price controls on gasoline and crude oil. Secretary of Transportation Drew Lewis moved to aid U.S. automobile manufacturers by giving them tax breaks and reduced regulation. Secretary of Energy James Edwards denied the existence of a fuel crisis and looked toward dismantling his own department. Under the Reagan administration the size and influence of the Department of Education and the Department of Health and Human Services were reduced. Anne Gorsuch Burford, head of the Environmental Protection Agency, was an uncompromising opponent of federal regulation, as were other high-level Reagan officials. The most controversial of these administrators was Secretary of the Interior James G. Watt, who had earlier headed a political lobby that favored exploiting the public domain. Watt seemed bent on reversing the conservation gains of the past two decades. He opened federal lands to coal and timber production, narrowed the scope of the wilderness preserves, and sought to make a million acres of offshore potential oil lands available for drilling. Watt's policies and provocative public statements kept him in the middle of controversy until he finally resigned in 1983.

Despite its conservative rhetoric, the Reagan presidency was not immediately successful in advancing its social philosophy in such areas as restricting abortions, outlawing busing and affirmative action, providing federal support for private and parochial education, and making possible prayer in the public schools. Congress and the courts were not as cooperative in this regard as they might have been, and Reagan himself appeared reluctant to wage an all-out battle in areas that might prove divisive and politically dangerous. Still, the administration was not inactive on some of these fronts. For example, it attacked the Internal Revenue Service's policy of denying tax-exempt status to private schools that discriminated on the basis of race. It was not disposed to support an extension of the 1965 Voting Rights Act, though it finally endorsed a revised version of the law. The president enjoyed a notable triumph when he appointed the first woman—the conservative Sandra Day O'Connor—to the Supreme Court, thereby bringing together conservative and liberal symbols.

Meanwhile, Reagan's restorative economic measures had not worked, at least in the short run. Indeed, a serious recession was in progress by the end of 1981, brought on by the administration's tight monetary policy. In 1982 unemployment increased to more than 10 percent, and the budget deficit was estimated at $110 billion. The downturn finally induced the president to approve an increase in business and excise taxes—"a down payment on the deficits." But Reagan continued to insist that his economic policies would ultimately work. The recession did bring inflation under control, with the inflation rate dropping from 12 percent in 1980 to 3.5 percent in 1984.[2] But the process was painful: nearly two years of recession, a record number of bankruptcies, and unemployment approaching 11 percent of the work force. Recovery began in 1983, and by year's end the economy was in a buoyant state. The inflation rate was about 4 percent, the GNP increased an impressive 4.3 percent, and unemployment had declined to 8 percent. The administration naturally took credit for the recovery. The only gloomy aspect of this rosy picture was a projected budget deficit of almost $200 billion.

Foreign Policy and the Crusade
Against International Communism

"The organizing principle of Ronald Reagan's defense and foreign policies," Robert Dallek has written, "is anti-Sovietism—the need to confront and overcome the Soviet Communist danger in every part of the globe." Reagan's view of Soviet communism, Dallek notes, "unchanged since the 1950s, is of a ruthless, power-mad movement bent on the creation of a 'one-world Communist state' in which individuals and the traditional Western concepts of freedom and morality count for nothing." The Californian's obsession with the threat of international communism seemed to represent a global extension of his inner fears of government authority and social change and of his struggle to defend freedom and morality at home. In Reagan's eyes, the Soviet Union embodied the evils of overweening government, atheism, and a lack of moral standards. Like the Moral Majority and many other American conservatives, he saw anticommunism as "a crusade to restore traditional assumptions about God, family, and country to a central place in American life."[3] The other goal of this crusade was to thwart the Russians' determination to export their totalitarian system to all parts of the world. Most of the president's national security and foreign policy advisers shared these attitudes. Secretary of State Alexander Haig, his successor George Shultz, Secretary of Defense Caspar Weinberger, National Security Adviser Richard Allen, and Ambassador to the United Nations Jeane Kirkpatrick all had an exaggerated fear of Soviet power and control.

President Reagan and Secretary Haig adopted a firm anticommunist line from the beginning of the new administration; they used tough language in referring to the Soviet Union and demonstrated a taste for confrontation. Reagan characterized the Soviet leaders as men who "reserve unto themselves the right to commit any crime, to lie, to cheat." He insisted that the SALT II agreement would have to be revised before it could be ratified. He moved ahead to implement Carter's plans to base cruise and Pershing II missiles in Western Europe. Reagan emphasized, as he had during the campaign of 1980, the imperative need to expand American military forces to meet the Soviet threat. Charging that the Carter administration had allowed the Russians to gain strategic superiority over the United States, Reagan proposed the largest and most expensive peacetime military buildup in American history. He recommended a military program that would cost $136 billion in 1981–82 and almost a trillion dollars over five years. This massive program would include the development of nuclear weapons, the expansion of the surface fleet and of tactical airpower, the creation of a Rapid Deployment Force begun by Carter for possible use in the Near East and elsewhere, and much more. Reagan ordered the B-1 bomber into production and announced his decision to push ahead with the construction of the neutron bomb, which was "designed to kill as many people as a regular hydrogen bomb ten times its size, and yet cause less damage to nearby buildings." Although military spending had begun to go up during the Carter years, increasing 5 percent after Afghanistan, the buildup under Reagan was unprecedented in the post–World War II era. Congress agreed to virtually all of the president's defense proposals, authorizing 98 percent of his appropriation requests in 1981 and 96 percent in 1982.

In practice the Reagan administration discovered that it frequently had to bow to realities in dealing with the Soviet Union. While criticizing SALT II, Reagan observed the limits it imposed, as did his Russian counterpart. American wheat surpluses encouraged the president in April 1981 to lift Carter's embargo on grain shipments to the Soviet Union. In September 1983, the administration concluded the biggest grain sale in history to the USSR. By 1985 Reagan had abandoned nearly all of the restrictions on Russia instituted by Carter. When Soviet pressure in December 1981 caused Poland's Communist rulers to declare martial law, to outlaw the independent trade union Solidarity, and to imprison its leader Lech Walesa, Reagan had to content himself with verbal attacks on the Russians. In 1982 the president prohibited the sale of equipment by U.S. firms to the Soviet Union for the construction of a pipeline linking its natural gas wells with Western Europe. The United States eventually abandoned this embargo after its European allies registered strong protests. The intensifying arms race between the two superpowers encouraged the development of an antinuclear war movement in the United States and Europe. A nationwide poll in the spring of 1982 showed that 57 percent of the respondents favored an immediate freeze on the testing, production, and deployment of nuclear weapons. A bipartisan resolution in Congress urging such a freeze gathered strong support. By the spring of 1982, President Reagan began to respond to this pressure, declaring his commitment to arms control. He accepted a modest reduction in the defense increase for 1983, in part because of the recession. After the death of Leonid Brezhnev in November 1982, Reagan proposed an interim agreement limiting United States and Soviet medium-range missiles in Europe to a fixed and equal number of warheads. Nothing came of this ploy, however; the new Soviet leader, Yuri Andropov, rejected it because it would have forced the destruction of existing Russian missiles in exchange for proposed American ones.

Despite evidence from authoritative sources that the United States and the Soviet Union were roughly equal in their possession of land- and sea-based missile warheads and that the United States was ahead when aircraft weapons were counted, the Reagan administration pushed ahead with its military buildup. While the arms-limitation talks languished, the arms race went on. Reagan succeeded, after a long struggle, in getting congressional approval to begin production of the MX, with an understanding that there would be a new "basing mode." In the spring of 1983 Reagan, citing the continued growth of Soviet military power, called for a 10 percent increase in American defense appropriations for 1984. He proposed the development of a new "star-wars" technology that would make it possible for the United States to destroy enemy missiles in space.

The president's harsh estimate of the Soviet Union seemed to be confirmed in mid-September 1983, when a Russian jet fighter shot down a South Korean commercial plane that had strayed over Soviet territory in the western Pacific, killing 269 people, including 60 Americans. Insisting that the plane was on an American intelligence mission, Soviet leaders refused to accept any blame for its loss or to show any remorse. In November the United States began deploying Pershing and cruise missiles in Great Britain and West Germany, according to the NATO agreement of December 1979. In retaliation the Russians walked out of the arms-control talks, which had earlier been resumed by the two superpowers.

Meanwhile, the Reagan administration's anti-Communist obsession found a consuming focus in Central America and particularly in El Salvador and Nicaragua. Carter had decided in January 1981 to extend military aid to the government of El Salvador, which was being challenged by a leftist insurgency. Reagan and Haig claimed that the rebels in El Salvador were being supplied by Sandinista radicals in Nicaragua, and that the overthrow of the Nicaraguan dictator Anastasio Somoza in 1979 had been supported by the Soviet Union and Cuba. Haig described a Marxist plot to take over all of Central America. The administration feared that Nicaragua would become another Cuba, providing the Russians with both a military base and a center for the export of revolution to neighboring countries. Reagan and his advisers were also alarmed at the possibility that a Communist victory in Central America would lead to an outpouring of refugees from that region to the United States, exacerbating the problem of illegal immigrants at home.

The administration sent advisers and increasing amounts of military aid to the government of El Salvador in its continuing struggle against the rebel forces. Many Americans, remembering Vietnam, questioned the wisdom of U.S. involvement in Central America, and Congress, led by the Democratic-controlled House, forced the chief executive to certify periodically that the Salvadoran government was making progress in stamping out the so-called death squads and in safeguarding human rights. The administration insisted that progress was being made, and it hailed the holding of elections in El Salvador in March 1982. It was even more optimistic two years later when José Napoleon Duarte, a moderate, won the presidential election. In the meantime, the Reagan government was providing covert assistance to the counterrevolutionaries ("contras") against the Sandinista government of Nicaragua, which American leaders held responsible for the civil war in El Salvador. Equipment, training, and financial support were provided to the contras through the CIA.

Mounting criticism of his Central American policy led the president, in the autumn of 1983, to appoint a bipartisan blue-ribbon commission to "investigate" the entire Caribbean situation and recommend a course of action. Henry Kissinger was named to head the commission, which presented its report in February 1984. The report acknowledged the vital need for long-term social and economic reforms in the region and proposed $8.5 billion in aid over the following three years. But it also called for a "significantly larger program of military assistance," since the Soviet Union and Cuba were said to be the hidden forces behind Nicaragua and the El Salvadoran guerrillas. In late October 1983, the Reagan administration had received another boost when it sent a military force to invade the independent island of Grenada (a British Commonwealth nation). A left-wing coup resulting in the death of the prime minister and other officials brought the American invasion and a speedy restoration of order. The administration claimed that its gunboat diplomacy was necessary in order to protect American civilians, including hundreds of medical students on the island, and because Barbados and Jamaica had asked the United States to intervene. Actually, Reagan and his advisers were motivated in large part by anti-Communist considerations. They had become deeply suspicious of the existing government of Grenada, since it had permitted Cuban construction workers to build an airfield on the island and had signed military agreements with Communist bloc countries. In any case, the American people, recalling the humiliation of the Iranian hostage episode, applauded the administration's display of military muscle in the Caribbean.

American preoccupation with what the French call *mal soviétique* was similarly evident in the Middle East during the early 1980s. Determined to contain the Soviet threat in that region, the Reagan administration attempted to revive the Camp David peace process as a means of stabilizing conditions in the area. It had little success in those efforts. After mid-1982, U.S. policy in the Middle East was dominated by an escalating crisis in Lebanon. The problem in that small nation was that no single force was able to control the country. Christian and Moslem factions struggled for supremacy, while Syrian troops occupied the northern section of the country and the Palestinian Liberation Organization had established itself in the southern portion, facing the Israeli border. This volatile situation led the Israelis to invade Lebanon in early June 1982 in order to crush the PLO. The Israeli troops drove northward and then besieged West Beirut, where refugee camps held thousands of Palestinians and provided a base for PLO soldiers. The United States managed during the next few weeks to work out an agreement for the peaceful evacuation of Yasser Arafat and his PLO forces, and Reagan soon announced that he was sending 800 Marines to Lebanon as part of an international peacekeeping force.

What was originally planned as a thirty-day stay by the Marines lasted for a year and a half. The United States tried to produce agreements among the contending Lebanese factions, but this proved impossible, and it began to seem that the U.S. Marines were really trying to stabilize the new government led by the Christian Amin Gemayel, whose government was opposed by the Shiite Moslems and several other groups. The peacekeeping forces thus found themselves caught in the cross fire of the civil war. Meanwhile, the United States tried without success to persuade Israel and Syria to agree to a mutual withdrawal of forces. Back home Reagan was subjected to growing criticism by Congress, which questioned his authority to keep troops in Lebanon, and by the public, which was hard put to understand the American purpose in the strife-ridden country. These doubts were heightened on October 23, 1983, when a truck loaded with explosives crashed through a security post and exploded inside a Marine barracks, killing 241 sleeping men. Reagan refused to get out of Lebanon in spite of the outcry that followed this tragedy. Not until early the next year did he finally order the withdrawal of American troops from Lebanon. The Middle East problem remained as intractable as ever.

As the presidential election campaign of 1984 approached, Ronald Reagan could claim a number of successes in the domestic arena, and he had reversed the post-Watergate decline in presidential power. But his foreign policies had fared less well, although he could point to a dramatic increase in America's military strength and a strategic balance with the Soviet Union. In the process, however, he had given impetus to the nuclear-arms race. Nevertheless, in February 1984 there was talk of resuming Soviet-American arms negotiations, or even of a summit meeting, prompted by the accession of a new Soviet leader, Konstantin Chernenko, and the fact that President Reagan would soon be involved in a campaign for reelection.

THE PRESIDENTIAL LANDSLIDE OF 1984:
A CONSERVATIVE TRIUMPH?

Ronald Reagan's reelection prospects looked good during the early months of 1984. Economic recovery was in full swing, foreign affairs had assumed a less hazardous outlook, and the president's popularity remained gratifyingly high. Reagan dominated the Republican party, which was strongly united in support of his reelection. When the GOP convention assembled in Dallas, Reagan and Bush were renominated without opposition.

The road to the Democratic nomination was, in comparison, long and difficult. One of the early developments in the nomination process was the withdrawal in December 1982 of Senator Edward Kennedy, widely regarded as a leading contender. Eight other Democrats eventually sought the nomination: former vice president Walter Mondale, George McGovern, ex-governor of Florida Reubin Askew, the black leader Jesse Jackson, and Senators Alan Cranston of California, John Glenn of Ohio, Gary Hart of Colorado, and Ernest F. Hollings of South Carolina. Mondale seemed to be the strongest candidate, but he was upset in the New Hampshire primary by Hart, who identified his candidacy with "new ideas" and attacked Mondale for catering to organized labor and other "special interest groups." The field of competitors gradually shrank as the state caucuses and primaries were held, finally leaving only Mondale, Hart, and Jackson in the race.

Mondale set out to rally the major elements of the Democratic coalition behind his candidacy, while Hart talked about the Democratic party of the future and the need to streamline social services and defense programs, as well as stressing such "New Politics" themes as environmental reform. Jackson, an eloquent minister and former associate of Martin Luther King, Jr., spoke for the forces of black protest. Although Hart won a number of primaries in New England and the western states, he had some difficulty in explaining his "new ideas," and Mondale gradually moved into the lead in the struggle for delegates. Jackson conducted a spirited race but was never a real possibility for the nomination. By the time the Democratic National Convention met in San Francisco, Mondale had won a majority of the delegates, and he was nominated on the first ballot. He then created a sensation by selecting Representative Geraldine A. Ferraro of New York for the vice-presidential place on the ticket. Ferraro, an able politician with a strong liberal record, attracted large crowds and proved to be an effective campaigner.

The Democratic preconvention campaign had been a bruising struggle for Walter Mondale, and it left the party in a weakened

The great communicator delivers his weekly radio address (*Jack Kightlinger, the White House*)

condition for the main event in the autumn. To win the nomination, one scholar has observed, the former vice president "had to endure an unbelievably grueling delegate selection process, with Gary Hart mobilizing Yuppies against him and Jesse Jackson preempting his normal base of support among black voters. Mondale had to go hat in hand, in public, to the labor unions, to 'special' interests, to the National Organization for Women—indeed, to anyone who would listen to his case."[4]

Reagan, in contrast to his Democratic challenger, began the campaign with several great advantages, including his incumbency. The economy promised to help him, and he had apparently stopped losing ground on foreign policy. He was certainly a popular president, and even people who disagreed with his handling of certain issues found him an appealing person. His personality was a decided asset. The president also benefited from impressive public approval of his leadership. According to *Washington Post*/ABC News polls, 72 per-

cent of those asked said Reagan had "strong leadership qualities."
Only 49 percent said that about Mondale.

Reagan conducted a very effective campaign, emphasizing optimism and opportunity. Avoiding specifics, he forecast a continuation of prosperity and a bright future. Mondale, as the underdog,
attacked the president for the huge increase in the federal deficit
and for having sponsored domestic policies that favored the well to
do and penalized the poor and the minorities. He said frankly that
if elected he would raise taxes—and that Reagan would do likewise.
Mondale waged a forceful and energetic campaign, but the nature of
his attack frequently made him appear somber and mean-spirited.
Reagan described his opponent's platform as a vision of "dreary
mediocrity" and talked about his own America as an "opportunity
society." In his basic speech the president declared, "I think there's
a new feeling of patriotism in our land, a recognition that by any
standard America is a decent and generous place, a force for good in
the world. And I don't know about you, but I'm a little tired of
hearing people run her down." Mondale's response was that the
election "is about values. I refuse to cut loose from my history and
desert the beliefs I have always fought for. I would rather lose a race
about decency than win one about self-interest."

The polls showed Reagan ahead from beginning to end. Few informed observers thought Mondale had any chance to win. As the
campaign proceeded, the Democrats' only hope seemed to rest on
two televised debates scheduled for October 7 and October 21.
Mondale clearly won the first of these confrontations. Vigorous and
refreshed, he was on the attack from the opening bell. The president, on the other hand, seemed old, tired, and confused; his answers were poorly focused, and he delivered a rambling closing
statement. The first debate probably closed the gap between Mondale and Reagan. But in the second debate the president looked refreshed and was ready with his answers. He held his own against
his Democratic challenger, which was all his campaign needed.
Meanwhile, Ferraro and Bush had also engaged in a televised debate,
which most voters considered a draw.

It was apparent that Mondale would lose the election, but the
extent of his defeat was a surprise. Reagan and Bush won by a landslide, receiving 54.5 million votes (59 percent) to 37.6 million (41
percent) for the Democratic ticket. The electoral college vote was
an overwhelming 525 to 13, with the Republicans carrying every
state except Mondale's Minnesota and the District of Columbia.
Reagan cut deeply into the traditional Democratic coalition; only
blacks remained faithful to the party of Franklin D. Roosevelt. Al-

though Reagan did well among almost all groups, he proved less attractive to traditional Democratic elements such as blacks, Jews, Hispanics, and people with incomes under $10,000 a year. More women voted for Reagan than for Mondale, but there was a "gender gap" of about 8 percent, attributed by some analysts to Ferraro's role in the campaign. The president's personal popularity was clearly a significant factor in his phenomenal victory. And, as the political scientist Nelson W. Polsby says, "The economic news improved; we cut our losses and got [our] troops out of Lebanon; the President went to China to get his picture taken at the Great Wall; and we had a splendid little war with Grenada."

While Ronald Reagan demonstrated his own extraordinary political appeal in the election of 1984, the results of that contest were ambiguous in other respects. Unfortunately for the Republicans, Reagan ran far ahead of his ticket. While the GOP retained control of the Senate, the Democrats gained 2 seats in that body while losing a net of only 14 seats in the House.[5] After the Reagan landslide, there were 34 Democratic governors to 16 Republican governors. Political analysts are divided over the question of whether Reagan's victories in 1980 and 1984 are part of a realignment of the political parties—a fundamental shift in voter affiliation that would last through several elections. Despite the decline in party identification and the growth of independentism, the Democrats are still the majority party in terms of party preference and registration. The polls suggested that only a small percentage of voters supported Reagan because he is a conservative. Nevertheless, it is possible that Reagan's appeal has an ideological component that puts the Democrats at a popular disadvantage, and a clear-cut GOP majority may emerge in future elections.

Much will depend on whether Reagan succeeds in rebuilding the national government along conservative lines. The venerable Roosevelt coalition seems to be disintegrating, and the Republicans are enjoying great success in presidential elections, having won six of the nine contests since 1952 and four out of the last five. Perhaps, as some scholars have suggested, there are two separate constituencies in contemporary American politics—one for the presidency and one for Congress and state and local offices. That would help explain Reagan's landslide victory in 1984. "The president's constituency," Theodore J. Lowi writes, "is a personal constituency involving a direct and immediate relationship between the president and the mass public. To a tremendous extent voters take into account the personal attributes of the presidential candidates, particularly when one of those candidates is the incumbent president."

THE CHARACTER OF CONTEMPORARY AMERICA

"Our nation is poised for greatness," Ronald Reagan declared in his second inaugural address on January 21, 1985. "There are no limits to growth and human progress when men and women are free to follow their dreams." The president made it clear that he intended to adhere to the conservative principles that had guided his first administration. Once again he condemned big government and vowed to resume his fight to transfer governmental authority from the federal to the state and local levels. He called for a major assault on domestic spending in 1985, a constitutional amendment mandating a balanced budget, and a move toward an anti-missile defense system designed to render offensive nuclear weapons "obsolete." In his State of the Union message a few weeks later, Reagan asserted that the budget deficit could be wiped out through "economic growth," not increased taxes. He continued to speak out against abortion, to support prayer in the schools, and to endorse a tuition tax credit, presumably as a means of injecting competition and choice into a school system under increasing criticism. Reagan's budget recommended a further increase in military spending and reductions in a wide range of social programs.

The administration enjoyed some successes in 1985, particularly involving defense and military aid measures. Congress once again voted its approval of the MX missile program, though not at the level sought by the Pentagon. After voting against further aid to the Nicaragua contras, the House of Representatives reversed itself and approved "humanitarian" assistance to the guerrillas (which many observers suspected would be used for military purposes). The Senate also approved this assistance.[6]

But Reagan's proposals also encountered stiff resistance. He was forced to compromise on his budget recommendations.[7] The president and most members of Congress agreed on the necessity of reducing the budget deficit, estimated at more than $200 billion in 1985, and a cut of at least $50 billion in the next year's deficit was accepted by the administration and congressional leaders of both parties. After a long battle, Reagan finally agreed to the demand by House Democrats that social security cost-of-living adjustments not be tampered with and that other social services receive more money than proposed by the administration. Military spending would increase, though not as much as the chief executive recommended. Concern over the mounting budget deficit led Congress in December 1985 to pass a measure sponsored by Senators Philip Gramm, Warren Rudman, and Ernest Hollings. The Gramm-

Rudman-Hollings Act, which became effective in March 1986, provided a schedule for balancing the federal budget by 1991. If Congress and the president were unable to agree on the annual budget reductions, the act would require automatic cuts in most domestic and military programs. President Reagan endorsed the scheme but was obviously afraid that it might result in substantial reductions in military spending. Meanwhile, Reagan had announced, with great fanfare, a tax reform and simplification plan. Although he and other administration leaders promoted the scheme in a series of speeches, it appeared to be heading for an early death. Prospects for genuine tax reform had improved by mid-1986, however, following passage of a Democratic bill by the House and approval of a different proposal by the Senate Finance Committee.[8]

Some aspects of Reagan's deregulation campaign, notably environmental protection regulation, ran into strong opposition from Congress, environmental advocacy groups, and challenges in the courts. On another question, the pressure for nuclear-arms control persuaded the president to resume negotiations with the Russians and to meet with Mikhail Gorbachev, the new Soviet leader, in Geneva in the autumn of 1985. The two men got along well, but little if any progress was made in reducing the arms race. By the summer of 1986, however, there were indications that Reagan and Gorbachev would eventually agree to hold another summit meeting on disarmament.

Only time will tell whether Reagan will be able to create a conservative majority party and a national government fashioned along the conservative lines he advocates. It was apparent by the mid–1980s, however, that these accomplishments would not be easy. One of the areas of uncertainty was the economy. In some respects the recovery from the recession of 1981–82 was impressive. The rate of economic growth for fiscal 1983 averaged 5 percent and for fiscal 1984, 6.2 percent. Unemployment dropped from a peak of 10.6 percent in December 1982 to 7.1 percent in June 1984. Inflation had been checked, and interest rates finally began to come down. Yet the United States was left with serious economic problems. Among these was the federal deficit, which tripled between 1976 and 1985 and reached $2 trillion in 1986. Another problem was the increasing U.S. trade deficit—over $100 billion in 1984, rising to an estimated $150 billion in 1986. The country was also caught in a stubborn farm recession, which had started in 1980 and was hastening a radical and painful restructuring of the American agricultural system.[9] Defaults on international debts and the instabilities of U.S. financial institutions were other sources of concern. Economic growth lost much of its steam in 1985, and activity in the industrial sector was sluggish. The operating rate in American factories declined during the first half of 1985, and in May of that year it was down to about 80 percent of capacity. Some of the nation's industrial weaknesses had been accumulating for a long time. For example, in the early years following the Second World War, the United States was producing more steel than Western Europe, Japan, and the Soviet Union combined, but a generation later, it was importing steel from Japan while U.S. mills were closing and unemployment in steel-making communities approached 50 percent.

In order to be successful, the Reagan administration will also have to overcome major political challenges in international affairs and at home. Will it be able to negotiate a satisfactory arms-reduction treaty? Will it help find solutions to dangerous trouble spots like Central America and the Middle East? Can it find a solution to the frightful problem of international terrorism?[10] In dealing with domestic issues, will the administration succeed in diminishing the federal bureaucracy, in removing federal regulations while still protecting consumers and disadvantaged groups, and in maintaining the health of the economy?

Will the Republicans be able to attract new voters and create a thoroughgoing majority party? Only in the South has there been conclusive evidence of party realignment during the last two decades. Cultural issues like school prayer and abortion, zealously promoted by the Moral Majority and right-to-life groups, may prove divisive and counterproductive. There are other political trends that seem likely to complicate the problems of both major parties: growing political apathy (only slightly more than half of the eligible voters cast ballots in 1980), the increasing importance of single-issue politics, the decline of party identification and the growing number of independents, and the influence of the mass media in making the political parties seem less pertinent and the personalities of candidates more important.

Students of contemporary American society also point to the existence of profound cultural problems in the 1980s. The nation's society is, for one thing, deeply divided and unequal. Poverty is increasing. The Census Bureau reported in 1983 that 35 million Americans (15.2 percent of the population) fell below the poverty line. Ironically, some observers noted, the War on Poverty and related social policies of the last two decades have actually hurt the poor they were intended to help. The black family, especially in ghetto areas, seems to be disintegrating, and the gap between the average income of whites and blacks is increasing. There appears to be a general loosening of social bonds and a decline of cohesive community. Hundreds of hamlets and small towns have disappeared in recent years, taking with them schools, churches, and other rural institutions that were once the source of ideals and values for millions of Americans. Meanwhile, a swelling tide of illegal aliens has been creating "an invisible subculture outside the boundaries of law and legitimate institutions." American society is increasingly segmented. Kevin Phillips talked about "the Balkanization of America": "the congealing of the melting pot and the re-emergence of ethnicity; the proliferation of sexual preferences and religious cults; the new political geography of localism and neighborhoods; the substitution of causes for political parties; the narrowing of loyalties; the fragmentation of government; the twilight of authority." Christopher Lasch, in a book entitled *The Culture of Narcissism: American Life in an Age of Diminishing Expectations* (1978), argued that the United States has become a "dying culture," in which the demands of corporate life and the consumer culture have displaced religion and tradition with an overriding concern with self-esteem and instant gratification.

These examples of troublesome tendencies in American life in the 1980s point up the extent of the nation's change since World War II. Social change has been especially striking during the last two decades. According to a recent article in *U.S. News & World Report*, "in virtually no aspect of life does the U.S. of the early 1980s resemble what it was in the relatively simple days of the late 1950s." The two decades from Eisenhower to Reagan, *U.S. News* declared, represented "a period of change so dramatic that it has left many Americans both dazzled and bewildered." The magazine identified ten dominant forces that were involved in this transformation: a maturing society, the lure of the Sunbelt, the computer revolution, increasing foreign competition, women on the move, the rise of minorities, declining superpowers, government under fire, the education boom, and a flurry of medical miracles. Among the more arresting points in the article were these: the population of the South grew by 20 percent and that of the West by 24 percent in the 1970s; 6.7 million personal and home computers were sold in 1983 alone; today more than two-thirds of American women between 25 and 44 are employed, women outnumber men on college campuses, and 6 million more women than men voted in the presidential election of 1980; and a society dominated by white values a generation ago has evolved into a much more diversified social order.

But if powerful new forces and dismaying circumstances in the 1970s and 1980s seemed to be transforming the United States into a radically different nation, there were nevertheless strong continui-

Astronaut Sally K. Ride communicates with ground
controllers from the earth-orbiting space shuttle
Challenger (*NASA photograph*)

ties between the older America and contemporary society. Much of
the past persisted in the postwar period, and older attitudes and
values demonstrated remarkable vitality. Although events after
1945 overtook Americans with breathtaking speed, they were far
less revolutionary than were developments in many other parts of
the world. Indeed, the nation's basic institutions proved extraordinarily durable. One strain of continuity was offered by organized
religion, which was characterized by renewed vigor and continuing
diversity. Another was the persisting faith in and commitment to
education. The resurgence of conservatism in recent years is no
doubt another indication of the American concern for the preservation of traditional institutions and values. Nor was that all. The
structure of American society retained many of its familiar prewar
features. Thus Richard Polenberg concludes, in *One Nation Divisible: Class, Race, and Ethnicity in the United States Since 1938*

(1980), that "behind the appearance of uniformity ... differences along class, racial, and ethnic lines persisted. While they had changed dramatically over a forty-year period, these distinctions continued to shape the lives of most Americans."

Change and continuity in the postwar period were accompanied by many noteworthy achievements and long-needed social reforms. The early postwar years avoided a repetition of the terrible prewar depression, a development many people expected. Nor have we suffered a nuclear holocaust. American technological innovations have been spectacular. The United States has made unparalleled economic and material advances since the war. Its political structure has been greatly democratized. It has made remarkable progress in protecting the rights of minorities and women. "The travail of liberalism," William E. Leuchtenburg suggests, "derived in no inconsiderable degree from its accomplishments. Each achievement awakened new expectations and made the nation more aware of unexplored shortcomings."

At the same time, few periods in American history have been as disconcerting and as troubling as the years since World War II. "If there are any readily recognizable characteristics of the new era," C. Vann Woodward wrote of the early postwar period, "they are the fortuitous, the unpredictable, the adventitious, and the dynamic— all of them charged with surprise." Developments like the Vietnam War and Watergate were deeply upsetting to Americans. There were also other sources of anxiety. An energy "crisis" seemed to jeopardize the prospect of continued industrial growth. A consumer movement began to protest against the quality of goods and services produced by the U.S. economic system. An environmental crusade, stimulated by rapid economic and population growth, called attention to the extensive pollution of air and water. Thoughtful citizens began to question the desirability of economic growth itself. Economic growth, they suspected, frequently brought with it unsuspected and adverse side effects whose cumulative impact might be more deleterious than beneficial to society. Some observers began to talk about "the end of the American era." In their lower expectations and new recognition of uncongenial realities and of the role of contingency in human affairs, Americans were moving closer to the basic outlook of most people everywhere.

Still, Americans continue to seek their identity in the future as well as in the past. The grand American experiment in the search for liberty and security was far from finished as the nation celebrated the bicentennial of its independence and approached the 200th anniversary of its constitution. It remained unbelievably rich and powerful, with a vigorous and inventive population, an extraordinarily well-developed economy, and a social order that has retained enormous stability in spite of the challenges and disappointments of the last two decades. There was still hope that the nation's vast resources and lofty ideals would enable its people to deal more successfully with the age-old problems of poverty, human rights, environmental deterioration, and the loss of community.

NOTES

1. Alonzo L. Hamby, *Liberalism and its Challengers: FDR to Reagan* (1985), p. 353.

2. Inflation, as measured by what economists call the GNP deflator, declined from about 9 percent in 1981 to 4.3 percent in 1982, 3.8 percent in 1983, and 3.5 percent in 1984.

3. Robert Dallek, *Ronald Reagan: The Politics of Symbolism* (1984), p. 133.

4. Nelson W. Polsby, "Did the 1984 Election Signal Major Party Realignment?" *The Key Reporter* 50 (Spring 1985): 3.

5. In the Ninety-ninth Congress (1985–86), the Republican margin in the Senate was 53 to 47, while the Democratic edge in the House was 253 to 182.

6. In 1986 both houses of Congress voted to authorize $100 million in aid to the contras with few strings attached.

7. The budget compromise was agreed to by the two houses of Congress and the president in early August. Its major provisions for fiscal 1986 included no significant tax changes; allowing military spending to rise with inflation; full cost-of-living adjustments for social security and other government benefit programs; reduced spending for a variety of domestic programs such as Amtrak and mass transit programs; and the ending of general revenue sharing for local governments in fiscal 1987. The size of the 1986 budget was $968 billion, with defense receiving $302 billion. The compromise included a $55 billion deficit-reduction package that would still add at least $172 billion to the national debt.

8. A compromise income-tax overhaul was finally agreed upon in the fall of 1986. It provided for lower rates, fewer deductions, and higher corporate taxes. The act reduced the number of individual tax brackets from about fourteen to two basic rates of 15 percent and 28 percent. The measure cut individual taxes an average of 6.1 percent but confronted millions of people who had gained from targeted deductions with tax increases. The Reagan administration could take considerable credit for this reform, along with Senator Robert Packwood of Oregon, Representative Dan Rostenkowski of Illinois, and other congressional leaders. Reagan hailed the enactment as historic and said it "satisfies my requirements for meaningful tax reform."

9. The deepening agricultural crisis finally forced Congress to pass major new farm legislation in late 1985. The legislation authorized a farm program that would cost more than $50 billion over the next three years. Even so, it made some reductions in price supports, in an effort to move agriculture toward a more "market oriented" future, and reorganized the nation's farm credit system.

10. Provoked by continuing acts of terror, including attacks on the Rome and Vienna airports that cost the lives of several Americans, the Reagan administration launched a series of punitive actions against Libya, whose strong man, Muammar Kaddafi, was identified as the perpetrator of the Rome and Vienna assaults. In a surprise move in April 1986, the United States carried out devastating air strikes against selected targets in Tripoli and Benghazi. How effective this resort to military force would be on international terrorism was not immediately apparent.

SUGGESTIONS FOR FURTHER READING

Scholarly literature on Ronald Reagan and his administration is still quite limited. Two books that provide a good introduction to the man and his politics are Lou Cannon, *Reagan* (1982), and Robert Dallek, *Ronald Reagan: The Politics of Symbolism* (1984). Frank Van Der Linden, *The Real Reagan* (1981), is a sympathetic biography; Laurence I. Barrett, *Gambling with History* (1983), provides a critical perspective. See also Ronnie Dugger, *On Reagan: The Man & His Presidency* (1983), and Rowland Evans and Robert Novak, *The Reagan Revolution*, cited in chapter 16. The Reagan policies are examined in Fred I. Greenstein (ed.), *The Reagan Presidency: An Early Assessment* (1983); John L. Palmer and Isabel V. Sawhill (eds.), *The Reagan Experiment: An Examination of Economic and Social Policies under the Reagan Administration* (1982); and Palmer and Sawhill (eds.), *The Reagan Record: An Assessment of America's Changing Domestic Priorities* (1984). For the fortieth president's own ideas, see Ronald Reagan, with Richard G. Hubler, *Where's the Rest of Me?* (1965), and appropriate volumes in the *Public Papers of the Presidents* series.

David W. Reinhard's *The Republican Right Since 1945* (1983) throws light on the conservative wing of the GOP from the death of Franklin D. Roosevelt to the election of Ronald Reagan. Other aspects of the conservative revival are explored by Donald Warren, *The Radical Center: Middle Americans and the Politics of Alienation* (1976); Peter Steinfels, *The Neoconservatives: The Men Who Are Changing America's Politics* (1979); and Alan Crawford, *Thunder on the Right: The "New Right" and the Politics of Resentment* (1980). Various features of Reagan's domestic policies are considered by Martha Derthick and Paul J. Quirk, *The Politics of Deregulation* (1985); William Greider, *The Education of David Stockman and Other Americans* (1982); Ronald Brownstein and Nina Easton, *Reagan's Ruling Class: Portraits of the President's Top 100 Officials* (1982); Robert Lekachman, *Greed Is Not Enough: Reaganomics* (1982); and Michael J. Boskin, *Reaganomics Examined: Successes, Failures, Unfinished Agenda* (1985).

Brief assessments of Reagan's foreign policy can be found in Ambrose, *Rise to Globalism*; LaFeber, *America, Russia and the Cold War*; and Weisberger, *Cold War, Cold Peace*, all mentioned earlier. Walter LaFeber's *Inevitable Revolutions* (1983) is helpful on Central American developments. Alexander Haig, Jr., *Caveat: Realism, Reagan, and Foreign Policy* (1984), throws light on Reagan's early approach to international questions.

The campaign of 1984 is analyzed in a comprehensive work edited by Michael Nelson, *The Elections of 1984* (1985). But see also Jack Germond and Jules Witcover, *Wake Us When It's Over: Presidential Politics of 1984* (1985), and Ellis Sandoz and Cecil V. Crabb, Jr. (eds.), *Election 84: Landslide Without a Mandate?* (1986). Other political trends in the 1980s are touched on by Walter Dean Burnham, *The Current Crisis in American Politics* (1982); Randall Rothenberg, *The Neoliberals: Creating the New American Politics* (1984); and Theodore J. Lowi, *The Personal President: Power Invested, Promise Unfulfilled* (1985). Social and cultural issues are explored in Christopher Lasch, *The Culture of Narcissism: American Life in an Age of Diminishing Expectations* (1978); Richard Louv, *America II* (1983); Robert Reich, *The Next American Frontier* (1983); Charles Murray, *Losing Ground: American Social Policy, 1950–1980* (1984); and Nathan Glazer (ed.), *Clamor at the Gates: The New American Immigration* (1985).

Index

Recent America: The United States Since 1945 was copyedited by Barbara Armentrout. Production editor was Brad Barrett. Ann Sutherland and Martha Kreger proofread the copy. The text was typeset by Graphic Composition, Inc., and printed and bound by Edwards Brothers, Inc.

The cover and text were designed by Roger Eggers. Cover illustration: UNTITLED, Willem de Kooning, 1961. (Photo by Muldoon Studio.) Rose Art Museum, Brandeis University, Waltham, Massachusetts, Gift of Julian J. and Joachim Jean Aberbach.